NEW YORK | 400

JOHN THORN
EDITOR

MELANIE BOWER
PICTURE EDITOR

RUNNING PRESS
PHILADELPHIA • LONDON

Printed in China

9 8 7 6 5 4 3 2 1
Digit on the right indicates the number of this printing

Library of Congress Control Number: 2009920757

ISBN 978-0-7624-3649-1

Designed by Joshua McDonnell

Edited by Cindy De La Hoz

Typography: Monkton & Mercury

Running Press Book Publishers
2300 Chestnut Street
Philadelphia, Pennsylvania 19103-4371

Visit us on the web!
www.runningpress.com

CONTENTS

INTRODUCTION

OUR CITY

BY MICHAEL R. BLOOMBERG, MAYOR

Birthdays tend to sneak up on us, making us marvel at how old we have become no matter how young we feel. That is certainly true for New York, impossibly old at 400 for a city so vital and with such exciting prospects, even in this time of upheaval. The great Casey Stengel once said of an aging ballplayer, "His future is behind him." This was meant as a put-down, but for New York it is a useful reminder, since our history is such an important part of our future. The openness and tolerance, the opportunity and ambition, and the inventiveness and perseverance that have always defined our history continue to shape our future. The history of New York is, in many ways, the history of America. So many of our nation's greatest innovations happened here first. So many of our toughest urban challenges were confronted here first. And so many of the nation's immigrants—who spread out across the country—came to New York, first. Those immigrants, and their sons and daughters, made New York an international city—but also the quintessential American city. New York City lives and breathes the nation's core values, and we embody America's founding spirit of personal freedom and equal opportunity. That is why we remain a destination for anyone with a dream, whether from a foreign land or the American heartland. It is why this city, at its 400th birthday, continues to be young and entrepreneurial. We are New Yorkers, all of us who live here or once did, or visited the city and were captivated by it. It is for us—and all who might wish to become New Yorkers—that the Museum of the City of New York has created this 400th birthday gift. Here we see the City at its highest—and lowest—moments. The successes we have enjoyed have proven that anything—and everything—is possible. And the difficulties that we have overcome fill us with appreciation for where we are today—and optimism for where we might go tomorrow. As the person fortunate enough to be Mayor as the city marks its 400th birthday, I recommend this book to anyone who loves New York—and anyone who would like to know how it came to be the capital of the world.

PREFACE

BY MIKE WALLACE

BIRTHDAYS ARE OCCASIONS FOR PEOPLE TO CELEBRATE THEIR LATEST SWING AROUND THE SUN. SOMETIMES INDIVIDUALS ALSO USE THEM TO REFLECT ON THEIR LIVES TO DATE, AN INCLINATION THAT SEEMS TO WAX STRONGER AS THEY APPROACH DECENNIAL MILESTONES. CITIES, BEING LONGER-LIVED, TEND TO UNDERTAKE THEIR SPECIAL COMMEMORATIONS ON A CENTENNIAL BASIS. NEW YORK, HAVING COMPLETED TWENTY SCORE SOLAR ORBITS, CERTAINLY HAS SOMETHING TO KICK BACK ABOUT, AND IS INDULGING, ACCORDINGLY, IN A FOUR HUNDREDTH BIRTHDAY BASH. AS A CONTRIBUTION TO THE MORE REFLECTIVE SIDE OF THESE PROCEEDINGS, THE MUSEUM OF THE CITY OF NEW YORK, AN INSTITUTION DEDICATED TO PRESERVING AND PONDERING GOTHAM'S PAST, DECIDED TO CONSTRUCT AN *AIDE-MÉMOIRE*—THE EQUIVALENT OF A FAMILY PHOTO ALBUM THAT INDIVIDUALS TAKE OUT OF THE CLOSET (OR SUMMON UP ON THEIR COMPUTER SCREENS) WHEN THEY WISH TO RECALL IMPORTANT POINTS IN THEIR LIVES, AND PERHAPS MUSE ABOUT WHERE THEY ARE IN LIGHT OF WHERE THEY'VE BEEN. WE ASKED SIXTEEN HISTORIANS OF NEW YORK TO DESCRIBE SOME ASPECT OF A PERIOD THEY HAVE STUDIED CLOSELY. WE WANTED NOT DRY SURVEYS THAT "COVERED" AN ERA BUT LIVELY PORTRAITS THAT EVOKED PARTICULAR MOMENTS—DEPICTIONS THAT WHEN STRUNG TOGETHER WOULD PROVIDE A MINI-RETROSPECTIVE OF THE CITY'S CENTURIES-LONG SAGA. THEY RESPONDED HANDSOMELY. JAAP JACOBS STARTS US OFF IN THE 1660S, IN NEW AMSTERDAM, BY INTRODUCING THE DUTCH WEST INDIA COMPANY'S TINY AND TENUOUS OUTPOST, FROM THE PERSPECTIVE OF ITS MARTINET DIRECTOR GENERAL, PETRUS STUYVESANT. SARA GRONIM JUMPS DOWN THE TIME LINE TO THE 1750S, OFFERING A TOUR OF THE NOW SUBSTANTIAL TOWN, HAVING BECOME A MAJOR PROVINCIAL PORT IN THE BRITISH EMPIRE. EDWIN BURROWS FOCUSES IN ON NEW YORK DURING THE AMERICAN REVOLUTION WHEN, OCCUPIED BY BRITISH FORCES BETWEEN 1776 AND 1783, IT BECAME THE HELLISH PRISON—AND GRAVEYARD—OF THOUSANDS OF CAPTURED REBELS. NANCY ISENBERG TAKES US ON A STROLL ABOUT THE REBUILT AND TRANSFIGURED 1790S TOWN, visiting its new and elegant venues in the company of that stylish sophisticate, Aaron Burr.

We then fast forward a generation to the 1830s, and Patricia Cline Cohen's exploration of the brouhaha over the rapid growth of prostitution, the unexpected corollary of a surge in commerce brought on by the opening of the Erie Canal, which drew great numbers of single young men and women from the countryside to what had become the nation's largest city. Overseas immigrants further swelled the population in the 1840s–50s, among them a contingent of Cubans whose community, sketched by Lisandro Pérez, was far smaller than its Irish and German counterparts, but as deeply rooted in the city's economy, being an outgrowth of the Caribbean sugar trade. The manifold tensions in this mushrooming metropolis erupted during the Civil War in the Draft Riots of July 1863, whose causes and consequences are scrutinized in Owen Gutfreund's contribution.

Thirty years farther on, Daniel Czitrom takes us through the Tenderloin district, thronged in the 1890s by a male clientele sampling the red-light pleasures of a vice economy that thrived, despite condemnation by moral reformers, thanks to the protection afforded by machine politicians and crooked cops. Lew Erenberg revisits the city's pleasure precincts, now relocated in Times Square, Harlem, and Greenwich Village: first in the 1910s, when cabarets, night clubs, and lobster palaces catering to men and women flourished; and then in the 1920s when the same establishments, criminalized by Prohibition, either folded or went underground, protected (or owned) by organized gangsters. The 1930s repealed Prohibition but ushered in Depression, and with it the massive misery and homelessness chronicled by Ella Howard. The New Deal, so largely a product of New Yorkers, was able to alleviate these hard times but not to end them. It took a world war to do that, and in a close up set in 1940–1941 I look at how Franklin Roosevelt's arms buildup provided jobs for unemployed New Yorkers—though not for the city's African-Americans, who responded to discrimination in the defense factories with a massive direct action campaign.

The postwar city of the 1940s and 1950s is the beat of Phillip Lopate, who finds the era's triumphalist mood well founded; Gotham had become the headquarters of the United Nations and the country's major corporations, and had given rise to astonishing accomplishments in the arts, architecture, music, and the life of the mind. There were, however, undertows at work subverting this self-confident prosperity, which first became evident in the 1960s when, as Clarence Taylor explains, African-Americans accelerated efforts to integrate the city's schools and job markets. Then, in the 1970s, as Joshua B. Freeman recounts, deindustrialization, suburbanization, and recession pitched the city into near bankruptcy. The consequences, though in general catastrophic, were at times creative, as illustrated by the amazing efflorescence of film, theater, dance, art, and music (including hip hop, which would soon sweep the planet). Developments in the art world during the 1980s are the subject of a close-up by Jed Perl. The recovery of the city during the 1980s and 1990s, David Dyssegaard Kallick suggests, was due in considerable measure to the tremendous resurgence of immigration to Gotham from around the world, and he paints us a picture of how these newcomers are getting on in the first decade of the twenty-first century.

I hope these jaunts to the past will prove intriguing and entertaining in their own right, but would like to suggest that the information they contain can be put to other purposes as well. Rather as the photos and jpegs of a family album can be rearranged to tease out or highlight the patterns of a particular life, so these samplings of New York's past can be redeployed to illuminate various trajectories the city has traveled over the centuries.

Consider, for instance, what they reveal about the city's changing position on the planet. New York's four hundred years have been largely coterminous with the emergence of a new world order launched in the wake of Columbus' voyages. In the 1500s and 1600s Europe, paced by Spain and Portugal, established by conquest and commerce the first truly globe-girdling empires, suturing together parts of the globe (Europe, Asia, Africa, the Americas) that previously had modest or zero connections. This was the *real* beginning of globalization—a term conventionally (and I believe inappropriately) applied only to recent decades when the velocity of movements of capital, culture, and peoples along these long-established circuitries accelerated dramatically.

From its foundation, New York's development was tightly bound up with this new world order of international empires and colonies. As the Jacobs piece reminds us, New Amsterdam in 1660 was a colony of the Dutch Republic—formerly a satrapy of Spain and now a would-be rival empire—and the town's marginal and fragile status was related to the Dutch empire's far greater attentiveness to more profitable ventures in Brazil, Africa, and Indonesia. New York's position improved drastically, Gronim's data suggests, when it was forcibly shifted from Dutch empire to that of England, the newest entrant in the imperial sweepstakes. The city thrived by shipping food down to England's newly acquired Caribbean sugar islands, and serving as a military base for operations against yet another rival empire, that of the French in Canada.

Prosperity did not prevent New Yorkers from eventually joining the anti-imperial rebellion of the 1770s, which helps account, Burrows argues, for the ferocity of Britain's treatment of POWs. After briefly becoming capital of the newly independent United States—a moment captured by Isenberg—the city began trading with colonies of the Spanish Empire, notably Cuba, with consequences described by Pérez. During the Civil War, New York merchant elites, initially reluctant, joined in crushing the Confederacy, in part to prevent the South from re-appending itself to the British Empire as a cotton-supplying neo-colony, but they left the actual fighting to Irish refugees from that same British empire, thus triggering the Draft Riots described in detail by Gutfreund. In the twentieth century, New York emerged as the financial and cultural capital of a new American empire, which achieved global primacy after the Second World War, as Phillip Lopate recounts. Being capital of the world had manifold benefits, but came with attendant perils, so Joshua Freeman notes, in a heightened vulnerability to perturbations in the global economy, as evidenced by the perfect financial storm now raining on our birthday parade.

In a similar way, material extracted from our *aide-mémoire* could afford insight into the evolution of New York's macroeconomic base, from fur trading (Jacobs), to shipping and manufacturing (Gronim), to trade with Europe (Isenberg) and Latin America (Pérez), and on down to becoming a financial complex and corporate headquarters (Lopate). One could also cobble together an account of Gotham's *underground* economy over the years by dipping into the discussions of prostitution, gambling, political corruption, and organized crime offered by Cohen, Czitrom, Isenberg, and Erenberg.

There's a whole other narrative embedded here about the city's lengthy reckoning with race, whose notable plot points include: New Amsterdam's pioneering of a traffic in slaves (Jacobs); British New York's widespread use of slave labor, development of race-based justifications for doing so, and ferocious suppression of suspected revolts (Gronim); the city's ongoing involvement with Southern slavery even after it ended its own, and its reliance locally on the cheap labor of free blacks, which together fed the anti-black savagery of the Civil-War era (Gutfreund); the emergence of the New Negro and arrival of white slummers in 1920s Harlem (Erenberg); the launching of the modern civil rights movement by A. Philip Randolph's 1940s March on Washington, which extended into the desegregation struggles of the 1950s, the black uprisings of the 1960s, and the hip-hop movement of the 1970s (Wallace, Taylor, Lopate, Freeman).

There are many other pathways these contributions light up: the ups and downs of life in a boom-bust capitalist city; the differential impact of varying wars; the centrality of immigration; New York as a crucible of cultures high and low and as a media and entertainment center (witness the treatment of newspapers, books, magazines, theater, vaudeville, film, and radio in these pages). But as it is the job of a preface to whet the appetite, not sate it, I leave the reader to enjoy the fruits of our scholars' labors, and extend to her or him my best wishes for a happy 400th.

"NEW YORK, NEW YORK"

BY JOHN THORN

Welcome to New York, the city whose only constant through four centuries has been relentless, roaring change—hills flattened, ponds filled, streams diverted, buildings demolished, neighborhoods dismantled, all in the name of progress. "Under Construction" might be a better motto for the city than the one on its official seal, *Sigillum Civitatis Novi Eboraci*, which translates numbingly as "Seal of the City of New York." Only one building survives from the city's Dutch period (Wyckoff House in Brooklyn, 1652); a bare handful from the British colonial years; and surprisingly few, by the standards of other great cities the world over, predate the Civil War. The constant charge has been to "Make it new." Yet more has endured in New York City over four hundred years than meets the eye. This is a haunted city, enriched in every moment by all that has gone before—at the same locations, or by practitioners of the same trades, or for the same causes. In this city that never sleeps (one of its myriad nicknames, as we will revisit below), it is the past that is always present. Isaac Newton Phelps Stokes, whose six-volume *Iconography of Manhattan Island* was an inspiration for this book, wrote late in life of a vivid recurring dream: I usually start from some point in the modern city, and on my way—perhaps to keep an appointment at some other well-known point—I am tempted to try a short-cut. I wander over the hills and valleys, and often through virgin forests, and sometimes come out on the shore of the Hudson or the East River where I recognize the topography from the old maps, and take great pleasure in searching for landmarks which I know exist—or at least existed at the time pictured in my dream. Sometimes I find them, and am thrilled by the discovery, but curiously they are almost never inhabited. Although the streets are sometimes populated, I generally pass unnoticed—apparently unseen! Phelps Stokes was an architect and an activist for decent urban housing, not a dotty antiquarian who spent all his time in archives. But his joy was to imagine himself freed from the constraints of time, walking the city of old but in the present moment. We hope that with the aid of this book you too may share his dream.

Even if you are a lifelong New Yorker, for a moment imagine yourself a tourist—but in four dimensions rather than three. Let this unwieldy tome be your armchair guide to sensing the city as our forebears experienced it—the sights, the smells, the cries—treading the same turf at different times.

In compiling this book, beyond the grounding of sixteen historical essays traversing the city's four centuries, the Museum of the City of New York has aimed to present, through its vast and largely unpublished collections, everyday life as it might have been experienced by an ordinary citizen, rather than focusing on political and footlight celebrities. We have preferred the frank street scene to the noble landmark, the uncommon view to the famous one, and especially pictures that tell stories you may not have heard before. The captions in the earlier periods, particularly, may run to greater length because, as Mrs. Schuyler Van Rensselaer aptly put it a century ago, "a special quality of interest pertains to the city of New York in its early years by reason of the preeminence it has since achieved; for it is with places as with men—the greater their importance in adult life the greater is the interest that attaches to their birth and antecedents, the incidents of their youth, and the influence that moulded their spirit and shaped their destinies." Whether short or long, all of the captions are the efforts of this editor, who stands upon the shoulders of many yet is solely responsible for any gaffes.

Many images from the archives have not been displayed in decades, if ever, so this book forms not only a visual history of New York but also a virtual tour of the archives of the Museum of the City of New York—one that would be impossible to offer to any real-world visitor. The aim has been to provide a panoramic view of the city and its people, principally through the selected images and secondarily through the volume's essays and captions. Because this is a graphic history of the city, the text accompanying an image will be sometimes about the history and sometimes about the graphic. Engravings, lithographs, and paintings present the image of the city in its first two centuries, although some later views, even a photograph or two, make their way into these chapters (the book is organized chronologically by the date depicted, not the date the image was executed). Photographs begin to portray the city by the mid-nineteenth century and increasingly become the cityscape artist's medium of choice.

Especially in regard to photographs, which most often are untitled, the editor may provide a title descriptive of the image content. When such titles were not devised by the photographer nor accompanied the photographs when first published, they are offered between brackets. The dimensions of paintings are offered in inches.

We have not directed our efforts at scholars or collectors or art historians, though it is hoped they will find much here to please them. This book is for you—current resident, former inhabitant, visitor, or descendant—because all who ever loved New York may call themselves New Yorkers. The result, we believe, forms a unique pageant of the greatest city in the world.

Would a city by any other name be as sweet? Many evidently have thought so, for New York has been called the Big Apple, Fun City, and the Melting Pot. It has been the City of Golden Dreams, the Capital of the World, and the City So Nice, They Named It Twice (though it might have to share that last one with Walla Walla). As early as 1784 George Washington dubbed New York the Seat of Empire, which soon became the enduring Empire City. But the most richly evocative of all the city's nicknames may be one that, like Yankee Doodle, was originally intended by its English coiners as an insult: Gotham.

"Three wise men of Gotham went to sea in a bowl," went the Mother Goose rhyme; "if the bowl had been stronger, then my rhyme had been longer." Mother Goose, or *Songs for the Nursery*, was first published in London in 1760, based upon English and French sources, including Charles Perrault's *Contes de ma mère l'oye* (1697). But the origins of Gotham may be traced back even further, to 1460, when the "Foles of Gotham" were first mentioned in print. A century later, the absurd doings of the people of that village seven miles from Nottingham, in England were collected in a book, *Merie Tales of the Mad Men of Gotam*.

In sixteenth century Gotham the perceived idiocy of the villagers was legendary. One absurdity attributed to them was the building of a thornbush around the cuckoo bird to secure eternal spring; another was an attempt to rid themselves of an eel by drowning it. But the archetypal tale of Gothamite conduct was when King John intended to establish a hunting lodge nearby. The villagers, fearful of the cost of supporting the court, feigned imbecility when the royal messengers arrived. Wherever the king's men went, they saw the fools of Gotham engaged in some lunatic endeavor. When King John selected another spot for his lodge elsewhere, the wise men of Gotham boasted, " . . . more fools pass through Gotham than remain in it."

How did this tale come to epitomize New York? Early on, our English cousins began to refer to those "fools" who sailed from the mother country (the aforementioned three men in a tub) to make their fortunes in New York as residents of the "New Gotham," the new-world capital of greed.

But then as now, a New Yorker's allegiance to his or her city was unshakable. You could not insult New York to a New Yorker because he was so secure in his belief that he resided in the best place in the world. And in turning his back on aristocracy and primogeniture and instead dedicating himself to the single-minded pursuit of money, he asserted his membership in a utopian meritocracy.

A Hessian in Rhode Island wrote to his brother in 1777:

> New York . . . is one of the prettiest, pleasantest harbor towns I have ever seen. For the houses are not only built fine and regular in English style, most of them like palaces, but they are all papered and most extensively furnished. For that reason it is too bad that this land, which is also very fertile, is inhabited by such people, who from luxury and sensuous pleasure didn't know what to do and so owe their fall to naught but their pride. Everyone at home who takes their part and thinks they had good cause for rebellion ought in punishment to spend some time among them and learn how things are here (for the meanest man here can, if he will only do something, live like the richest among us). . . . For though the majority are descended from runaway vagabonds expelled from other places, yet they are so stuck up and make such display, especially in New York, as perhaps nowhere else on earth. . . . The worst thing about it is that at the king's express command the troops must treat these folk most handsomely—though at heart they are all rebels. . . .

More than a century earlier, Daniel Denton had written in *A Brief Description of New York*: "Here those which Fortune hath frowned upon in England, to deny them an inheritance amongst their brethren, or such as by their utmost labors can scarcely procure a living—I say such may procure here inheritances of lands and possessions, stock themselves with all sorts of cattle, enjoy the benefit of them whilst they live, and leave them to the benefit of their children when they die."

So New Yorkers adopted Gotham as their model, the city of "wise fools" who knew more than their English lords. Travelers might note that New York was not only crass but also dirty and crowded and mongrelized; residents would nod in agreement and set about their business. They liked their city just the way it was.

CHAPTER I | 1609–1664

THE ELUSIVE SHIFTING SAND

JAAP JACOBS

"Do you like him?" a colleague recently asked, after I had talked about Petrus Stuyvesant for fifteen minutes. I fell quiet. "So you do like him?!" he exclaimed. But the reason I didn't immediately answer was that the question seemed somewhat inappropriate. I don't think a biographer has to like or dislike his or her protagonist. Especially not when it concerns people from the seventeenth century, a time in which characters and their traits seem so different from ours. Of course, that hasn't stopped some historians from passing judgments that are less detached than might be expected from scholars.

Stuyvesant's name translates as "shifting sand." In a parallel to this identification, the question of who he is can and has been answered in many ways. And the ways often reveal more about the author than about the subject. A random selection: Stuyvesant was an intolerant colonial ruler who stopped Lutherans from obtaining their own minister, who had Quakers whipped, and who tried to evict the Jews from New Amsterdam. He was a slave driver, who introduced the trade in human cargo at Curaçao and had few qualms about selling enslaved people in North America. He was a hothead who in his tantrum tore up official documents and thus showed disrespect to the States General, the highest authority in the --Dutch Republic. He was a fighting man who lost his right leg to a Spanish cannonball and stomped around Manhattan trying to deny the colonists their lawful right to local government. He was the founder of New Amsterdam, later renamed New York. He was a stubborn Frisian who was so loyal to his Amsterdam superiors that the population of New Amsterdam had to force him to surrender the town to overwhelming English forces. And despite all of that his name still rings a bell nowadays, both in the United States and in the Netherlands. It can't all be due to the Stuyvesant brand of cigarettes or the Dutch travel organization ("Stuyvesant! Discover the World!"). Or can it?

Despite this ambiguous reputation, he has been the focus of my attention for years. The biography I am writing of him goes beyond the man himself to address how the Dutch governed their Atlantic colonies. Obviously, that is a question that could be answered in another format than a biography, but government and personal authority are so intertwined in the seventeenth century that I came to believe that a biography would provide the most comprehensive approach to the issue. I was interested in the "classical decades" of the Dutch Atlantic World, in which parts of Brazil (1630–1654) and North America (1621–1664, 1673–1674) were under control of the Dutch West India Company. Those are the decades that Jan De Vries, the American historian of Dutch descent, has labeled the first and second Dutch Atlantic Economy. The Dutch Atlantic Empire was at its zenith and the foundation was laid for the less extensive territorial presence of the Dutch Republic in later centuries. The two biographical options I had were Count Johan-Maurits van Nassau-Siegen, for seven years governor-general of Dutch Brazil, and Petrus Stuyvesant, director of Curaçao (1642–1644) and director general of New Netherland (1647–1664). As the latter covered a longer timeframe and as I was already familiar with the New Netherland sources, the choice was obvious. Johan-Maurits could wait.

When I began researching Stuyvesant, all the varying accounts of his reputation appeared an obstacle. I wanted to return to the original sources to find for myself what the real truth was. Yet gradually the interaction between "historical reality," to use that distinctly nonpostmodern phrase, and the later fiction became a separate and interesting subtheme, if only because of its richness—not only in America, but also in the Netherlands. The Frisian county of Weststellingwerf alone boasts three monuments to the man: a statue in Wolvega, a memorial along the Peter Stuyvesant Road near Scherpenzeel, and a pillar near the church of Peperga. Stuyvesant is obviously important to this sparsely populated rural county, which regularly organizes events that bear his name. He is one of the best known sons of this region. The old Dutch Reformed Church in Peperga, where Stuyvesant's father once preached the word of God, has not been used for religious services for years. It has changed hands a couple of times and has even been offered for sale to the City of New York. The small building embodies the difficulties facing a minister in this area. It is not known for certain where the Stuyvesant family lived when Pieter was born in 1611 or 1612. Likely in Peperga, but possibly in Blesdijke, a few miles up the road, where the vicarage once stood.

Stuyvesant junior entered the university at Franeker, but soon left it to join the Dutch West India Company, which especially in its early years bore a strong anti–Spanish stamp. For the son of a minister, possibly borne along by the euphoria that engulfed the Dutch Republic when the news broke of the taking of a Spanish-silver fleet by Admiral Piet Heyn, the West India Company was an obvious choice. Stuyvesant became a *commies,* a commissary within the civil branch of the Company. He was never a soldier, as is sometimes inferred from the fact that he had a leg missing. His duties as a West India Company official entailed the supervision of operations of the military branch of the company. In 1635 he served on the Brazilian archipelago Fernando de Noronha. Nowadays it is a natural park with a vulnerable ecosystem and is a veritable paradise for scuba divers. But in the seventeenth century the Dutch presence caused an ecological disaster. The ships' rats had found their way to land and feasted upon the local flightless birds. Then, as rats do, they multiplied and soon swarmed all over the main island. In an attempt to counter the rats, the Dutch deployed cats, which unsurprisingly also multiplied, quickly becoming pests in their own right. Fernando de Noronho has no public memory of Stuyvesant. The only reason we know he was actually there is that his father asked the Amsterdam directors of the West India Company to move him to a better place.

That better place was Curaçao. Stuyvesant was appointed commissary of the cargoes and spent the warm tropical evenings exchanging verses with one of his colleagues, Johan Farrett. Stuyvesant's poetry is extant in a manuscript in the Amsterdam Maritime Museum and his poems are signed "Virtue bears joy." The signature may reflect on the man's personality, but the poetry is not in his own hand.

After the demise of the director of Curaçao, thirty-year-old Stuyvesant was appointed his successor. He probably had lodgings somewhere in Fort Amsterdam. That fort, at the entrance of the natural harbor of Willemstad, is still the seat of government, to which the function of museum has been added. The local high school, the Peter Stuyvesant College, boasts a statue of its namesake. But what meaning could a white, seventeenth-century governor hold for Curaçao students of the twenty-first century?

Using Curaçao as a port of departure, Stuyvesant visited several places in the Caribbean. He went to St. Kitts to obtain provisions and was in charge of a raid on the Venezuelan coast to annoy the Spanish and enlarge the Curaçao livestock with a booty of 3,000 goats and sheep. A raid to the north was also in the cards. The target, the Spanish-held island of Saint Martin, was decided upon only once the expedition had set sail. The fort near present-day Philipsburg had only a small garrison and the Dutch overpowered their foes easily. Yet an immediate assault was risky: A siege aimed at forcing the enemy to choose between starvation and surrender seemed the better option. Even so, the fort had to be bombarded, so the Dutch decided to position a battery on a nearby hill. The cannons of the fort replied to the Dutch fire. The second Spanish volley hit the right leg of Stuyvesant, who was placing a flag on the battery. Johan Farrett waxed lyrical about the shot-off leg in a poem: "What crazy cannonball comes pounding on your leg, My dear Stuyvesant, and makes you fall to ground?"

With Stuyvesant out of action the siege was continued for a couple of weeks, but when it became clear that starving the fort would not work, the Dutch fleet returned to Curaçao. That is where, according to lore, Stuyvesant's leg was amputated and buried. The story is probably apocryphal, but it is indicative of the rich layers of mythology that have covered Stuyvesant's life. It is much more likely that his right leg was amputated on board one of the ships at Saint Martin and fed to the sharks.

In any event, in Curaçao Stuyvesant had no leg to stand on. His wound would not heal in a tropical climate and he decided to return to the Dutch Republic. He stayed with his sister and her husband in the small village of Alphen aan den Rijn. Apart from recuperating, he found time to fall in love with the sister of his brother-in-law. After a speedy courtship, the couple was married in the Walloon Church of Breda. The marriage register lists his new position: director of New Netherland. The decision to appoint Stuyvesant was made in Amsterdam, in a building still known as the West India House. In the twentieth century a statue of Stuyvesant was erected in the courtyard.

There are several more statues of Stuyvesant in America. In the upstate New York city of Kingston a very martial version can be found. Kingston was called Wiltwijck, the place of the Indians, in the Dutch days. During the wars with the Esopus tribe, Stuyvesant issued a veritable challenge. The Indian negotiators told him they didn't want war: they had done nothing wrong, were not angry, and did not want to fight—the aggression emanated from young braves who were out of their control. Stuyvesant answered that if these young braves were eager to fight, a battle could be arranged. He would pit a soldier against each one of them in a collective duel; it would not do for the young bloods to quench their anger on Dutch farmers, their wives, and children, who could not fight. The Indians found themselves unwilling to take up the challenge. Yet Stuyvesant's intimidating tactics did not buy a long peace. A couple of years later the Indians massacred Wiltwijck and Stuyvesant had to send in a group of soldiers. He did not take up command himself but appointed an experienced military man, Marten Kregier, instead. A martial statue for Kregier in Kingston might have been more appropriate.

Further north up the Hudson River, the remains of Fort Orange lie under highway overpasses built in the 1970s. One of the walls bears a plaque marking the spot of the fort. "Oranje boven" ("Up with Orange"), some Dutch tourist has scrawled on it in orange paint. Stuyvesant had been here too, at Fort Orange and the town of Beverwijck (now Albany). The New York State Archives hold most of his correspondence, which is being translated by Charles Gehring and Janny Venema as part of the New Netherland Project. Many of the documents have only barely survived the ordeal of flame and water, a result of the 1911 Capitol Fire. Stuyvesant's own handwriting would be difficult to read even if his letters were intact, as he had a very scribbly hand. It is a stroke of luck for his biographer that most of the official correspondence was written by well-trained scribes.

Back on Manhattan. Up the stairs in the New-York Historical Society I stare at the well-known portrait, the only seventeenth-century depiction on which all the later iconography is based. Stuyvesant seems to smile with his thin lips, as though my attempts to recover who he was were destined to be futile. The society holds some other family heirlooms, paintings of relatives, and his silver stamp. Some parts of the pear tree that he is supposed to have brought to the New World in 1647 are in the collection as well; another is in the collection of the Museum of the City of New York. The tree survived until 1867, when it was hit by a truck. The remains have become relics, worshiped in the temples of public history. Yet the seventeenth-century sources only list a ship called *The Peartree* and that is possibly the origin of yet another myth.

Stuyvesant Square holds a park with yet another Stuyvesant statue, sculpted by someone with a partly Dutch name, Gertrude Vanderbilt Whitney. Stuyvesant would not recognize this part of what used to be his bowery. He would not have liked it either: It is surrounded by the Beth Israel Medical Center, St. George's Episcopal Church, a Quaker Meeting House, and St.

Mary's Catholic Church of the Byzantine Rite. But no church of his "true Reformed religion."

A few blocks to the south lies St. Mark's-in-the-Bowery, built on the spot where once the chapel of Stuyvesant's bowery stood. This is where he is buried. The door of the church publicizes a ballet performance within its walls. Dancing on Stuyvesant's grave! In the churchyard stands a bust of Stuyvesant, donated by Dutch Queen Wilhelmina in the early twentieth century. In the wall of the church a tombstone is visible. It is a replica and gives the wrong year of his birth, 1580 instead of 1611 or 1612. The family vault inside the church was sealed with concrete after the demise of the last descendant. After Stuyvesant's death, minister Henricus Selijns wrote:

EPITAPH

For Petrus Stuyvesant,
late General of New Netherland

Stir not the sand too much, for there lies Stuyvesant,

Who erst commander was of all New Netherland.

Freely or no, unto the foe, the land did he give over.

If grief and sorrow any hearts do smite, his heart

Did die a thousand deaths, and undergo a smart

Insuff'rable. At first, too rich; at last, too *pauvre*.

Stir not the sand too much. Is the history of my protagonist so distant that it endures only in the meanings that many attach to it in the present? Am I trying to grasp the elusive shifting sand? Visiting the places where Stuyvesant has been, those places of memory, does not make me like him. I think my opinion of him has shifted and perhaps I am even beginning to understand him. I understand his formalistic way of thinking in governmental and judicial matters. I do not share his antipathy towards Jews or Quakers, but I see how it emanates from his desire for unity in the tender colonial society in his care. He was old fashioned in that, even for the seventeenth century.

I admire him for the way in which he embodied personal leadership. In late 1659 a number of colonists living in distant places on Manhattan fled to New Amsterdam out of fear of an Indian attack. Stuyvesant mounted his horse and rode out to boost their morale and convince them that it was better to fortify their villages than flee to the city. He knew he had to do this personally and did so, despite being feverish at the time. He knew the effect his presence would have.

I understand Stuyvesant's indignation when during a public meeting he was unexpectedly confronted by an adversary with an order from the States General to return to the Dutch Republic. The insolence of that provocation angered him and he found it difficult to control himself.

And I see how adept he was at playing the governmental and political game, how he could delegate where possible and intervene where needed. But if he would be transported to the twenty-first century by some time warp, would I like him? His arrogance, his sarcasm, his self-assuredness would make that difficult. But I would like to talk with him.

(RIGHT) **THE CASTELLO PLAN, 1660:** Jacques Cortelyou, surveyor general of the province of New Netherland, drew up a map in 1660 for Petrus Stuyvesant to send back home to the directors of the West India Company. This plan was subsequently lost, but a watercolor copy from about 1667 by Johannes Blaue survives. This watercolor was sold to Cosimo III de' Medici (1642–1723), probably in Amsterdam in 1669 when he and Prince Orsini visited that city to purchase art objects for Florence. It was discovered in 1900, within the archives of the Villa Castello. Shown here is a Fratella Alinari copy of the watercolor that was given to the Museum of the City of New York by La Biblioteca Medicea Laurenziana. Note the clearly delineated path of modern-day Broadway; it had long been a major Native American trail north. 49.150.

JAAP JACOBS (PH.D. LEIDEN UNIVERSITY 1999) HAS TAUGHT AT LEIDEN UNIVERSITY, THE UNIVERSITY OF AMSTERDAM, CORNELL UNIVERSITY, THE UNIVERSITY OF PENNSYLVANIA, AND OHIO UNIVERSITY. HE HAS PUBLISHED EXTENSIVELY ON NEW NETHERLAND. HIS LATEST BOOK IS *NEW NETHERLAND: A HISTORY OF THE DUTCH COLONY ON THE HUDSON* (CORNELL UNIVERSITY PRESS). HE IS CURRENTLY WORKING ON A BIOGRAPHY OF PETRUS STUYVESANT.

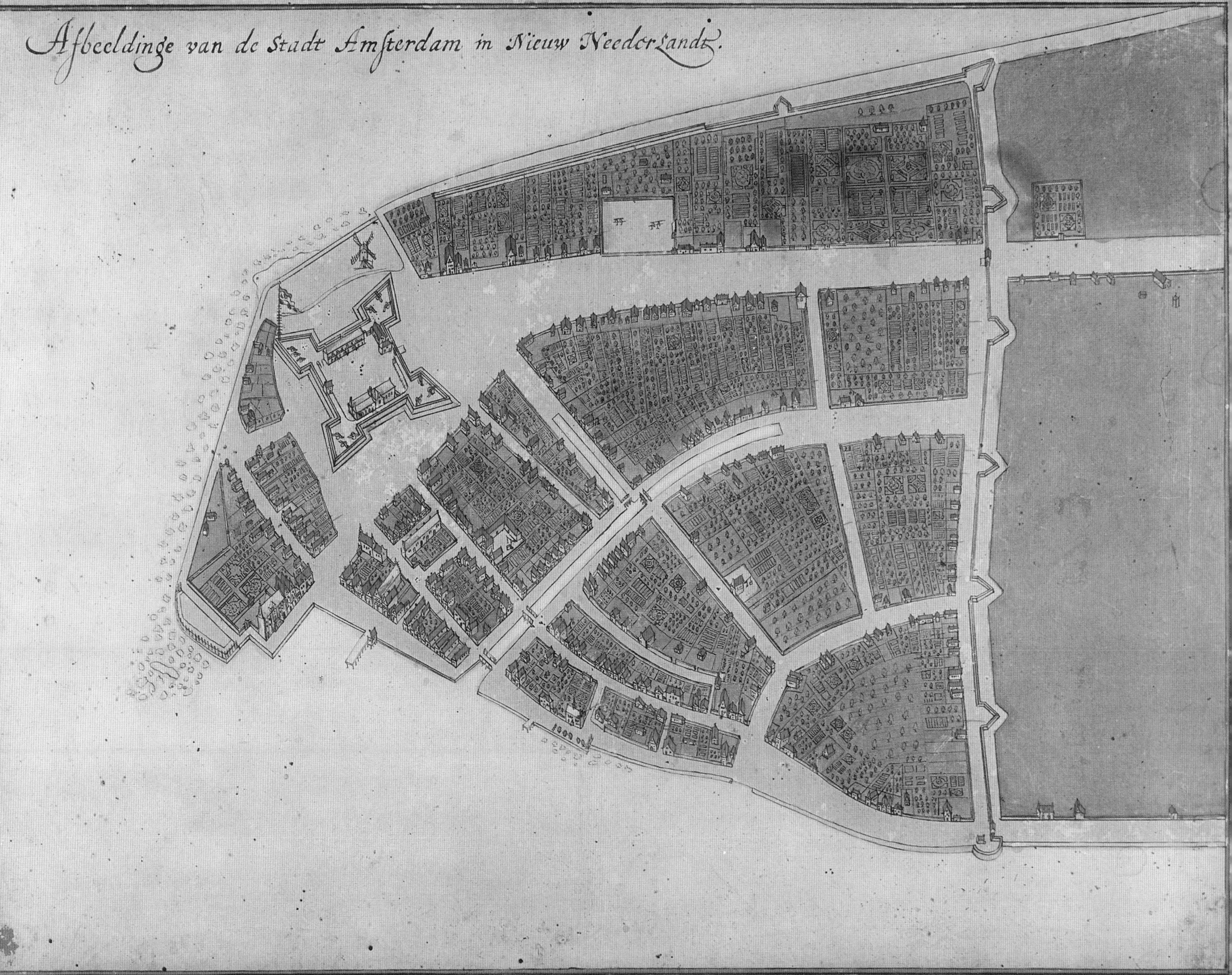
Afbeeldinge van de Stadt Amsterdam in Nieuw Neederlandt.

NEW YORK, 1650: This etching is a modern imagining of old New York, ultimately published in a portfolio titled *Three Hundred Years of New York, Twelve Etchings* by Anton Schutz (1894–1977), published by the New York Graphic Society in 1926. "About this time," the artist wrote, "there are four windmills mentioned in New Amsterdam. . . . In the middle ground is the first fort, protection against the Indians, in the distance Governor's Island and the New York Bay." GIFT OF MRS. ROBERT W. HIGBIE, JR. 59.210.9.

THE HALF MOON, 1609: Here is a fanciful nineteenth-century woodcut view of an encounter between Native Americans and the crew of Henry Hudson's *Half Moon*, anchored by the Palisade cliffs. Robert Juet, a crew member, entered in his journal for September 11, 1609 [as translated in 1841]: "Was fair and very hot weather. At one o'clock in the afternoon, we weighed and went into the river, the wind at south-south-west, little wind. . . . Then we anchored and . . . the people of the country came aboard of us, making show of love, and gave us tobacco and Indian wheat, and departed for that night; but we durst not trust them." PRINT ARCHIVES.

THE TREATY BETWEEN GOVERNOR MINUIT AND THE ABORIGINES, 1626: William Howland (1822–1869) was a wood engraver of historical re-creations such as this depiction of the sale of Manhattan Island, legendarily for goods costing the Dutch sixty guilders, in 1840s currency translation a mere twenty-four dollars. Pieter Minuit (1594–1638), the colony's Director, struck a deal with the Native Americans. The purchase was understood differently by both parties, the natives having no concept of ownership of real estate. PRINT ARCHIVES.

AN INDIAN VILLAGE OF THE MANHATTANS, PRIOR TO THE OCCUPATION BY THE DUTCH, CA. 1600: Though we commence the history of New York for purposes of this volume with the arrival of the first Europeans in 1609, the Munsee branch of the Lenape (later named by Europeans the Delaware Indians) could argue for a date far earlier. *Manhattan* is a phonetic interpretation of a word in the Munsee dialect meaning (among other offered etymologies) "hilly island." Some of the Lenape trails would survive as urban thoroughfares, while others would be obliterated by the grid plan. LITHOGRAPH BY GEORGE HAYWARD. PUBLISHED IN *VALENTINE'S MANUAL*, 1858.

DANCE ON THE BATTERY IN THE PRESENCE OF PETER STUYVESANT, CA. 1650: Asher B. Durand (1796–1886) was inspired to paint this fanciful scene from Washington Irving's comic *History of New York* (1809), in which the author, writing under the pseudonym "Diedrich Knickerbocker," wrote of "a young vrouw, of great figure in the gay world, and who, having lately come from Holland, of course led the fashions in the city, made her appearance in not more than half-a-dozen petticoats, and these too of most alarming shortness. An universal whisper ran through the assembly, the old ladies all felt shocked in the extreme, the young ladies blushed, and felt excessively for the 'poor thing,' and even the governor himself was observed to be a little troubled in mind." Durand exhibited the painting in 1838 at the National Academy of Design and sold it to Thomas H. Faile, a local businessman. OIL ON CANVAS, 1838. 32 x 46½. GIFT OF JANE RUTHERFORD FAILE THROUGH KENNETH C. FAILE. 55.248.

(RIGHT) **THE PROTOTYPE VIEW, 1650–53:** This splendid view of the little settlement around the Battery was first published in I. N. Phelps Stokes' monumental six-volume *Iconography of Manhattan Island* (published 1915–28). Discovered in the State Archives at The Hague, it was dubbed the "prototype view" because Stokes believed it to be a 1670 copy of a known view from 1650 that has not survived. Nineteenth-century print from the watercolor. THE J. CLARENCE DAVIES COLLECTION. 34.100.29.

NIEUW AMSTERDAM OFTE NUE NIEUW IORX OPT' TEYLANT MAN

NIEUW
op t Eylan
D
C
E
B
F
A
G
A. Het Fort B. de Kerck C. de Wintmolen D. dese Vlagge wert op gehaelt als daer Schepen in de Haven k

NIEUW AMSTERDAM OP T' EYLANT MANHATTANS, CA. 1651: This inset of New Amsterdam is part of a larger map titled *Novi Belgii Novæque Angliæ* (Map of New Belgium and New England). One of at least thirty-one "Visscher Views" that were published as late as the mid eighteenth century, this map was executed by Nicolaes Visscher (1649–1702) in 1685. The view bears a legend at the bottom: A. *Het Fort* (the fort); B. *de Kerck* (the church); C. *de Wintmolen* (the Windmill); D. *dese Vlagge wert op gehaelt als daer Schepen in de Haven kommen.* (This flag was hoisted whenever ships came in the harbor.); E. *t' gevangen huys* (the jail house); F. *de H. Generaels huys* (the Director General's house); G. *t' Gerecht* (the gallows); H. *de Kaeck*, to the left of F (the kitchen); I. *Compagnies Pachuys* (the company's storehouse); K. *Stadts Herberch* (the town's inn). THE J. CLARENCE DAVIES COLLECTION. 29.100.1572.

THE GRAFT OR CANAL, 1659: This nineteenth-century engraving depicts the canal and fishing bridge that ran down present-day Broad Street until 1676, when the canal was filled in. Heer Graft (sometimes spelled Heeren Gracht)—Lord's Canal, named after one of the main canals in Amsterdam—was the name given by the Dutch to the part of the street that ran between present-day Beaver and Pearl Streets in 1657. Like all later views of New Amsterdam, this sketch may be challenged for its sentimentality and questionable accuracy; all the same it is not without value to those who today would wish to envision the Dutch city. THE J. CLARENCE DAVIES COLLECTION.

(RIGHT) **MAP OF THE ORIGINAL GRANTS OF VILLAGE LOTS, 1642:** The full title is the best descriptor: "Map of the Original Grants of Village Lots from the Dutch West India Company to the inhabitants of New Amsterdam, now New-York, lying below the present line of Wall Street. Grants commencing A.D. 1642, Located from historical & legal records by Henry Dunreath Tyler. New York 1897." This map owes much to a version that appeared in *Valentine's Manual* forty years earlier. Depicted are property lots with dimensions, names of owners, and year of grant, 1642–58. *Henry D. Tyler's Colored Wall Maps: No. I.*, Dunreath Publishing Co. 1897. GIFT OF AN ANONYMOUS DONOR. 26.272.

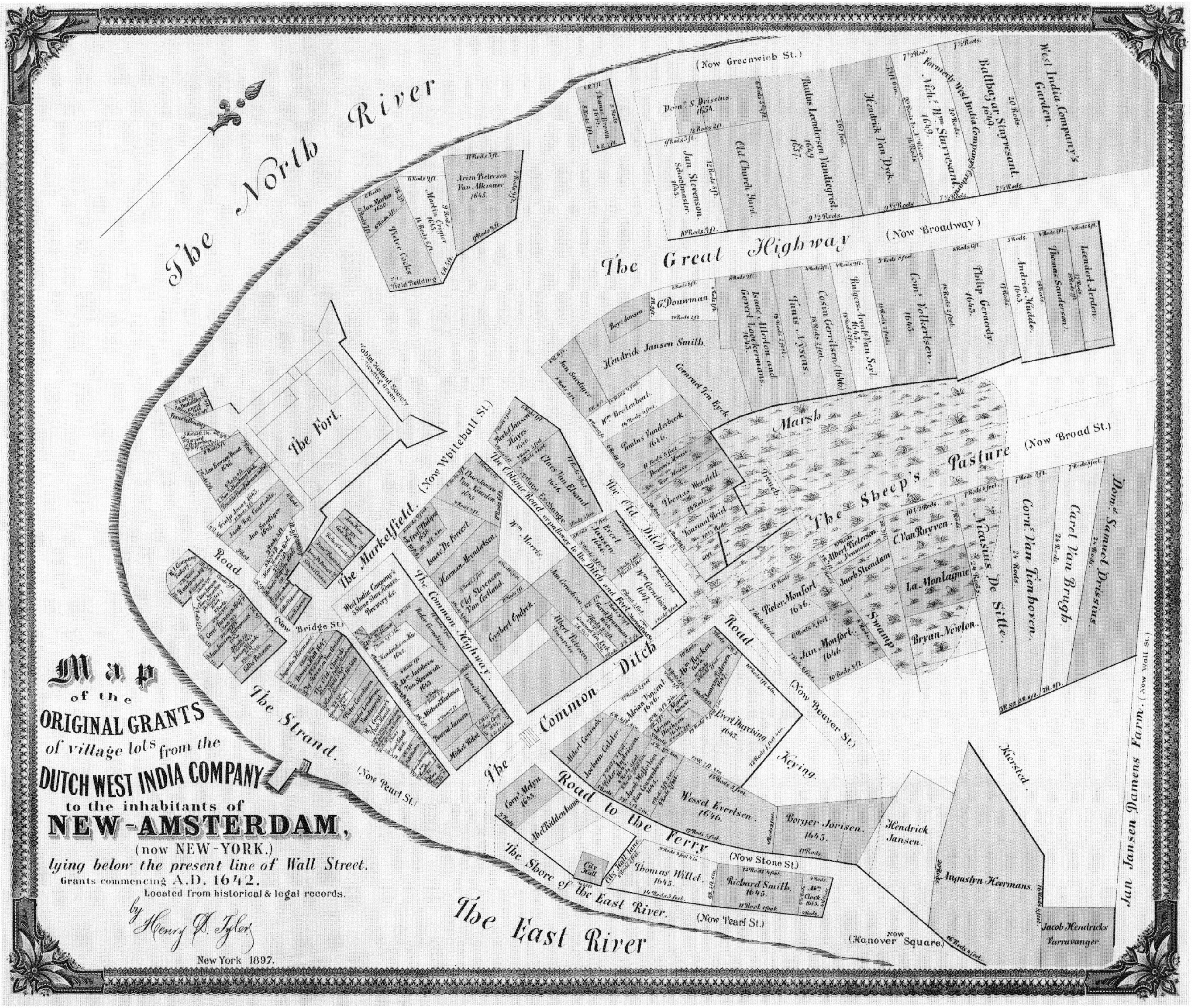

Map
of the
ORIGINAL GRANTS
of village lots from the
DUTCH WEST INDIA COMPANY
to the inhabitants of
NEW-AMSTERDAM,
(now NEW-YORK,)
lying below the present line of Wall Street.
Grants commencing A.D. 1642.
Located from historical & legal records.
by Henry B. Tyler
New York 1897.
The North River
The East River
(Now Greenwich St.)
The Great Highway
(Now Broadway)
The Fort.
The Marketfield.
(Now Whitehall St.)
The Common Highway.
The Old Ditch
The Common Ditch
The Sheep's Pasture
(Now Broad St.)
Marsh
Swamp
Road
(Now Beaver St.)
The Strand.
(Now Pearl St.)
The Road to the Ferry
(Now Stone St.)
The Shore of the East River.
(Now Pearl St.)
Now (Hanover Square)
(Now Wall St.)
Jan Jansen Damens Farm.
West India Company's Garden.
Balthazar Stuyvesant. 1649.
Nich's W^m. Stuyvesant. 1649.
Hendrick Van Dyck.
Paulus Leendersen Vandiegrist. 1649 1657.
Dom^e. S. Drissius. 1654.
Old Church Yard.
Jan Stevenson. Schoolmaster. 1643.
Arien Pietersen Van Alkmaer 1645.
Martin Crigier 1643.
Jan Martin 1650.
Pieter Cocks
Field Building
Leendert Aerden.
Thomas Sanderson.
Andries Hudde. 1643.
Philip Geraerdy. 1643.
Cor^s. Volkertsen. 1643.
Rutgers Arentz Van Seel. 1643.
Cosin Gerritsen (1646)
Tunis Nyssen.
Isaac Allerton and Goverd Loockermans. 1643.
G. Douwman
Boye Jansen
Hendrick Jansen Smith.
Jan Snediger
Gerrit Ten Eyck.
W^m. Bredenbent.
Paulus Vanderbeeck. 1646.
Thomas Wandell.
Toussaint Briel
Roeloff Jansen Haves.
Claes Van Elsland 1646.
Isaac De Forest.
Harman Meyndertsen.
Olof Stevensen Van Cortland.
Gysbert Opdyck.
W^m. Morris
Jan Cornelisen
Albert Pietersen. Trumpeter.
W^m. Goudisen 1647.
West India Company's 5 Stone Store Houses. Brewery &c.
Michiel Paulusen
Barent Jansen
Michel Tadens
Pieter Cornelisen.
Abel Riddenhaus
Cor^s. Melyn. 1645.
City Hall
Thomas Willet. 1645.
Richard Smith. 1645.
Wessel Evertsen. 1646.
Borger Jorisen. 1643.
Evert Duycking 1645.
Adrian Vincent 1646.
Jochem Calder.
Albert Coninck.
Keying.
Hendrick Jansen.
Augustyn Heermans.
Kiersted.
Jacob Hendricks Varravanger
Pieter Monfort. 1646.
Jan Monfort. 1646.
Jacob Steendam
C. Van Ruyven.
La Montagne
Bryan Newton.
Nicasius De Sille.
Cor^s. Van Tienhoven.
Carel Van Brugh.
Dom^e. Samuel Drissius.
Jacob Roy Constable.
Jan Snediger 1645.
Francis Douty
Trench

Petrus Stuijvesant:

LAND GRANT SIGNED BY PETRUS STUYVESANT, 1664: On May 15, 1664, Petrus Stuyvesant signed in bold hand a grant of land in Brooklyn to Thomas Lambertse of Pearl Street. Also signing was Cornelis van Ruyven, secretary of the Council. INK ON PARCHMENT. GIFT OF DELANCEY KOUNTZE. 33.307.

(RIGHT) **FIRE CURTAIN, LIBERTY THEATER:** In an odd reminder of New York's beginnings, four hundred years ago, the fire curtain at the now vanished Liberty Theater (open to the public from 1904 to the 1980s, at 234 West 42nd Street) depicted Henry Hudson's *Half Moon*. Photographer Andrew Moore tells the story, "One day while leaving the IRT at 42nd Street, I noticed how the renovation of the New Victory Theater had added the original projecting entrance stair from the days of David Belasco. My interest was piqued by this nostalgic reconstruction, and through some city contacts, I was allowed access to all the closed theaters in Times Square during a six-month period in 1995–96. Of the nine theaters along 42nd Street between 7th and 8th Avenues, two were undergoing preservation and renovation, while the rest remained as empty shells, some utterly stripped, the others in fair condition at best. I've always enjoyed the architecture of theaters, but what struck me was the silence of these once throbbing spaces in the heart of Manhattan. After nearly a century of audiences, workers, and performers circulating through them, the theaters now had the barrenness of gigantic skeletal remains." Today the remains of the Liberty are part of the New 42nd Street entertainment complex. PHOTOGRAPH BY ANDREW MOORE, 1996. GIFT OF THE PHOTOGRAPHER. 01.18.2.

PHOTO I.D.

CHAPTER II | 1665–1763

OPEN CITY

NEW YORK AS A PORT TOWN IN THE MID-EIGHTEENTH CENTURY

Sara Stidstone Gronim

From its beginnings, New York was a port, and as such it was far from a sedate, tradition-bound town. Rather, New York was open to a host of influences from elsewhere. Goods, people, ideas: all flowed into the port, sometimes welcomed by New Yorkers and sometimes not. As residents of a port town, New Yorkers encountered both innovation and opportunities, and threats to the familiar, the comfortable, and the safe. Because it was a port, New York was particularly subject to events in the wider Atlantic world—the vagaries of trade, the strains and opportunities of war. Even the weather in other places influenced New York. This vulnerability to changes elsewhere, this porosity, the mingling of the delightfully new and the dangerous, all made for a boisterous, contentious, and ultimately unsettled town.

The townscape reflected its nature as a port. By 1750 New York had grown to about 12,000 residents, its streets paved with cobblestones and lined with handsome brick houses and dozens of shops, much like towns anywhere around the rim of the North Atlantic. At the same time the townscape was very much shaped by trade. The East River was lined with docks, wharfs, and shipyards, and nearby parts of town were filled with the workshops of coopers and sail makers, the long sheds of ropewalks, and the warehouses of chandlers with their varied array of goods used by ships at sea. Ports draw people in from many places. The people who walked the streets of New York had origins in the Netherlands, England, Scotland, Ireland, Germany, and France. Eleven different Protestant denominations erected churches in the town and a congregation of Jews built a synagogue. Fully a fifth of New Yorkers had origins in Africa, and most of this group was held in slavery. There were Moslems from West Africa, Portuguese-speaking Catholics from Angola, Madagascar Africans speaking the languages of the Indian Ocean. From all over the world people had flowed into the port—willingly or not. There they mingled, sometimes happily and sometimes not.

The eighteenth century was a time of inventions, innovations, and discoveries all over the Atlantic world, and news of these came to New York. By 1725 New Yorkers had their own weekly newspaper, and by the 1740s they had three. In them they could read about a grate that made fires less smoky, a method of desalinizing sea water, and a canvas tunic with corks for sailors swept overboard. In 1745 London-trained Anthony Lamb opened a shop that sold improved sextants, compasses, and similar instruments for land surveyors and sea captains. Improvements to ship design and rigging made the routes plied by New Yorkers somewhat faster and more reliable. By 1755 the packet service between Falmouth, England, and New York was so improved that news and letters seemed to fly across the Atlantic.

In 1730, Nicholas Bayard built the first sugar house in the city, the first of many to process raw sugar into the white crystals for which there was such demand. Rum distilleries, too, became common in the city.

The openness of a port meant that those New Yorkers who so desired could avail themselves of new opportunities. The example of "tar water" illustrates how an innovation developed elsewhere could be embraced by New Yorkers. Tar water was a solution of spring water that was mixed with pine tar until the spirituous resins of the tar impregnated the water. The tar was then allowed to settle out and the water could be imbibed as medicine. In the 1730s an account of its use to ward off smallpox in South Carolina appeared in a London newspaper. The London story was reprinted in a New York newspaper and sometime thereafter New Yorkers tried tar water out for themselves. James Alexander, a prominent lawyer, began to take it in hopes of staving off the gout and kidney stones to which he was prone. "Yet it soon had an unexpected Effect," he wrote a friend. "For two years past and more I had almost continually a Looseness, with wind in the Stomack and Guts which often swelled me up . . . After three or four days using the tarr water, I found that my Looseness was gone, was not troubled with wind as before [and] I got a keen appetite Such as I remember not to have had these twenty years." Cadwallader Colden, the colony's surveyor general, had his own successes with tar water treating fevers in his family and read about similar successes in Ireland. In 1745, he reported these happy outcomes in the *New-York Weekly Post-Boy*. Thus was tar water, originating in South Carolina and first reported on in London, made part of the healing repertoire of New Yorkers.

Some New Yorkers became aware of a new cultural style that was coming into fashion in places like London and Edinburgh, an orientation to life that was urbane and sophisticated. By the mid-eighteenth century, New York had taken on some of the attributes of a more elegant town, with coffee houses for conversation, and the Bowling Green laid out for evening strolls. Nonetheless, the Scottish-born physician Alexander Hamilton, visiting New York City in 1744, complained that despite such amenities the men he met seemed mostly to value hard drinking and bawdy humor and were indifferent to the cultivation of the finer virtues.

In the 1750s, a group of locally born young men sought to transform the culture of New York. Three young lawyers, William Livingston, William Smith, Jr., and John Morin Scott, took the lead, hoping to reform the culture of, at the very least, men who provided political and social leadership for the colony. In 1752 and 1753 the trio published the *Independent Reflector* with essays full of suggestions for improving New York. They promoted the establishment of New York City's first college in 1754, King's College (now Columbia), to offer young men the gentleman's education available elsewhere. And they organized the New York Society Library, a private lending library, which they hoped would become the center of intellectual life in New York.

But most New Yorkers were uninterested in such erudition. Rather than the fashion for intellectual sophistication, they embraced fashionable consumption, abundantly available in a port town. Advertisements in newspapers and news in family letters attest that New Yorkers had also cultivated a passion for elegance. Shops offered patterns for the latest styles from London, along with an array of beautiful fabrics, and dressmakers advertised their ability to make them up. John Baptiste Guerbois "from Paris" offered to teach young New Yorkers French, and eager New York families hired itinerant dancing masters to turn their ducklings into swans.[2] The town erected an impressive new building, the Royal Exchange, with rooms for balls and concerts. Wealthy New Yorkers erected imposing mansions and built spacious seats in the nearby countryside. Gerardus Duyckinck advertised landscapes and seascapes to adorn New Yorkers' homes, and Theophilus Hardenbrook advertised that he could design interiors for all sorts of rooms in styles "Arabian, Chinese, Persian, Gothic, Muscovite, Paladian, Roman Vitruvian, and Egyptian."[3] By the 1750s theater companies from London came regularly to New York City to perform. The plays New Yorkers saw were the same ones seen by Londoners, such as *Othello* and *The Beaux' Stratagem*. At times it seemed that any association with elegance was a selling point. One Dr. Stork, claiming that he had attended "her royal highness the Princess of Wales," informed New Yorkers that they, too, could have such fashionable care.[4]

Not that elegance was the only import into the colony. Plenty of more modest New Yorkers jostled for room at traveling pantomimes, Punch and Judy shows, and displays of exotica from all over the world. In 1728, New Yorkers could see a lion exhibited at a fair. In 1751 they could admire a tightrope-walking monkey; in 1754 they could gawk at an alligator; in 1756 a twenty-one foot snake killed in the Alleghenies; in 1757 a buffalo; and in 1763 an elk. Sometimes people showed off local curiosities, too. In 1732, for example, a woman pulled up a radish and, the *New-York Gazette* reported, found that it had "the Appearance of a Child's Hand and Fingers," which she found "surprisingly strange." Preserved in alcohol and put on display where an "Abundance of People resort daily to see it," the radish "continues in the shape and colour of a human Hand and Five Fingers with Sinews and Joynts, which," the paper claimed, "open and shut."[5] In 1751, someone exhibited a live porcupine—it's uncertain how exotic New Yorkers found that. George Hopkins the next year was probably more successful with his exhibit of a seven-legged calf.

In the eighteenth century, one of the most dramatic innovations that lent itself to such shows was the unfolding understanding of electricity. Benjamin Franklin's experiments were reported respectfully in the New York press, as well as the honors that ensued. By the 1740s men with such interests had developed a range of equipment with which they could do experiments, experiments that then could be demonstrated to the public. The first man to visit New York with such demonstrations was Archibald Spencer, a Scottish physician who toured colonial ports in 1744. Richard Brickell gave electrical demonstrations in 1748, Lewis Evans and Ebenezer Kinnersley of Philadelphia in 1751 and 1752 respectively, and an Irish Quaker, William Johnson, in the 1760s. Johnson directed his advertisements to "Ladies and Gentlemen," promising them "a rational and agreeable entertainment." Johnson, then, distanced his performance from the kind of curiosity-showing that appealed to the lower sorts, and hoped his electrical demonstrations would encourage the kind of cosmopolitan sophistication that Livingston and his set longed for. "[T]he knowledge of Nature tends to enlarge the Mind," proclaimed Johnson, "and gives us more noble and exalted Ideas of the God of Nature."[6] Nonetheless, it's hard to know exactly how ennobling and exalting Johnson's audience found his electrical show. One of his demonstrations was the "Salute Repuls'd," in which a lady's cheeks and lips were charged so that no man could kiss her, no matter how hard he tried. Whatever Johnson's intentions, his audience may well have seen this as being as much fun as watching a monkey performing on a tightrope, and certainly more interesting than a porcupine. Nonetheless, high and low, the circulation of new inventions, medicines, goods, and entertainments enlightened and amused New Yorkers.

Not everything that entered the port was so welcome. A port is porous, and all sorts of people drifted into the town. In good times employment opportunities were brisk but even then some hung about on the fringes. Alongside the visible economy was a shadow one in which people traded castoff or, more often, stolen goods, the clothes, silverware, jewelry, and other sundries so prized by New Yorkers. Taverns that catered to sailors, servants, and slaves were often rowdy though, truth be told, more than a few wealthy New Yorkers contributed to the mayhem. Oliver DeLancey, scion of one of New York's wealthiest merchant families, was a noted tavern brawler, while Adolphe Philipse, scion of another, was known for his voracious sexual appetite. All in all, authorities had steady work moving against pickpockets, burglars, counterfeiters, and other disturbers of property and peace.

Slavery, too, had taken root in New York. Although initially it had been an ad hoc practice, with real possibilities for freedom, white New Yorkers soon shifted to making slavery a permanent condition. Thus they ensured a stable labor force, which they then justified in terms of "race," a new idea that asserted that human beings were divided into natural groups with inherent characteristics. In this they followed the lead of other slaveholding colonists, enacting laws that severely constrained slaves' lives modeled on the slave codes developed in places like Jamaica and South Carolina. As advertisements for runaway slaves attest, African-descended people in New York in fact lived lives much like many modest New Yorkers. They worked as servants, assisted in shops, and engaged in the many varieties of craftwork. The very frequency of ads for runaway slaves is also testimony to how often they resisted their enslavement.

However, the anxiety and anger white New Yorkers felt toward those slaves who so resisted culminated in the most horrific event to occur in colonial New York. The setting was the edgy atmosphere of early 1741, after New Yorkers had struggled through a long trade depression in the 1730s and endured a particularly harsh winter in 1740–41. In late February, the house of merchant Robert Hogg was robbed. John Hughson, a man who ran a public house that catered to the "lower" sort—sailors, servants, slaves—was found with the stolen goods and he, his wife, an Irish woman who lived with them, and two slaves who frequented the house, were indicted for the theft. So far, the incident was simply one among many stemming from New York's underground economy of petty theft and the trade in stolen goods.

However, as the investigation of these five proceeded, a fire broke out at the fort and burned the soldiers' barracks and the governor's house to the ground.

The next week there was another fire, and the week after that three more. In all, by early April, ten fires were set in the town by a person or persons unknown. Hughson's servant now let something unexpected slip: these fires had been set as part of a conspiracy to burn the town, kill as many inhabitants as possible, and take their possessions. By August, accusations of participation in this alleged conspiracy spiraled upward until, in the end, 133 people—twenty of them white and 113 black—stood trial. White New Yorkers particularly loathed those men among the accused whom they themselves held in slavery. They had been, as one judge claimed, "treated here with tenderness and humanity"; hence their efforts (whatever they may have been) to overthrow their enslavement, as one of the prosecuting attorneys said, could only be attributed to "monstrous ingratitude."[7] Four of the accused whites were convicted and hanged, with another six banished from New York. Among the accused slaves, seventy were sold out of the colony and thirty-one were executed. Cruelly, half of the convicted slaves were executed by being burned alive. The so-called Conspiracy of 1741 was as dramatic and harsh an incident as the Salem witch trials in Massachusetts fifty years before, fueled by the increasing acceptance among white New Yorkers of the idea of separate races, however much black New Yorkers resisted.

Disease came, too. Some ships sailed into port with the visibly ill, and the coming and going of people and goods from the hinterlands meant that epidemics spread easily. Suspect ships were quarantined off Bedloe's Island and in the winter of 1759–60 a "pest house" was built there. Happily, in the 1730s, New Yorkers learned of the novel procedure of inoculation for smallpox, news of which came from the Ottoman Empire. Inoculation almost always gave people a mild case of smallpox that they survived but nonetheless they developed lifelong immunity. As more and more New Yorkers took up inoculation, smallpox, at least, was to some modest degree less threatening. But nothing protected New Yorkers from epidemics altogether.

Lastly, even more so then than now, New Yorkers were subject to the variability of weather, wind, and tides. Every local almanac included tide tables and the dates of full moons, for tides determined sailing times and full moons allowed night sailing. Harsh winters, such as that of 1740–41, caused widespread suffering in a town where firewood grew dear and employment slacked off. New Yorkers' trade was overwhelmingly in foodstuffs from the hinterland: flour and bread, apples and cider, cheese and salt meat, pickled oysters and dried fish, most of it bound for the sugar plantations of the West Indies. Drought, late springs, or heavy rains in the surrounding countryside threatened the port's prosperity. But it wasn't only local weather that affected New Yorkers. The rhythms of trade were affected by weather elsewhere. From late March to June there was a great rush of outbound ships to the West Indies, leaving once the harbor was free of ice but hurrying to beat the hurricane season to the south. And in October and November, when shipping might be expected to slacken off, there was an inbound rush, for the sugar crop came to market then. A port was always subject to the turn of the seasons, vulnerable to the fluctuations of the weather, and of necessity attuned to the climate of distant places.

In the eighteenth century New York was a port, with all that the nature of a port implies. The inhabitants themselves were a heterogeneous assortment of ethnicities, religions, and occupations, with some families in the town for generations but many as newcomers or transients. Fashions and amusements came and went, but so did epidemics and abrupt changes of fortune. Some new ideas and practices, such as smallpox inoculation or better ways to rig a ship, were of clear benefit, but others, such as race and slavery, only bred conflict. Whatever decorum Livingston and his friends might have wished for, New York was steadfast only in its openness to elsewhere.

(RIGHT) **A VIEW OF FORT GEORGE WITH THE CITY OF NEW YORK FROM THE SOUTHWEST, CA. 1735:** The depicted stronghold is the old Fort Amsterdam, built in 1626 by the Dutch, renamed Fort James after the British takeover of 1664, and renamed again for George in 1714. It survived even after the American revolutionaries set it aflame in 1776. This "Carwitham View" is named for its engraver, John Carwitham ("I. Carwitham, sculpt."). Trinity Church may be seen at the left. BEQUEST OF MRS. J. INSLEY BLAIR IN MEMORY OF MR. AND MRS. J. INSLEY BLAIR. 52.100.30.

SARA STIDSTONE GRONIM IS AN ASSOCIATE PROFESSOR OF HISTORY AT THE C.W. POST CAMPUS OF LONG ISLAND UNIVERSITY. SHE HAS PUBLISHED A NUMBER OF ARTICLES ABOUT COLONIAL NEW YORK, INCLUDING ARTICLES ON MAPPING, ON SMALLPOX AND INOCULATION, AND ON THE BOTANIST JANE COLDEN. HER BOOK *EVERYDAY NATURE: KNOWLEDGE OF THE NATURAL WORLD IN COLONIAL NEW YORK* WAS PUBLISHED BY RUTGERS UNIVERSITY PRESS IN 2007.

I. Carwitha

A View of FORT GEORGE *with the* CITY *of* NEW YORK *from the* S W.

Printed for Carington Bowles Map & Printseller, at No. 69 in St. Pauls Church Yard, London.

VIEW OF NEW AMSTERDAM, 1673: In 1897 William Loring Andrews wrote of this fanciful engraving on copper ("N. Amsterdam, ou N. Iork in Ameriq"): "This print is enclosed in a border, and one-third of the picture on the left hand side is covered with tropical trees and plants and with human figures presumed to represent the aboriginal inhabitants of the country. The section of the city which is visible is virtually the same as that in Allard's view [see page 35, "Totius Neobelgii Nova Et Accuratissima Tabula (Restitutio View), c. 1674]. The only important variation to be noted is that there is one less pier upon the water front." PUBLISHED BY PIETER MORTIER, CA. 1700. ARTIST UNKNOWN. BEQUEST OF MARGARET D. STEARNS. 89.77.1.

VIEW OF NEW YORK, CA. 1673 (THE SCHENK VIEW): In 1673 the Dutch Republic briefly regained control of the city from the English, to whom they had lost it in 1664. By treaty in November 1674 the Dutch ceded title back to England. It was this brief restitution of Dutch rule to the city that Peter Schenk depicted in 1702. His view of New Amsterdam is copied from the prototype view on the Restitutio View (see page 35). COPPER ENGRAVING. THE J. CLARENCE DAVIES COLLECTION. 29.100.1689.

(RIGHT) **TOTIUS NEOBELGII NOVA ET ACCURATISSIMA TABULA (RESTITUTIO VIEW), CA. 1674:** This map was originally published ca. 1651 as "Novi Belgii Novæque Angliæ (Map of New Belgium and New England), by Nicolaes Visscher. The Dutch reconquest of 1673 led Carel Allard to reissue the map, replacing Visscher's depiction of Nieuw Amsterdam with the current "Restitutio View" of the city formerly known as Nieuw Jorck. CARTOGRAPHER AND PUBLISHER, CAREL ALLARD. THE J. CLARENCE DAVIES COLLECTION. 18 x 21. 29.100.2199.

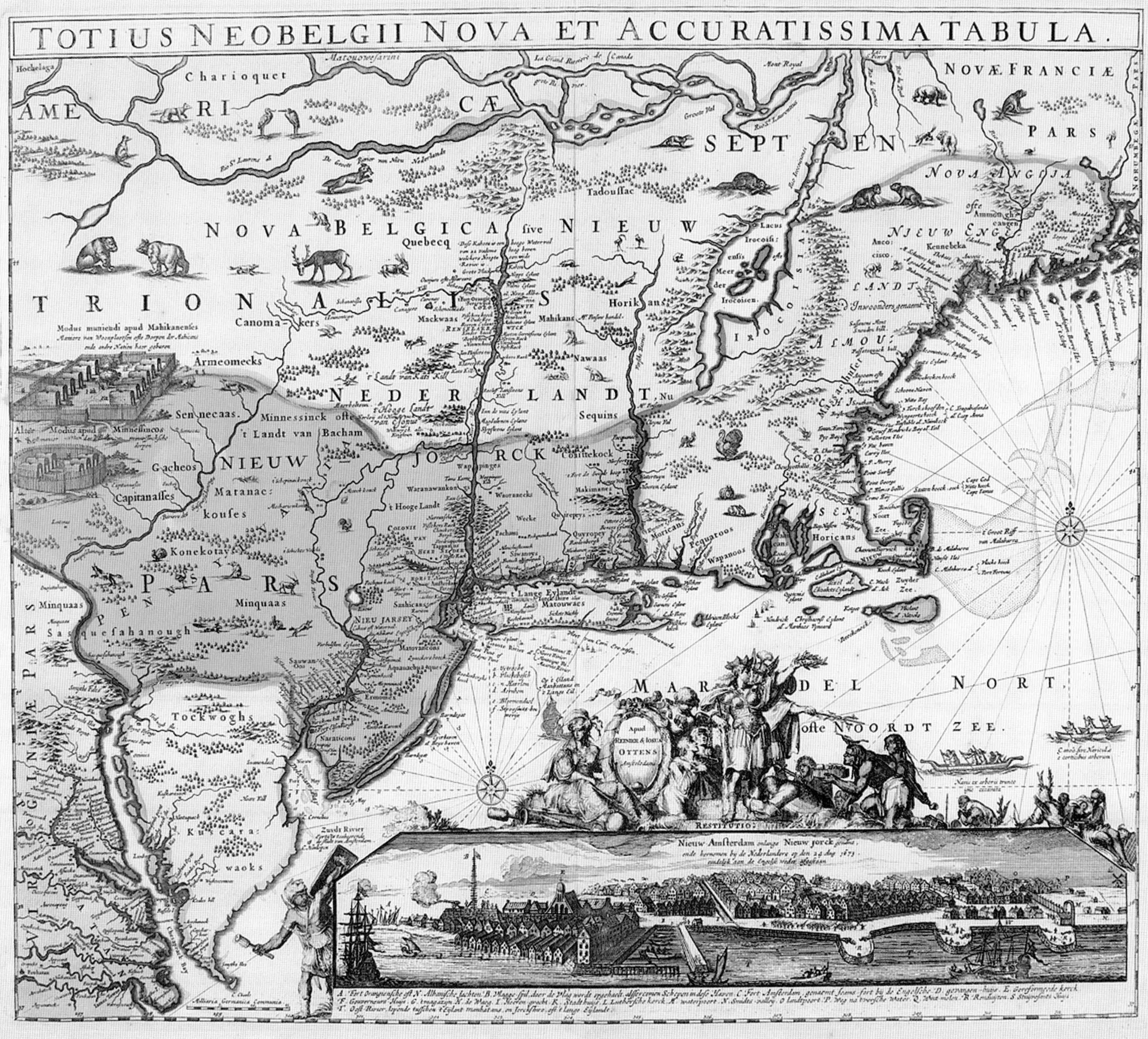
TOTIUS NEOBELGII NOVA ET ACCURATISSIMA TABULA.
AMERICÆ SEPTENTRIONALIS
NOVÆ FRANCIÆ PARS
NOVA ANGLIA
NOVA BELGICA sive NIEUW NEDERLANDT
NIEUW ENGELANDT
NIEUW JORCK
PARS
Chariorquet
Tadoussac
Quebecq
Canomakers
Armeomecks
Sennecaas.
Minnessinck ofte 't Landt van Bacham
Gacheos
Capitanasses
Matanac: kouses
Konekotay
Minquaas
Sasquesahanough
Tockwoghs
Kuscara: waoks
Mackwaas
Mahikans
Nawaas
Sequins
Wappinges
Waranawankon
't Hooge Landt
Wauranecks
Weeke
Makimanes
Quiripeys
Horikans
Pequatoos
Wapanoos
Horicans
Irocoisen
Kennebeka
Nieuw Amsterdam
NIEU JARSEY
't Lange Eylandt
Matouwacs
Manovaacons
Aquamachukes
Naraticons
Sawwanoos
MAR DEL NORT ofte NOORDT ZEE.
VIRGINIÆ PARS
Apud REINER & IOSUA OTTENS Amstelodami
RESTITUTIO.
Nieuw-Amsterdam onlangs Nieuw Jorck genaemt, ende hernomen by de Nederlanders op den 24 Aug. 1673
Modus muniendi apud Mahikanenses

No. 1 The residence of Jacob Leisler on "the Strand" (now Whitehall Street, N.Y.)
THE FIRST BRICK DWELLING ERECTED IN THE CITY.

THE RESIDENCE OF JACOB LEISLER ON "THE STRAND," 1679: The English Revolution of 1688 bitterly divided the populace of New York. In 1689, Jacob Leisler, who headed the anti-Catholic burghers and artisans, seized New York's Fort James in the name of the Protestant William and Mary, who had seized the crown of England at the invitation of Parliament. The sitting governor, Francis Nicholson, seemed unwilling to accept the new monarchs' authority. Worse yet, rumors flew that he, former governor Thomas Dongan, and some Jacobite supporters of James were plotting to seize the city in league with the French. Leisler claimed to be taking power in the name of the new monarchs. When his group divided into factions, however, Leisler and his cohorts were labeled "Cromwellians." Leisler refused to surrender the fort until he saw the new governor's commission, proving he was a legitimate emissary of William and Mary. By then it was too late. When he did, he surrendered but on May 16, 1691, the rival faction persuaded the governor to order Leisler's execution for treason. His dismembered body was buried opposite the place of his execution. In 1695, by parliamentary act, his name was cleared and three years later, with the encouragement of William III, his remains were removed to the new Dutch church in Garden Street (now Exchange Place). This unsigned lithograph of Leisler's house, the first brick dwelling in the city, is based on a 1679 pen-and-ink drawing by Jaspar Danckaerts in *Journal of a Voyage to New York, 1679–1680*. ARTIST AND LITHOGRAPHER UNKNOWN. PUBLISHED IN *SHANNON'S MANUAL*, 1869.

(RIGHT) **PART OF NEW YORK, 1742:** This appears to be an extract from "A Plan for the City and Environs of New York as they were in the Years 1742, 1743, and 1744. Drawn by David Grim in the 76th year of his age." The illustration's label reads: "Part of New-York in 1742 shewing [sic] the site of the present Park; the Collect and little Collect Ponds; and a portion of the west side of Broadway. Drawn by David Grim in 1813." In other words, the map and the illustration reflect the old man's recollection of the streets of his youth some seventy years earlier! Note Jacob Leisler's grave as well as the line marking the Palisades, a wall erected in 1745 to ward off an anticipated French attack. LITHOGRAPHER UNKNOWN. PUBLISHED IN *VALENTINE'S MANUAL*, 1856.

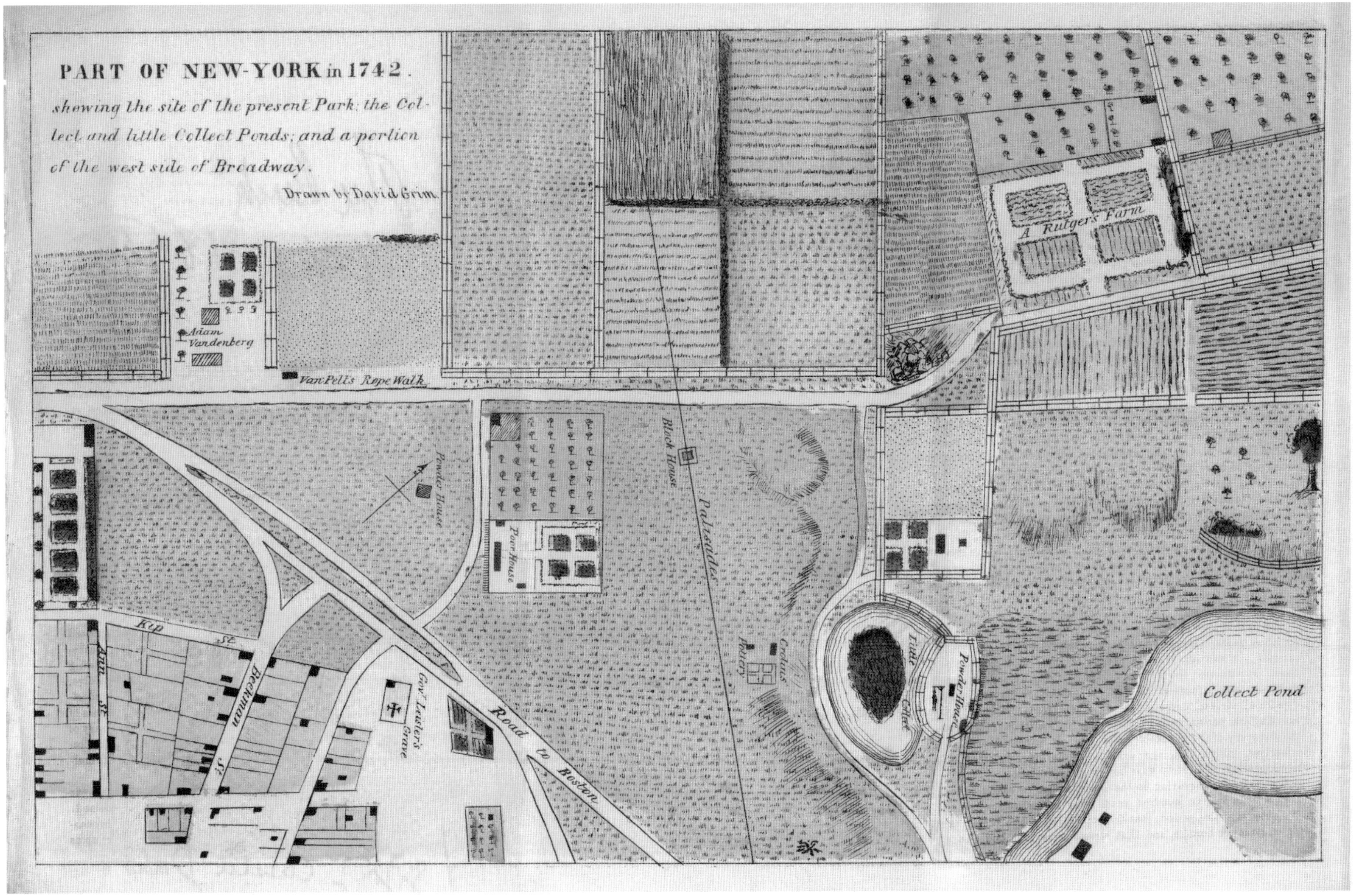
PART OF NEW-YORK in 1742.
showing the site of the present Park; the Collect and little Collect Ponds; and a portion of the west side of Broadway.
Drawn by David Grim.
A. Rutgers Farm
Adam Vandenberg
Van Pell's Rope Walk
Powder House
Poor House
Block House
Palisades
Kip St.
Ann St.
Beekman St.
Gov. Leister's Grave
Road to Boston
Crolius' Pottery
Little Collect
Powder House
Collect Pond

This CHURCH was founded A D 1727 & finish'd A D 1731
The Rev'd Mr Walter Du Bois & Mr Henry Boel Ministers
To the Honourable
RIP VAN DAM. Esq
PRESIDENT of His Majesty's Council for the PROVINCE of NEW YORK
This View of the New Dutch Church is most humbly
Dedicated by your Honour's most Obedient Serv't Wm Burgis

(LEFT) NEW DUTCH CHURCH, "THE RIP VAN DAM VIEW," 1731: This lively engraving (note the coach barely evading the pedestrian) is distinguished as the first known close-up view of a New York building. The New Dutch Church (later to be known as the Middle Dutch Church) stood at the corners of Nassau and Crown (now Liberty) Streets and was completed in 1729–31, when it would have been logical to publish a commemorative piece. Rip Van Dam, to whom the piece is dedicated, was acting governor of the province from July 1731 to August 1732. The church underwent many transformations—including serving as a prison and a riding school during the Revolutionary War—before being demolished in 1882. GIFT OF MRS. JAMES GARRETSON IN MEMORY OF HER HUSBAND. 55.249.1.

VIEW OF NEW AMSTERDAM, 1673: This curious allegorical view reflects the period of the Restitutio views of New York of 1673–74 (see pages 35), when the Dutch briefly regained control of the city. The colored copper engraving was executed by Aldert Meyer and published by Carel Allard in Amsterdam ca. 1700, as part of their *Orbis Habitabilis oppida et vestitu* (Cities and Costumes of the Inhabited World). THE J. CLARENCE DAVIES COLLECTION. 29.100.1652.

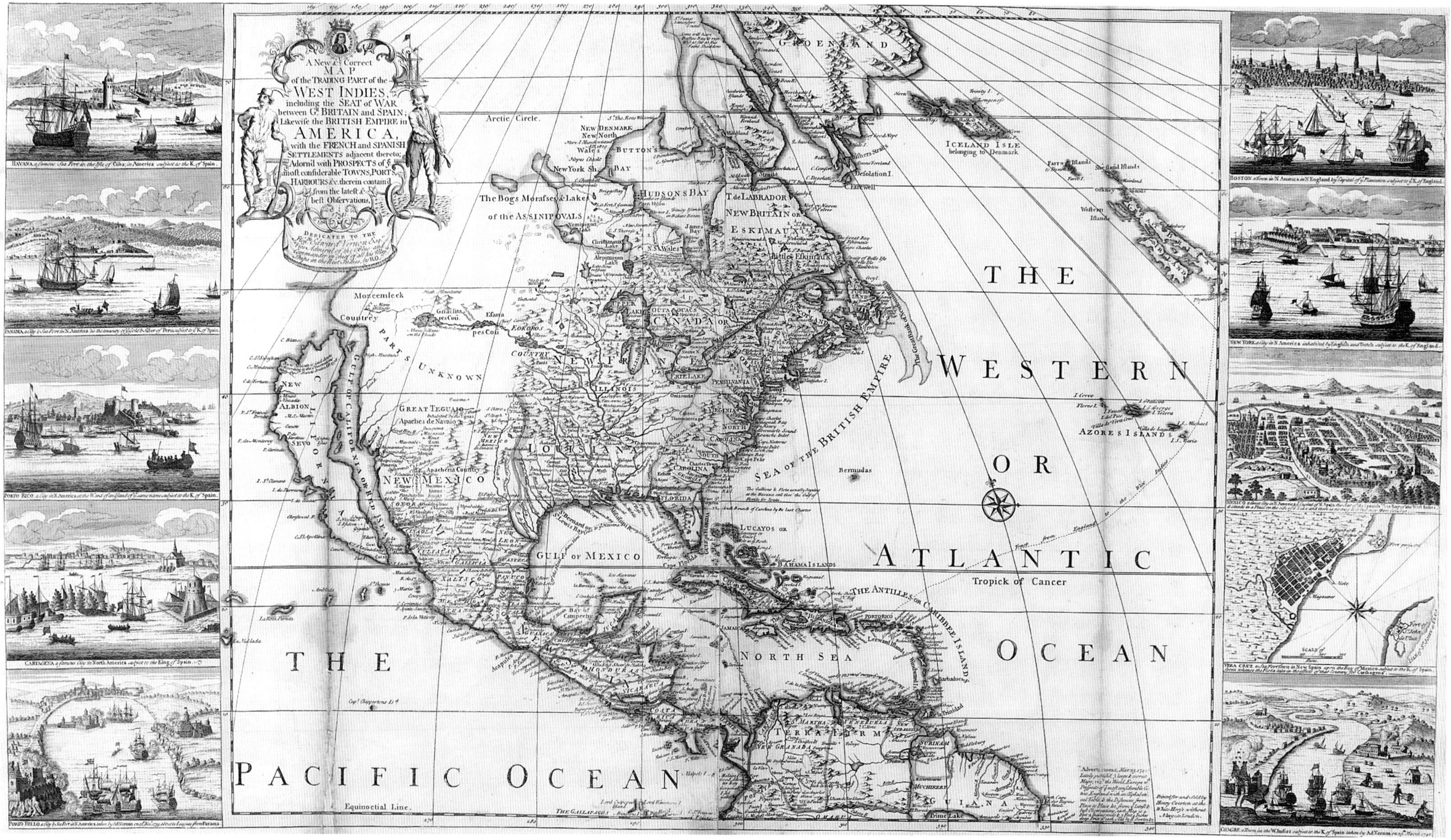

A NEW & CORRECT MAP OF THE TRADING PART OF THE WEST INDIES, 1741: The full description of this 1741 print is "A New & Correct Map of the Trading Part of the West Indies, including the Seat of War between Gr Britain and Spain; likewise the British Empire in America, with the French and Spanish Settlements adjacent thereto; Adorn'd with Prospects of ye most considerable Towns, Ports, Harbours &c. therein contain'd from the latest & best observations. 1741. Dedicated to the Honble. Edward Vernon Esqr., Vice Admiral of the Blue and Commander in chief of all his Majs. ships in the West Indies, by H.O." Printed for and sold by Henry Overton at the White Horse without Newgate London." Of special interest is the second panel from the top at the right: "NEW YORK a City in N America inhabited by English and Dutch subject to the K. of England." THE J. CLARENCE DAVIES COLLECTION. 29.100.2193.

A SOUTH EAST VIEW OF THE CITY OF NEW YORK IN NORTH AMERICA, 1763: In the distance we can see at the right the spire of the original Trinity Church, the dome of the town hall, the prison, and at the center King's College (now Columbia University). This was "drawn on the SPOT by Cap' Thomas Howdell of the Royal Artillery," but that palm tree is clearly a flight of fancy. This fine view from the famously rare *Scenographia Americana* series was taken from a point that today corresponds to the corner of Varick and Beach Streets. Engraved on copper by Pierre Charles Canot, after a drawing by Capt. Howdell made in about 1763. London: printed for John Bowles, Robert Sayer, Thos. Jefferys, Carington Bowles, and Henry Parker, 1768. GIFT OF MISS EDITH ALLEN CLARK, GIVEN IN MEMORY OF HER BROTHER, P.A. CLARK. 51.48.2.

STADTHUYS OF NEW YORK IN 1679: The Dutch City Hall at Pearl Street and Coenties Slip, built as a stone tavern in 1641–42, continued to serve as the seat of government in the transition to English rule. It was not razed until 1700. This is a nineteenth-century Louis Oram redraft of a watercolor by Jaspar Danckaerts (*Journal of a Voyage to New York, 1679–1680*, with Peter Sluyter). WATERCOLOR ON PAPER, 12⅞ x 10¼. THE J. CLARENCE DAVIES COLLECTION. 29.100.1634.

PEARL STREET ABOVE COENTIES SLIP, 1718: This watercolor on paper is attributed to Abram S. Hosier, an artist who flourished in New York from the 1830s up through the 1880s. He executed many city views for the multivolume *History of New York* by Mrs. Martha J. Lamb and Mrs. Burton Harrison, which was first issued in 1877. He also executed drawings for Benjamin Lossing's historical volumes. This charming nineteenth-century view depicts the city of 1718, when the Dutch influence was still strong. THE J. CLARENCE DAVIES COLLECTION. 29.100.1635.

NEW YORK FROM THE EAST: THE POPPLE VIEW, 1733: This splendidly detailed engraving is copied from Henry Popple's *Map of the British Empire* (1733), Sheet 4, which offered city views of Quebec and New York. 15⅝ x 11. THE J. CLARENCE DAVIES COLLECTION. 29.100.1520.

NEW YORK FROM THE NORTH, FROM THE LABADIST VIEW, 1679: This is a nineteenth century Louis Oram reconfiguration of a pen and ink drawing by Jaspar Danckaerts and Peter Sluyter that appeared in *Journal of a Voyage to New York, 1679–1680*. The original is commonly known as the Labadist General View of New York, named for a communal religious sect founded by Jean de Labadie; Danckaerts and Sluyter were followers. Phelps Stokes declared in 1930, “Can there be anyone so callous, and so lacking in romance,

THE JAGGED ROCKS OF THE OLD FORT, 1675: "The harbor was full of rocks," wrote artist Anton Schutz in 1926, "the seas around the city uncharted. At the left the fort with the first Dutch Church, in the middle the growing city, in the background is South Street, developing as harbor." Schutz was not quite correct in this, for there was no South Street until the 1790s; in the 1670s the street running along the East River would have been Pearl Street. At the right, adds editor Henry Collins Brown, is "the salient attraction . . . the stern of the good ship Britannica, now a melancholy wreck, cast upon the jagged rocks of the old fort." This etching was published in a portfolio titled *Three Hundred Years of New York, Twelve Etchings* by Anton Schutz (1894–1977), published by the New York Graphic Society in 1926. GIFT OF MRS. ROBERT W. HIGBIE, JR. 59.210.8.

PETER KALM'S TRAVELS IN NORTH AMERICA IN 1748–51: In his visit to the city the Swedish botanist observed that "New York is generally reckoned very healthy. . . . In the chief streets there are trees planted . . . and during the excessive heat afford a cooling shade. I found it extremely pleasant to walk in the town, for it seemed like a garden." His account was also notable for its attention to the Jewish community: ". . . there are many Jews settled in New York, who possess great privileges. They have a synagogue and houses, and great country seats of their own, property, and are allowed to keep shops in town. They have likewise several ships, which they freight, and send out with their own goods. In fine, they enjoy all the privileges common to the other inhabitants of the town and province." This is the frontispiece to the Utrecht edition of Kalm's *En resa til Norra Amerika*, published in English in 1770 as *Travels in North America, &c.* Note the New York vignette at the top right. THE J. CLARENCE DAVIES COLLECTION. 29.100.1539.

THE OLD STONE HOUSE, LONG ISLAND, 1699: The Old Stone House at Gowanus in Brooklyn was built by Claes Vechte beside the Gowanus Creek in 1699. In August 1776, as part of the largest battle of the Revolutionary War, the Battle of Long Island, the Continental Army engaged here with 2,000 British and Hessian soldiers who held the house against revolutionary assaults, inflicting many casualties. The house, which stood at what is now Fifth Avenue and Third Street, was demolished in 1897. In 1930–34 it was rebuilt using some of the original brick and is now part of the Historic House Trust. Nathaniel Currier (1813–88) signed this lithograph but his long-time partner James Ives (1824–95) did not, so we may say of this undated rare image that it was published no later than 1856 and no earlier than 1846, when Louis Grube created an oil painting upon which the lithograph clearly is based. THE HARRY T. PETERS COLLECTION. 56.300.385.

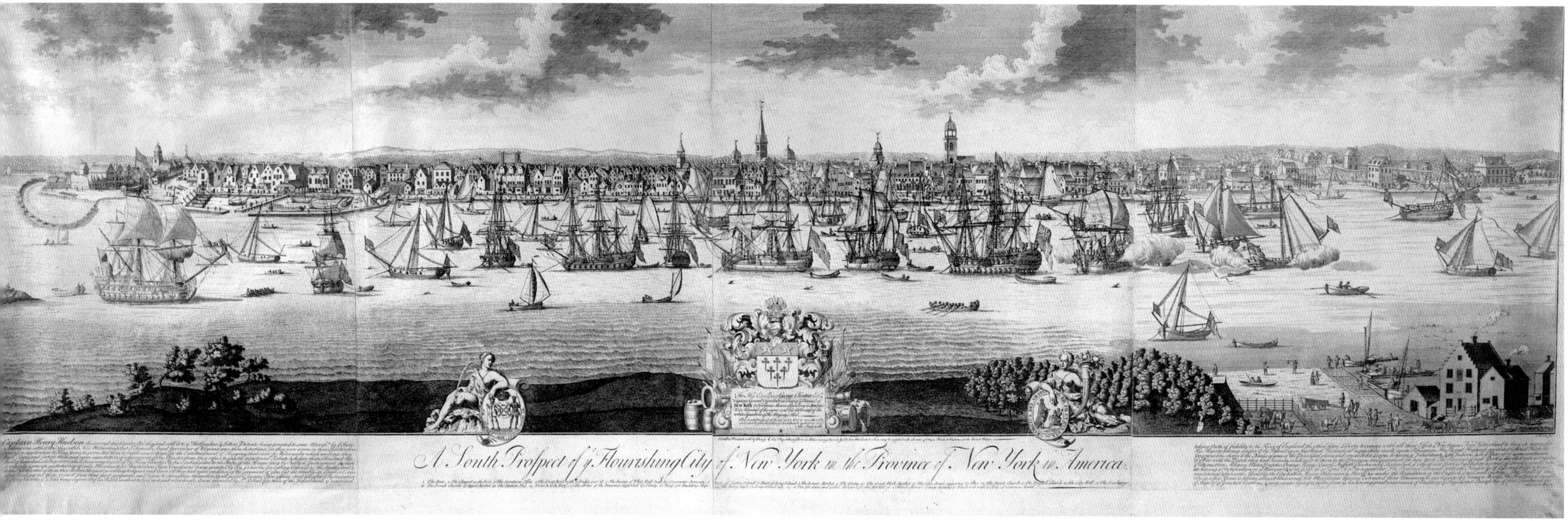
A South Prospect of ye Flourishing City of New York in the Province of New York in America.

THE BAKEWELL [BURGIS] VIEW OF NEW YORK FROM BROOKLYN HEIGHTS, 1717: The Original of "A South Prospect of ye Flourishing City of New York in the Province of New York in America" was drawn by William Burgis of Boston and engraved by John Harris of London and measured over six feet. The 1746 engraving by Thomas Bakewell, depicted here, added information to the skyline; another issue, in reduced format for the August 1761 issue of *London Magazine*, revised the data once again. William Loring Andrews remarks with truth: "The importance of this engraving in the pictorial annals of our city cannot well be over-estimated. It is beyond question an accurate representation of the place it claims to depict, and in the key at the foot of the print is embraced the name of every building of note of which the city at that time could boast." The great number of ships in the harbor may reflect the birthday of King George I on June 4 of that year. GIFT OF MRS. WILLIAM SLOANE. 40.421.1.

(FAR LEFT) **MOSES LEVY, 1720–28:** Between 1720 and 1735 Gerardus Duyckinck (1695–1746) painted several portraits of the Levy-Franks family, offering a glimpse into the lives of a noteworthy family at a time when New York's Jewish community comprised only about seventy-five families. Many of these were merchants. The German-born Moses Levy was a real-estate investor who also owned a fleet of merchant ships. He was married twice; the first time in 1695 to Richa Asher, and then in 1718, to Grace Mears, who had been born to English parents in Jamaica. OIL ON CANVAS ATTRIBUTED TO GERARDUS DUYCKINCK, 43¼ x 34¾. BEQUEST OF ALPHONSE H. KURSHEEDT. 36.343.1.

(NEAR LEFT) **GRACE MEARS LEVY, 1720–28:** When her husband Moses died in 1728, Grace Mears Levy opened a retail shop. Through the marriage of her daughter Bilhah Abigail to merchant Jacob Franks, the Levy family was extended, as was the range of linked portraits. OIL ON CANVAS, ATTRIBUTED TO GERARDUS DUYCKINCK I. BEQUEST OF ALPHONSE H. KURSHEEDT. 45 x 36. 36.343.2.

MARY SPRATT PROVOOST ALEXANDER, CA. 1750: The portrait depicts the wife of James Alexander, attorney general for the province of New York in 1721–23. But in New York circles she was generally known as Mrs. Provoost, for even during her second marriage she continued the business ventures in dry goods and real estate of her first husband, Samuel Provoost. This oil on canvas was painted almost two decades later by John Wollaston, (active 1742–75), sometime after the celebrated artist left England for New York in 1749 and before he departed for Pennsylvania, Maryland, and Virginia in 1752. GIFT OF WILLIAM HAMILTON RUSSELL. 30¼ X 25¼. 50.215.4.

CHAPTER III | 1764–1783

THE GIBRALTAR OF AMERICA

Edwin G. Burrows

From 1776 to 1783, New York served as the principal base and nerve center of British operations in the Revolutionary War. It was the "Gibraltar of America," as one officer proudly called it. In addition to the soldiers and sailors who thronged the city, there were Loyalist refugees from every colony and rising numbers of runaway slaves. By 1779, this influx had boosted the civilian population to a record 33,000. Somehow, virtually all of these multitudes found a place to live in the square mile below Chambers Street, which in those days marked the town's northern frontier. Often overlooked in accounts of British-occupied New York are the thousands of captured American insurgents, civilian as well as military, who would be brought to the city for detention for supporting the Revolution. By the end of 1776, as a result of the fighting on Long Island and Manhattan, at least 5,000 Americans had been shoehorned into a hastily assembled collection of churches and public buildings, including the almshouse, the jail, and even City Hall (then located on Wall Street). Conditions in these makeshift prisons were frightful. The prisoners never had enough clothing, blankets, or firewood. Their rations—when they received rations—consisted mostly of rotten pork or beef and scraps of moldy bread. Some inmates were said to be so hungry they ate rats, shoes, and even the lice that covered their bodies. Most lost weight quickly and virtually all exhibited the bleeding gums, tooth decay, open sores, and listlessness symptomatic of scurvy. The filth was appalling. Survivors told of floors slick with human excrement and of air so fetid that candles wouldn't stay lit. Not surprisingly, typhus, dysentery, and other infectious diseases ran rampant, and men died so quickly that burial details could barely keep up. No one knows for sure, but it is likely that by early 1777, six or seven of every ten prisoners had perished—a mortality rate roughly twice that of the infamous Confederate stockade in Andersonville, Georgia. (In World War I, only 3.6 percent of U.S. prisoners died in POW camps. In World War II the figure rose to 11.3 percent, and in Korea to 37.8 percent.)

Seventeen-year-old Levi Hanford, a Connecticut militiaman who became a British prisoner in March 1777, wound up in one of the most notorious of New York's Revolutionary War prisons: a five-story "sugar house" on Crown (now Liberty) Street, just east of Nassau, in what is today the lower Manhattan business district. The building had been confiscated from the redoubtable Livingston family, who built it in the early 1700s as a manufacturing plant for loaf sugar and rum. Massive stone walls and small, dungeon-like windows made the building serviceable as a prison. Although a sizeable majority of the eight hundred-odd Americans confined there over the winter of 1776–77 were long dead by the time Hanford arrived, British operation in New Jersey, Westchester, and Connecticut soon brought in hundreds of replacements. As spring turned to summer, Hanford recalled, the stench became overpowering, and the air grew so oppressively thick it was hard to breathe. "Our allowance of provisions," he added, "was a scanty supply of pork and sea-biscuit" — too scanty to keep a man going for very long:

> The pork was old and unsavory, and the biscuit was such as had been wet with sea-water, and being damaged, was full of worms and very mouldy. It was our common practice to put water in our camp kettle, then break up the biscuit into it, and after skimming off the worms, to put in the pork, and then, if we had fuel, to boil the whole together.

If the men had no fuel, they gobbled down the revolting mixture anyway. "Starved as we were," Hanford mused, "there was nothing in the shape of food that was rejected, or that was unpalatable." In late October, after seven months in the sugar house, Hanford was transferred to the ill-named *Good Intent*, a transport recently converted for use as a prison ship and now riding at anchor in the Hudson River. There he discovered 200 more Americans crammed below decks, starving and dying like flies in the sepulchral gloom. "The air was exceedingly foul, close, and sickening," he said later. "No wonder that pestilence in all its fury began to sweep us down." Within two months, half the Americans were dead.

Hanford's transfer from Livingston's sugar house to the *Good Intent* was a sign that the booming population of American captives in the occupied city had compelled British authorities to begin moving the overflow onto an assortment of vessels anchored in the waters around Manhattan. Already there were prisoners on the *Prince of Wales*, a decrepit warship anchored over in Wallabout Bay, on the Brooklyn side of the East River, near a hospital ship named *Kitty* (which burned in mid-October 1777, quite possibly set ablaze by the prisoners themselves). At some point in the course of that year, the *Judith* and the *Myrtle*, two transports anchored in the Hudson opposite Trinity Church, began to receive prisoners, as did the *Jersey* and the *Good Hope*, a pair of hospital ships hitherto reserved for the use of His Majesty's forces. American captives would also be confined in the brigs of at least nine other vessels not officially designated as prisons or hospitals: the *Eagle*, *Felicity*, *Isis*, *Richmond*, *Otter*, *Dispatch*, *York*, *Vigilant*, and *Mercury*.

Because changing weather conditions often required them to find new anchorages, few if any of these ships remained in the same place for more than two or three months at a time. Initially, the *Good Hope* lay in the Hudson, somewhere along the city's west side, perhaps near the *Good Intent*; some reports place the *Jersey* there as well, though others find her at various locations in the East River. But when the Hudson began to freeze in December, the *Good Hope* and the *Good Intent* were brought around Manhattan to Wallabout Bay, where they joined the *Prince of Wales* and several other ships that cannot now be identified. The *Jersey* followed at some point over the winter (if she wasn't there already), and by the spring of 1778 she was serving as the first stop for captives destined for the prison ships anchored nearby.

Aboard the *Good Intent*, meanwhile, Hanford fell sick and was transferred again, this time to the military hospital in the Brick Presbyterian Church. The so-called "hospital" was no improvement, however. "Disease and death reigned there in all their terror," he remembered. "I have had men die by the side of me in the night, and have seen fifteen dead bodies sewed up in their blankets and laid in the corner of the yard at one time, the product of one twenty-four hours." And worse, horribly worse:

> Every morning, at eight o'clock, the dead-cart came, and the bodies of those who had died the day previous were thrown in. The men drew the rations of rum to which they were entitled, and the cart was driven to the trenches of the fortifications, where they were hastily covered. . . . On one occasion, I was permitted to go with the guard to the place of interment, and never shall I forget the scene that I there beheld. They tumbled the bodies promiscuously into the ditch, sometimes even dumping them from the cart, then threw upon them a little dirt, and away they went. I could see a hand there, a foot there, and there again a part of a head, washed bare by the rain, and all swollen, blubbering, and falling to decay.

At any time in this ordeal, Hanford might have reconsidered his initial enthusiasm for the Revolution and won his freedom by enlisting in the British service. Yet he rebuffed every overture by enemy recruiters, and when finally exchanged in May 1778—one of the relatively few who lasted as long as thirteen months in captivity—he went home, rejoined his old unit, and resumed the fight. Instead of weakening his resolve, Hanford's stint as a prisoner of war had made him more determined than ever to send the redcoats packing.

Approximately 200,000 Americans bore arms against the Crown between 1775 and 1783, at least 18,200 of whom—according to the most recent estimate—became prisoners of war. But that figure represents only men wearing the uniform of the Continental forces or serving in one of the state militias. It doesn't include thousands of nonuniformed personnel—privateers caught preying on British shipping and civilians rounded up for taking part in revolutionary committees or speaking out against the Crown. If we take them into account as well, it is likely that between 24,800 and 32,000 patriots fell into British hands by 1783. Like Levi Hanford, the great majority of them were held in and around New York City, under conditions so atrocious that as many as 18,000 (almost 60 percent) perished; fully *two and a half times* the 6,800 who are thought to have fallen in battle. In other words, more Americans gave their lives for independence in New York than anywhere else in the country.

There's no evidence that the British intended the deaths of so many prisoners. Still, they had often threatened to hang every American taken in arms against the Crown, and after the debacle at Lexington and Concord in April 1775, followed by their Pyrrhic victory at Bunker Hill in June, the men and officers of His Majesty's forces in America were out for blood—impatient, as a captain in the King's Own Regiment put it, "to scourge the rebellion with rods of iron," even if it meant "almost extirpating the present rebellious race." The green light for war of extirpation would come in August 1775, when the king issued a Proclamation for Suppressing Rebellion and Sedition that enjoined his loyal subjects throughout the realm to suppress "all traitorous Conspiracies and Attempts against Us, Our Crown and Dignity." Parliament finished the job in March 1777 by adopting a measure, dubbed "North's Act" after Prime Minister Frederick North, that suspended *habeas corpus* and authorized the prosecution of captured rebels for treason or piracy, as circumstances required. Not surprisingly, the officials charged with the care and feeding of prisoners in New York—Joshua Loring, Commissary of Military Prisoners, and David Sproat, Commissary of Naval Prisoners—were at best indifferent to the fate of their charges (why pamper traitors on their way to the gallows?). Moreover, every time General George Washington protested, his British counterparts, especially generals Sir William Howe and Sir Henry Clinton, denied any wrongdoing, even when presented with irrefutable evidence that their provost marshal, Captain William Cunningham, beat and starved prisoners for his own sadistic amusement.

It is important to keep in mind, too, that the British were under no formal obligation to take better care of captured Americans. The growth of nation-states in early modern Europe had brought a degree of predictability to the conduct of war and given rise to certain precepts and customs bearing on the treatment of prisoners—that disarmed adversaries shouldn't be executed, humiliated, tortured, or mutilated; that they shouldn't be denied ransom, prosecuted as criminals, or enslaved; that they shouldn't be denied appropriate food, clothing, and shelter. But none of this had been codified in multinational treaties or conventions, nor would it be for more than a century. The "rules of war" or "law of arms" explicated by classicists and jurists were largely theoretical and essentially unenforceable. They weren't rules or laws at all, strictly speaking, merely optimistic guidelines for mitigating the severity of armed conflict between purportedly civilized princes. Whether they even applied in cases of domestic insurrection or rebellion was (and still is) open to question.

There were, however, social constraints on the conduct of officers, because everywhere in eighteenth-century Europe, military rank remained intimately connected to inherited property and privilege. Only someone entitled by birth to the deference of others was thought capable of leading men in war: Gentility, not expertise, constituted the foundation of an officer's authority. This was no theoretical abstraction. In Britain, army officers purchased their commissions at prices so steep that the service essentially belonged to the few hundred wealthy families who ran the country. Officers thus tended to believe they had more in common with their counterparts across the field than with the men they led, and out of that belief had emerged an unwritten code of honor that precisely regulated their behavior toward one another in war. Importantly, the code required them to behave with genteel "complaisance" toward prisoners of all social ranks. It also allowed for the release of captured brother officers on "parole"—their solemn promise, usually though not necessarily given in writing, to stay out of the fight until exchanged. In principle at least, common soldiers didn't qualify for parole because they weren't gentlemen and couldn't be counted on to keep their word.

The trouble was that the American army seemed, especially at the beginning of the war, like an undisciplined rabble led by men without the social status necessary for genuine officers. The Americans themselves admitted as much. As General Richard Montgomery had remarked before the invasion of Canada in 1775, "I wish some method could be fallen upon of engaging *gentlemen* to serve; a point of honor and more knowledge of the world, to be found in that class of men, would greatly reform discipline, and render the troops much more tractable." Opinions changed as the war developed, but it remained a nice question as to whether men who in civilian life had been merchants and tradesmen, even plain farmers, deserved the courtesies ordinarily due real gentlemen in uniform—and if captured, whether it was appropriate to exchange them, rank for rank, as if they were social equals. When a captain of the Royal Welch Fusiliers heard rumors that an exchange of officers might take place after the Battle of Brooklyn, it distressed him to think "we should treat with them as if on an equality."

Indeed, the very sight of "men calling themselves officers" (Lord George Germain's tart phrase) could provoke acts of flagrant intimidation and violence against American prisoners that would have been condemned in Europe. In the fighting that raged around New York in 1776–77, captured American officers in particular were regularly robbed and beaten by indignant soldiers. Said one Hessian after the Battle of Brooklyn: "Among the prisoners are many so-called colonels, lieutenant colonels, majors, and other officers, who, however, are nothing but mechanics, tailors, shoemakers, wigmakers, barbers, etc. Some of them were soundly beaten by our people, who would by no means let such persons pass for officers."

In the spring of 1780, Americans woke to a new horror: the prison ship *Jersey*. Easily the biggest and deadliest of her kind in the Revolutionary War, the *Jersey* claimed so many lives during her brief time in service that for generations she would serve as the single most widely recognized symbol of British cruelty toward captured patriots.

Launched in 1736, the *Jersey* had seen decades of service in the Mediterranean as a fourth-rate frigate before the navy converted her to a hospital ship around 1771. (In the Royal Navy, a fourth-rate, or large frigate, was a three-masted ship mounting fifty to seventy cannons on two decks below the main deck and carrying a crew of around four hundred.) She came to New York with the rest of the fleet in the summer of 1776 or shortly thereafter. As one of the largest vessels in port at forty-one feet at the beam and 144 feet stem to stern, her great black hull would have been a familiar sight to the residents of the city. To convert her for use as a prison ship, she was anchored permanently in Wallabout Bay and "hulked"—stripped of her masts, canvas, lines, ordnance, figurehead, rudder, and any other reusable equipment. Her gunports were then sealed and replaced by two rows of small, square air-ports, barred with iron lattices, for the benefit of the prisoners confined on the lower decks. Aft, on the quarterdeck, a large awning or tent was erected to shelter the thirty-odd marines assigned to guard the prisoners. Directly below the quarterdeck were the officers' cabin and various storerooms. Between the quarterdeck and forecastle lay an area of the gun deck known as the spar deck, much of which was now occupied by the pens where officers kept pigs for their own consumption. The forward part of the gun deck was reserved for the galley. Below the gun deck lay the middle deck, a cavernous, vile-smelling, vermin-infested space where the prisoners passed time, ate, and slept shoulder to shoulder. Still more prisoners dwelled like troglodytes on the dank lower deck, at or near the water line. The only way to reach topside from the holds was up a narrow ladder and through a heavy grated hatchway, always shut tight at sundown.

Exactly when the *Jersey* began to receive prisoners is unclear. It may have been when she was still in service as a hospital ship—a report reached Philadelphia as early as June 1779 that 512 captives were languishing in her holds—but once she became a prison hulk, the numbers soared and conditions rapidly deteriorated. Among her first prisoners was John van Dyke, a furloughed artilleryman who had had the misfortune to be traveling on a brig that was taken by the enemy frigate *Iris*. He and the others were taken to New York and consigned to the *Jersey* toward the end of May 1780. "When I came on board," Van Dyke recalled, "her stench was so great . . . I thought it would soon kill me." The rations he received were "so short a person would think it was not possible for a man to live on." Once, Van Dyke came back from the galley with a piece of salt pork so small that he and his five messmates had only one mouthful each and nothing else for the entire day; another time, they had only some "soup" that consisted of "brown water, and fifteen floating peas" to hold them for twenty-four hours. Each week, his mess received three pounds of flour containing mysterious green lumps along with a pound of "very bad raisins." Mashed together and boiled in a bag, it made a pudding. That day became "Pudding day."

Although Captain van Dyke's memoir would not be published until long after his death, American newspapers soon gave their readers plenty of comparable stories about the *Jersey* to contemplate. Most frequently reprinted was a deposition taken from George Batterman, who said that when he was sent aboard in the autumn of 1780, the *Jersey* held an astonishing 1,100 prisoners—almost three times her normal component of seamen. To soften them up for Royal Navy recruiters, he added, their rations were reduced to a pint of water and eight ounces of "condemned bread" per day, plus eight ounces of meat *per week*. One of Batterman's fellow prisoners that fall was Silas Talbot, a privateer captain out of Providence already well known for wreaking havoc with enemy shipping and later commander of the U.S.S. *Constitution* ("Old Ironsides"). Twenty-three years after the experience, Talbot described a world below decks from which it is a miracle anyone emerged sane, let alone alive:

> THERE WERE NO BERTHS OR SEATS, TO LIE DOWN ON, NOT A BENCH TO SIT ON. MANY WERE ALMOST WITHOUT CLOATHS. THE DYSENTERY, FEVER, PHRENZY AND DESPAIR PREVAILED AMONG THEM, AND FILLED THE PLACE WITH FILTH, DISGUST AND HORROR. THE SCANTINESS OF THE ALLOWANCE, THE BAD QUALITY OF THE PROVISIONS, THE BRUTALITY OF THE GUARDS, AND THE SICK, PINING FOR COMFORTS THEY COULD NOT OBTAIN, ALTOGETHER FURNISHED CONTINUALLY ONE OF THE GREATEST SCENES OF HUMAN DISTRESS AND MISERY EVER BEHELD. IT WAS NOW THE MIDDLE OF OCTOBER, THE WEATHER WAS COOL AND CLEAR, WITH FROSTY NIGHTS, SO THAT THE NUMBER OF DEATHS PER DAY WAS *REDUCED TO AN AVERAGE OF TEN*, AND THIS NUMBER WAS CONSIDERED BY THE SURVIVORS A SMALL ONE, WHEN COMPARED WITH THE TERRIBLE MORTALITY THAT HAD PREVAILED FOR THREE MONTHS BEFORE.

Numerous contemporary accounts confirm the accuracy of Talbot's assertion that prisoners on the *Jersey* were treated with unparalleled "severity and inhumanity;" that they received only a few ounces of bad meat per week; that they fought "like wild beasts to get near the small air ports, that they might breathe;" that "seven or eight died every twenty-four hours;" that hundreds enlisted with the Royal Navy in a desperate bid to save themselves. Christopher Vail's unpublished narrative, composed years later but based on a journal he kept during the war, corroborates the overcrowding, hunger, sickness, and hellish filth. "There was only one passage to go on deck in the night," he recalled, and the guards would allow only two men up at a time. "Many of the Prisoners were troubled with the dysentery and would come to the steps and could not be permitted to go on deck, and was obliged to ease themselves on the spot, and the next morning for twelve feet around the hatches was nothing but excrement." As bad as the nauseating stench was the noise: "There was all kinds of business carried on," Vail wrote, "some playing cards, others swearing, stealing, fighting, some dying &c." *Many* dying, in fact: Death visited the lower decks so often that the men handled corpses as casually as they would sacks of grain or animal carcasses:

> WHEN A MAN DIED, HE WAS CARRIED UP TO THE FORECASTLE AND LAID THERE UNTIL THE NEXT MORNING AT 8 O'CLOCK WHEN THEY WERE ALL LOWERED DOWN THE SHIP'S SIDES BY A ROPE ROUND THEM IN THE SAME MANNER AS THO' THEY WERE BEASTS. THERE WAS 8 DIED OF A DAY WHILE I WAS THERE. THEY WERE CARRIED ON SHORE IN HEAPS AND HOVE OUT THE BOAT ON THE WHARF THEN TAKEN ACROSS A HAND BARROW, CARRIED TO THE EDGE OF THE BANK WHERE A HOLE WAS DUG 1 OR 2 FEET DEEP AND ALL HOVE IN TOGETHER.

Christopher Hawkins, Vail's fellow prisoner, likewise wrote in his autobiography of the rampant dysentery that left him and others covered with "bloody and loathsome filth" by morning, of fisticuffs between demoralized prisoners, of savage whippings, of one man so hungry he ate the lice from his shirt. A third captive, Ebenezer Fox, a seventeen-year-old seaman, aptly described the *Jersey* in the late summer of 1781 as a "floating Pandemonium."

The story of New York's Revolutionary War prisons and prison ships dropped out of sight in the twentieth century, a victim of (among other things) improved Anglo-American relations. It deserves to be revived, however, because it enlarges our understanding of how the United States was made—not merely by bewigged Founding Fathers, of whom we have heard so much in recent years, but also by thousands upon thousands of mostly ordinary people who believed in something they considered worth dying for.

Their suffering, moreover, left an enduring mark on international law. Between 1782 and 1787, American diplomats negotiated treaties of amity and commerce with foreign powers that took unprecedented steps toward mitigating the evils of war. Agreements struck with the Netherlands, Sweden, and Morocco, for example, required negotiation before the use of force, curbed privateering, and regulated the exercise of search and seizure on the high seas. The 1785 treaty with Prussia negotiated by Thomas Jefferson, John Adams, and Benjamin Franklin even included provisions designed specifically "to prevent the destruction of prisoners of war." Among other things, the parties stipulated that in the event of armed conflict between them, captives taken by either:

> . . . SHALL NOT BE CONFINED IN DUNGEONS, PRISON-SHIPS, NOR PRISONS, NOR BE PUT INTO IRONS, NOR BOUND, NOR OTHERWISE RESTRAINED IN THE USE OF THEIR LIMBS; THAT THE OFFICERS SHALL BE ENLARGED ON THEIR PAROLES WITHIN CONVENIENT DISTRICTS, & HAVE COMFORTABLE QUARTERS, & THE COMMON MEN BE DISPOSED IN CANTONMENTS, OPEN & EXTENSIVE ENOUGH FOR AIR & EXERCISE, AND LODGED IN BARRACKS AS ROOMY & GOOD AS ARE PROVIDED BY THE PARTY IN WHOSE POWER THEY ARE FOR THEIR OWN TROOPS; THAT THE OFFICERS SHALL ALSO BE DAILY FURNISHED BY THE PARTY IN WHOSE POWER THEY ARE, WITH AS MANY RATIONS; & OF THE SAME ARTICLES & QUALITY AS ARE ALLOWED BY THEM, EITHER IN KIND OR BY COMMUTATION, TO OFFICERS OF EQUAL RANK IN THEIR OWN ARMY; & ALL OTHERS SHALL BE DAILY FURNISHED BY THEM WITH SUCH RATION AS THEY ALLOW TO A COMMON SOLDIER IN THEIR OWN SERVICE.

Even if the conduct of their own countrymen had sometimes fallen well short of acceptable, the three American negotiators understood that the new nation must pledge itself to treat future prisoners of war with the decency and humanity never accorded them by the British—that what set the United States apart from the former mother country and all the other tyrannies to come was only this commitment to basic human rights.

(RIGHT) **ATTACK ON FORT WASHINGTON, 1776:** Having been routed in the Battle of Long Island, the Continental Army retreated across the East River to the southern tip of Manhattan, an indefensible spot. The troops thence repaired north to Fort Washington, located at what is now Fort Washington Avenue and 183rd Street, a five-sided position surrounded by three lines of entrenchment. After a four-hour resistance to a furious assault, the fort was taken. At the top, extreme left appears the Morris-Jumel Mansion, which is still standing. This house was erected by Col. Roger Morris in about 1765 and was used as Washington's headquarters just prior to the attack on the fort. "A View of the Attack against Fort Washington and Rebel Redouts near New York on the 16th of November 1776 by the British and Hessian Brigades. Drawn on the spot by Thos. Davies, Capt. Royal Artillery." Collotype print after the Davies watercolor. THE ARTHUR H. SCRIBNER COLLECTION. 41.62.106.

EDWIN G. BURROWS IS DISTINGUISHED PROFESSOR OF HISTORY AT BROOKLYN COLLEGE OF THE CITY UNIVERSITY OF NEW YORK. HE IS THE AUTHOR OF *FORGOTTEN PATRIOTS: THE UNTOLD STORY OF AMERICAN PRISONERS DURING THE REVOLUTIONARY WAR* (BASIC BOOKS, 2008). HE IS ALSO THE CO-AUTHOR OF *GOTHAM: A HISTORY OF NEW YORK CITY TO 1898*, WHICH WON THE PULITZER PRIZE FOR HISTORY. FOR THE PAST FIVE YEARS BURROWS HAS BEEN A DISTINGUISHED LECTURER FOR THE ORGANIZATION OF AMERICAN HISTORIANS. HE SERVES ON THE BOARD OF THE DYCKMAN FARMHOUSE MUSEUM IN MANHATTAN AND IS A FELLOW OF THE SOCIETY OF AMERICAN HISTORIANS. HE LIVES IN NORTHPORT, NEW YORK WITH HIS WIFE AND TWO CHILDREN.

View of the Attack against Fort Washington and Rebel Redouts near New York on the 16 of November 1776 by the British and Hessian Brig.

Drawn on the Spot, by Thos. Davies Capt. R. R. of Artillery.

LANDING OF THE BRITISH FORCES IN THE JERSEYS, 1776: The full title of the engraving by Thomas Davies, published for the edification of the royalists, was "The landing of the British forces in the Jerseys on the 20th of November 1776 under the command of the Rt. Honl. Lieut. Genl. Earl Cornwallis." However, the original drawing of the troops clambering up the wooded Palisades was supposed to have been done by Lord Rawdon, who served at the time as engineer officer on Cornwallis's staff. PRINT ARCHIVES.

(RIGHT) **PORTRAIT OF ALEXANDER HAMILTON AS A SOLDIER, 1776:** Alexander Hamilton served with distinction at the battles of Trenton and Princeton in 1776. Marriage to Elizabeth Schuyler linked this low-born man of genius with one of New York's most powerful and high-toned families. In 1789 he became the nation's first Secretary of the Treasury. Alonzo Chappel (1828-87) painted this portrait ca. 1857, more than a half century after his subject's death in a duel at Weehawken with Aaron Burr. 18 x 14. GIFT OF MRS. ALEXANDER HAMILTON AND GENERAL PIERPONT MORGAN HAMILTON. 18 x 14. 71.31.5.

Collection des Prospects.
Die Anlandung der Englischen Trouppen zu Neu Yorck.
Debarquement des Troupes engloises a nouvellè Yorck.
Gravé par François Xav. Habermann
Se vend à Augsbourg au Négoce coṁua de l'Academie Imperiale d'Empire des Arts libereaux avec Privilege de Sa Majesté Imperiale et avec Defense ni d'en faire ni de vendre les Copies.

DISEMBARKATION OF ENGLISH TROOPS AT NEW YORK, 1776: An entirely fictitious view of a real event of September 17, 1776, when 30,000 British troops landed in New York. The title shown in reverse at the top indicates that this print was an optical or perspective view meant to be exhibited in a peep-show box consisting of a mirror and a convex lens, enhancing the sense of depth. Engraver Franz Xaver Habermann had never visited New York, so it is not surprising that the streetscape looks decidedly European. THE J. CLARENCE DAVIES COLLECTION. 29.100.2024.

Collection des Prospects.
Gravé par Francois Xav. Habermann
Der Einzug der Königlichen Völcker in Neu Yorck.
L'Entré triumphale de Troupes royales a Nouvelle Yorck.

TRIUMPHAL ENTRY OF ROYAL TROOPS IN NEW YORK, 1776: Another optical view, this colored engraving by Habermann is as fanciful as his others of New York. THE J. CLARENCE DAVIES COLLECTION. 29.100.2127.

RESIDENCE OF ROGER MORRIS (WASHINGTON'S HEADQUARTERS), 1776: More celebrated for its later occupant, adventuress Mme. Elizabeth Jumel, this house served as General Washington's headquarters for five weeks in September-October 1776. Lieutenant Colonel Roger Morris built it in 1765. In 1785 it became a tavern (Calmut Hall) and President Washington and his cabinet had dinner there five years later. Steven Jumel purchased it in 1810 and in the year after his death in 1832, his widow Eliza married seventy-seven-year-old Aaron Burr. It endures today as the Morris-Jumel Mansion, the oldest house in Manhattan. The watercolorist, Thomas Worth, is famous for his work with Currier and Ives. 13¾ x 12. THE J. CLARENCE DAVIES COLLECTION. 29.100.2444.

WASHINGTON'S FAREWELL TO THE OFFICERS OF HIS ARMY: AT THE OLD TAVERN, CORNER OF BROAD AND PEARL STREETS, DECEMBER 4, 1783: The scene is "Francis's [Fraunces] Tavern at Broad Street, New York, Decr 4th 1783." The key participants in the farewell scene are named in the border (left to right): Steuben, Knox, Washington, Clinton, and Hamilton. The poignant parting words: "With a heart of love and gratitude I now take leave of you. I most devoutly wish that your latter days may be as prosperous and happy as your former ones have been glorious and honorable." LITHOGRAPH BY CURRIER AND IVES, PUBLISHED 1876. GIFT OF GERALD LEVINO. 58.84.6.

FRAUNCES TAVERN, 1776: This engraving by Samuel Hollyer (1826–1919) was one of a series of Old New York views created between 1905 and 1914 to commemorate a New York that had largely vanished. Yes, one can still go to Fraunces Tavern and bend an elbow not far from where George Washington lifted a glass of wine in tribute to his officers. But the museum, tavern, and restaurant of today at 54 Pearl Street are in a network of buildings substantially restored in 1904 from the original, built in 1719. THE J. CLARENCE DAVIES COLLECTION.

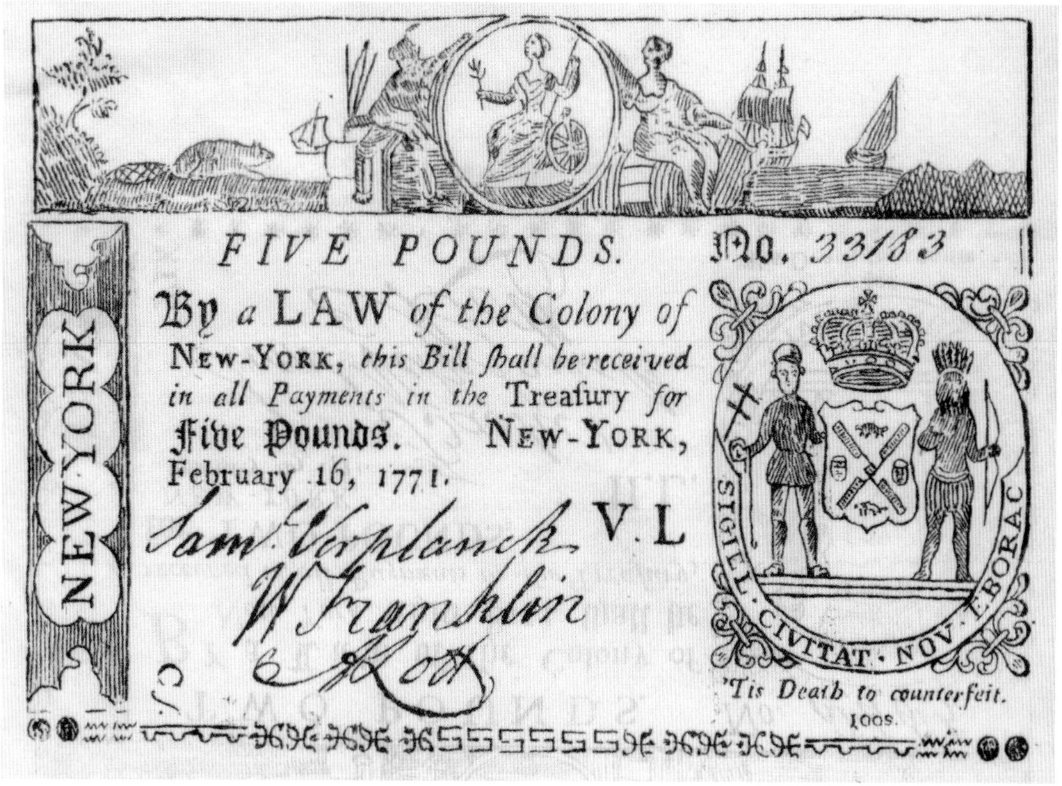

CURRENCY, 1771: "By a Law of the colony of New-York, this Bill shall be Received in all payments in the treasury, for Five Pounds. New-York, February 16, 1771." Signers were Samuel Verplanck, Walter Franklin, and A. Lott. On this date £120,000 in bills of credit receivable for taxes were issued. The newly cut decorative top border (by Elisha Gallaudet of New York City) shows the seal of the City of New York at right. At the top is the seated Britannia in a roundel with an Indian holding a bow and arrows and the New World to the right. To the left is a figure of Commerce seated on a barrel and holding a lyre with ships behind her. The notes were printed by Hugh Gaine on thin laid paper. There was extensive counterfeiting of this issue; some forged bills still turn up in auctions today. PRINT ARCHIVES.

(RIGHT) **PLAN OF NEW YORK AND ENVIRONS TO GREENWICH &C., 1766:** This copper engraving is a later version of an exceedingly scarce plan drawn in 1766. According to Captain John Montresor's notes, the survey was made between December 16, 1765 and February 8, 1766, in the aftermath of the Stamp Act riots, at the bequest of the Commander in Chief, General Thomas Gage. On December 8, Montresor noted in his journal: "The Sons of Liberty as they term themselves, openly defying powers, office, and all authority sole rulers." On the 17th he added: "Placards seditious and infamous as ever." Army officer Bernard Ratzer drew a version of the plan; this view was for a time thought to have preceded Montresor's. DRAWN BY JOHN MONTRESOR, ENGRAVED BY P. ANDREWS. REPRINTED IN *HARPER'S WEEKLY* FEBRUARY 19, 1876. THE J. CLARENCE DAVIES COLLECTION. 29.100.2601.

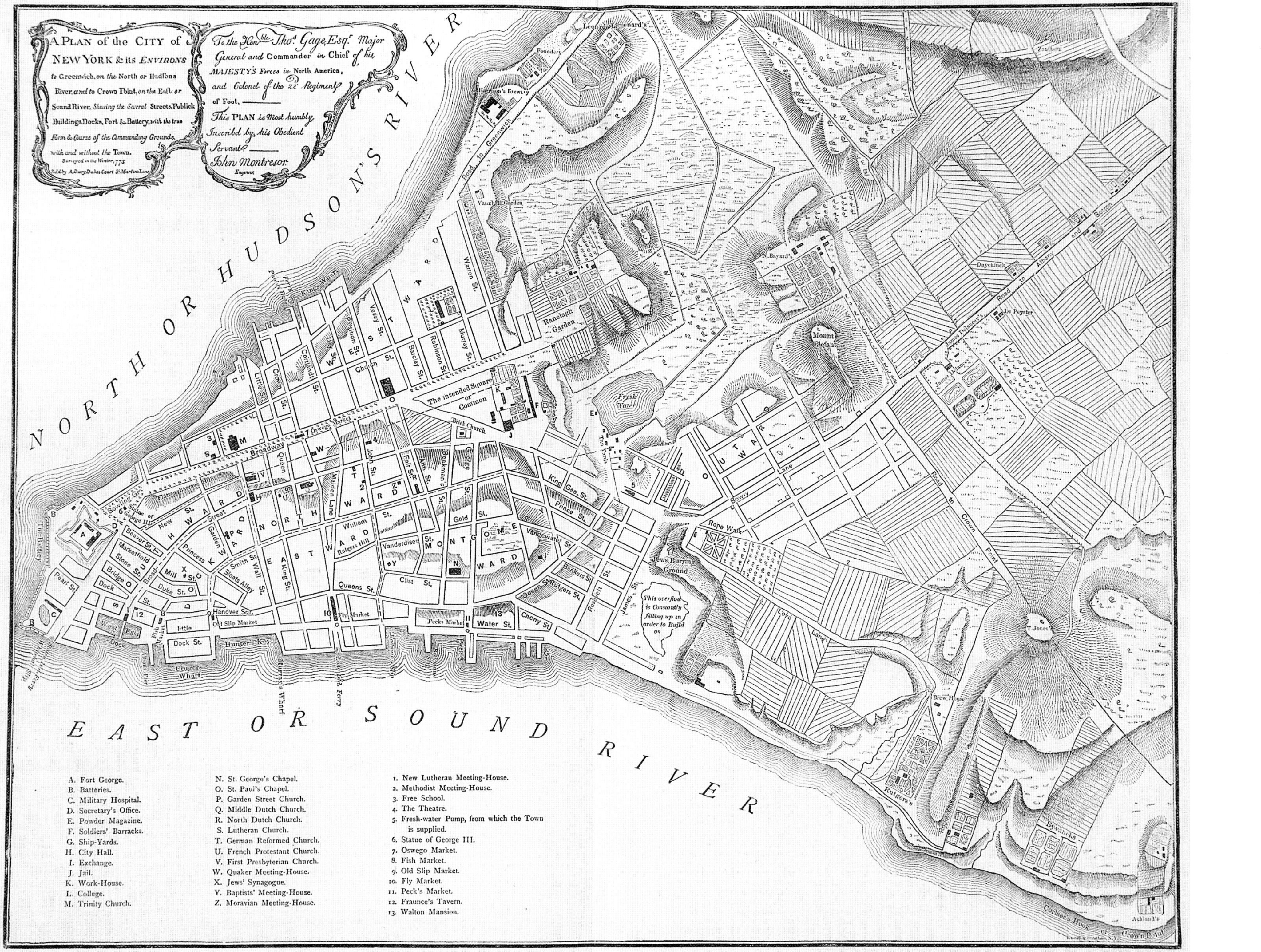
A PLAN of the CITY of NEW YORK & its ENVIRONS to Greenwich, on the North or Hudsons River, and to Crown Point, on the East or Sound River, Shewing the Several Streets, Publick Buildings, Docks, Fort & Battery, with the true Form & Course of the Commanding Grounds, with and without the Town.
Surveyed in the Winter, 1775
Sold by A. Dury Dukes Court St. Martins Lane
To the Hon.ble Thos. Gage, Esqr. Major General and Commander in Chief of his MAJESTY'S Forces in North America, and Colonel of the 22d Regiment of Foot, ——
This PLAN is Most humbly Inscribd by his Obedient Servant ——
John Montresor.
Engineer
NORTH OR HUDSON'S RIVER
EAST OR SOUND RIVER
A. Fort George.
B. Batteries.
C. Military Hospital.
D. Secretary's Office.
E. Powder Magazine.
F. Soldiers' Barracks.
G. Ship-Yards.
H. City Hall.
I. Exchange.
J. Jail.
K. Work-House.
L. College.
M. Trinity Church.
N. St. George's Chapel.
O. St. Paul's Chapel.
P. Garden Street Church.
Q. Middle Dutch Church.
R. North Dutch Church.
S. Lutheran Church.
T. German Reformed Church.
U. French Protestant Church.
V. First Presbyterian Church.
W. Quaker Meeting-House.
X. Jews' Synagogue.
Y. Baptists' Meeting-House.
Z. Moravian Meeting-House.
1. New Lutheran Meeting-House.
2. Methodist Meeting-House.
3. Free School.
4. The Theatre.
5. Fresh-water Pump, from which the Town is supplied.
6. Statue of George III.
7. Oswego Market.
8. Fish Market.
9. Old Slip Market.
10. Fly Market.
11. Peck's Market.
12. Fraunce's Tavern.
13. Walton Mansion.

VIEW of HARLAEM from MORISANIA in the PROVINCE of NEWYORK Septemr 1765.
65

VIEW OF HARLAEM FROM MORISANIA IN THE PROVINCE OF NEW YORK, SEPTEM[R] 1765: Originally Morrisania (its current spelling) was the estate of the Morris family in Westchester County. In 1840 a railroad was permitted to run through it, and in 1855 Morrisania Village was founded. In 1874 Morrisania was annexed to New York City, which then consisted only of Manhattan; today it is part of the Bronx. The church here shown was destroyed during the Revolution, rebuilt in 1788, and finally demolished in 1825. The ferry across the Harlem River, established in 1667, appears in the foreground. Copied from the original manuscript in the British Museum, for Mr. George H. Moore, Librarian of the New-York Historical Society. LITHOGRAPH BY GEORGE HAYWARD. PUBLISHED IN *VALENTINE'S MANUAL*, 1863.

BULL'S HEAD TAVERN ON THE BOWERY, 1783: Located between Bayard and Pump (now Canal) Streets, this tippling spot had been a favorite haunt for cattle drovers, butchers, and sporting men since 1756. For Evacuation Day, when the British at last relinquished control of New York, generals George Washington and George Clinton hoisted glasses of ale before linking up with General Henry Knox for the procession southward. The famous old haunt endured in its spot on the Boston Post Road until 1826, when it was moved to Third Avenue and 26th Street. Its former spot was then taken by the Bowery (Thalia) Theater and, following a fire, the Atlantic Garden. This nineteenth-century watercolor on paper is attributed to Abram S. Hosier. A woodcut modeled on it appeared in *Munsey's* magazine in April 1898. THE J. CLARENCE DAVIES COLLECTION. 29.100.2775.

(RIGHT) **CERTIFICATE OF MEMBERSHIP IN THE SOCIETY OF THE CINCINNATI, 1783:** Instituted by officers of the American Army after the peace of 1783, the Society's purpose, according to Charles S. Davies, was "to perpetuate the mutual feelings of patriotism, benevolence, and brotherly friendship created by a common experience of the hardships encountered in achieving the freedom of their country." The American and French officers and their descendants adopted for their association "the name and example of the Roman citizen-soldier who had laid down in peace arms assumed only for the public defense. It was Washington personified under the image of the Roman Cincinnatus." William Bainbridge was inducted into this noble order in the year of its founding, with this certificate signed by Washington. Other New York members were Chancellor Livingston, Gouverneur Morris, Rufus King, Stephen Van Rensselaer, the naval commanders Bainbridge, Biddle, Stewart, Hull, and Perry, and Generals Jackson, Scott, Brown, Cadwallader, Taylor, Worth, and Wool. INK ON PARCHMENT. GIFT OF DUNKIN STERLING. 45.76.

Be it known that **Commodore William Bainbridge** of the Navy of the United States
Member of the Society of the **Cincinnati**; instituted by the Officers of the American Army, at the Period of its Dissolution, as well
nmemorate the great Event which gave Independence to North America, as for the laudable Purpose of inculcating the Duty
ying down in Peace Arms assumed for public Defence, and of uniting in Acts of brotherly Affection, and Bonds of perpetual Friendship,
Members constituting the same.

In Testimony whereof I, the President of the said Society, have hereunto set my Hand at Mount Vernon
in the State of Virginia this tenth Day of December in the
Year of our Lord One Thousand Seven Hundred and Eighty five and in the tenth
Year of the Independence of the United States.

By order,

H Knox Secretary.

G Washington President.

Granted
8th December 1810

A South West View of the City of New York, in NORTH AMERICA. § Vue de Sud Ouest de la Ville de New York, dans L'AMERIQUE SEPTEN

Drawn on the SPOT by Cap.t Thomas Howdell, of the Royal Artillery. Engraved by P. Canot.

(LEFT) SOUTH WEST VIEW OF THE CITY OF NEW YORK, 1763: The vista is observed from the southern slope of Mount Pitt, near the present-day intersection of Henry and Montgomery Streets. This was the highest point of that part of the city, which "commanded a magnificent prospect, extending on the east beyond Hellgate, on the west over the city and the bay to the shores of Staten Island and New Jersey, and on the south over the East River and the heights of Long Island." In later years this elevation was graded down. This was drawn by Captain Thomas Howdell and engraved by Pierre Charles Canot in 1768. BEQUEST OF MRS. J. INSLEY BLAIR IN MEMORY OF MR. AND MRS. J. INSLEY BLAIR. 52.100.29.

JOHN STREET METHODIST CHURCH, 1768: Titled "The First Methodist Episcopal Church in America," or alternately "Wesley's Chapel, John Street, New York," this image was first published by Joseph Beekman Smith as an engraving in 1824 and subsequently published in several versions, including a colored engraving by Lewis Delnoce in 1868. "The walls were constructed of ballast-stone, and the face was covered with a light blue plaister." Opened to the public by Reverend Philip Embury on October 30, 1768, the chapel was erected on Golden Hill, subsequently renamed John Street, and survived until 1840. In the following year a new church was built and assumed the name of "old John Street." THE J. CLARENCE DAVIES COLLECTION. 29.100.2158.

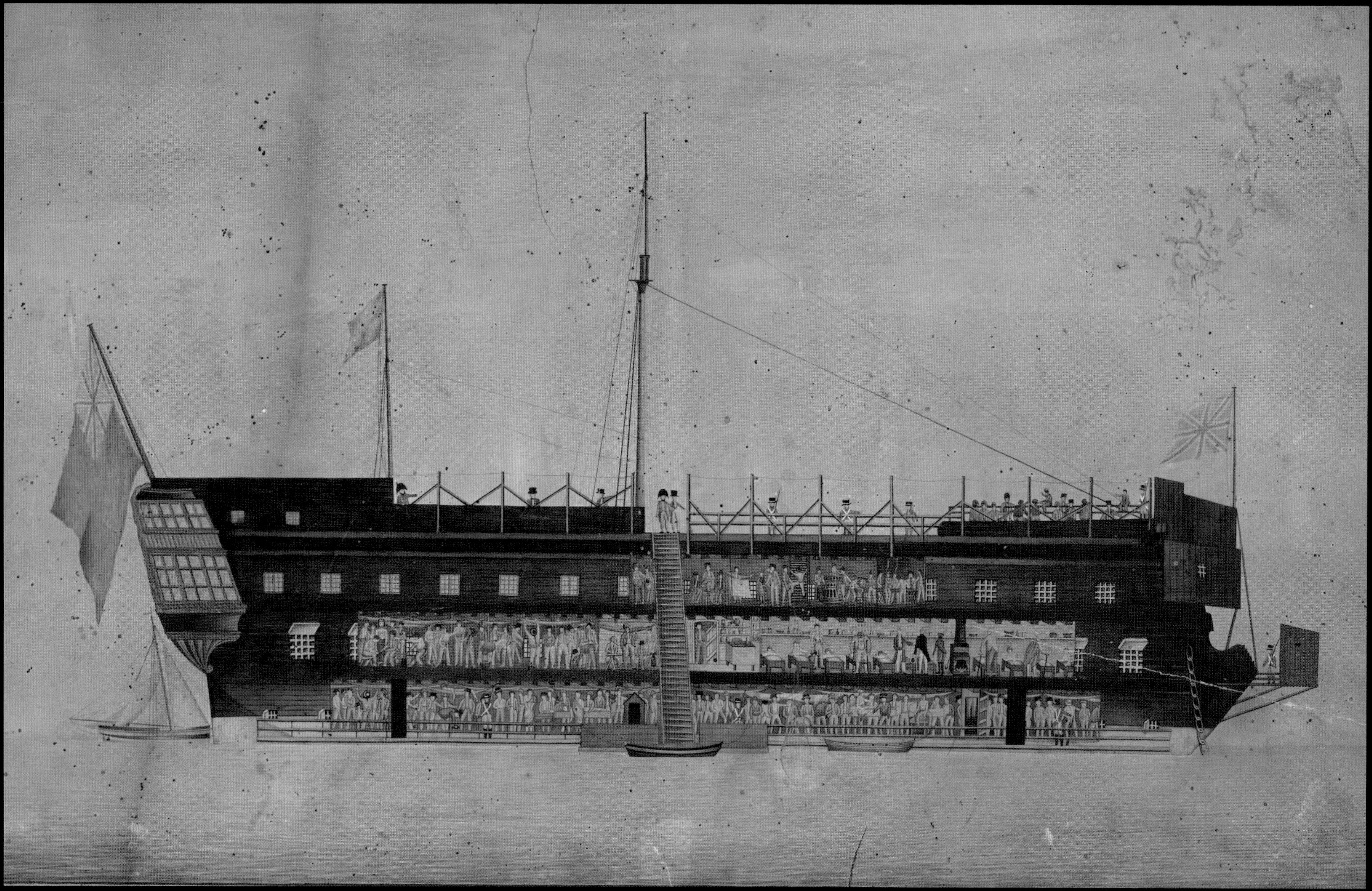

PRISONERS OF WAR (DETAIL ON RIGHT): The name of the British prison ship is unknown, as is that of its artist, who wrote in French on the border of this watercolor on paper, "My God, Have you forgotten me?" GIFT OF MRS. EDITH GREGOR HALPERT. M41.3.

CHAPTER IV | 1784–1811

"THE MAN ABOUT TOWN"

MEN AND STYLE IN AARON BURR'S NEW YORK

NANCY ISENBERG

IN 1807, AS AARON BURR STOOD TRIAL FOR TREASON IN RICHMOND, VIRGINIA, A YOUNG WRITER RECORDED HIS IMPRESSIONS OF THIS NOTORIOUS NEW YORKER. THAT OBSERVER WAS TWENTY-FOUR-YEAR-OLD WASHINGTON IRVING, WHO HAD NOT YET ACHIEVED HIS FULL STATURE AS AN INTERNATIONALLY ACCLAIMED AUTHOR. IRVING HAD KNOWN THE SEASONED POLITICIAN FOR YEARS, ACTIVELY SUPPORTING HIS CAMPAIGN FOR GOVERNOR OF NEW YORK IN 1804. HE KNEW EXACTLY THE QUALITIES PEOPLE SAW IN BURR—QUALITIES THAT GAVE THE ASCENDANT, AND NOW DISCREDITED, VICE PRESIDENT HIS DASHING, MASCULINE STYLE.[1] FOR IRVING, ONE SCENE CAPTURED BURR AT HIS BEST. IT WAS THE MEMORABLE ENCOUNTER OF THE DEFENDANT AND HIS MAIN ACCUSER, GENERAL JAMES WILKINSON. ARRIVING SEVERAL WEEKS AFTER CRIMINAL PROCEEDINGS HAD BEGUN, THE HAUGHTY, PORTLY COMMANDER OF U.S. FORCES STRUTTED INTO THE COURTROOM IN FULL MILITARY REGALIA. AS IRVING DESCRIBED, "SWELLING LIKE A TURKEY-COCK, AND BRACING HIMSELF UP FOR THE ENCOUNTER OF BURR'S EYE," WILKINSON WAS NO MATCH FOR AARON BURR. AS THE GENERAL'S NAME WAS CALLED OUT, BURR TURNED, AND "LOOKED AT HIM FULL IN THE FACE WITH ONE OF THOSE PIERCING REGARDS, SWEPT HIS EYE OVER HIS WHOLE PERSON FROM HEAD TO FOOT," AND THEN "COOLLY" RESUMED HIS CONVERSATION WITH HIS COUNSEL, AS THOUGH NOTHING OF CONSEQUENCE HAD TRANSPIRED. RELISHING THE MOMENT, IRVING SUMMED IT UP simply: "The look was over in an instant; but it was an admirable one." What made this well-timed glance so effective? There was "no affectation or disdain" in it; it seemed completely natural, firm and manly, and nearly effortless. Burr displayed ease and finesse in dismissing his adversary with a mere look.[2]

Irving's Burr cut a striking figure. Dressed in black satin for his trial, standing barely five feet six inches, he exuded elegance. A successful Wall Street attorney in the years following the Revolution, he had a reputation for intelligent and witty conversation. He admired smart women and gained a large following of personal friends and devoted political supporters. His coolness under pressure belied the fact that his entire way of life was at stake at that moment in Richmond. He would be found innocent of all charges, and yet rumor and the stigma of public disgrace were to strip him of his vaunted social standing in the nation at large and, as important to him, in his home state. He would never regain his place in the political limelight or return to the ranks of respectable society.[3]

Not long before, Burr had been Gotham's version of the "man about town." But then, in July 1804, he was forced into exile after his duel with Alexander Hamilton, which had resulted in his rival's death. To escape possible prosecution, Burr was obliged to leave behind a thriving social scene in which he was a major player. Manhattan had flourished in the fifteen years since George Washington's inauguration. As the nation's capital from 1789 to 1790, New York City became the center of financial speculation. Grand edifices appeared downtown, and a rising mercantile class demanded entertainment. Elegant public spaces celebrated gentility, and new theatrical venues offered weekly amusement, creating a New York *bon ton*. City Hall was remodeled using a "modern" design by the French architect Pierre Charles L'Enfant. Renamed Federal Hall, it was ready just in time for Washington to stand on its balcony as he was sworn in as the first president of the United States.[4]

In rapid succession, other new public structures appeared in lower Manhattan that imitated the metropolitan tastes of London and Europe. The City Hotel on Broadway opened its doors in 1794, providing 137 rooms for guests, an elegant ballroom, public parlors for intimate gatherings, a bar, and the largest circulating library in the nation. That same year, New Yorkers watched the rise of the Tontine Coffee House, a proud four-story, brick-and-stone structure at the corner of Wall and Water Streets, which served as a meeting place for merchants, politicians, and speculators. Here, prominent leaders with proud family legacies made deals among themselves and with ambitious newcomers. They drank coffee, socialized informally, and shared news and gossip.[5]

Two other new structures catered to the recreational tastes of New Yorkers. In 1794, Ricketts' Equestrian Circus opened a new building on Broadway, treating its clientele to spectacular pantomimes and daring feats of horsemanship. The most lavish building of all was the Park Theatre, which made its debut in 1798. Situated across from today's City Hall, and costing $130,000, the Park Theatre had 200 seats and an unusually spacious stage. It was dramatically adorned with sumptuous scenery, which led one newspaper to praise it for an "elegance and effect" never seen before in America.[6]

Private wealth and the desire for more spurred real estate investment, but so did New York City's temporary role as the nation's capital. In 1790, the State of New York built the Presidential Mansion near fashionable Bowling Green. New York's elite and well-heeled Federalist politicos wanted to be seen showcasing a style of dress and manners suited to national officeholders. The Washington administration encouraged this kind of public display. The President and Mrs. Washington soon convened what became known as the "Republican Court," holding formal weekly receptions, or levees, which, as one attendee wrote, attracted everyone who was "fashionable, elegant, and refined in society." The "rabble" was not invited. No one spoke of democracy.[7]

New Yorkers also attended concerts, balls, and banquets at the City Hotel. They ate ice cream, watched fireworks, and strolled among "curious plants and shrubs" at the various English-style pleasure gardens that dotted the early urban landscape. In his travel narrative, Englishman John Lambert described lower Broadway as the fashionable center of the city. The wealthy lived in mansions and townhouses near the Battery, while up a few blocks stood a succession of fancy stores, displaying "Italian and European goods" in their shop windows. Every day, from eleven to three, the gentry would promenade along the whole of Broadway, exchanging courtesies and engaging in small talk, creating what Lambert called the "genteel lounge" of New York.[8]

Gotham's man about town had many haunts available to him by the turn of the century. He might be found hobnobbing at a private dinner party, discussing with the hostess the latest novel he had read; or he might be sipping cups of java at the Tontine Coffee-House, while convincing a close friend to sign a promissory note, or to buy shares in a land company, or to back some other grand speculative venture. He might be seen and heard giving a clever and patriotic toast at a public banquet. Or he could be found demonstrating his elegant deportment while dancing at the City Hotel.

The man about town was rarely alone. He was often accompanied by his coterie of male friends. Washington Irving and his college-educated older brothers Peter, William, and Ebenezer, along with several other New Yorkers including the satirist and novelist James Kirke Paulding, formed a group alternately known as the "Lads of Kilkenny," the "Nine Worthies," and the "Ancient Club of New York." They convened at Dyde's public house near the Park Theatre, and by 1807, had established themselves as astute observers and social critics. Washington Irving's first published work consisted of his Jonathan Oldstyle letters, which appeared in his brother Peter's Burrite newspaper, the *Morning Chronicle*. The Irving brothers and Paulding followed up with the *Salmagundi* essays, offering a "mixed dish" of social and political satire. One of their favorite subjects: the foibles of young men about town.[9]

The strange twists and turns of male fashion formed the centerpiece for both Oldstyle and *Salmagundi*. Irving penned a blistering critique of those "male bucks" and "modern beaus" who affected a studied carelessness and "slovenliness of dress." Wearing a "large hat, large coat, large neckcloth, large pantaloons, and large boots," he sneered, these so-called gentlemen could be found "lounging along the streets in the most apparent listlessness," or sauntering into a ballroom, "dressed up in the mammoth style," entertaining the ladies with the "common slang of the day."[10]

Irving directed the same kind of ridicule at "fashionable duelists." Most young men were "poor shots," he wrote in 1803, and were content with only one discharge; but others recklessly took to the field, ready to "either conquer or die," and were typically saved by the sanity of their seconds, who resolved to intervene after the first shot. All in all, the farce of dueling would be less common, he concluded, if the public was "admitted *to the show*." These proud young gladiators would be cut down in size if the world could see how foolish they really were.[11]

Barbed jabs such as these tell us that the man about town invited both admiration and disdain. His excesses of display, whether he was bounding around the city in large, unkempt dress, or engaging in fashionable duels, provoked a barrage of ridicule. Fashionable men who spent too much time with women, mastering the art of tea-party conversation, were just as likely to be mocked. The tailor, barber, and dancing master were this young man's best friends, one writer explained in New York's *The Weekly Visitor*, or *Ladies Miscellany* in 1804; and with his constant efforts to please the ladies, another writer claimed, he "almost becomes himself a lady."[12]

New Yorkers were quick to borrow from an older figure in English satire, who was labeled, interchangeably, beau, dandy, fop, and pretty fellow. The foppish man was a dangerous sexual hybrid feeding fears of social instability common among elites of London and New York. Fops were dismissed as men of glittering surfaces without substance. They were accused of cultivating feminine airs and theatrical gestures, only in the hope of seducing unwitting female prey. Behind a mask of sociability, such men might be libertines in disguise.[13]

This satirical picture had some foundation in reality. Social and sexual commerce commingled in New York's urban landscape. A man about town might attend a concert, stroll along the battery, and then visit one of the many brothels in town. In 1794, the Frenchman Moreau de Saint-Méry was shocked to discover that New York, though a young city compared to those in Europe, already had "whole sections of streets given over to street-walkers for plying their profession" and "many house of debauchery." Prominent men had mistresses and illegitimate children. In the 1790s one could buy condoms at a local bookstore in Philadelphia, and possibly in New York as well, suggesting that both reading and sex were genteel pastimes.[14]

One of the most prominent families in New York, the Livingstons, came to own a dozen brothels. Though Chancellor Robert Livingston held the highest legal office in the state, his younger brother John became, without embarrassment, a noted whoremaster. Elite New Yorkers were hardly puritanical. In 1797, Alexander Hamilton openly admitted to having an adulterous affair. Burr himself kept a secret cache of sexually explicit letters, tied up with a red string, and labeled "Put," which he told his daughter to destroy if he did not survive the duel with Hamilton. The word *putage* was a legal term for prostitution, and so Burr's shorthand may well have been a reference to such liaisons.[15]

Though he was socially adept and physically mobile, the man about town spent considerable hours at home. An elite man with political ambitions transformed his residence into a personal stage. Hamilton built "The Grange," his country manor home in upper Manhattan. In what became Greenwich Village, Burr purchased the Richmond Hill estate, a sprawling 160 acres with English-style gardens, abundant meadows, and a manmade pond which graced the entrance to the grounds. The mansion had two stories, Ionic columns, and Chinese Chippendale railings around the porch. He filled his home with the finest furnishings: chintz curtains, large mirrors, an elegant tea service, Brussels carpet, card tables, a piano-forte, and a large bathing tub.[16]

Burr cultivated the ambiance of a French salon at Richmond Hill. The large library, picture gallery, and gracious dining room were all suitable for entertaining. Fascinating guests graced his home, including the French philosopher-historian Constantin-François Chasseboeuf, the Comte de Volney; and the chief of the Mohawks, London-educated Joseph Brant. Notably, Burr also opened his home to John Vanderlyn, a young American destined for international fame as a painter. He supplied a room to the Englishman John Davis while Davis penned a travel narrative of the United States. More than a home, Burr's Richmond Hill was a cosmopolitan *entrepôt*, a way station for foreign travelers, French exiles, artists, and Burr's friends and family.[17]

Ultimately, Burr's home was a symbol of spectacular loss. He sold all his furnishings in 1797 to cover mounting debts from various speculative ventures. Eventually, the property became the possession of John Jacob Astor, who reaped vast profits by subdividing the land into smaller lots as Greenwich Village grew and prospered.[18]

In many ways, the man about town was a creation of New York's outward-aiming commercial enterprises, financial networks, and transatlantic connections. His tastes were European, looking to London or Paris for latest styles in the food, fashion, and architecture. As the political party system took shape in the 1790s, producing hard-fought campaigns and men jockeying for local and national office, partisan differences shaped cultural tastes. John Lambert observed that some of the ladies of New York wore their party allegiances literally on their sleeves. Those who favored the Jeffersonians dressed "*à la mode Françoise*," while Federalists favored "*la mode Angloise*." Though the men were indistinguishably dressed in black, their choice of dancing partners suddenly took on political meaning.[19]

Social capital was the man about town's greatest asset. Using his silver tongue and debonair style, he circulated his talents in the parlors and public haunts of the New York elite. Conservatives were quick to attack these mobile men for their lifestyle. They warned against confidence men lurking in coffee houses. They scoffed at Chesterfieldian beaux, who—they imagined as the manipulators of good manners, trained in the treachery of female seduction.[20]

In 1807, the year of Burr's treason trial, an anonymous writer cast the defendant as the "epitome" of "Chesterfield and the graces." To the ladies, he is "all attention . . . he gazes on them with complacency and rapture;" he displays "those captivating gestures . . . those dissolving looks . . . and insinuating eloquence" that take the "soul captive." Men and women fell under his hypnotic sway, or so his critics claimed.[21]

Burr's admirers saw him in a far more positive light. He was a man of the Enlightenment, of refined sensibility and good taste, of eloquence, and a commanding presence. This is what Washington Irving observed in 1807, as he watched Burr calmly dispatch his adversary with one subtle but perfect glance. For Irving, Burr represented an American version of the London maverick Beau Brummell, who was known for his glossy boots, his meticulous grooming in the style of a military man, and his understated though fascinating repartee and moving gestures. The "incomparable Burr," as he was called, projected an image of disciplined audacity. If one were to think of a contemporary cult figure who embodies "cool" (movie legends like Humphrey Bogart and Clint Eastwood come to mind), the quality they exude is comparable to what Burr was said to possess in his generation.[22]

The iconic man about town marked New York City's rejection of its provincial past. He was a modern man who indulged the epicurean pleasures of friendship and conversation. He was so smooth that he could be easily caricatured, his excesses made to appear the core of his being. Articulate, bold, curious, and cosmopolitan he loomed large. Though often surrounded by male friends (as long as his credit remained good), he was as likely to be seen in the company of smart, stylish women. He was the quintessential New Yorker.

NANCY ISENBERG IS PROFESSOR OF HISTORY AT LOUISIANA STATE UNIVERSITY AND AUTHOR OF *FALLEN FOUNDER: THE LIFE OF AARON BURR* (VIKING, 2007), WHICH WAS A FINALIST FOR THE *LOS ANGELES TIMES* BIOGRAPHY PRIZE AND WINNER OF THE 2008 OKLAHOMA CENTER FOR THE BOOK NONFICTION AWARD. HER FIRST BOOK, *SEX AND CITIZENSHIP IN ANTEBELLUM AMERICA* (UNIVERSITY OF NORTH CAROLINA PRESS, 1998), RECEIVED THE 1999 SHEAR (SOCIETY FOR HISTORIANS OF THE EARLY AMERICAN REPUBLIC) BOOK PRIZE. SHE IS CURRENTLY WORKING ON *MADISON AND JEFFERSON*, FOR RANDOM HOUSE, TO BE COAUTHORED WITH HISTORIAN ANDREW BURSTEIN.

THE CORNER OF WARREN AND GREENWICH STREETS DURING THE SNOW, 1809: Anne-Marguérite-Henriette Rouillé de Marigny, otherwise known as the Baroness Hyde de Neuville, arrived in New York with her husband in 1807, having been banished from France for participation in a royalist conspiracy against Napoleon. In January 1809 she painted this charming watercolor with pencil view of the silent streets of snowy New York, where sleigh-riding and sledding had been a winter tradition since their introduction by the Dutch. The City Council, as late as 1908, mandated that sleighs be equipped with bells

CITY HALL (FEDERAL HALL), 1790: This view is noteworthy for depicting the exterior of the Federal Hall on Wall Street, as remodeled by Pierre L'Enfant in 1788-89 for the accommodation of Congress (note the extension at the rear of the Hall). "A Perspective View of the City Hall in New York Taken from Wall Street" is also known as The Tiebout City Hall View. Drawn and engraved on copper by Cornelius Tiebout, likely between 1790 and 1793. As City rather than Federal Hall appears in the original title, the view must have been issued after August 12, 1790, when the nation's capital was moved from New York to Philadelphia. THE J. CLARENCE DAVIES COLLECTION. 29.100.1692.

UNION HILL, FORDHAM, CA. 1790: Stephen DeLancey acquired a mill property in Fordham in 1731 and seven years later his son Peter brought a bride, Elizabeth Colden, daughter of Lt. Gov. Cadwallader Colden, to the family manse. Upon Stephen's death in 1741 the property was willed to Peter, whose alliance with the Coldens permitted him to become the political ruler of Lower Westchester. The widowed Mrs. DeLancey took residence at a new home, Union Hill, sometime after 1770. Its location was near what is now the intersection of Fordham Road and the Grand Concourse. WATERCOLOR ON PAPER, 12¾ x 17¾. GIFT OF MRS. FREDERICK S. WOMBWELL. 49.233.

(RIGHT) **NEW YORK FROM HOBUCK FERRY HOUSE NEW JERSEY, 1796:** The ferry house and the ferry franchise were the property of John Stevens, who bought both in 1784 and before long made the Elysian Fields of Hoboken the favored pleasure excursion for New Yorkers. This beautiful aquatint by Alexander Robertson, etched by Francis Jukes and published in 1800, was based on a June 1796 sketch by his brother Archibald. The Scottish émigrés were accomplished artists who founded the Columbian Academy of Art on Liberty Street, where John Vanderlyn received early training. THE J. CLARENCE DAVIES COLLECTION. 29.100.2130.

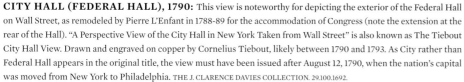

VOLUNTARY AID

These are to Certify that George Warner is pursuant to Law nominated and appointed one of the Firemen of the City of New York

July 2nd 1787

Rob. Benson Clk

Godwin Sculpt

Lith. for D.T. Valentine's Manual for 1863, by A.Brown & Co. 47 Nassau St. N.Y.

(LEFT) **CERTIFICATE APPOINTING GEORGE WARNER A FIREMAN OF THE CITY OF NEW YORK, 1787:** On March 19, 1787, an act for the better extinguishing of fires in the city of New York passed in the state legislature. "That it shall and may be lawful, to and for the mayor, aldermen and commonalty of the city of New York, in common council convened, or the major part of them, and they are hereby required to nominate and appoint a sufficient number of strong, able, discreet, honest and sober men, willing to accept, not exceeding three hundred in number, of the inhabitants, being freeholders or freemen of the said city, to have the care, management, working and using the fire engines, and the other tools and instruments now provided, or hereafter to be provided, for extinguishing of fires within the said city; which persons so to be nominated and appointed, as aforesaid, shall be called, The Firemen of the City of New York . . . " George Warner, on July 2 of that year, was one of these original three hundred. Fire fighting in the city, however, remained, largely volunteer in nature until 1865. The vignette features a venerable Newsham fire engine, of the sort that had served the city since 1731. LITHOGRAPH BY A. BROWN & CO. PUBLISHED IN *VALENTINE'S MANUAL*, 1863. GIFT OF MRS. EDWARD H. VERNET. 29.122.

A VIEW OF THE FEDERAL HALL OF THE CITY OF NEW YORK, 1797: The subtitle of the lithograph reads: " . . . as appeared in the year 1797 with the Adjacent buildings thereto." The City Hall building, which had been remodeled in 1788–89 as Federal Hall, had not been the U.S. capital since August 12, 1790. At that time the capital moved to Congress Hall in Philadelphia where it remained the seat of government until November 17, 1800, when Washington, D.C. became the permanent home of the nation's capital. This lithograph by Charles Currier (brother of Nathaniel) ca. 1850, was designed after the painting of George Holland, which had been engraved for publication by H.R. Robinson in 1847. The great iconophile I. N. Phelps Stokes believes that this name should actually be Joseph Holland, an English artist employed in connection with the *Atlantic Neptune*. Currier's lithograph was meant for *Valentine's Manual* but was never reproduced therein. The original Federal Hall was demolished in 1812; the building that stands today under that name was built as the Custom House in 1842 and has been known as Federal Hall Memorial National Historic Site since 1939. THE J. CLARENCE DAVIES COLLECTION. 29.100.2379.

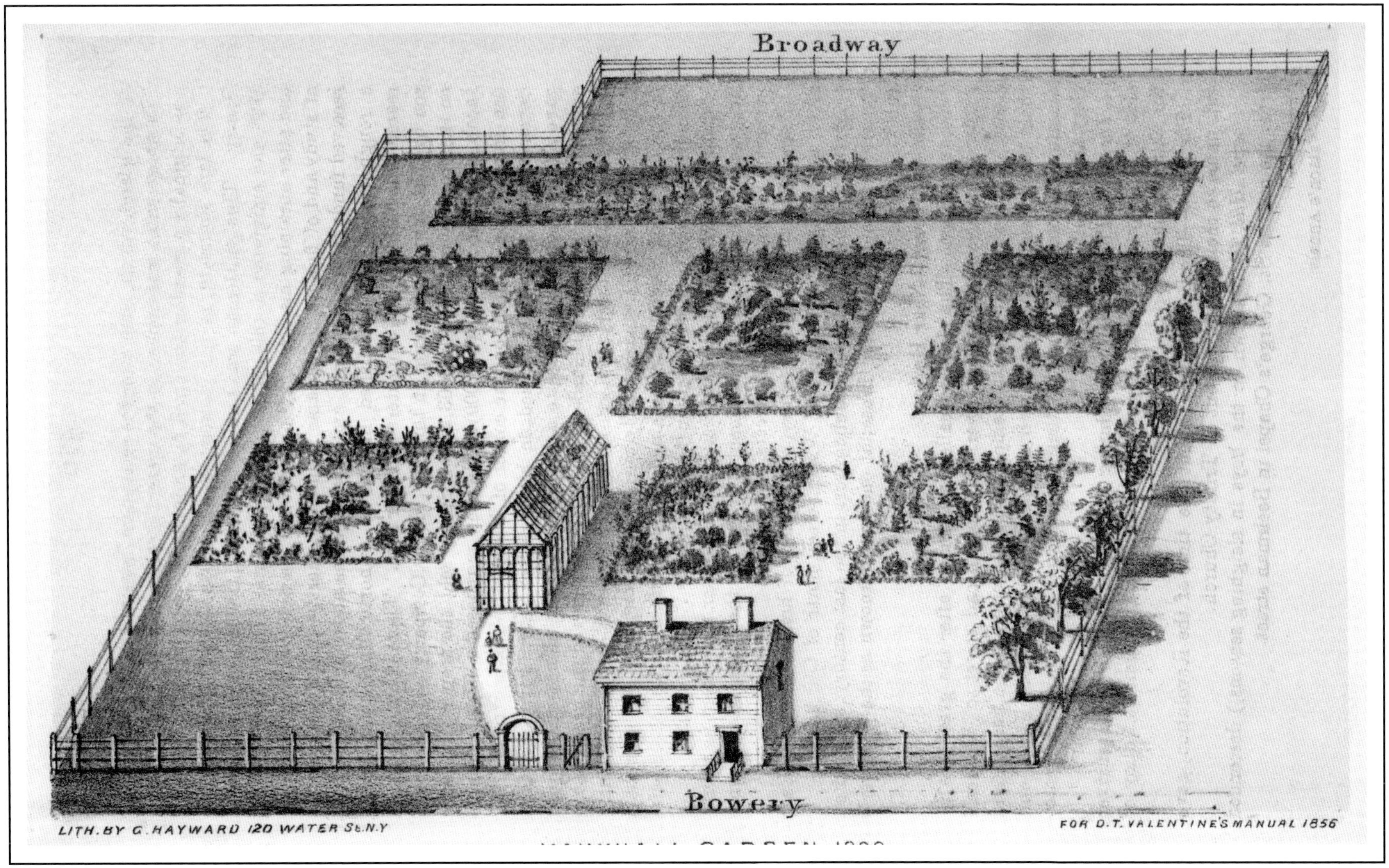

(LEFT) GOVERNMENT HOUSE, 1795: Intended as a presidential residence when it was erected in 1790, this building was named the Government House in 1791 when it was appropriated to the use of the governors of the State, beginning with Governor George Clinton. Fronting Broadway, the building went up on the spot where the southwest bastion of Fort George, razed in 1787, had stood since 1626. Government House was itself razed not long after, in 1815, to make way for fashionable private residences. On this historic site today stands the National Museum of the American Indian in the former U.S. Custom House Building. Watercolor painted and engraved by John Scoles (1772?–1853) for *The New-York Magazine; or, Literary Repository*, 1795. THE J. CLARENCE DAVIES COLLECTION. 29.100.1783.

VAUXHALL GARDEN, 1803: John Lambert, in his *Travels Through Canada, and the United States of North America, in the Years 1806, 1807, & 1808*, noted the city's pleasure gardens: "New York has its Vauxhall and Ranelagh; but they are poor imitations of those near London. They are, however, pleasant places of recreation for the inhabitants. The Vauxhall garden is situated in the Bowery Road about two miles from the City Hall. It is a neat plantation, with gravel walks adorned with shrubs, trees, busts, and statues. In the centre is a large equestrian statue of General Washington. Light musical pieces, interludes, &c. are performed in a small theatre situate[d] in one corner of the gardens: the audience sit in what are called the pit and boxes, in the open air. The orchestra is built among the trees, and a large apparatus is constructed for the display of fire-works. The theatrical corps of New-York is chiefly engaged at Vauxhall during summer." LITHOGRAPH BY GEORGE HAYWARD, PUBLISHED IN *VALENTINE'S MANUAL*, 1856.

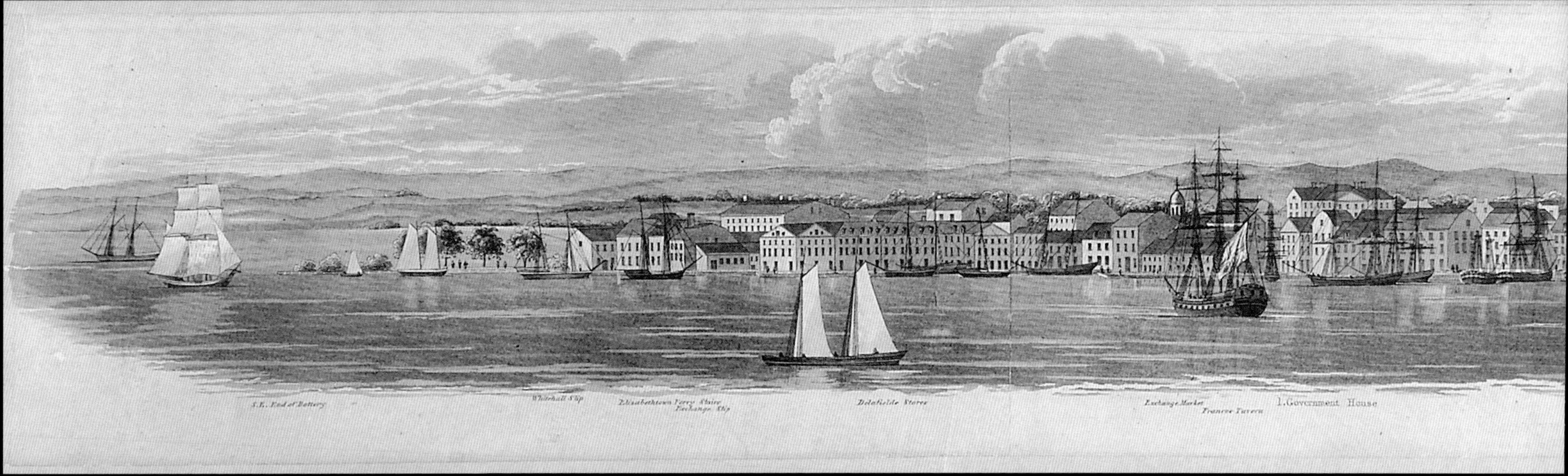

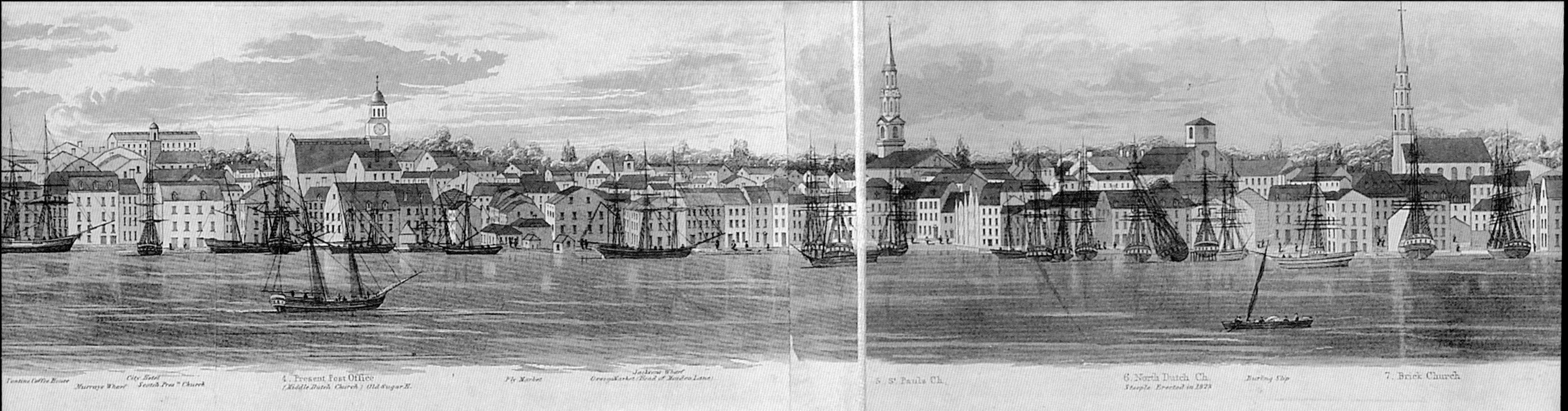

onsieur C.B. Julien de St. Memin with a Pantograph invented by himself.

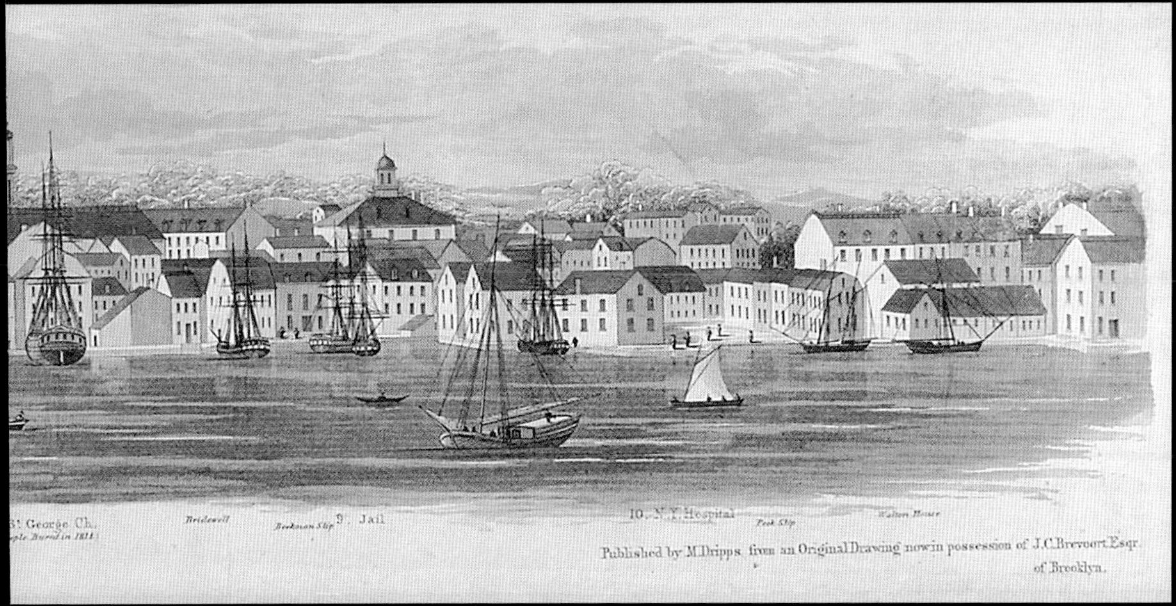

ST.-MÉMIN VIEW OF NEW YORK, 1798: The full title of this monumental panorama is "A View of the City of New-York from Brooklyn Heights, foot of Pierrepont St. in 1798, by Monsieur C. B. [Charles Balthazar] Julien [Févret] de St.-Mémin, with a Pantograph Invented by Himself." At right one reads: "Prepared by M. Dripps for *Valentine's Manual* 1861, from an Original Drawing now in possession of J. C. [Carson] Brevoort Esqr of Brooklyn." Stokes, however, noted that this panorama was enlarged directly from an engraved view by St-Mémin himself, executed in 1796. In any event, he states, "This panoramic view, on account of its size, and because of the accuracy of the drawing, gives the best depiction which we have of the East River front of New York at the close of the eighteenth century. It is also one of the few early views to give the names of the important buildings." THE J. CLARENCE DAVIES COLLECTION. 29.100.2127.

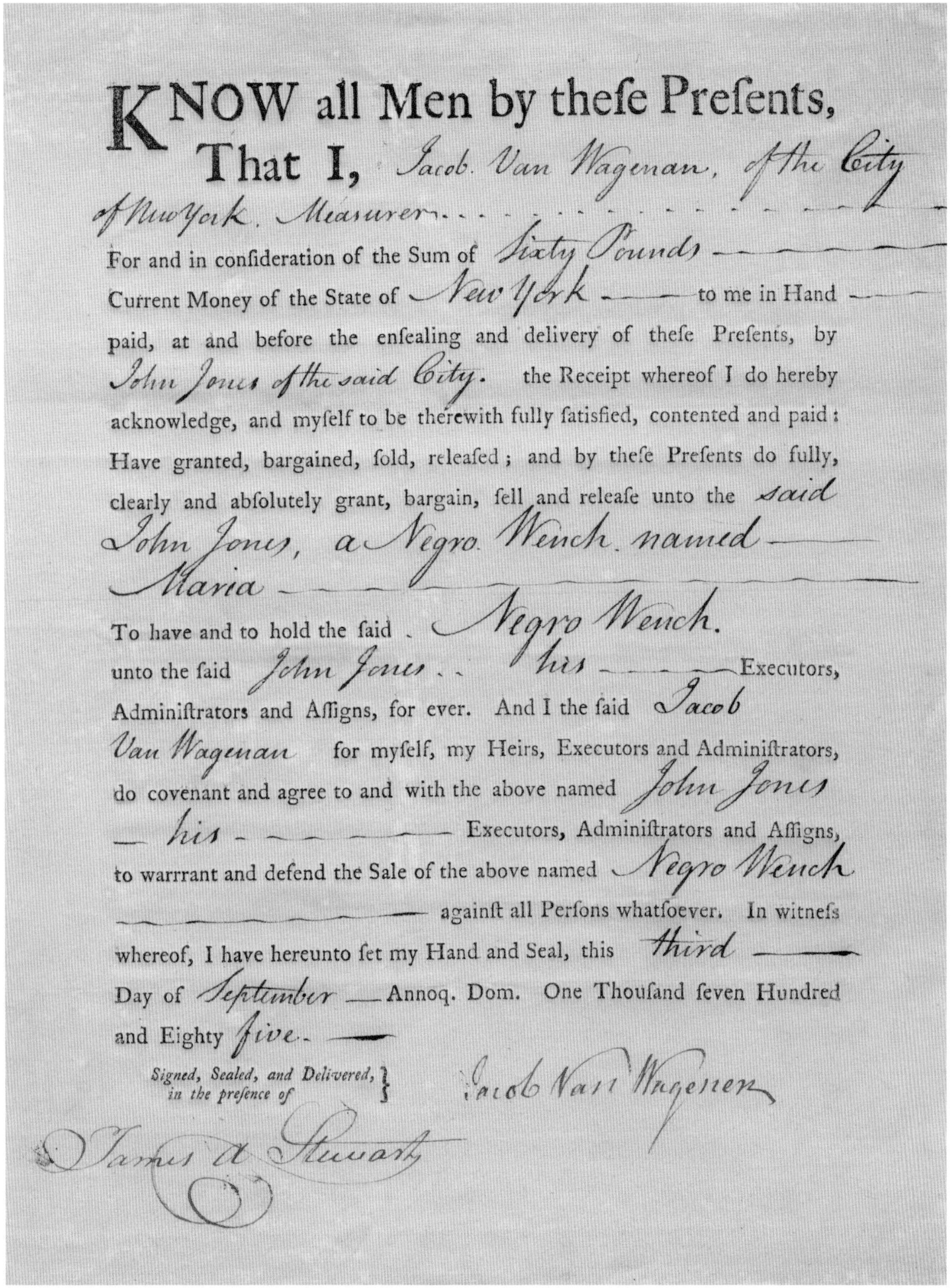
KNOW all Men by thefe Prefents,
That I, Jacob Van Wagenan, of the City of New York. Measurer
For and in confideration of the Sum of Sixty Pounds
Current Money of the State of New York to me in Hand paid, at and before the enfealing and delivery of thefe Prefents, by John Jones of the said City. the Receipt whereof I do hereby acknowledge, and myfelf to be therewith fully fatisfied, contented and paid: Have granted, bargained, fold, releafed; and by thefe Prefents do fully, clearly and abfolutely grant, bargain, fell and releafe unto the said John Jones, a Negro Wench named Maria
To have and to hold the faid Negro Wench. unto the faid John Jones his Executors, Adminiftrators and Affigns, for ever. And I the faid Jacob Van Wagenan for myfelf, my Heirs, Executors and Adminiftrators, do covenant and agree to and with the above named John Jones his Executors, Adminiftrators and Affigns, to warrrant and defend the Sale of the above named Negro Wench againft all Perfons whatfoever. In witnefs whereof, I have hereunto fet my Hand and Seal, this third Day of September Annoq. Dom. One Thoufand feven Hundred and Eighty five.

Signed, Sealed, and Delivered, in the prefence of

Jacob Van Wagenen

James A Stewart

BILL OF SALE OF SLAVE MARIA FOR SIXTY POUNDS, 1785: By this chilling document of September 3, 1785, title to the "Negro wench" Maria is transferred from Jacob Van Wagenan to John Jones, as if she were a tract of land or a horse. Slavery was not outlawed in the state until 1827—New York was the third to last Northern state to do so. It had been a powerful and pernicious part of the city's economy since the colonial period. GIFT OF MRS. NEWBOLD MORRIS. 34.86.2.

(RIGHT) **THE NEW YORK FEDERAL TABLE, 1787:** On July 23, 1788 the city staged a "Federal Procession in Honor of the Constitution of the United States" culminating in a grand dinner at Bayard's House. Horsemen with trumpets were followed by artillery and field pieces; then foresters with axes, gardeners, and musicians; then tailors and brewers and coopers and butchers—seemingly all of New York was involved in the parade. Tanners and curriers, skinners and glovers. Cordwainers and carpenters, confectioners and cutlers. Bearers of the motto "*Concedat Laurea Lingue,*" expressive of the superiority of civil over military honors. The flag, embellished with the Genius of America, crowned with a wreath of thirteen purple plumes, ten of them starred, representing the ten States which had ratified the Constitution. All these forces converged upon the Bayard House. As Frank Moss described the scene in *The American Metropolis*: "The two principal sides of the building provided for this entertainment consisted of three large pavilions, connected by a colonnade of about one hundred and fifty feet front, and forming two sides of an obtuse angle; the middle pavilion majestically rising above the whole, terminating with a dome, on the top of which was a figure of Fame with her trumpet, proclaiming a new era, and holding in her left hand the standard of the United States, and a roll of parchment, on which was inscribed, in large characters, the three remarkable epochs of the late war; Independence, Alliance with France, Peace." This is a copy from an original sketch by David Grim of that dinner for *Valentine's Manual*, 1856. The design for the pavilion had been provided by Major Pierre Charles L'Enfant. The "Bunker Hill" noted in the drawing was not the battle site outside Boston but another name for Mount Pleasant, near the present intersection of Grand and Centre Streets. PRINT ARCHIVES.

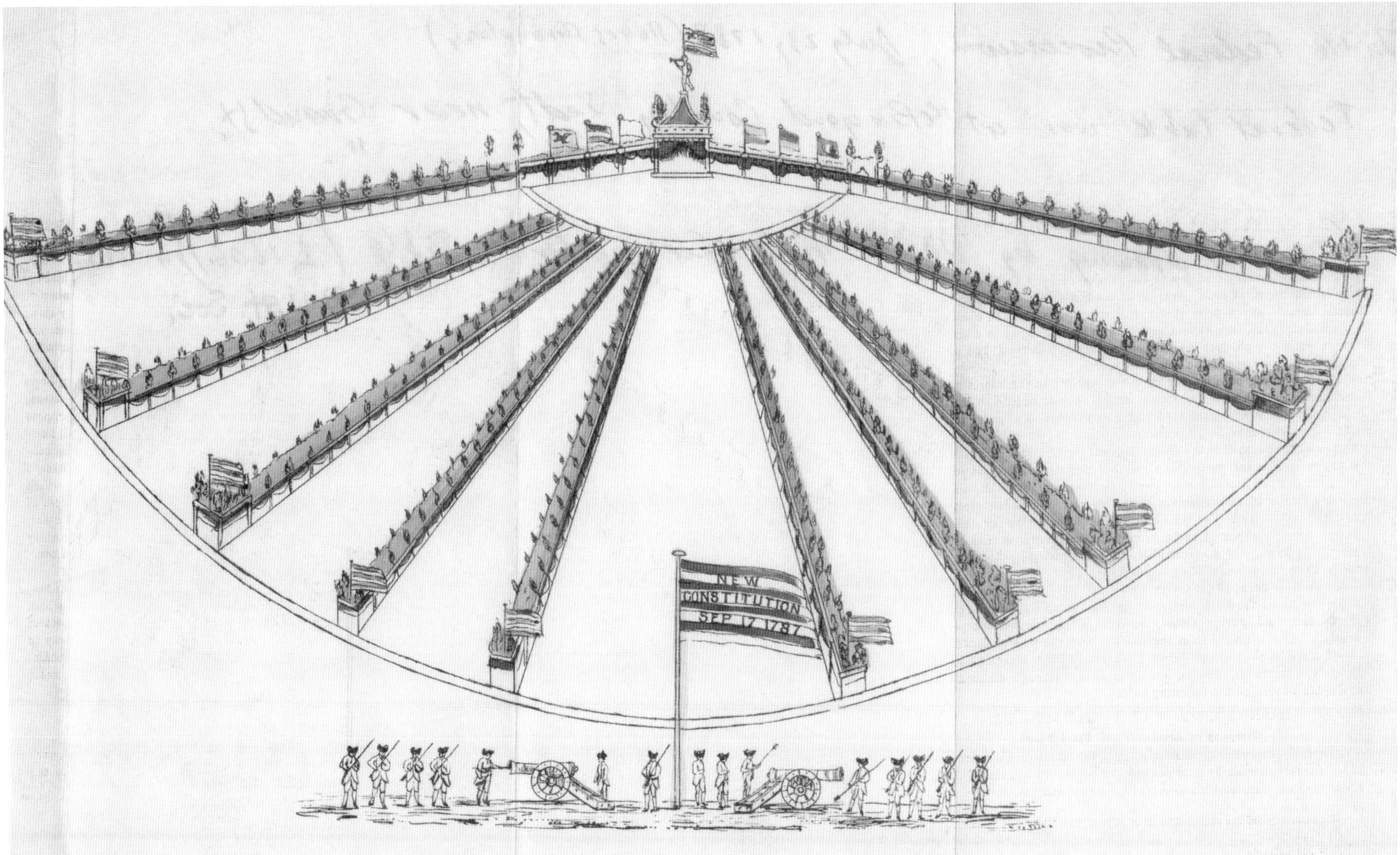

The New-York Federal Table, as seen from Bunker Hill.

Copied from an original sketch by David Grim, for D. T. Valentine's Manual 1856.

DRAWELL AT MORRISSANIA [SIC], CA. 1798: On May 8, 1697, Benjamin Fletcher, Captain-General and Governor-in-Chief of the Province of New York, issued a royal patent in the name of William II of England to Lewis Morris, for the Manor of Morrisania, comprising some 1,920 acres located in what is the southern part of the Bronx but was then part of Westchester County. In 1762 the manor had devolved to Lewis Morris III, one of the signers of the Declaration of Independence, and he held this land until his death in 1798. WATERCOLOR ON PAPER BY ARCHIBALD ROBERTSON, 14¾ x 20¼. THE J. CLARENCE DAVIES COLLECTION. 29.100.2498.

CORNER OF CANAL AND BROADWAY, LOOKING EAST, 1807: John Banvard (1815–91) came to fame as a painter of moving panoramas. In 1846 he debuted a 15,840-square-foot painting of the Mississippi River, which he cranked through rollers for two hours in a touring lecture and exhibition. But he had begun life more modestly in New York, where he painted watercolors such as this one. The house was built by Jesse Mead before the Revolution and was torn down in 1820. The bridge was on Broadway where it crossed Canal Street. 11¼ x 8¼. GIFT OF MISS EDITH M. BANVARD. 46.282.1.

CORNER OF BROADWAY AND PEARL STREET, LOOKING NORTH, 1789: This watercolor by John Banvard depicts the home built by his father, Daniel. The tree in front of the house was directly on the corner of the two streets. When Daniel Banvard died in 1831, John Banvard went west to commence a career as an itinerant painter. His work on a showboat—painting scenic art for productions aboard the Floating Theatre, in 1833—set him on the path to celebrity. 11¼ x 8¼. GIFT OF MISS EDITH M. BANVARD. 46.282.5.

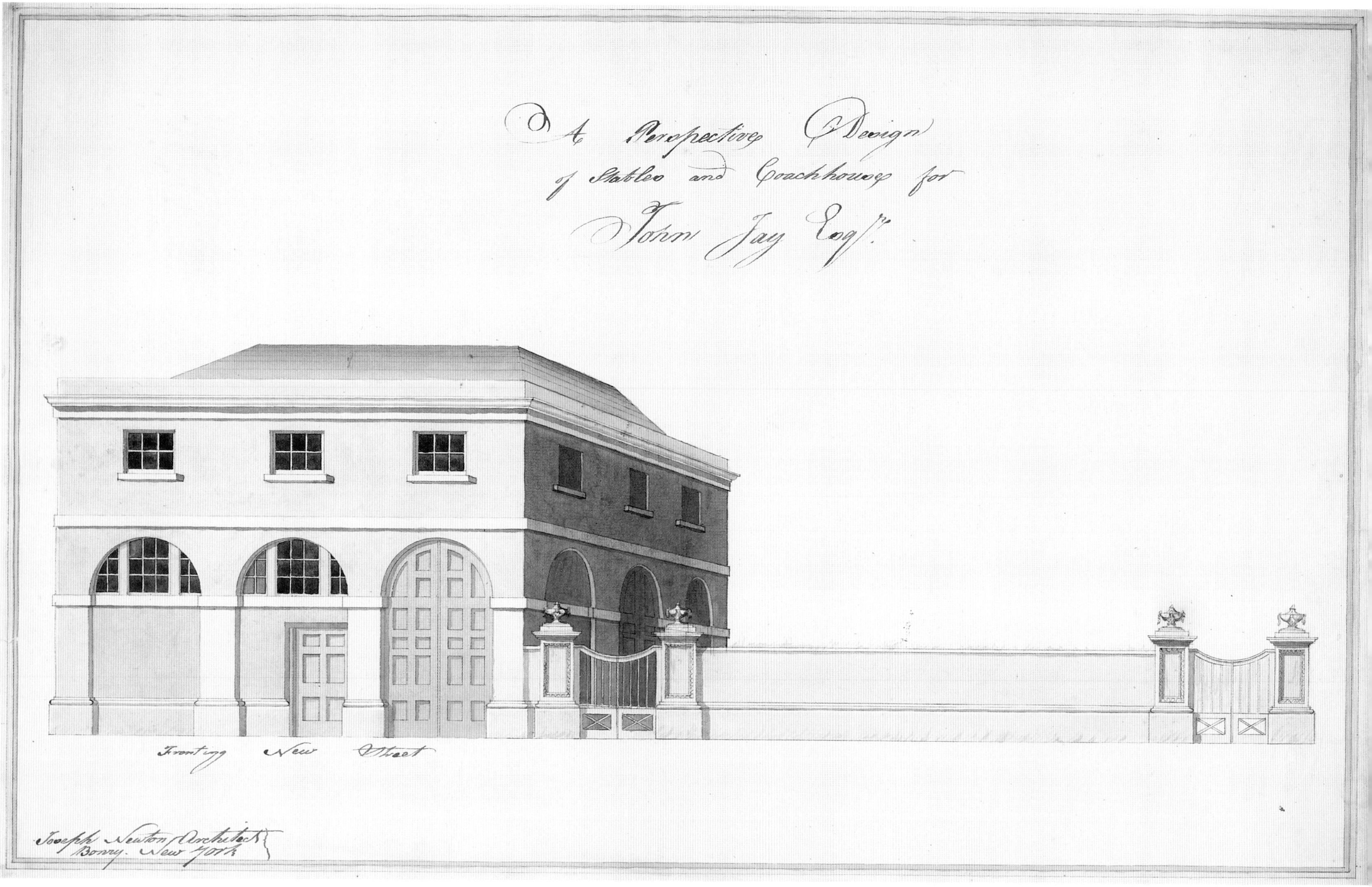
A Perspective Design
of Stables and Coachhouse for
John Jay Esqr.
Fronting New Street
Joseph Newton Architect
Bowry. New York

ELIZABETH SCHUYLER HAMILTON, 1787: Elizabeth Schuyler married Alexander Hamilton at Schuyler Mansion (Albany) in 1780. She bore him eight children and outlived him by fifty-three years. This oil portrait, the only one during her husband's lifetime, was painted by Ralph Earl under peculiar circumstances. Several members of the recently formed Society for the Relief of Distressed Debtors, including Elizabeth Schuyler Hamilton, sat for their likenesses at the prison where the financially embarrassed Earl was being detained. 31¾ x 27¾. GIFT OF MRS. ALEXANDER HAMILTON AND GENERAL PIERPONT MORGAN HAMILTON. 71.31.2.

(LEFT) A PERSPECTIVE DESIGN OF STABLES AND COACH-HOUSE FOR JOHN JAY ESQ., CA. 1786: John Jay's house was built in 1786 at 52 Broadway. The stables fronted onto New Street. When Jay was elected governor in 1795, he relocated to Government House. DRAWING BY ARCHITECT JOSEPH NEWTON, 15 x 23½. GIFT OF MRS. FREDERICK DE WITT WELLS. 52.49.A.

CHAPTER V | 1812–1841

ANTEBELLUM NEW YORK

THE CAPITAL CITY OF SEX

PATRICIA CLINE COHEN

On a cold Sunday morning in April 1836, news of a brutal murder circulated briskly throughout the lower wards of New York City. Homicides were rare in the booming city, numbering fewer than a dozen per year. This one was particularly riveting, however, because the young victim was a prostitute at an elegant brothel whose regular clientele reached up into the mercantile ranks of the city. Who had taken an axe to the head of the beautiful twenty-three-year-old Helen Jewett? And who was she, really? Jewett was her last of a string of false names, and newspapers whipped up their readership by running conflicting stories of her early life and the calamitous departure from virtue that turned her into a "fallen woman." Normally, illicit sex was not a permissible topic of public conversation among the polite classes of antebellum America. But the mystery and shock of Jewett's death unleashed the unspeakable and generated impassioned newspaper coverage about the sex trade for the next several months. Was she an injured innocent, a soiled dove spoiled by wicked and licentious men? Or was she a sexually autonomous—even sexually aggressive—female out to take revenge on men? Jewett's murder launched a debate about youth and sex, and it put a human face on prostitution, bringing it into close focus in the press.

Commercialized sex was of course not new in the 1830s. It was an old but hidden story in most port cities along the Atlantic coastline, where mariners and business travelers disembarked from ships, perhaps far from home, and found sex partners for a price. Up to the 1810s, prostitutes in New York conducted their business in sailors' dives near the docks around Corlears Hook, in rundown neighborhoods such as the Five Points, or in the occasional discreet brothel near the thoroughfares of urban commerce. Females in the trade most often were down-on-their-luck women lacking the economic support of a father or husband. Their sex-for-money activity wasn't strictly speaking against the law. Instead, authorities exercised selective policing of prostitutes under general vagrancy laws, applicable to a range of public disturbances by both men and women. It was an authority of broad discretion. As long as nonmarital sex did not seem to be destabilizing or pose a threat to public order, as long as it remained closeted in the margins of society, it was generally ignored and even well tolerated in New York City.

Starting around 1820, the commercial sex trade began to grow in scope and luxury, in tandem with the rapid commercial development of New York City. Multiple upscale brothels were built by a few wealthy real estate developers, located in streets just off

Broadway, between Chambers Street to the south and Canal Street to the north. A coterie of madams, entrepreneurs usually in their forties and fifties, headed these all-female households. Some madams rated prominent spots on the city's tax list, and a highly successful few reportedly amassed thousands of dollars alleged to be invested with brokers on Wall Street. By the 1830s there were hundreds of such establishments, many of them located on streets lined with churches, middle-class residences, and schools. Helen Jewett had lived in at least four of these high-end brothels in her four-year career in the city.

Yet in many ways, Jewett was indistinguishable from the mass of young people migrating to New York City. Like thousands of others from New England and upstate New York, the Maine native came to New York City at the age of nineteen, in response to attractive economic opportunities. Thousands of rural young men from their mid-teens to early twenties made the same move to take jobs as clerks and stock boys, the entry-level rungs of the ladder that could lead to mercantile success. Young women also came in droves, hoping to become shop girls, milliners' assistants, seamstresses, or domestic servants. Jewett, a shoemaker's daughter, left a five-year stint as a domestic servant with an elite Maine family to seek enhanced prosperity in the nation's largest city.

New and easy forms of transportation facilitated the youthful migration stream, allowing parents to feel confident that sheltered, village-reared youngsters could safely navigate their passage to big cities. A multitude of stagecoach lines operated frequently over well-maintained roads, connecting the hinterlands with New York City. The famed Erie Canal, completed in 1825, brought passengers from Buffalo and points between to Albany, where steamboats took them down the Hudson River to New York City. Smaller New England canals such as the Blackstone brought central Massachusetts into easy contact with steamboats out of Providence, Rhode Island, churning their way on the Long Island Sound to the city. By 1835, the beginnings of passenger railroads further increased the flow to New York. The city's population shot up to 270,000 inhabitants by 1835, an increase of nearly 70,000 in five years.

Not all of the incoming young people found an easy path upward. Antebellum New York no longer operated on the system of formal apprenticeship of earlier generations, where a written contract bound a youth to a master, who supplied job training, substitute parenting, and room and board. In the 1820s and 1830s, young people were much more on their own—and more than a few failed to find their footing. Young men bunked together in crowded boarding houses with minimal adult supervision. Girls seeking domestic work expected to board with their employers; jobs in the needle trade typically came with rooms over the stores. Without parental supervision, young men on their own were in danger of succumbing to the temptations of the city. For young women who failed to find legitimate work, turning to prostitution for a living became a very real temptation.

Helen Jewett differed from most young female migrants to New York in that she had no desire to seek low-paid women's work. She had already made the jump from servant to prostitute during brief stays in Portland and Boston, and quick success fed her ambition. The glittering, fast-growing metropolis on the Hudson offered by far the most attractive opportunities for a life as a high-paid prostitute. The nation's first city of commerce, transportation, and publishing was now unequivocally the nation's first city of sex merchandising.

In New York's fancy brothels, prostitution was remarkably lucrative. The young women in Helen Jewett's establishment typically charged patrons $3 to $5 apiece—this at a time when female workers in the needle trades earned just $2 to $3 in total for a sixty-hour workweek. Brothel madams made their money by charging high rents, on the order of $10 a week, to each of the girls in their establishments. They also sold expensive food and drink to the patrons. In turn, the madams paid rent to the owners of the properties, but that transaction covered only living space; it didn't cover protection. Police office records detail how the women in these brothels called on official authorities (night watchmen and police constables) to assist them with unruly patrons. Jewett and many other women showed no reluctance to pursue legal complaints before magistrates of the Police Court against harassers, attackers, or clients who cheated them. In this early phase of lucrative prostitution, women (and not pimps or mobsters) managed the sex trade.

Women like Helen Jewett were thus independent operators, able to set their conditions of employment and, when needed, control clients with help from city authorities. Most often, clients in Jewett's kind of brothel did not require police intervention, because it was in their interest to keep their sexual adventures private. Clients came from all rungs of the business classes, from unmarried clerks up to owners of firms. Others were country merchants in town on buying trips, often escorted to brothels by "drummers," the term for young men who drummed up business for New York mercantile firms by furnishing access to sex. Men of respectable reputations evidently felt assured that a code of silence protected them from public exposure. Imagine the anxiety, then, when newspapers reported that a trunk containing some four dozen letters from clients had been impounded by the police after Jewett's murder.

By the early 1830s, the stepped-up visibility of prostitution in New York led some bold citizens to break the customary silence about illicit sexual behavior. Anti-prostitution activists took their inspiration from the Second Great Awakening, a new nationwide evangelical movement that rocked several Protestant denominations. A central tenet of the Second Great Awakening was that Christian perfectionism would soon arrive and usher in a thousand-year reign of Christ on earth. Revivalists hoped to speed the coming of the millennium by tackling immorality wherever they found it: alcohol abuse, irreligion, Sabbath desecration, and not least of all, male sexual licentiousness, seen as the driving force behind the increase in prostitution.

One early effort of reformers involved calculating the enormity of the problem using statistics. A newly formed Magdalen Society run by evangelicals issued a report in 1830 asserting that over 10,000 public prostitutes worked in the city. If each fallen woman met with three men a day, the reformers figured, the result would be more than ten million visits for illicit sex a year. "Magdalen Facts" like these were meant to shock the respectable classes, and shock they did. The report generated explosive publicity. As one incredulous newspaper editor pointed out, these numbers suggested that a third of all unmarried women in the city were unchaste and ruined, while every adult male must be visiting prostitutes at the rate of three times per week. (Modern scholars estimate the prostitute population in the 1830s to be 2,000–3,000 women, or perhaps 5–7 percent of all unmarried women.) Other critics worried that such high numbers paradoxically normalized illicit sex: if so common, then what's the shame?

Female members of the Magdalen Society charted a less controversial course to eradicate sexual sin. They founded an asylum offering temporary refuge to young women who voluntarily left the sex trade. Bowing to the reformers' conviction that they were victims of male lust, several dozen young women received training in domestic duties and needlework at the asylum. Magdalen Society members then placed the reclaimed girls as servants with kindly families willing to give them a second chance. But the rates of success remained low, recidivism was high, and in any case the small number of girls who could be housed and treated stayed well under fifty, just a drop in the large bucket of sexual sin in the city.

The chaplain of the Magdalen Society opted for bolder action and began making surprise visitations to brothels, to preach to the inmates and chastise the male clients. The Reverend John R. McDowall published a detailed record of his visitations—including brothel locations—in a new monthly periodical. As with the statistics of sin, McDowall's brothel tours caused a sensation. Critics charged that his columns provided a directory pointing men to dissipated locations. By 1835 the young minister faced church disciplinary action as well as a civil grand jury charge of promoting immorality.

A group of female evangelicals took over McDowall's periodical and reoriented it to a nationwide female readership, in an attempt to warn young women of the dangers of coming to New York City. Calling themselves the New York Female Moral Reform Society, the editors promoted discussion of specific sexual dangers to women—perilous courtship practices, wolves on steamboats and railroads, seduction warning signs, and the like. The emphasis was on saving young women from the fateful fall, rather than on rescuing them after the fact. By 1840, over 1,400 affiliate societies in New York and New England filled the journal's columns with accounts of their local meetings. The Moral Reformers got political too, organizing a massive petition campaign to criminalize seduction in the state of New York. In 1848 they finally succeeded: a convicted seducer of an innocent woman might face a five-year term in state prison—unless he married his victim, in which case all was forgiven.

Moral Reform women pioneered in female networking, a dozen years before the first woman's rights movement in U.S. history emerged, and they set high standards to protect women. But, like McDowall, they also were subject to plenty of criticism. The predictable response was that any and all discussion of sex only planted bad ideas in inexperienced minds and thus increased licentiousness. One cynical newspaper editor suggested that the Moral Reformers' periodical was too indecent to be read in Helen Jewett's brothel—it would make the prostitutes blush!

Perhaps the sharpest criticism was delivered by a set of satirically inclined young male editors whose newspapers imitated the moral reform model, wagging a collective finger of reproach at sexual sin. In this case, imitation was far from flattery: Their real purpose was to excavate New York's seamy underground and deliver a true tour of the brothels. The first entry in this field appeared in 1838, a weekly called the *Polyanthos*. It wrapped itself in the flag of morality and devoted many column inches to full-throated exposés of reverend rakes and immoral abortionists in the city. Soon the coverage tipped, and the exposés of brothels took on breathless tones of admiration and excitement. The *Polyanthos* editor faced obscenity and libel charges and spent six months in jail, but on release he continued with his potent mix of shock and titillation.

The same disingenuous ruse of righteousness appeared in the title of an 1839 directory of brothels, *Prostitution Exposed; or, Moral Reform Directory*, which listed exact addresses and trumpeted the histories and charms of the "ladies of pleasure" in each establishment. Full-blown satire on moral reform arrived in 1841–42, with a series of competing weeklies titled the *Rake*, the *Whip*, the *Libertine*, and the *Flash*. The youthful editors protested that their public-spirited purpose was to expose evil—all while explaining exactly where to find sex, obscene books and prints, and illegal pugilism matches. These frisky papers with their profiles of prostitutes and ratings of brothels garnered a large circulation, attracting customers on the streets and in saloons, oyster bars, barbershops, and steamboats. They were also shipped in bulk to scores of towns and cities as far as two hundred miles away. If New York's national reputation for racy sex needed any further buttressing, these scurrilous papers provided it.

By 1840, antebellum New York had become a contentious battleground in debates over sexual morality. Was prostitution to be tolerated and treated as if invisible, or was it a menace to be eradicated? Were men alone to be blamed for it, or did women participate willingly? What was its relation to the burgeoning economy and to parental responsibilities? Helen Jewett's murder midway through the 1830s landed these debates in the headlines, but the issues were already at play in the campaign taken up by the moral reformers and shouted down by their critics fearful of any discussion of sex. In turn, the satirical weeklies twisted the debate inside out and in effect asserted the rights of New Yorkers to a public pleasure culture.

Helen Jewett's murderer was a denizen of that pleasure culture. A young clerk from a good family in Connecticut, he lived in an all-boy boarding house and hung out in brothels, using money pilfered from his employer to pay his tab. He saw Jewett regularly and wrote her love letters that were moody and dark. He then grew tired of her and killed her. Jewett's friends at her brothel placed him at the scene on the fateful night, but the judge and jury overruled that evidence and found the young man innocent.

For decades to come, New York continued to be the nation's capital city of sex.

PATRICIA CLINE COHEN IS PROFESSOR OF HISTORY AT THE UNIVERSITY OF CALIFORNIA, SANTA BARBARA. SHE IS THE AUTHOR OF *THE MURDER OF HELEN JEWETT: THE LIFE AND DEATH OF A PROSTITUTE IN NINETEENTH-CENTURY NEW YORK* (KNOPF, 1998); *THE FLASH PRESS: SPORTING MALE WEEKLIES IN 1840S NEW YORK* (UNIVERSITY OF CHICAGO PRESS, 2008; COAUTHORED WITH HELEN LEFKOWITZ HOROWITZ AND TIMOTHY J. GILFOYLE). SHE IS CURRENTLY WRITING A BOOK ABOUT MARY GOVE NICHOLS AND THOMAS L. NICHOLS, HEALTH, MARRIAGE, AND SEX REFORMERS IN NEW YORK CITY IN THE 1840S AND 1850S.

THE REAL ELLEN JEWETT, 1836: Essayist Patricia Cline Cohen writes, "In the wake of Helen [a.k.a. Ellen] Jewett's murder, New York newspapers vied in their coverage of the crime to uncover the true life story of the dead prostitute. How could such a beautiful and cultured young woman fall from virtue and embrace vice? Jewett's string of five aliases and her penchant for spinning contradictory stories of her life complicated the efforts to pin her down. But artistic depictions of the young woman allowed for her to be pinned up, literally. This colored lithograph reportedly adorned walls in barbershops. Jewett appears in highly fashionable dress, carrying a letter. Newspapers had already told of her daily trips to the post office and of the trunk of letters found in her room. At least two other disturbing lithographs showed her post-mortem, in flimsy bedclothes." LITHOGRAPH BY H. R. ROBINSON AFTER A DRAWING BY F. COFFEY. MUSEUM PURCHASE. 95.94.13.

RICHARD P. ROBINSON, 1836: Essayist Patricia Cline Cohen writes, "The young man charged with Jewett's murder was Richard P. Robinson, a nineteen-year-old clerk who worked in a store on Maiden Lane. The occasion of this sketch was Robinson's arraignment in court in May 1836. Robinson's very youthful face and figure lent some credibility to his claim of innocence, and his high-powered attorney, Ogden Hoffman, called him an 'innocent boy' repeatedly in court. Robinson's father sat in the Connecticut State Legislature, and his New York City employer, Joseph Hoxie, cut a modest figure in city politics at the alderman level. Hoffman, Hoxie, and Robinson Sr. flanked the accused at his five-day trial in June; the jury took fifteen minutes to come back with a verdict of 'Not Guilty.' LITHOGRAPH BY H. R. ROBINSON AFTER A DRAWING BY F. COFFEY. MUSEUM PURCHASE. 95.94.14.

ERIE CANAL CELEBRATION, NEW YORK, 1825: This oil on canvas is one of only three known by the celebrated lithographer Anthony Imbert (1794–1824). It focuses on a scene at the end of the day's festivities of November 4, 1825, when a fleet of American ships sailed in salute around the British war ships *Swallow* (foreground) and *Kingfisher* (distant). The occasion was the opening of the Erie Canal (or "Clinton's Ditch," as it was termed with derision from the announcement of its plan). Governor DeWitt Clinton, shown here aboard the *Seneca Chief*, ceremoniously poured a keg of Lake Erie water into the Atlantic to symbolize the

A VIEW OF THE
Magnificent and Extraordinary
Fire Works
Exhibited on the N.Y. CITY HALL, on the Evening of
the Celebration of THE GRAND CANAL, November 4th 1825
BY RICHD WILLCOX, ENGINEER, &c.
R. Willcox Invt & del.
Prud'homme Sc.
EXPLANATION.
The City Hall was illuminated with 1542 wax candles,-454 lamps, and 310 variegated lamps; total 2.306. —— To eclipse this great effusion of light was not within the powers of ordinary Fire-works: —Hence extraordinary means were employed,—which consisted of 13 compounded Gerbs, each containing 58 lbs. of brilliant Chinese and Diamond fires, which changed alternately. These fires were supported by a back-ground of Spur Fire, which projected 1500 Brilliant Stars, intersecting each other in fanciful directions. During the evening were projected 320-4lb. Rockets; 30-9lb, and 24-20lb. Rockets;—total 374: with a great variety of minor amusing pieces. The general bursts of simultaneous applause from a great concourse of citizens afford the best panegyric on the decided superiority of these Fire Works,—both as to Extraordinary Grandeur and Brilliant Display.

VIEW OF THE FIREWORKS AT CITY HALL, NOVEMBER 4, 1825: This view marks the completion of the Erie Canal on October 26, 1825 and the arrival of the first flotilla of boats to sail from Buffalo to New York. "Explanation" underneath the view of City Hall states that the illumination consisted of "1,542 wax candles, 454 lamps, and 310 variegated lamps; total 2,306" whose "great effusion of light" could be eclipsed only by extraordinary fireworks." The latter are described, itemized, and characterized as superior, "both as to Extraordinary Grandeur and Brilliant Display." DESIGN BY WILLCOX. ENGRAVING BY JOHN FRANCIS EUGENE PRUD'HOMME. 30.28.3.

BROADWAY AND CITY HALL, LOOKING NORTH FROM ANN STREET, 1819: In 1824 Baron Axel Leonard Klinckowström, a young engineer sent by the Swedish government to study railroad construction, published his travel letters from the United States. "New York is not as clean," he wrote, "as cities of the same rank and population in Europe; in spite of the fact that the police regulations are good, they are not enforced and one finds in the streets dead cats and dogs, which make the air very bad; dust and ashes are thrown out into the streets, which are swept perhaps once every fortnight in the summer; only, however, in the largest and most frequented streets, otherwise they are cleaned only once a month. . . ." When engraved for publication of Klinckowström's letters, this charming view, drawn in 1819, was enhanced to reflect his notions by the addition of some of the feral pigs that, by eating household refuse, formed the core of the city's street sanitation system. WATERCOLOR. 15½ x 22⅜. BEQUEST OF MRS. J. INSLEY BLAIR IN MEMORY OF MR. AND MRS. J. INSLEY BLAIR. 52.100.8.

NIGHT-FALL. ST. THOMAS CHURCH, BROADWAY, NEW YORK, CA. 1837: On Sunday, October 12, 1823, a new Protestant Episcopal congregation was organized in a meeting room at 44 Broome Street. In July 1824, in accord with the resolutions of that congregation, the cornerstone for the new St. Thomas Church was laid at the intersection of Broadway and Houston Street. By 1866 this part of town had turned seedy, impelling the worshippers to build a new church, which endures, at 53rd Street and Fifth Avenue. In 2000 an unnamed editorialist for the *New York Times* wrote of this atmospheric cityscape, "Three tides of traffic now cross each other at Broadway and Houston, and every pedestrian who pauses there for a light carries within him an intuitive sense of the city's volume, its voltage, just as the pedestrians in Harvey's watercolor [depicted here] surely did. That is perhaps the only thing that has not changed in 165 years. That, and on fair summer nights, the pale western sky." WATERCOLOR BY GEORGE HARVEY, 8¼ X 13¾. BEQUEST OF MRS. J. INSLEY BLAIR IN MEMORY OF MR. AND MRS. J. INSLEY BLAIR. 52.100.11.

THE RESERVOIR, BOWERY, 1831: This is half of one of the nineteen double plates of various buildings and views of New York drawn and engraved by various artists and published in 1831 by George Melksham Bourne. Stokes said of what is today termed the Bourne Views, "It is the largest and most beautifully executed series of New York views ever made, and deserves more attention than it has yet received." This view of the octagonal reservoir on the Bowery and 13th Street, erected in 1829 to deliver water for firefighting by iron pipe, is here depicted separately from the other half of the double plate. ENGRAVED ON COPPER BY HATCH & SMILLIE. THE J. CLARENCE DAVIES COLLECTION. 29.100.1536.

LA GRANGE TERRACE, LAFAYETTE PLACE, 1831: Also known as Colonnade Row, this spectacular row of nine adjoined buildings, of which four remain, formed the city's first apartment building. It was of a decidedly high-toned nature (although all the stonework was executed by prisoners at Sing Sing). Among the residents were Washington Irving and John Jacob Astor. Built by Albany's Seth Greer in 1831, the design of this row was originally attributed to Greer as well. Later scholarship has revealed that the architectural firm of Ithiel Town and Alexander Jackson Davis, with junior member James H. Dakin, actually created the plans. The image depicted here is Dakin's, published in *Views in New-York and its Environs from Accurate, Characteristic & Picturesque Drawings, Taken on the spot, expressly for this work, by [James H.] Dakin, Architect.* PRINTED BY PEABODY & CO. THE J. CLARENCE DAVIES COLLECTION. 29.100.1610.

(RIGHT) **STREET CRIES, SCARF OR KERCHIEF, CA. 1814:** This glorious toile survivor of distant days testifies to the vibrant commercial life of the streets of New York, when the distinctive cries for hot corn, ripe watermelons, baked pears, and buttermilk ("butter-milleck") could be heard anywhere in town. Clams and oysters came in from Rockaway, as well as sand for use on wooden floors. "Here's White Sand: Choice Sand: Here's Your Lily White S-A-N-D: Here's Your Rock-A-Way Beach S-A-N-D." LINEN, PRINTED WITH RED INK. THE J. CLARENCE DAVIES COLLECTION. 29.100.0613.

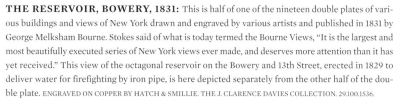

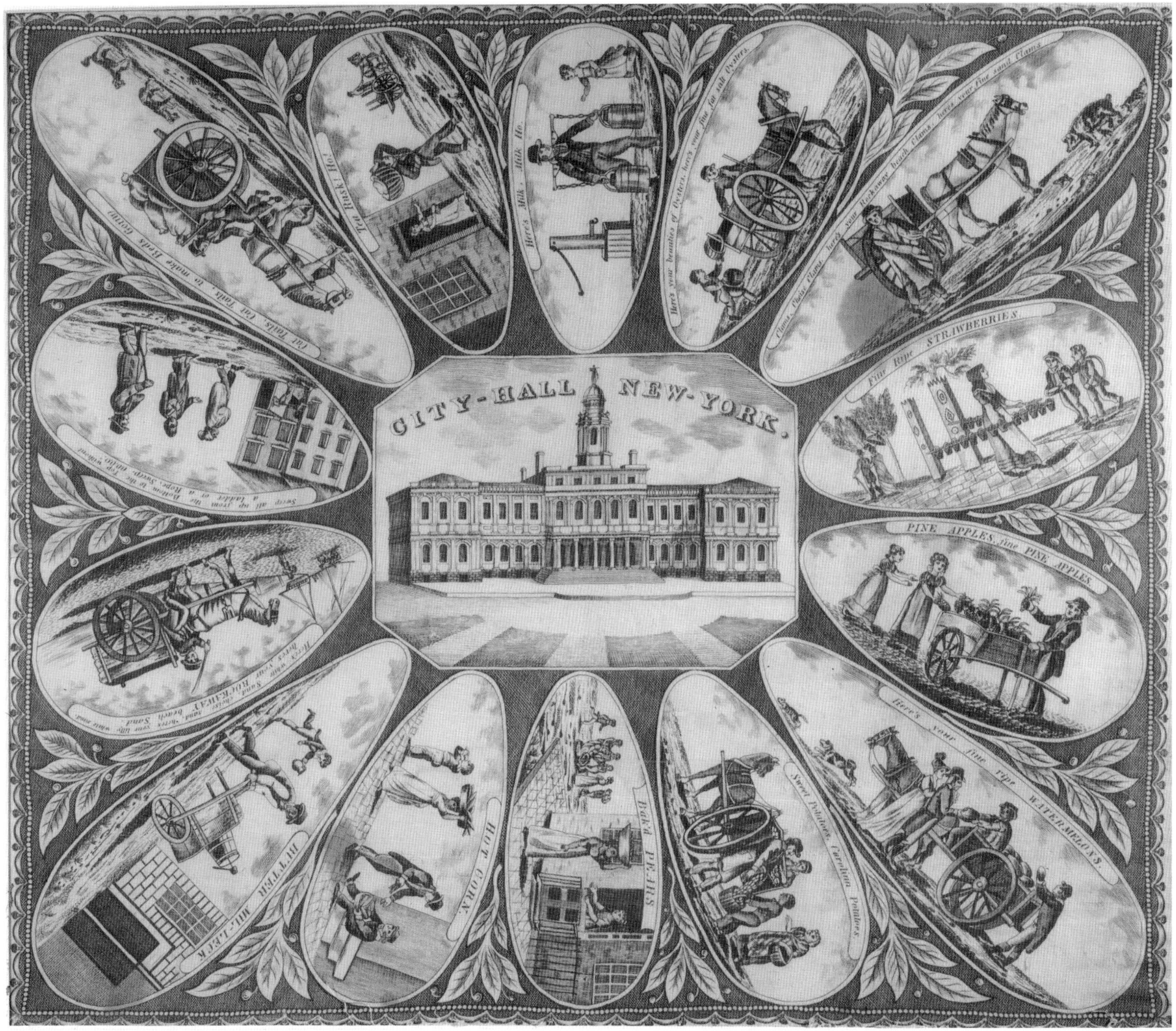
CITY-HALL NEW-YORK.
Here's Milk, Milk Ho.
Tea Rusk! Ho!
Fine Ripe STRAWBERRIES
PINE APPLES, fine PINE APPLES
Here's your fine ripe WATERMELONS.
Sweet Potatoes, Carolina Potatoes.
Bak'd PEARS
HOT CORN
BUTTER MILK

NEW YORK FROM GOVERNORS ISLAND, 1820: First named Noten Eylant ("Island of Nuts") by Dutch explorer Adriaen Block, Governor's Island has become the name familiar to New Yorkers since 1784, when the United States made the area an army post. The circular fortification visible at the right is Castle Williams, built in 1808-10. This aquatint is plate twenty of the celebrated *Hudson River Port Folio*, based upon drawings made by William Guy Wall in 1820. Although the ambitious project was never completed, the result was, according to William S. Reese, "often considered the finest American color plate book of the 19th century. The twenty plates . . . trace the course of the Hudson River from north to south, concluding with a view of New York harbor." DRAWN BY WILLIAM G. WALL, PRINTED BY JOHN HILL, PUBLISHED BY HENRY J. MEGAREY. THE J. CLARENCE DAVIES COLLECTION. 29.100.2165.

NEW YORK FROM WEEHAWK, CA. 1823: A writer in the *Commercial Advertiser* of July 2, 1823 noted of this and other scenes published by William Guy Wall that "views taken by Mr. Wall are the most accurate descriptions that we have seen. One of them is taken from Brooklyn Heights, near the Distillery of the Messrs. Pierponts, and the other from the Mountain at Weehawk. Mr. Wall at first made a drawing from the high land back of Hoboken; but the view from Weehawk is far preferable, as it not only affords a commanding prospect of the city but also of the whole of our beautiful harbor, with all the islands, &c." William G. Wall drew (and published) this from an engraving by John Hill. A later but identical edition (1828) was published by G. & C. & H. Carvill, 1828. 29.100.2163.

Wm I. Bennett Pinxt et Sculpt

FULTON ST. & MARKET.

(LEFT) **FULTON ST. & MARKET, 1834:** This view of Fulton Street was drawn about 1834, and it shows the market that was erected in 1821–22 on the East River looking down Fulton Street to the North Dutch Church, whose tower is seen in the distance. Fulton Market was abandoned as a city market in 1914, though the adjoining Fulton Fish Market thrived until 2005. The print is one of three drawn and engraved by William J. Bennett as the first of four "parts" of a projected series. Only the first of these parts was published—by Henry J. Megarey in *Megarey's Street Views in the City of New-York.* THE J. CLARENCE DAVIES COLLECTION. 29.100.2160.

CITY HALL PARK, NORTH END, 1825: The first New York Museum was established by the newly formed Tammany Society in 1790 right inside City Hall (the building called Federal Hall, on Wall Street; not the subsequent Mangin-designed City Hall), suddenly capacious with the removal of the Federal Government seat to Philadelphia. It soon outgrew this space and the constraints of Tammany affiliation, however, and by 1810 it had wound up in the hands of John Scudder, a young naturalist. He died in 1821 but his son continued the management in new quarters at the north end of City Hall Park, expanding the collection by 1826 to a claimed 150,000 curiosities: "live mud turtles, a Baltimore oriole, an iguana, various minerals, and the bed curtains belonging to Mary Queen of Scots." His principal competition was Charles Willson Peale's New York Museum, but Scudder won out, finally selling to P. T. Barnum in 1841. This view shows the west elevation of the old Almshouse, which had been converted in 1816 for the use of a number of institutions, including the American Museum, which occupied the west section of the building until 1830. McSpedon & Baker lithographed a version of this image for *Valentine's Manual,* 1855. THE J. CLARENCE DAVIES COLLECTION. 29.100.1895.

This
ACTUAL MAP
AND COMPARATIVE PLANS
Shewing 88 years growth of the City of
NEW YORK,
Is inscribed to the
Citizens
BY THE PROPRIETOR
David Longworth
1817
CITY HOTEL
New York Hospital 124 feet front and 86 feet Broad built of Granite
Asylum 88 ft front and 60 ft deep Built of granite
New York Institution 200 feet front Built of Brick
REFERENCES.
NORTH RIVER
EAST RIVER
CASTLE CLINTON
NORTH FORT
FORT GANSEVORT
CORLAERS HOOK
BROAD WAY
BOWERY
THIRD AVENUE
SECOND AVENUE
FIRST AVENUE
AVENUE B
MARKET PLACE
THIRD WARD
FIFTH WARD
EIGHTH WARD
SIXTH WARD
SECOND WARD
FOURTH WARD
SEVENTH WARD
TENTH WARD
Scale of one mile
PLAN OF NEW YORK in 1729 Surveyed by James Lyne
KINGS FARM
COMMON
THE GUIDE
THROUGH THE
CITY OF NEW-YORK
IS
LONGWORTH'S
EXPLANATORY MAP AND PLAN,
With an alphabetical list of all its streets, lanes, allies, wharves, public slips, and buildings, &c.
BRIEF HINTS FOR Guessing.
Published by David Longworth 11 Park 1817.

(LEFT) THE ACTUAL MAP AND COMPARATIVE PLAN, CA., 1817: "Longworth's Map of New York," as it is known, shows "88 years growth of the city of New York," aided by an inset of a "Plan of New York in 1729, surveyed by James Lyne." Engraved by James D. Stout and G. B. King and printed by Daniel Fanshaw, it was published by David Longworth, a key figure in the publishing scene of his day and a name well known to researchers today for his New York City register and directory. Commencing in 1796, his annual publication provided his patrons with up-to-date information on commercial concerns, major institutions, and city residents, embellished with vignettes of City Hall, the Asylum, New York Hospital, the New York Institution, and the City Hotel. Though he died in 1821, Longworth's directory continued under his son, with its last number issued in 1843. THE J. CLARENCE DAVIES COLLECTION. 29.100.2192.

THE GREAT FIRE OF THE CITY OF NEW YORK, 16 DECEMBER 1835: We offer multiple views of this calamitous blaze because it was so influential in shaping the city. Families were ruined and fortunes lost. The wooden buildings of the city, many dating back to the seventeenth century, were decimated. The economic boom that had begun with the opening of the Erie Canal ten years earlier was about to careen into the Panic of 1837. Yet a new New York, one of solid brick and masonry, was in the offing. This lithograph published by H. R. Robinson may be the finest depiction of the event, and it is one of the rarest and most interesting views. Drawn by Alfred Hoffy, it also has the singular virtue of offering an exceedingly rare key to the heroes issued with the plate. THE J. CLARENCE DAVIES COLLECTION. 29.100.2305.

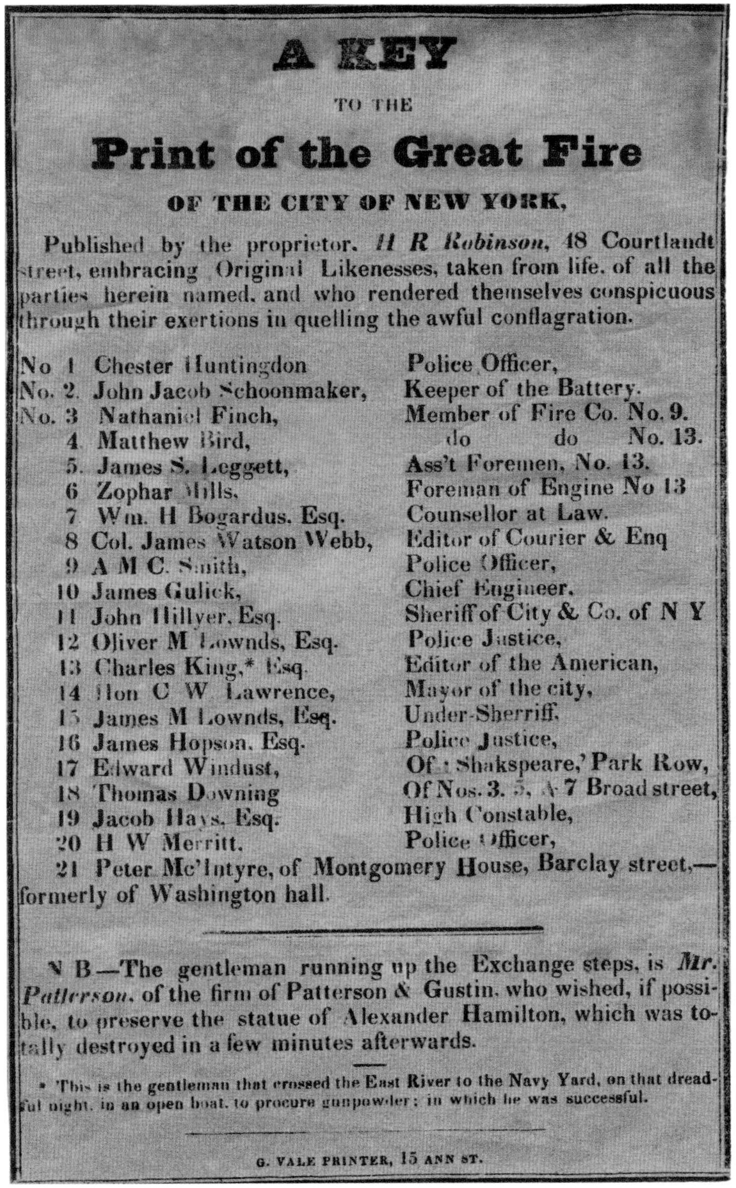

A KEY

TO THE

Print of the Great Fire

OF THE CITY OF NEW YORK,

Published by the proprietor. *H R Robinson*, 48 Courtlandt street, embracing Original Likenesses, taken from life, of all the parties herein named, and who rendered themselves conspicuous through their exertions in quelling the awful conflagration.

No 1	Chester Huntingdon	Police Officer,
No. 2.	John Jacob Schoonmaker,	Keeper of the Battery.
No. 3	Nathaniel Finch,	Member of Fire Co. No. 9.
4.	Matthew Bird,	do do No. 13.
5.	James S. Leggett,	Ass't Foremen, No. 13.
6	Zophar Mills,	Foreman of Engine No 13
7	Wm. H Bogardus. Esq.	Counsellor at Law.
8	Col. James Watson Webb,	Editor of Courier & Enq
9	A M C. Smith,	Police Officer,
10	James Gulick,	Chief Engineer,
11	John Hillyer, Esq.	Sheriff of City & Co. of N Y
12	Oliver M Lownds, Esq.	Police Justice,
13	Charles King,* Esq.	Editor of the American,
14	Hon C W Lawrence,	Mayor of the city,
15	James M Lownds, Esq.	Under-Sherriff.
16	James Hopson, Esq.	Police Justice,
17	Edward Windust,	Of 'Shakspeare,' Park Row,
18	Thomas Downing	Of Nos. 3. 5, & 7 Broad street,
19	Jacob Hays, Esq.	High Constable,
20	H W Merritt.	Police Officer,

21 Peter Mc'Intyre, of Montgomery House, Barclay street,—formerly of Washington hall.

N B—The gentleman running up the Exchange steps, is *Mr. Patterson*, of the firm of Patterson & Gustin, who wished, if possible, to preserve the statue of Alexander Hamilton, which was totally destroyed in a few minutes afterwards.

* This is the gentleman that crossed the East River to the Navy Yard, on that dreadful night, in an open boat, to procure gunpowder; in which he was successful.

G. VALE PRINTER, 15 ANN ST.

A KEY TO THE PRINT OF THE GREAT FIRE, 1835: PRINTED BY G. VALE. THE J. CLARENCE DAVIES COLLECTION. 29.100.2306.

FULTON FIRE INSURANCE Co
Painted on the spot by
Nicolino Calyo

(LEFT) BURNING OF THE MERCHANTS' EXCHANGE, NEW YORK, DECEMBER 16TH & 17TH, 1835: The Great Fire of 1835 destroyed 674 buildings, virtually the entire downtown business district. The loss of the Merchants' Exchange—the colonnaded hulk at the center, its cupola already destroyed—seemed particularly crushing. Designed by Martin Euclid Thompson in 1825 and erected two years after, it had seemed the symbol of Wall Street's vigor in the years after the opening of the Erie Canal. "The splendid edifice," wrote diarist and New York mayor Philip Hone, "& one of the ornaments of the city & is now a heap of ruins &c. When the dome of this edifice fell in, the sight was awfully grand. In its fall it demolished the statue of Hamilton executed by [Robert] Ball Hughes, which was erected in the rotunda only eight months ago by the public spirit of the merchants." (Hughes's plaster model survives in the Museum of the City of New York's collection.) At the lower left of the gouache on paper rendering of the conflagration is the artist, Neapolitan émigré Nicolino V. Calyo. He depicted himself at an easel situated on the roof of the Bank of America building. Below him is signed "Painted on the spot by / Nicolino Calyo." 13 X 20½. BEQUEST OF MRS. J. INSLEY BLAIR IN MEMORY OF MR. AND MRS.J. INSLEY BLAIR. 52.100.7.

VIEW OF THE RUINS AFTER THE GREAT FIRE IN NEW-YORK, DECEMBER 16TH & 17TH, 1835: One of several views of the Great Fire by Nicolino Calyo from different vantage points, this view is from Exchange Place, looking east. The ruin on the left is the Garden Street Church as it was rebuilt in 1807 and is the only depiction we have of that edifice. In the belfry of the burned-out church had resided the cornerstone of the original seventeenth-century chapel, which had been situated within the bounds of Fort George; it perished in the blaze. L. P. Clover published this engraving by William J. Bennett. GIFT OF MRS. LANCASTER MORGAN IN MEMORY OF HER HUSBAND. 47.182.2.

CUSTOM HOUSE, NEW YORK.

DESIGNED BY ITHIEL TOWN AND ALEXANDER JACKSON DAVIS, ARCHITECTS.

CUSTOM-HOUSE, N.Y. – PLAN OF THE PRINCIPAL FLOOR.

SHEWING THE PAVED FLOOR, COUNTERS AND SIDE-WALK.

LENGTH 180 FT. BREADTH 90.

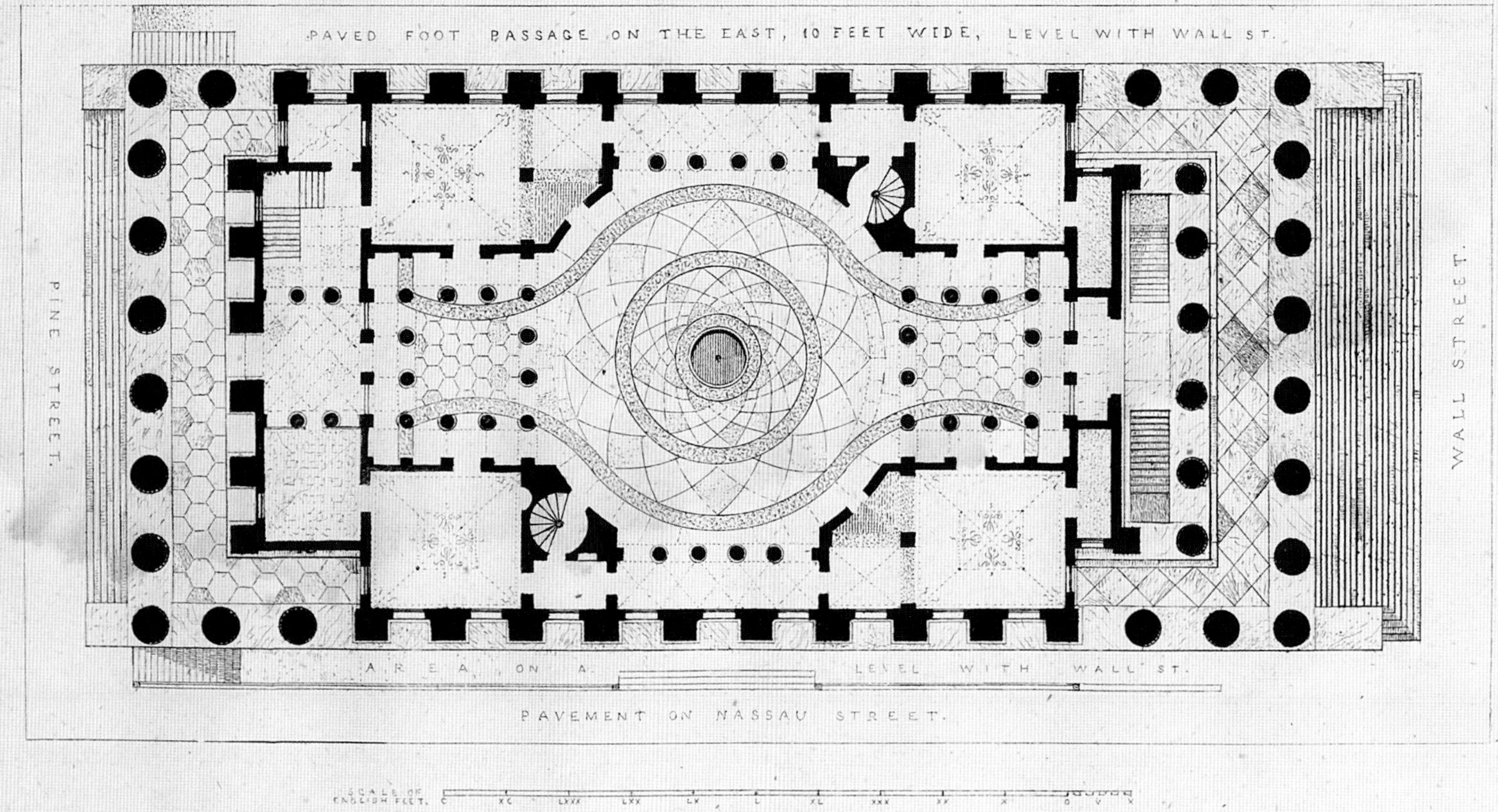

LITH. PRESS OF STODART & CURRIER.

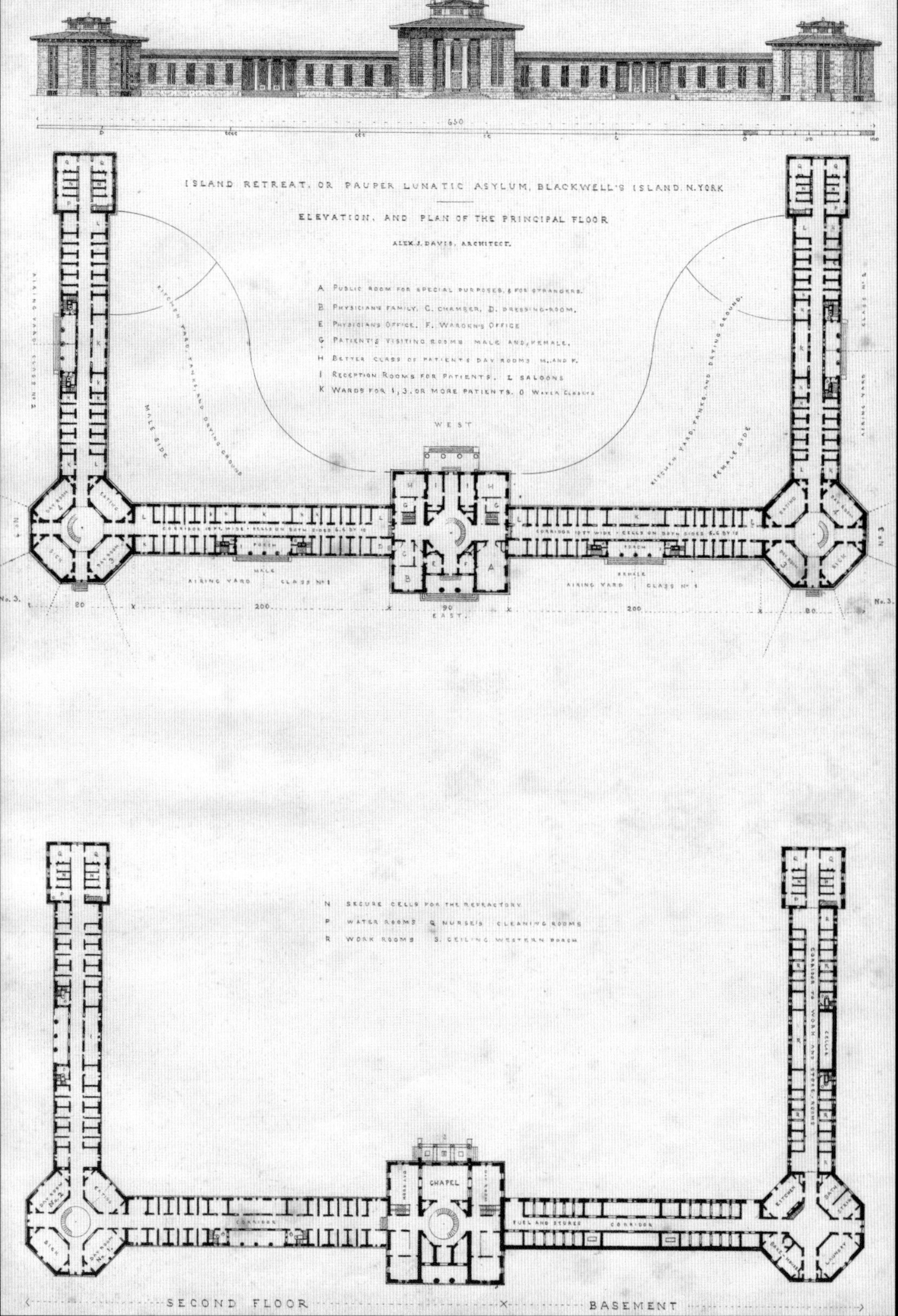

(PREVIOUS SPREAD) CUSTOM HOUSE, NEW YORK, CA. 1834: This Custom House was built on Wall Street between 1833 and 1842 from the plans of architects Ithiel Town and Alexander Jackson Davis on the site of the old Federal Hall, where George Washington had been inaugurated as President in 1789 and where the nation's seat had briefly been. It served as the Custom House until 1862. In the following year it became the U.S. Sub-Treasury. The Davis and Town Custom House survives—once again named Federal Hall—but as a national memorial, familiar to Wall Street strollers for its grand columns and the huge bronze statue of Washington in the center of the front steps. A portion of the full title of the print, "Lith. Press of Stodart & Currier," permits us to date it. Currier commenced his lithographic career with partner Stodart in 1834 but by the following year was on his own. GIFT OF JOSEPH B. DAVIS. 35.257.8A & B.

ISLAND RETREAT, OR PAUPER LUNATIC ASYLUM, BLACKWELL'S ISLAND, CA. 1835: Alexander Jackson Davis was commissioned to design an asylum for lunatics and paupers to replace the old Bloomingdale Asylum. Francis R. Kowsky wrote: "Davis received $300 in 1834 for drawing the plans, which the Board of Aldermen approved in 1835. The large, two-story U-shaped structure . . . faced Manhattan. . . ." Parts of the Davis plan went unbuilt for budgetary reasons, but some remnants of the structure endure on what is today Roosevelt Island (formerly Welfare Island, and before that Blackwell's). LITHOGRAPH BY NATHANIEL CURRIER. THE GERALD LEVINO COLLECTION. 57.100.71.

MANHATTAN COMPANY RESERVOIR, 1825: The Manhattan Company, headed by Aaron Burr, was incorporated in 1799 following the yellow fever epidemic of the previous year. Its purpose of "supplying the City of New York with pure and wholesome water" was not fulfilled, but Burr's personal ambitions were, as a clause in the company's charter permitted it to establish the Manhattan Company, which eventually became the Chase Manhattan Bank and later J. P. Morgan Chase. By 1842 the Manhattan Company's meager output through the wooden pipes it laid had been superseded by the Croton system. This Egyptianate reservoir stood on the north side of Chambers Street between Broadway and Park Row. The bronze figure over the entrance, supported by four Doric columns, was "Oceanus, one of the sea-gods, sitting in a reclining posture on a rising ground pouring water from an urn which forms a river and terminates in a lake." This was the physical embodiment of the

TAMMANY HALL, 1830: The Tammany Society or Columbian Order, which became the power behind the city's Democratic Party, was founded on May 12, 1789. The name comes from Tamanend, a Lenape tribe leader. The society adopted many Native American words, going so far as to call its hall a *wigwam* and its leader a *sachem*. Soon after its founding, Tammany came under the influence of Aaron Burr and it worked for the election of Jefferson as president in 1800. The hall depicted here was its first, built on Frankfort Street in 1811. It moved to 14th Street in 1867. LITHOGRAPH BY GEORGE HAYWARD. PUBLISHED IN *VALENTINE'S MANUAL*, 1858.

THE PARK, 1827: In 1827 no New Yorker required further explanation about which location was referenced by "The Park." The center of the city's history and social life was the park south of City Hall. Known as the Commons in the years before the Revolution, City Hall Park was the city's public forum where political factions and citizens with grievances spoke their minds. Here the fashionable and the rough, youthful strollers, and ballplayers (at center, in the distance) might all mingle peaceably. LITHOGRAPH BY McSPEDON & BAKER. PUBLISHED IN *VALENTINE'S MANUAL*, 1855.

THEATER TICKETS, CA. 1840: The Bowery Theatre was established in 1826 to rival the Park Theatre, which had been the fashionable venue since it opened on Park Row in 1798. Frances Trollope described the Bowery Theatre, in *Domestic Manners of the Americans*, as "superior in beauty [to the Park]; it is indeed as pretty a theatre as I ever entered, perfect as to size and proportion, elegantly decorated, and the scenery and machinery equal to any in London. . . ." The two tickets depicted here for The Bowery Theatre (see page 145) bear the marks of Thomas Hamblin, who commenced to manage it in August 1830, and A.W. Jackson, to whom Hamblin handed the reins of the New Bowery Theatre after a fire in 1845. The signature of William Niblo appears on the remaining ticket, which is for a Grand Concert at his eponymous Garden. It recalls a time of transition in the city's popular entertainment, from the pleasure gardens like Ranelagh and Vauxhall, in which format Niblo's venture had commenced in 1828, to an enclosed theater that endured several fires and relocations in its long life (1829–95). THEATER COLLECTION

THE HERALD
THE COURRIER and ENQU
THE DAILY

(LEFT) **READING ROOM OF THE ASTOR HOUSE, 1840:** The Astor House, built in 1834–36 from an Isaiah Rogers design at the behest of merchant prince John Jacob Astor, stood at Broadway between Vesey and Barclay Streets until 1926. At the time of its construction it was regarded as the finest hotel in the country. The Astor House offered gas lighting, running water, seventeen bathrooms, two showers, and a reading room for boarders that stocked daily papers from around the nation. Located above the main entrance, the reading room permitted patrons to look down at "the thronging procession of human heads, sweeping up and down, and clattering over the pavement below," as Benjamin Robinson wrote. Those who preferred a seat by the fireplace might smoke and spit to their hearts' content, as depicted here in Nicolino Calyo's watercolor and ink on paper. 9½ x 12. ACQUIRED THROUGH THE MRS. ELON HOOKER ACQUISITION FUND. 41.3.

BRANCH BANK OF U.S., 1825: The lithograph of this dazzling structure was designed by Martin Euclid Thompson, drawn by Alexander Jackson Davis—like Thompson a partner in the architectural firm topped by Ithiel Town—and published by Anthony Imbert in *Views of Public Buildings in the City of New York* (1827). In 1915 the structure at 15½ Wall Street was demolished but the facade, after decades in storage, has been re-erected in full in the American Wing of the Metropolitan Museum of Art. Interestingly, another of the works Davis depicted for Imbert's book—John Vanderlyn's Rotunda of 1819—has also been substantially recreated at the Met. MUSEUM PURCHASE WITH THE NEW YORK STATE STOCK EXCHANGE FUND. 38.299.7.

FASHIONABLE
BEAVER HATS
LEONARD BOND'S
HAT WARE-HOUSE
FASHIONABLE
BEAVER HATS
TERMS CASH
BOND
BOND

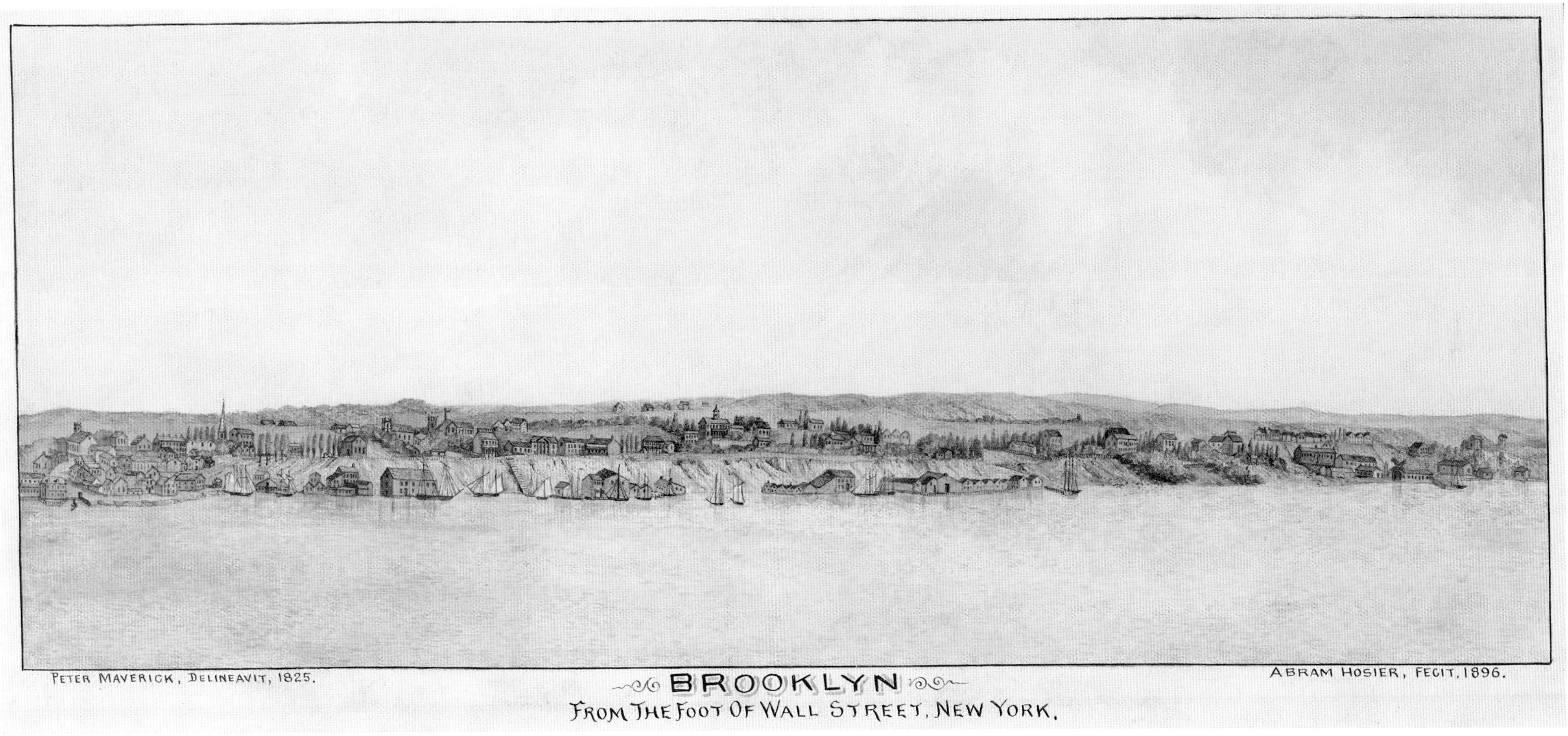

PETER MAVERICK, DELINEAVIT, 1825.
BROOKLYN
FROM THE FOOT OF WALL STREET, NEW YORK.
ABRAM HOSIER, FECIT, 1896.

(LEFT) **LEONARD BOND'S HAT WARE-HOUSE, CA. 1828:** Leonard Bond's hat store was located at 208 Chatham Street in 1828 and Number 8 Bowery in the following year. Beaver stovepipe hats were *de rigueur*, as was cash on the barrelhead. This charming if crude watercolor by Alexander Jackson Davis provides a rare view of a store interior of the day. 7½ x 8¾. GIFT OF JOSEPH B. DAVIS. 35.257.1.

BROOKLYN, FROM THE FOOT OF WALL STREET, 1825: Brooklyn was New York's sleepy rival city to the east. Watercolor on paper by Abram Hosier, 1896, based upon an engraving by Peter Maverick, Jr. of 1825. Before the advent in 1880 of the photomechanical (halftone) process of reproducing photographs, engraved images like this were the mass media of their era and for artists just about the only way to make money from their skill, either as the painter of the original or the deliverer in copper, wood, or steel. THE J. CLARENCE DAVIES COLLECTION. 29.100.3540.

(LEFT) **WINTER SCENE IN BROOKLYN, NEW YORK, 1817–20:** Louisa Ann Coleman painted this scene of Front and James Streets in 1853. The work adds little but fresh color to the original by Francis Guy (1760–1820), which by that time may have been on display at the Brooklyn Institute, predecessor to the Brooklyn Museum. Walt Whitman called Guy's view "the most important and compact portrait of Brooklyn as it stood in 1820. . . . [It] forever will be invaluable as exhibiting the architectural character of the village at that period; and, in some degree for half a century previous." OIL ON CANVAS, 48 x 97. ANONYMOUS GIFT. 53.2.

SYNAGOGUE OF B'NAI JESHURUN, NEW YORK, CA. 1830: Congregation B'nai Jeshurun was founded in New York City in 1825 by a group of Ashkenazic Jews who broke off from the city's first synagogue, the Sephardic Shearith Israel. Only the second temple to be founded in New York, it opened its doors on Elm Street two years later, built in the Greek Revival mode fashionable in the period. J. R. BRADY, ARCHITECT; ALEXANDER JACKSON DAVIS, DRAWING; ANTHONY IMBERT, LITHOGRAPHER. THE J. CLARENCE DAVIES COLLECTION. 29.100.1611.

BROADWAY AND FULTON STREET, 1831: "City Hall in the Distance," the border advises us, but we should note also the rear of Scudder's American Museum, the side of St. Paul's posted with lottery notices, and the ubiquitous street vendors. This view was drawn by Charles Burton and engraved on copper by R. Lowe. GIFT OF HENRY SILL BALDWIN. 44.344.36.

(RIGHT) **THE ARRIVAL OF THE "GREAT WESTERN," 1838:** This steel engraving is precisely titled "Arrival of the *Great Western* Steam Ship off New York on Monday 23rd April, 1838." The port is a riot of vessels in greeting and the Battery is lined with a picturesque set of Gothamites—from swells and hawkers to dancers and musicians—as the *Great Western* marked the onset of the age of steam and iron and a long, slow retreat of sail. The smaller *Sirius*, the first ship to cross the Atlantic under the power of steam alone, reached New York a day ahead of the *Great Western* but to less fanfare. Philip Hone wrote in his diary entry for this day: "The Battery and adjacent streets were crowded with curious spectators, and the water covered with boats, conveying obtrusive visitors on board." Probable publisher W. & H. Cave of Manchester, England. BEQUEST OF MRS. J. INSLEY BLAIR. 36.18.1.

MANCHESTER

(LEFT) THE PARK THEATRE, CA. 1830: Nothing is known of the provenance of this fine gouache of the Park Theatre, located at 21, 23, and 25 Park Row, which in its first incarnation hosted a debut performance on January 29, 1798. In 1814 John Lambert wrote of that venue, "It contains a large coffee-room, and good sized lobbies, and is reckoned to hold about 1,200 persons. The scenes are well painted and numerous; and the machinery, dresses, and decorations, are elegant, and appropriate to the performances, which consist of all the new pieces that come out on the London boards, and several of Shakespeare's best plays." Comparing images of the original building with this one, we may safely say that this is the second Park Theatre, built in 1821 after a fire consumed the first. As the taste in popular entertainment coarsened somewhat in the next decade, the high-toned Park had to compete with the melodramatic and variety fare offered by the Bowery Theatre and Chatham Garden; unsurprisingly, the Park's clientele shifted too. By 1838 the *New York Herald* felt compelled to note, "On Friday night the Park Theatre contained 83 of the most profligate and abandoned women that ever disgraced humanity; they entered in the same door, and for a time mixed indiscriminately with 63 virtuous and respectable ladies. . . . Men of New York, take not your wives and daughters to the Park Theatre, until Mr. Simpson pays some respect to them by constructing a separate entrance for the abandoned of the sex." The Bowery Theatre, a cross-town rival of the Park, did have a separate entrance for the third balcony. THEATER COLLECTION.

CHATHAM SQUARE, 1812: Chatham Square, today in the heart of Chinatown, has a varied history, from the bucolic to the bilious (the former in the 1750s, the latter by the 1850s). From earliest times the rural Bowery Lane was associated with racing, trial running, and sale of horses, and until the end of the Revolution, Chatham Square was designated the principal place in the city for horse auctions. As Kenneth Dunshee wrote in *As You Pass By*, "After the horse market was banished the square was ordered enclosed with a picket fence and the walks filled with gravel. An appropriation for trees and planting for Chatham Square Park followed in 1812. But as early as 1816 the hustle and bustle of this junction of busy thoroughfares [seven roads lead into the square!] made it necessary for the authorities to order that the park and fence be removed and the area paved." This view depicts the days of that short-lived fence. LITHOGRAPH BY GEORGE HAYWARD. PUBLISHED IN *VALENTINE'S MANUAL*, 1864.

GROCERY AND TEA STORE, CROSBY AND SPRING STREETS, 1826: This scene depicts a busy corner in the course of everyday trade at a time—before the fire of 1835—when frame houses were the rule and brick buildings were too costly for common folk. The grocery at 83 Crosby Street was, according to the border, "owned and Occupied by Charles Dusenberry, Esq., [a trustee of the Bowery Savings Bank] and for several years thereafter." LITHOGRAPH BY GEORGE HAYWARD. PUBLISHED IN *VALENTINE'S MANUAL*, 1865.

MASONIC HALL, BROADWAY AND WORTH (NORTHWEST CORNER), 1830: Recalling the time of the Masonic Hall's construction in 1826, the *Express* observed "Who does not remember the glory and pomp with which the Masonic Hall, in Broadway, was thrown open, for the first time, to the public: when its light and beautiful Gothic tracery, its rich, antique groined ceiling, and all its gorgeous decorations were viewed by admiring thousands, as forming one of the most attractive edifices of the country?" At length the Masonic uses of the building waned, and the Gothic Hall, as it was dubbed, was given over for dress balls, Whig Party functions, public worship on Sundays and, in 1843, a bowling saloon and gymnasium. WATERCOLOR ON BOARD SIGNED "G. P. HALL & SON," 10 x 16. THE J. CLARENCE DAVIES COLLECTION. 29.100.2770.

NEW YORK BY GASLIGHT—HOOKING A VICTIM, CA. 1840: Even by the time of this lithograph, the oldest profession had long since established its customs and practices in New York City. Certain lunchrooms, saloons, oyster houses, and basement restaurants (as in the view) were well known to cater to sporting men and their sundry wants. Private rooms, hidden entrances and exits, private parties—all advertised in the respectable daily press as well as in "flash papers," racy weeklies whose specialty was the simultaneous denunciation of vice and the salacious detailing of it. George G. Foster, a reporter for the *New York Tribune*, published a book in 1850 with the very same title as this lithograph by Henry Serrell & S. Lee Perkins and named a chapter "Hooking a Victim." GIFT OF KARL SCHMIDT. 37.361.423.

(RIGHT) **AWFUL CONFLAGRATION OF THE STEAM BOAT LEXINGTON, 1840 (DETAIL):** This hurriedly prepared broadsheet memorialized the 139 persons who perished when the steamboat *Lexington* immolated in Long Island Sound on January 13, 1840, in a fire started by sparks igniting bales of cotton or some flammable material. But, apart from the "melancholy occurrence" and the entrepreneurial instinct of Nathaniel Currier, this modest lithograph is a monument in the history of American journalism. It was sold on the streets as an extra edition of the *New York Sun*—the first time an illustration had been distributed with the news of a breaking event. The *Sun* "extra" became so popular that Currier kept the presses running for some months as he also sold the lithos separately. DRAWING BY W.K. HEWITT. LITHOGRAPH BY NATHANIEL CURRIER. THE HARRY T. PETERS COLLECTION. 56.300.4.

Drawn by W. K. Hewitt

N. Currier, Lith & Pub. 2 Spruce St. N.Y.

Awful Conflagration of the Steam Boat **LEXINGTON** *In Long Island Sound on Monday Eve.g Jan.y 13th 1840, by which melancholy occurrence; over* 100 PERSONS PERISHED.

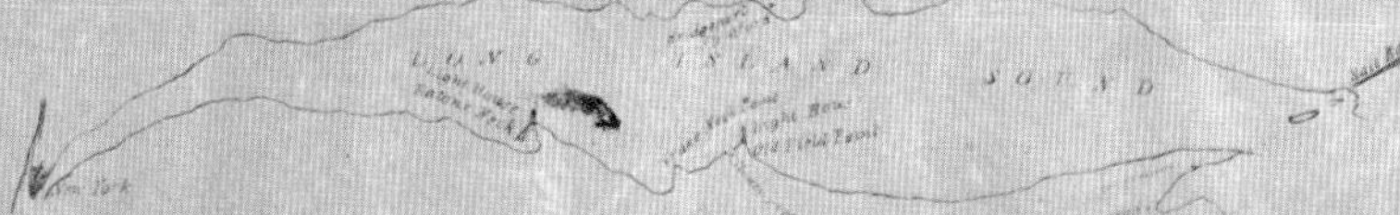

PASSENGERS.

Capt. Chester Hilliard of Norwich, the only passenger saved
Mr Isaac Davis, of Boston
Mr John Corey, of Roxboro', Mass
Mr Charles W Woolsey, of Boston
Mr John Brown, of Boston
Mr J Porter Felt, Jr, of Salem
Mr Abraham Howard, firm of Howard & Merry, Boston
Mr H C Craig, firm of Maitland, Kennedy & Co, N Y; (body found)
Mr Alphonso Mason, of Gloucester, Mass
Mr Charles Bracket, Clerk to N Bracket, N Y; (body found)
Mr Robt Blake, of Wrentham, Mass, President of Wrentham Bank
Mr Fowler, of New York
Mr Wm A Green, firm of Allen & Green, Providence; (body found)
Mr Samuel Henry, firm of A & S Henry, Manchester, England
Mr R W Dow, firm of Dow & Co, New York
Mr Charles H Phelps, of Stonington
The widow of Henry A Winslow, firm of Winslow & Co, New York
Mr John Winslow, of Providence
Mr Wm Winslow, ditto, father of the above. The three last mentioned persons were returning to Providence, with the corpse of Mr H A Winslow, who died in this city a few days previous
Rev Charles Follen, D D, of Boston; late Professor of German Literature of Harvard University
Mr Adolphus Harnden, Superintendant of Harnden's Express. He had in charge $20,000 in specie for the Merchants' Bank, Boston; and from forty to fifty thousand dollars in Bank notes
Mr Thomas White, of Boston, firm of Sands & White
Capt J D Carver, of Plymouth, Mass., of the barque Brontes
Mr Pierce, of Portland, mate of the Brontes.
Miss Sophia T Wheeler, daughter of Robt Wheeler, Greenfield, Mass
Capt E J Kimball
Capt B F Foster, late of the John Gilpin
These Captains had recently returned after several years' absence, and were on their way to visit their families at the East
Mr. Everett, of Boston, returning from the burial of a brother, who died here the previous week
Mr Royal T Church, of Baltimore
Mr Richard Picket, of Newburyport
Mr Bullard, of New York
Capt Theophilus Smith, Dartmouth, Mass
Mr Charles S Noyes, Clerk to C B Babcock, New York
Mr Albert E Harding, firm of Harding & Co, New York
Mr Henry J Finn, Comedian. He was a native of Virginia; his family resided at Newport, R I
Mr Charles L Eberle, of the Theatre
Mrs Russell Jarvis, of New York, and her two children, one about 12 and the other about 8 years of age. Mrs Jarvis was a daughter of Mr Thomas Cordis, of Boston
Capt John G Low, Agent for the Boston Underwriters; husband of the niece of Mr Cordis
Mr John Lemist, Treasurer of the Boston India Rubber Co. of Roxbury, Mass, uncle to Mrs Jarvis
Mr John W Kerle, of Baltimore
Mr Walker, of Baltimore, with Mr Kerle
Mr Weston, firm of Weston & Pendexter, Baltimore
Mr John G Brown, firm of Shall & Brown, N Orleans
Mr Stephen Waterbury, firm of Mead & Waterbury, N Y; (body found)
Mr J A Leach, Boston
Mr E B Fanen, New York
Mr N F Dyer, of Pittsburg, formerly of Braintree
Mr Nathaniel Hobart, of Boston
John Brown, a colored man
Mr H C Bradford, from Kingston, Jam
Mr Chas Lee, of Barre
Mr Jonathan Linfield, Stoughton, Mass
Mr Philo Upton, Egremont, Mass, (body found)
Mr Wm Gell, Stonington, Ct
[illegible], of Boston
[illegible]
Mr [illegible], of Cold Spring, New York.
[illegible] of the brig Clarion
James Walker and John Gordon, seamen, of Cambridgeport, from brig [illegible]
Wm B [illegible], of Williamsburg, L I, late of Worcester, Mass
[illegible], N Y, Clerk with Donnelly & Hyatt
Mr [illegible] of Brooklyn
Mr [illegible], nephew of [illegible], Esq
Mr [illegible], Vt [illegible] Franklin [illegible]
Mr [illegible], New York
Mr [illegible], of Philadelphia, Agent of the [illegible] Manufacturing Company; (body found)
[illegible] of Massachusetts,
[illegible]
Mr [illegible], New York, formerly of Boston
[illegible]
[illegible], Ct
[illegible], N J
Mrs Lydia Bates, widow of Mr James Bates, of Bordentown, N J, and their two children, Lydia C Bates and Jacob C Bates (Body of the boy found)
Mr Walker, whose parents reside in Belchertown, Mass (Possibly this may be the same person mentioned above as Mr Walker, of Baltimore)
Mr John Martin, and his son Gilbert Martin, recently from England.
William ——, an English boy.
Washington Cowen, street 21, New York City.
Benjamin D Holmes, copper-smith, Boston.
William Dexter, Boston
George O Swan, son of Judge Swan, of Columbus, Ohio. He was on his way to join the law-school at Cambridge, Mass
Mr John Ricker, Monroe, Me

BOAT'S COMPANY.

Capt Geo Childs, commander
Mr Jesse Comstock, clerk
H P Newman, steward
E Thurber, First mate
Mr Crowley, Second mate (saved)
Mr Stephen Manchester, pilot (saved)
Mr John Hoyt, baggage master
Mr Walker, barkeeper
Cortland Hemsted, chief engineer (body found)
Wm Quimby, 2d do
Martin Johnson, wheelman
R B Schultz, Geo Baum, Benj Cox, and Chas Smith, (saved) firemen
Chas Williams, Ben Laddie, C Humber, Joel Lawrence, three others, and a boy, deck hands
Job Sands (body found), Dan'l Aldridge, Mr Gilbert, Oliver [illegible], King Cade, Jos Bostin, John H Tab, E Parker, John Mason, [illegible] Adams, Isaac Putnam, colored waiters
Susan C Hutchins, chambermaid, colored
Joseph Robinson, cook, do
Oliver Howell, Second do do
Robert Peters, do
Henry Reed and another, coal-heavers

Total passengers - - - -	87—Lost 86	
Total attached to the steamboat	40—Lost 37	
	——127	——123

Saved 4—lost 123.

ROOT BEER SELLER, CA. 1840: A pristine, nearly complete set of Nicolino Calyo's *New York Street Cries, Chanters and Views* resides in the Museum of the City of New York's collection. Executed in the period 1840–44, the set of thirty-six watercolor views of New York street vendors was published in line engraving in *The Cries of New York* by John Doggett, Jr. in 1846. Certainly their beauty may be better appreciated in full color. In this scene the root beer seller offers his refreshment for three cents a glass, and to convey its quality he labels it "Knickerbocker," drawn from Washington Irving's pen name. Irving himself wrote in 1849: ". . . I find, after a lapse of nearly forty years, this haphazard production of my youth [Diedrich Knickerbocker]. . . become a 'household word,' and used to give the home stamp to everything recommended for popular acceptance, such as Knickerbocker societies, Knickerbocker insurance companies, Knickerbocker steamboats, Knickerbocker omnibuses, Knickerbocker bread, and Knickerbocker ice. . . ." 10¼ x 14. GIFT OF MRS. FRANCIS P. GARVAN IN MEMORY OF FRANCIS P. GARVAN. 55.6.8.

The Hot Corn Seller

THE HOT CORN SELLER, CA. 1840: Among Calyo's picturesque street criers, the hot corn seller was a particular favorite. In the fall of the year, the cry of "Hot Corn!" was abundantly heard all over the city in advance of the delicacy. Boiled in the husks while green, with the addition of a little salt this street corn is said to have made very pleasant eating. 11 x 10¼. GIFT OF MRS. FRANCIS P. GARVAN IN MEMORY OF FRANCIS P. GARVAN. 55.6.2.

THE MILKMAN, CA. 1840: "Here's Milk, ho!" Milkmen in those days went from door to door calling out that once familiar catchphrase. Milk was delivered twice a day in summer, and once in winter, in large tin kettles, some of which held more than twelve gallons. The milk was brought over by Brooklyn ferry in great quantities, some of it from several miles north of the center of New York. The milkmen of the 1820s usually wore a yoke, from which the tin kettles were suspended on each side by a chain. With these they went daily from door to door and delivered to their customers the daily allowance of the article they consumed. By 1840 the yoke had passed away, and carts of various forms were substituted. WATERCOLOR BY NICOLINO CALYO, 10¼ x 14. GIFT OF MRS. FRANCIS P. GARVAN IN MEMORY OF FRANCIS P. GARVAN. 55.6.11.

(RIGHT) **THE PALISADES, CA. 1820:** The Hudson River Palisades are an imposing remnant of the Triassic Period formed nearly two hundred million years ago. The Lenape word for these cliffs is "we-awk-en" (from which the New Jersey city derives its name), meaning "rocks that look like rows of trees." Their beauty may never have been captured better than in this, plate nineteen of the *Hudson River Port Folio*, which was painted by William Guy Wall, engraved by John Hill, and published by Henry J. Megarey. THE J. CLARENCE DAVIES COLLECTION. 29.100.2578.

W. G. Wall

Engraved by I. Hi

PALISADES.

No. 19 of the Hudson River Port Folio

CHAPTER VI | 1842–1860

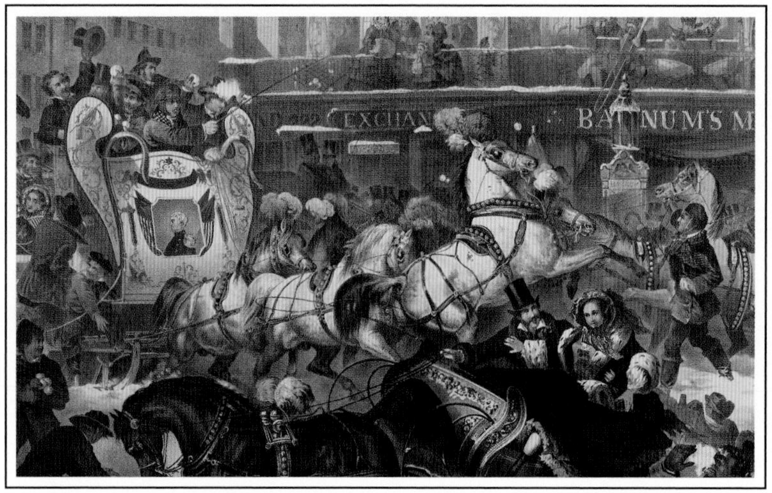

SUGAR, SLAVES,

AND THE RISE OF CUBAN NEW YORK

LISANDRO PÉREZ

IN THE EARLY MORNING OF MONDAY, FEBRUARY 17, 1845, PASSERSBY ON BARCLAY STREET, BETWEEN CHURCH AND WEST BROADWAY, HEARD LOUD NOISES FROM THE ROOFTOP OF THE BOARDINGHOUSE AT NUMBER 58. LOOKING UP, THEY SAW A MAN CLAD IN HIS PANTALOONS, SHIRT, AND SOCKS, SITTING ATOP A DORMER WINDOW, WAVING HIS ARMS WILDLY AND SHOUTING INCOHERENTLY. THOSE WHO LINGERED TO WATCH THE SPECTACLE STOOD HORRIFIED WHEN THE MAN SUDDENLY THREW HIMSELF OFF THE ROOF OF THE THREE-STORY STRUCTURE, A DISTANCE OF SIXTY FEET, LANDING HEADFIRST ON THE CURBSTONE BELOW AND DYING INSTANTLY. THE NEW YORK PRESS TOOK AN INTEREST IN THE TRAGEDY WHEN THEY LEARNED THAT THE VICTIM WAS GONZALO ALDAMA, A MEMBER OF A VERY WEALTHY CUBAN FAMILY, A YOUNG MAN, OBSERVED THE *NEW YORK HERALD*, "WITH BRILLIANT PROSPECTS BEFORE HIM." HIS SUICIDE WAS HARD TO UNDERSTAND. THE INITIAL EXPLANATION, PUT FORTH BY THE *BROOKLYN DAILY EAGLE*, WAS THAT GONZALO SUFFERED FROM TEMPORARY INSANITY, CAUSED BY A THUNDERBOLT THAT STRUCK VERY NEAR TO HIM ON SATURDAY NIGHT. IN THE BOARDINGHOUSE ALL DAY SUNDAY HE ACTED ERRATICALLY, EVEN VIOLENTLY, AS OTHER BOARDERS TRIED TO SUBDUE HIM. UPON FURTHER INVESTIGATION, THE *HERALD* CONCLUDED THAT IT WAS NOT A THUNDERBOLT, BUT AN IMPOSSIBLE LOVE THAT HAD FATALLY STRUCK THE YOUNG ALDAMA. GONZALO FELL IN LOVE IN HAVANA WITH A BEAUTIFUL, CHARMING, AND EDUCATED WOMAN SOMEWHAT OLDER THAN HE, BUT BELOW his family's social status. His father would not entertain the idea of Gonzalo marrying the woman and banished him to New York, ostensibly to study medicine. By all reports, Gonzalo arrived in the city with the intention of forgetting the woman. He was seen frequenting the theater, the opera, and the ballrooms. But Manhattan's best amusements failed to make him forget. He wrote repeatedly to his father, pleading for permission to marry the woman. A few days before his suicide, he received his father's irrevocable decision: Gonzalo could not return to Cuba until he renounced his romantic intentions. The *Herald* reporter concluded that the "warm and passionate and impetuous temperament of the Spaniard could no longer suffer and he therefore resolved to end his troubles."

Gonzalo's father was Domingo Aldama y Aréchaga, one of Cuba's wealthiest men. Born in Spain to a family of modest means, he migrated to Cuba determined to succeed in the island's expanding trade business. Eventually he achieved enough success to marry one of the daughters of his employer, Gonzalo Alfonso, an aristocrat, merchant, and sugar mill owner who had befriended the enterprising immigrant. Domingo made the most of his new social position and soon amassed a fortune from the booming business in sugar and slaves, acquiring his own mills as well as controlling interests in the island's major railroads and insurance firms. He built a palatial home in Havana, the first residence to be built outside the city's walls. The Aldama Palace, as it was called, still stands and is regarded as "the most acclaimed building in nineteenth-century Havana."

Gonzalo's younger brother, Miguel, was anointed the heir to the family fortune. He had been a good student, an obedient son, a responsible manager, and he married a woman from a prominent family. His brother Gonzalo, on the other hand, was troublesome and rebellious and intent on marrying unwisely. So Gonzalo was sent away—not to Spain, where Domingo was born, nor to France or England, nor even to Mexico or another nearby Latin-American country. He was sent to New York, where Domingo and Miguel sold their sugar and bought virtually everything they needed to furnish their new Havana palace. Gonzalo was already familiar with New York. As teenagers, Gonzalo, Miguel, and their cousin Gonzalo Alfonso visited Manhattan, arriving on May 24, 1836 aboard the *Norman* from Havana.

Gonzalo Aldama's story was repeated throughout the nineteenth century: New York as the place of refuge, exile, banishment, or escape for Cubans. The trade center on the Hudson became that world outside the island where Cubans went for an education, opportunity, wealth; to start a new life or forget an old one; to evade royal authority, plot a revolution; to experience freedom; to buy and sell. Many of those stories, like Gonzalo's, ended tragically. Others were steeped in heroism and sacrifice, and still others in opportunism and mendacity. But they all represent the building blocks of a New York community that by the middle of the nineteenth century was attracting increasing numbers of Cubans. Throughout most of the nineteenth century Cubans were by far the largest Spanish-speaking group in New York City and they represented the largest concentration of Latin Americans east of the Mississippi. Their numbers peaked in 1870 when nearly 3,000 Cuban-born people were living in what are now the five boroughs, with about 2,600 in Manhattan alone.

The story of Cuban New York, like most New York stories, starts with the port. As early as the 1820s there were more passengers arriving in the city from Cuban ports than the number of passengers arriving from all the other ports of Latin America and Spain combined, a pattern that would be sustained throughout most of the century. Underlying that passenger traffic were the extensive and longstanding trade relations between New York and Spain's island colony, commercial ties older than the United States itself. The brief British occupation of Havana in 1762 had opened up trade between Cuba and the English North American colonies.

But the real spark for New York's Cuba trade was the boom in the island's sugar production that started in the closing years of the eighteenth century and intensified throughout the first half of the nineteenth, transforming Cuba into the world's largest producer of sugar. Cuba was a Spanish colony, but by the start of the nineteenth century, its ports, especially Havana, were in the service of trade with the young American nation. In 1830 alone, 936 U.S. ships entered Cuban ports. Between 1835 and 1865 the total value of goods the United States exchanged with the island was exceeded by only three or four other countries in the world.

At first, New Orleans, Boston, Philadelphia, and Baltimore vied with New York for the flourishing Cuba trade. But in the end New York ended up with the lion's share of commerce with the island. The key to New York's dominance was its capacity to turn a hefty profit through the industrial processing of raw sugar. By 1860, the port of New York was handling almost two-thirds of all sugar entering the United States. Cuba exported raw brown sugar, marketable only to the poorest consumers. The real profit was made by selling it as refined white sugar and packaged in a large cone or loaf. The profitable refining process was done in New York, which even before the Cuba trade had established itself as the nation's refining center. In 1689 New York had the first sugar refinery in the North American colonies and by 1855 it had fourteen plants operating. From 1845 to 1860 the port of New York exported an average of 1.8 million pounds of refined sugar annually.

New York's exports to Cuba were, of course, much more diverse than the products arriving from Cuban ports. The island's increased population and wealth as a result of the sugar boom and its dramatic shift to a single-crop economy increased the demand for a wide range of manufactured products that New York could provide. Cuba had to import practically everything. Cuban planters bought machinery for their mills, fine linen and clothing for themselves, furnishings for their new mansions, carriages in which to ride around Havana, and large amounts of foodstuffs, especially flour, to feed their slaves.

The key players in New York's trade with Cuba were the counting houses that lined Manhattan's waterfront. A combination of trading office, warehouse, accounting firm, credit agency, bank, and investment manager, those mercantile establishments typically had employees or representatives operating out of offices in Havana and Matanzas. The counting houses cultivated relations with the Cuban planters, extending them credit, acting as their shipping and commission agents, selling their sugar, investing their money, and purchasing goods in New York on their behalf.

But the counting houses and their agents forged links between Cuba and New York that went beyond the commercial sphere, establishing the basis for a profound and extensive exchange not only of goods and money, but also of people and culture. On the back of the Cuba trade rode an extensive network of social contacts that would cement the New York-Cuba connection and provide the basis for the rise of a notable Cuban presence in the city by mid-nineteenth century. Spearheading that Cuban presence were boys and young men from wealthy Cuban families who were sent to New York for an education or for work experience, and the counting houses had a direct role in bringing them from Cuba. New York merchants would make arrangements for the sons of their Cuban clients to be enrolled in boarding schools in the New York area. They would meet them at the dock, buy their winter clothing and other necessities, pay for tuition and board, and even disburse periodic allowances to the students. The counting house would also temporarily employ young Cuban men in their own operations in New York—a sort of internship that would enable them to learn English and become familiar with modern business operations.

Of all the New York counting houses, the one that had the most profound and sustained influence on the Cuba trade was Moses Taylor and Company. Established in 1832 and located at 44 South Street, Taylor's counting house conducted business with Cuba for more than fifty years. The file the firm kept on boarding schools in the New York region, with brochures and letters from headmasters, was almost as large as the file it had on sugar refiners and sugar equipment manufacturers. Assuming the demanding role of caretaker in the United States for Cuban youngsters was a necessary burden for Moses Taylor and his associates, one that reflected their Cuban clients' interest in educating their children in the lives and ways of the country with which they conducted the bulk of their business. In 1850, one New Yorker estimated that nearly 2,000 young Cubans had already been educated in U.S. schools.

One of those young men was Cristóbal Madan, who in 1823 was an intern in a South Street counting house while he learned English in preparation for admission to a New York law school. The counting house belonged to Jonathan Goodhue, a New Englander who had moved to South Street from Salem and was engaged, years before Moses Taylor, in importing sugar from Cuba. Goodhue and Company was located at 44 South Street, the same address where Moses Taylor would later establish his counting house. Cristóbal's grandfather, of Irish descent, had migrated to Cuba from the Canary Islands to take advantage of the opportunities opened up by the island's sugar boom. Although they lived in Havana, the Madans owned mills in the Matanzas region of Cuba and sold their sugar in New York, primarily through Goodhue.

Many of the Cuban planter families intermarried, further consolidating their economic wealth. The Madans eventually formed part of the wealthy Alfonso-Aldama clan, the family of the ill-fated Gonzalo. It is not surprising that given their economic interests and increasing ties with the United States, the Alfonsos, Aldamas, Madans, and many other planter families favored annexing Cuba to the United States. The annexationist movement gained strength during the 1840s and early 1850s and was supported by U.S. southerners and their sympathizers who saw the annexation of Cuba as a way of adding another slave state to the Union. The motivations of the Cuban planters for favoring annexation were varied, but ultimately rested on their interest in saving slavery, which had become the basis of the sugar planters' wealth. By the 1840s, slavery was under siege, primarily from British abolitionists. Becoming a U.S. slave state seemed to offer the best guarantee for continuing the institution, with the added benefit that Cuba would become part of the nation where the planters sold their sugar and where they bought practically everything they needed.

New York, as might be expected, became a center for the Cuban annexationist movement, and one of its key players was Cristóbal Madan. By mid-century Madan was already in his early forties, dividing his time among his house in Havana, his family's sugar mills in Matanzas, and his residence in the fashionable Madison Square area of Manhattan. It was there that the 1850 U.S. Census found him, in a large household comprised of his wife, six children, and several servants (one of them, an Irish woman with Madan's ancestral surname, Madden). The four oldest of Madan's children, two boys and two girls, were the teenaged offspring of Madan's deceased first wife. The youngest two, a girl of four and the infant Julián, were the children of his second wife, Mary, listed in the 1850 census as a thirty-year-old native New Yorker.

Mary's maiden name was O'Sullivan, and she was the sister of John L. O'Sullivan, an influential New York Democrat, the editor of the *New York Morning News* and the *Democratic Review*, and a staunch supporter of U.S. expansionism. In an 1845 editorial in the *Democratic Review* on the annexation of Texas, O'Sullivan coined the term "manifest destiny" to refer to the expansionist sentiment that guided the subsequent acquisition of Oregon and more than half of Mexico's territory.

O'Sullivan traveled to Havana with the editor of the *New York Sun*, Moses Yale Beach, with the purpose of meeting secretly with a group of prominent Cuban planters who had clandestinely formed an organization called El Club de La Habana. Madan had set up the meeting with his Cuban relatives, Domingo Aldama and his son Miguel, at the recently built Aldama Palace. It was 1847, two years after Gonzalo's suicide. El Club had been created to advance the cause of Cuban annexation to the United States, largely by promoting the purchase of Cuba by the U.S. government.

Both Americans returned from Havana committed to annexing the island. As a newspaperman, Beach chose to make the cause a public one, and the *Sun* became the standard bearer of the cause of Cuban annexation to the United States. One of the most notable efforts of the annexationists in New York was the establishment of a pro-annexation bilingual newspaper, *La Verdad*, which appeared biweekly from 1848 to 1853 and to which Madan was a frequent anonymous contributor of essays. It was printed at the *Sun* and the editor was one Cora Montgomery, a pseudonym for a relative of Moses Yale Beach, Mrs. W. L. Cazneau. The *Sun* also supported armed expeditions to Cuba to wrest control of the island from Spain. The departure of one of those expeditions, led by Narciso López and organized largely in New York, was heralded in the *Sun*'s May 11, 1850 edition with the headline: "DEPARTURE OF THE EXPEDITION AGAINST CUBA!" The accompanying story announced the extraordinary event that "The Flag of Free Cuba" would be flown that morning in front of the *Sun*'s offices at the corner of Nassau and Fulton streets. It was reportedly designed and sewn in a Manhattan boarding house by a group of Cuban exiles. Never before had anyone seen a piece of cloth identified as a flag of Cuba. And yet, on a Manhattan street corner, it flew for the first time. Not just *a* Cuban flag, but *the* Cuban flag, the one that was subsequently adopted by the separatist movement and remains to this day, despite a turbulent history, the flag of Cuba.

The annexationist movement declined around 1855 after many of its proponents realized that the U.S. government was unwilling to risk its relations with Europe to annex Cuba and that it would continue to oppose the launching of expeditions from its own soil. The movement was practically nonexistent by the time of the U.S. Civil War.

The annexationist movement was, however, a harbinger of things to come as Cuban New York became more and more affected by the emerging conflict between Cubans and Spaniards over the future of the island. Other separatist movements arose and Spain countered with greater repression. Even Cristóbal Madan, who tried to keep a low profile, saw his life disrupted in the wake of Spain's response to the annexationist threat. A year after the debacle of the last annexationist expedition in 1851, the Spanish government sentenced *in absentia* the leading figures of the annexationist movement in New York, including Madan. Cristóbal was sentenced to ten years of supervised exile in Spain. Joaquín Madan traveled from Matanzas to Havana to plead with the authorities that the sentence against his son be lifted so that he could return to Cuba. On March 19, 1852, however, Cristóbal Madan was arrested in Havana. Without any regard for Madan's U.S. citizenship, General José de la Concha, the Spanish governor, ratified the sentence on June 5, and the man who had started out as a teenaged clerk at Goodhue and Company on South Street was banished to Spain.

As soon as he could, however, Cristóbal Madan made his way back to New York. For him, as for many Cubans, the city had replaced Spain as that "other place" beyond an island's constraining boundaries that sparks the imagination. It had become the place of reference for style, ideas, progress, culture, and economic advancement—in short, the place where horizons could be expanded beyond the possibilities available on a tropical island.

LISANDRO PÉREZ is Professor of Sociology at Florida International University (FIU) in Miami. In 1991 he founded FIU's Cuban Research Institute and served as its director until 2003. He has also served as the editor of the journal *Cuban Studies* and is the co-author of the book *The Legacy of Exile: Cubans in the United States*, published by Allyn & Bacon. Both the National Endowment for the Humanities and the Cullman Center for Scholars and Writers of the New York Public Library supported the research for his latest book: *Cubans in Gotham: Immigrants, Exiles, and Revolutionaries in Nineteenth Century New York*, under contract with New York University Press.

NEW YORK FROM THE STEEPLE OF ST. PAUL'S CHAPEL, 1849: Familiarly known as the "Papprill View of New York," this is in fact one of several engravings by Henry Papprill (1816–1903), and his most spectacular. Standing atop St. Paul's Chapel—one of the city's few Colonial buildings still standing—Englishman John William Hill painted a magnificent watercolor of the city looking east, south, and west. Among the highlights are Barnum's Museum at left; the spire of Trinity Church at center; and Brady's Daguerreian Miniature Gallery at center, foreground. COLORED AQUATINT AFTER ORIGINAL DRAWING BY HILL. ENGRAVED BY PAPPRILL. PRINTED BY HENRY J. MEGAREY. GIFT OF MRS. LOUIS J. HECTOR. 82.116.

VIEWS of NEW-YORK
Drawn by C. Autenrieth.
Published by Henry Hoff No 130 William St New-York
CITY HALL of BROOKLYN.
Entered according to Act of Congress in the year 1850 by Henry Hoff in the Clerks Office of the District Court of the Southern District of N. York

CITY HALL OF BROOKLYN, 1850: Here is a view from Henry Hoff's 1850 portfolio, *The Empire City of New York: Twenty Beautiful Colored Views of the Most Remarkable and Prettiest Places, Buildings, and Streets of New York and Brooklyn* (see also "Croton Water Reservoir," page 154). Brooklyn's City Hall is today known as Borough Hall, but is the same grand Greek Revival structure dominating Joralemon Street that was designed by Gamaliel King in 1846. ENGRAVED AFTER A DRAWING BY C. AUTENRIETH. BEQUEST OF MRS. J. INSLEY BLAIR IN MEMORY OF MR. AND MRS. J. INSLEY BLAIR. 52.100.23S.

(RIGHT) **NEW YORK (LOOKING SOUTH FROM UNION SQUARE), 1849:** A decade before this view was drawn, the *New York Mirror* noted that "around Union Place new blocks of houses, capacious and stately, are springing up with surprising celerity. . . . Fourteenth Street will doubtless be considered at the heart rather than the extremity of the town in the course of a few years." The remark was prescient, for in 1845 the *Herald* declared that "whole streets of magnificent dwelling houses have been erected in the vicinity of Union Square within the last year." This was drawn by C. Bachman, lithographed by Sarony & Major, published by John Bachmann. The relation between artist C. Bachman and artist-lithographer-publisher John Bachmann is unclear; this is the only city view bearing the name of the former. THE J. CLARENCE DAVIES COLLECTION. 29.100.1344.

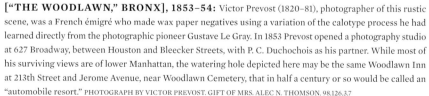

["THE WOODLAWN," BRONX], 1853–54: Victor Prevost (1820–81), photographer of this rustic scene, was a French émigré who made wax paper negatives using a variation of the calotype process he had learned directly from the photographic pioneer Gustave Le Gray. In 1853 Prevost opened a photography studio at 627 Broadway, between Houston and Bleecker Streets, with P. C. Duchochois as his partner. While most of his surviving views are of lower Manhattan, the watering hole depicted here may be the same Woodlawn Inn at 213th Street and Jerome Avenue, near Woodlawn Cemetery, that in half a century or so would be called an "automobile resort." PHOTOGRAPH BY VICTOR PREVOST. GIFT OF MRS. ALEC N. THOMSON. 98.126.3.7

[WOOD FRAME HOUSES], 1853: One of the Museum of the City of New York's earliest photographs, this unidentified view dates from 1853, Victor Prevost's first year in business as a professional photographer and one of only a few in the United States producing calotypes commercially. He was also a painter and an academician: the annual New York City directories of 1850–53 describe him as an artist, that of 1853–54 as a photographer, and those of 1855–57 as a chemist. PHOTOGRAPH BY VICTOR PREVOST. GIFT OF MRS. ALEC N. THOMSON. 98.126.2.10.

[BATTERY PLACE, BEFORE FILLING IN OF THE PARK], 1853: Battery Park was filled in to extend the tip of Manhattan south of Castle Garden, which since its creation above the walls of the Castle Clinton fortification in 1824 had been accessible only via a pier. P. C. Duchochois, who was partner to photographer Victor Prevost at the time the latter created this view, wrote in 1901: "I knew him in Paris, and when I came to New York in 1853 we formed a partnership. Our studio was in Broadway, between Houston and Blee[c]ker streets, pretty far up town then, but we did not succeed in making it pay; the time for photographers was not yet come, the beauty of Daguerreotype was reigning supreme." By this Duchochois meant that the artistry of a positive salt print pulled from a waxed paper negative seemed inferior to the dazzling clarity afforded by the original daguerreotype process, which created only one image from a photographer's work. GIFT OF MRS. J. WEST ROOSEVELT. 38.93.1.

SWEET WARBLER

(LEFT) FIRST APPEARANCE OF JENNY LIND IN AMERICA, CASTLE GARDEN, 1850: Jenny Lind (1820–87), "The Swedish Nightingale," was a sensation of previously unimagined dimension from the moment she reached New York's shores in September 1850. For months in advance she had been trumpeted by promoter P. T. Barnum as an exemplar of morality, tenderness, generosity, anti-Papist Protestantism, and of course, musicality. Her much anticipated performance was held on September 11, 1850 at Castle Garden, which following initial service as a fort, had been opened as a "place of resort" in the harbor, accessible by a boardwalk, in 1824. Kenneth Dunshee wrote of Miss Lind's advent: "The clamor for tickets would have been a scalper's delight. As it was, choice seats were auctioned at previously unheard-of prices. So great was the desire to see her that some people who failed to obtain tickets formed parties in rented rowboats and, resting on their oars, listened from the river outside of the Garden during the performance." The concert was a gold mine, yielding $26,238 in receipts, with Miss Lind dedicating her portion—some $12,600—to New York charities. LITHOGRAPH PUBLISHED BY N. CURRIER. THE J. CLARENCE DAVIES COLLECTION. 29.100.1871.

THE OLD BOWERY THEATRE, 1860: This theater, designed in the Greek Revival style by architect Ithiel Town, opened its doors as the New York Theatre on October 22, 1826 with the play *The Road to Ruin*. The title of the play was a path the theater seemingly pursued as it tried—with ballet, opera, and classical drama—to be as high-toned as the older Park Theatre. In 1828 it burned to the ground, but like a Phoenix rose anew as the Bowery Theatre, with a new, more popularly oriented bill of entertainments. Its history was marked by a continued penchant for flame—it burned down and was rebuilt in 1836, 1838, 1845, and 1923—yet it endured until 1929, sometimes known as the Thalia Theater but generally as the Bowery Theater. LITHOGRAPH BY SARONY, MAJOR & KNAPP FOR *VALENTINE'S MANUAL*, 1863.

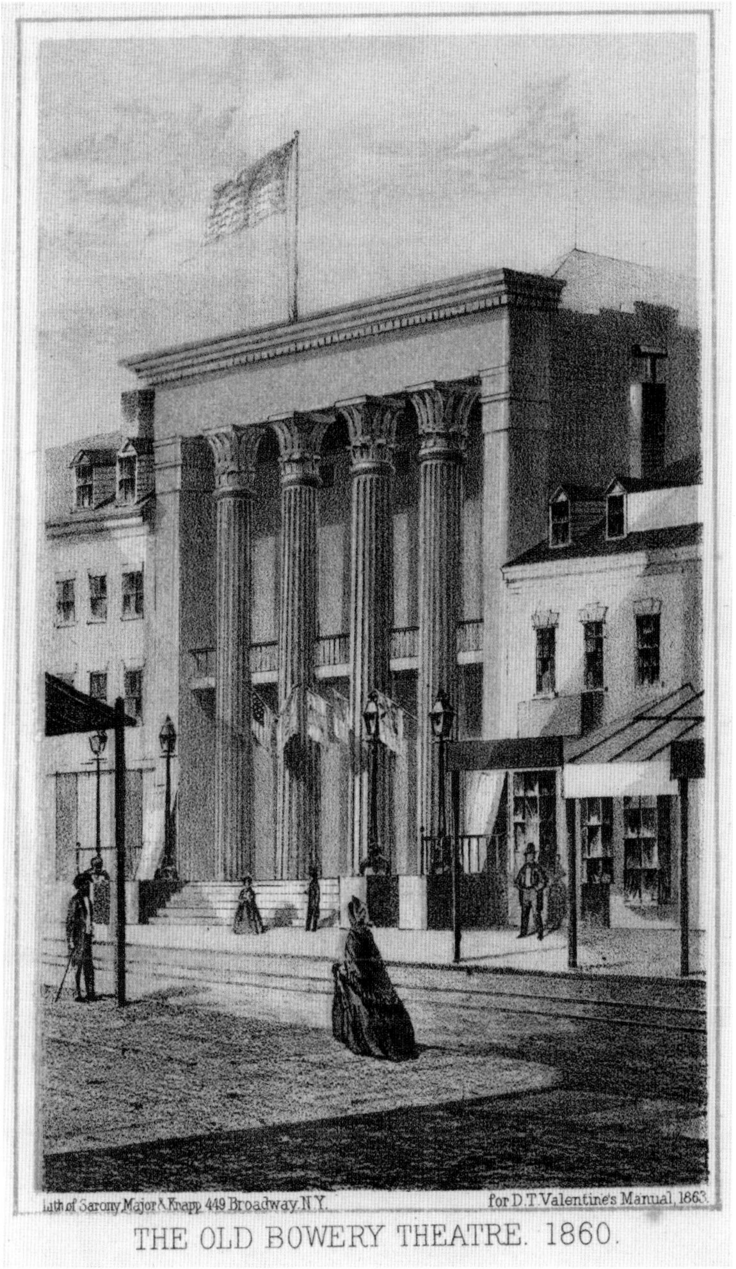

Lith of Sarony Major & Knapp 449 Broadway N.Y.
for D.T. Valentine's Manual, 1863.
THE OLD BOWERY THEATRE. 1860.

AUCTION IN CHATHAM SQUARE 1843: E. Didier exhibited this oil painting at the National Academy of Design in 1843, but it may depict an earlier period, when auction sales in Chatham Square were both common and legal. After 1820 all Chatham Square auction permits were revoked, at the instigation of merchants and storekeepers who were unable to compete with open-air *vendues* of crockery, baskets, and furniture. And yet some elements of city life in 1843 intrude: W. N. Seymour and H. Kipp and Company, the furniture businesses depicted on the far side of Chatham Square, are listed in directories of the period at, respectively, Nos. 4 and 7 Chatham Square. Perhaps the prohibition of auction sales was flouted like so many other city ordinances? OIL ON CANVAS, 22 x 27½. ANONYMOUS GIFT. 51.222.1.

(RIGHT) **NEW YORK CRYSTAL PALACE, 1853:** From the border: "These buildings constructed of iron and glass, are erected on Reservoir Square in the City of New York. The ground plan of the main building, forms an octagon, and is surmounted by a Greek cross, with a dome over the intersection. Dimensions, Main Building: extreme length 865 feet, extreme breadth 365 feet, height of dome to top of lantern 146 feet, entire space on ground floor 111,000 square feet, galleries 62,000 square feet. Dimensions, Additional Buildings: extreme length 451 feet, space on ground floor 22,872 square feet, space on gallery 9,480 square feet, whole area of buildings 5 acres or 205,352 square feet. Geo. J. B. Carstensen & Charles Gildemeister, architects." Note at left the 350-foot-high Latting Observatory, built for "the Exhibition of the Industry of All Nations" and like it a victim of fire, though two years earlier. Note also at right a bit of the Croton Water Reservoir. LITHOGRAPH BY NATHANIEL CURRIER. THE J. CLARENCE DAVIES COLLECTION. 29.100.2479.

…ER, DEL.

Entered according to Act of Congress, in the year 1853, by N. Currier, in the Clerk's Office of the District-Court of the Southern District of New York.

LITH & PUB BY N. CURRIER, 152 NASSAU ST.

NEW YORK CRYSTAL PALACE.

FOR THE EXHIBITION OF THE INDUSTRY OF ALL NATIONS.

THESE BUILDINGS CONSTRUCTED OF IRON AND GLASS; ARE ERECTED ON RESERVOIR SQUARE IN THE CITY OF NEW-YORK. THE GROUND PLAN OF THE MAIN BUILDING, FORMS AN OCTAGON, AND IS SURMOUNTED BY A GREEK CROSS, WITH A DOME OVER THE INTERSECTION.—

DIMENSIONS:
MAIN BUILDING.

EXTREME LENGTH	365 FEET.
EXTREME BREADTH	365 FEET
HEIGHT OF DOME TO TOP OF LANTERN	148 FEET.
ENTIRE SPACE ON GROUND FLOOR	111,000 SQUARE FEET
GALLERIES	62,000 SQUARE FEET.

DIMENSIONS:
ADDITIONAL BUILDING

EXTREME LENGTH	451 FEET.
SPACE ON GROUND FLOOR	22,872 SQUARE FEET.
SPACE ON GALLERY	9.480, SQUARE FEET.
WHOLE AREA OF BUILDINGS 5 ACRES, OR	205.352 SQUARE FEET.

GEO. J. B. CARSTENSEN, } ARCHITECTS
CHARLES GILDEMEISTER, }

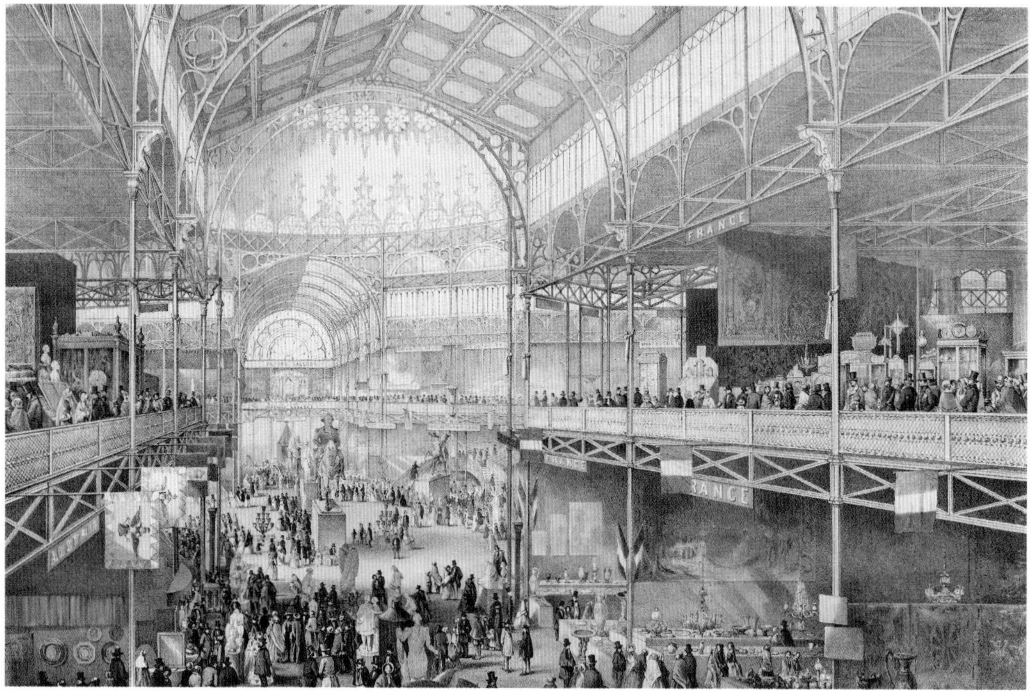

CRYSTAL PALACE, CA. 1853: Starting in the mid-nineteenth century, large trade fairs such as the Crystal Palace Exposition provided new venues for American art and inventiveness. The "New-York Crystal Palace for the Exhibition of the Industry of All Nations" was designed by Georg J. B. Carstensen and Charles Gildemeister, frankly modeled on the great hall of the same name that had opened in London's Hyde Park for the Great Exhibition of 1851. Both were cast iron and glass buildings of vast scale. New York's Crystal Palace stood on a site behind the Croton Distributing Reservoir, between Fifth and Sixth Avenues on 42nd Street (today's Bryant Park). President Franklin Pierce opened the New York version on July 4, 1853, inaugurating America's first World's Fair. The exhibition closed on November 1 of the following year, but the building continued to host trade shows until it was destroyed by fire on October 5, 1858. PAINTING BY W. S. PARKES, 1852–58. OIL ON GLASS BACKED WITH MOTHER-OF-PEARL, 34 x 46. GIFT OF MRS. SAMUEL S. SCHWARTZ. 64.94.

AN INTERIOR VIEW OF THE CRYSTAL PALACE, 1853: In the center one sees that the Picture Gallery sits atop the Machine Arcade, testifying to the era's optimism that art and industry could be united in service to the people. The artist, Charles Parsons (1821–1910), was a prolific chronicler of the city. With Lyman Atwater he produced almost all the New York City views published by Currier & Ives in the years following the Civil War. DRAWN BY CHARLES PARSONS. PRINTED BY ENDICOTT & CO. PUBLISHED BY GEORGE S. APPLETON. THE J. CLARENCE DAVIES COLLECTION. 29.100.2391.

(RIGHT) **THE DESTRUCTION BY FIRE OF THE NEW YORK CRYSTAL PALACE, OCTOBER 5TH 1858:** Advertised by the fair's promoters as a fireproof structure, the great glass and iron hall was destroyed by flame in fifteen minutes. According to the *Sun*, within a week of the calamity a certain industrious Mrs. Richardson set up an outdoor stand in the adjoining Palace Garden and sold relics of the conflagration, including "vitrified masses of glass, metals, &c., showing the intense heat which prevailed at the time of the destruction." PUBLISHED BY H. H. LLOYD & CO.; ALSO BY SPEARING & STUTZMAN. THE J. CLARENCE DAVIES COLLECTION. 29.100.2397.

THE DESTRUCTION BY FIRE OF THE

NEW YORK CRYSTAL PALACE.

October 5th 1858.

ublished by H. H. LLOYD & CO. ALSO BY SPEARING & STUTZMAN. APPLETONS BUILDING N.Y.

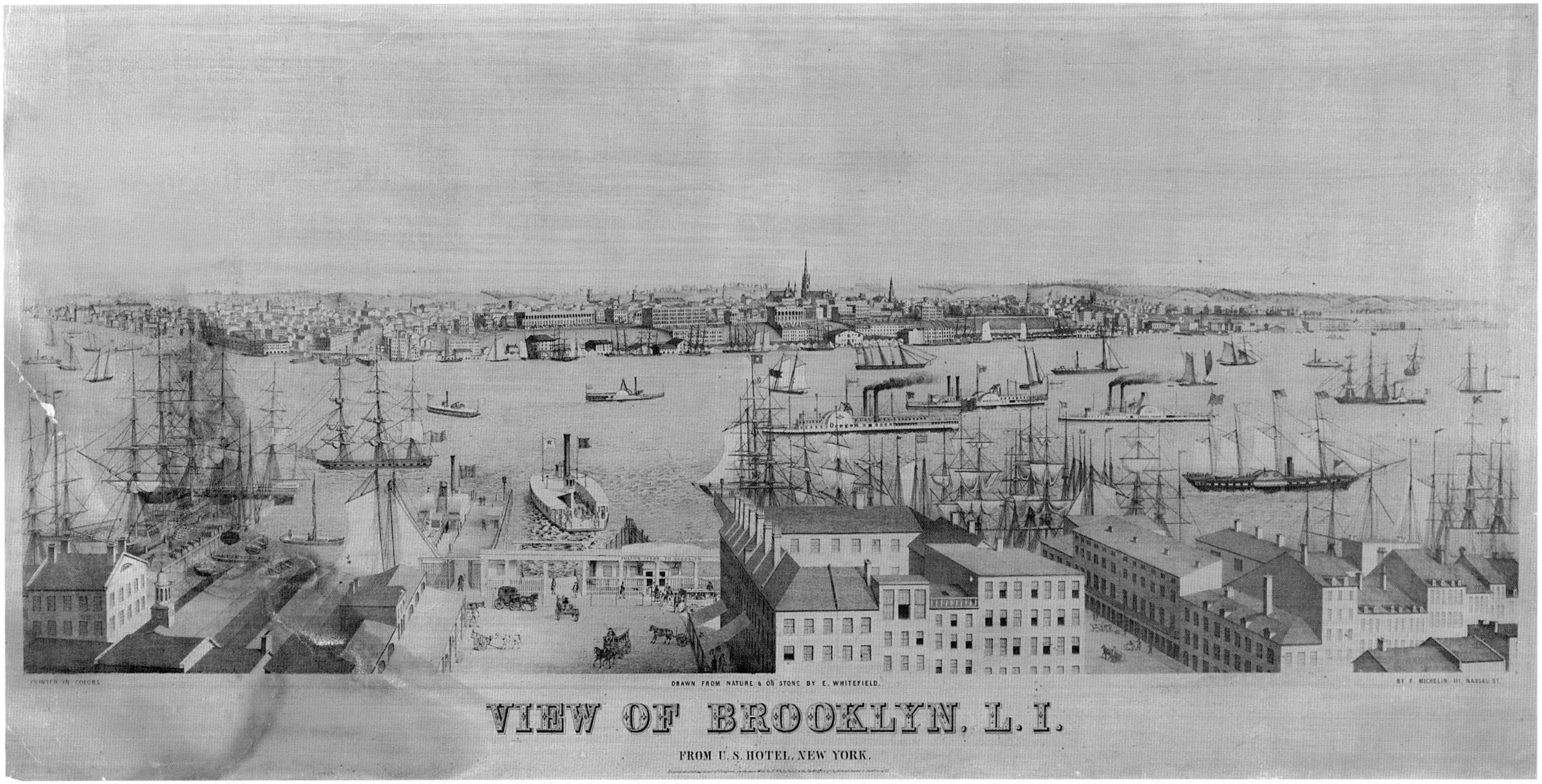
DRAWN FROM NATURE & ON STONE BY E. WHITEFIELD.
VIEW OF BROOKLYN, L. I.
FROM U. S. HOTEL, NEW YORK.

(LEFT) **[ROW HOUSE], 1853–54:** The location is unknown, but the stone facing on the frame house testifies to changing tastes and trends in the wake of the fires of 1835 and 1845. Even modest row houses now began to take on the trappings of commercial housing. The bluestone slabs that formed the sidewalks were quarried upstate and ported to New York via the Delaware and Hudson Canal leading to Kingston, and thence along the Hudson River. The bluestone walks would not be replaced by poured concrete until century's end. SALTED PAPER PRINT BY VICTOR PREVOST. GIFT OF MRS. ALEC N. THOMSON. 98.126.3.12.

VIEW OF BROOKLYN, L.I. FROM U.S. HOTEL, NEW YORK, 1846: Edwin Whitefield (1816–92) was one of the first traveling artist-publishers, making his drawings on the spot in such widespread locales as Quebec, New York, Chicago, and Louisville—and then securing sufficient subscribers to make publication worthwhile. These historically accurate if somewhat austere lithographs are known to collectors as the "Whitefield Views." In this staggeringly thorough view of Brooklyn, David William Moody added detail on new lithographic stone to Whitefield's watercolor, from the ships in the East River to the houses in Brooklyn. The New York slip of Fulton Ferry is in the foreground, with steamboats *Oregon*, *Worcester*, and *Rhode Island* among the craft in the river. DAVID WILLIAM MOODY, ARTIST. EDWIN WHITEFIELD, LITHOGRAPHER. FRANCIS MICHELIN, PRINTER. THE J. CLARENCE DAVIES COLLECTION. 29.100.3537.

WALL STREET, HALF PAST 2 O'CLOCK, OCTOBER 13, 1857: The scene depicted was a memorable one: at the height of a financial panic, all but one of the fifty-eight banks in the city had just suspended specie payments, which would not be resumed until December 12. The entire nation was thrown into a depression. In the center of the painting, wearing a light-colored coat, is stunned speculator Jacob Little; market manipulator Cornelius Vanderbilt stands at the extreme right. To relieve the suffering of the suddenly unemployed, the city embarked upon a public works program, including an acceleration of the work already commenced to create Central Park. PAINTING BY JAMES H. CAFFERTY AND CHARLES G. ROSENBERG. OIL ON CANVAS, 50 X 39½. GIFT OF THE HONORABLE IRWIN UNTERMYER. 40.54.

(RIGHT) **BROADWAY AT ANN STREET, BARNUM MUSEUM, 1855:** Phineas Taylor Barnum (1810–91), prince of humbugs and great showman, purchased Scudder's American Museum in 1841 and remade it in his outsize image. To a hall of biological and historical curiosities he added a lecture room, legitimate theater, and his own famous frauds and oddities, from Tom Thumb to conjoined twins Chang and Eng. In earlier years he had exhibited the Fee-jee Mermaid (cobbled together from fish parts) and Joice Heth, a superannuated African American exhibited at the advertised age of 161 years old as the "nursing mammy" of George Washington. The chaotic glory that marked Barnum's museum is here depicted in a chaotic street scene; Barnum himself may be seen with arm extended, raising his hat at the extreme left. The artist is presumed to be David Benecke. LITHOGRAPH BY THOMAS BENECKE. THE HARRY T. PETERS COLLECTION. 57.300.582.

EXCHAN
NUM'S MUSE

CROTON WATER RESERVOIR, 1850: Henry Hoff, a lithographer and publisher, issued a beautiful set of city scenes in *The Empire City of New York: Twenty Beautiful Colored Views of the Most Remarkable and Prettiest Places, Buildings and Streets of New York and Brooklyn*. One of these, depicted here in an oval frame, was of the Croton Reservoir, erected between 1837 and 1842 on Fifth Avenue, between 40th and 42nd Streets. Each of Hoff's colored lithographs was mounted onto a decorative card with a gold border and lettering. The data in the border of the full version of this image indicates that it was drawn by Charles Autenrieth. The drawing has also been attributed to the briefly prolific lithographer and artist John Bornet, but city directories offer no listing for him until 1852. THE J. CLARENCE DAVIES COLLECTION. 29.100.2103.

(RIGHT) **VIEW OF THE DISTRIBUTING RESERVOIR, 1842:** The Croton Aqueduct opened to public use on October 14, 1842, with a day-long celebration culminating in a fountain that spouted water to a height of fifty feet in City Hall Park. This overhead view of the Distributing Reservoir, a.k.a. the Croton Water Reservoir, was submitted for copyright less than two months later. It depicts one of the reservoir's secondary benefits—its lovely promenade. The border of the lithograph informs, more prosaically, that the reservoir "Extends from 40th to 42nd Str./And on the 5th Avenue 420 Feet./Covers 4 Acres." Additionally, "Depth of Water when filled, 36 Feet./Contains 21,000,000 of gallons./Height above [mean] tide, 114 feet." LITHOGRAPH BY NATHANIEL CURRIER. THE GERALD LEVINO COLLECTION. 57.100.56.

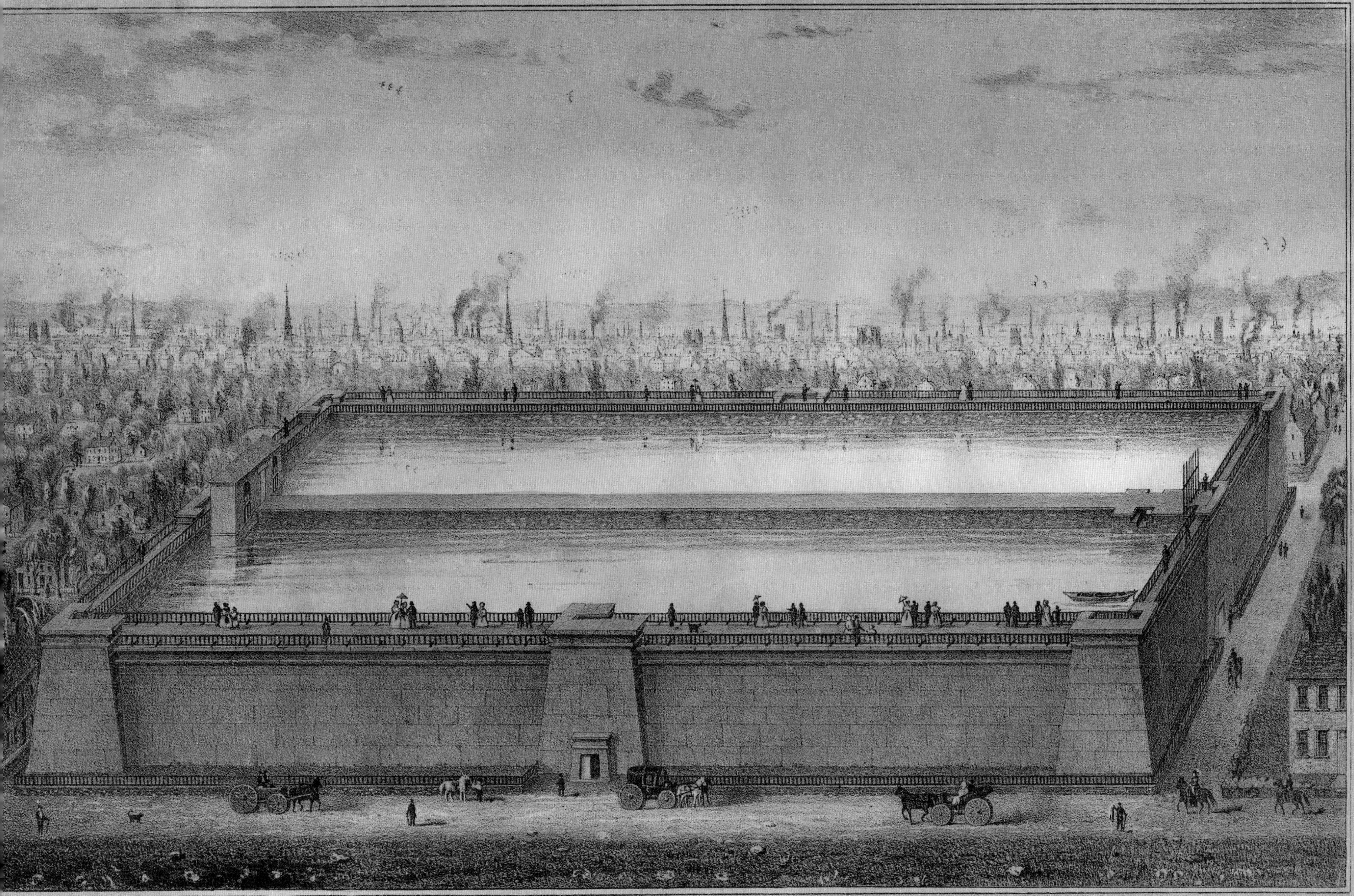

Extends from 40th to 42nd Str.
And on the 5th Avenue 420 Feet.
Covers 4 Acres.

VIEW OF THE DISTRIBUTING RESERVOIR.

ON MURRAYS HILL, — CITY OF NEW YORK.

Depth of Water when Filled 36 Feet.
Contains 21,000,000 of Gallons
Height above Tide 114 Feet

Entered according to Act of Congress A.D. 1842 by N. Currier in the Clerks Office of the District Court of the Southern District of New York.

Lith. & Pub. by N. Currier 2 Spruce St. N.Y.

SNUFF MILLS, BRONX, c. 1850: Built in about 1840 to replace an earlier building of the same function, the Lorillard Snuff Mill is the nation's oldest existing tobacco manufacturing building. Today it can be seen at the New York Botanical Gardens in the Bronx. Martha J. Lamb wrote in 1892: "The waterfall near the former Lorillard mansion, while adding beauty to the scene, also served the utilitarian purpose of furnishing power for the extensive snuff mills, which for nearly three generations were operated by the Lorillards, laying the foundation of their fortune, which still ranks high in this city of many millionaires." WATERCOLOR BY JAMES RENWICK BREVOORT, 9 x 9⅞. GIFT OF MRS. RUDOLF EICKMEYER. 38.217.

OLD SLIP, 1860: In 1709 a petition was granted establishing a dock and public landing place between Theobald's Slip and Burger's Path (the present Old Slip), which Burger Jorissen made to go down to the Strand. The "slips" on the East River shoreline were originally inlets that brought the waterfront a block or two inland. They were eventually filled in and became streets. (Old Slip today extends to South Street.) The building on the right is the Franklin Market, rebuilt in 1837–38 following the Great Fire of two years earlier. By 1860 the once vibrant market had become a shell of its former self. WATERCOLOR ON PAPER BY ACHILLES BEGODEN, 12⅞ x 9¼. GIFT OF MRS. J. INSLEY BLAIR. 38.419.4.

TWO VIEWS OF THOMAS BENNETT, ENGINE COMPANY NO. 8, CA. 1858: We know little of the proud member of Engine Company No. 8 portrayed in this double ambrotype, except that his name is Thomas Bennett and he was clearly proud of his affiliation. The Manhattan or Essex Engine Company, as Number 8 was formally known, was the last company established before the Revolutionary War in 1776. It had an elephant as its emblem and had its first headquarters near the Tan Pits, at the foot of what is now Maiden Lane, at one time known as Shoemakers' Pasture. The company made an excursion to Washington at the inauguration of President Franklin Pierce in March 1853, and it is possible that Tom Bennett accompanied them. Membership in one of New York's all-volunteer and often rowdy fire companies was a badge of social distinction among the city's working class before the Civil War. DAGUERREOTYPE, MAKER UNKNOWN. GIFT OF MRS. JOSEPH E. HILTON, GIVEN IN MEMORY OF HER UNCLE, THOMAS BENNETT. 52.304.1.

JOHN H. KEMP, 1860: This smartly uniformed lad seems too young to go off to war, and too cool to get far beyond dress drills—but off to war he surely went. He was part of New York's "Dandy Seventh," the 7th regiment New York State Militia, a crack infantry unit was also nicknamed the "Old Greybacks" because of their distinctive uniforms. A less complimentary term for the outfit was the "Silk Stocking" Regiment—an epithet revived a century later for application to Congressmen who represented the Upper East Side. DAGUERREOTYPE, MAKER UNKNOWN. GIFT OF MRS. ROBERT COLEMAN KEMP. 46.68.2.

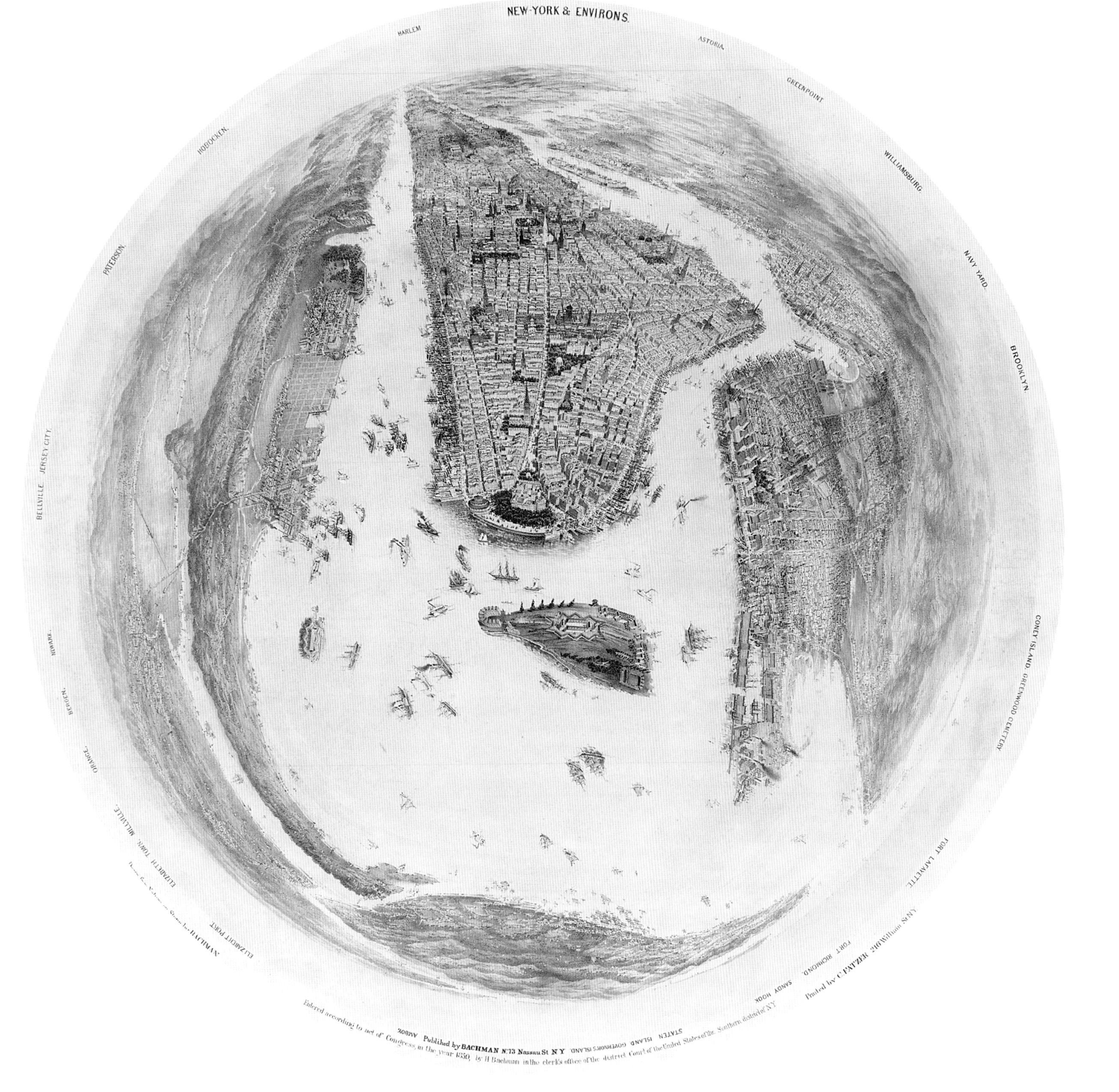
NEW-YORK & ENVIRONS.
HARLEM
ASTORIA
GREENPOINT
WILLIAMSBURG
NAVY YARD.
BROOKLYN.
CONEY ISLAND. GREENWOOD CEMETERY
FORT LAFAYETTE
FORT RICHMOND
SANDY HOOK
STATEN ISLAND
GOVERNOR'S ISLAND
AMBOY
ELIZABETH PORT
ELIZABETH TOWN. MILLVILLE.
ORANGE.
BERGEN.
NEWARK.
BELLVILLE JERSEY CITY.
PATERSON.
HOBOCKEN.
Published by BACHMAN N.º73 Nassau St N Y
Entered according to act of Congress, in the year 1859, by H Bachman in the clerk's office of the district Court of the United States of the Southern district of NY
Printed by C. FATZER 216 William St NY

(LEFT) NEW YORK AND ENVIRONS, 1859: In John Bachmann's dizzying aerial view we may construct New York as the world—not altogether differently from Saul Steinberg's modern-day *New Yorker* map of New York and the hinterlands west of the Hudson. On a microcosmic level, note that the water surrounding Castle Garden in earlier views has now been replaced by landfill. Also, Brooklyn seems more populous. GIFT OF JAMES DUANE TAYLOR. 31.24.

VIEW ON THE HARLEM RIVER, NY. THE HIGHBRIDGE IN THE DISTANCE, 1852: Depicted in the foreground is the Macomb's Dam Bridge (erected in 1813) and, at right, Robert Macomb's tollhouse on the Morrisania side. This dam-bridge was demolished in 1858 but the High Bridge, shown in the distance, still stands, though vastly altered (in 1927 the stone piers were replaced by steel). High Bridge was completed in 1848 as part of the plan to bring water to the city via the Croton Aqueduct System. This lithograph presents a puzzle, as it appeared in 1852 under this title and Currier's sole imprint, with Fanny Palmer as the artist. It also reappeared some years later (post-1856) with a credit to Currier & Ives. In a further complication, it also appeared in 1852 under another title: "Bass Fishing at Macomb's Dam, Harlem River, N.Y." LITHOGRAPH BY NATHANIEL CURRIER. THE HARRY T. PETERS COLLECTION. 57.300.68.

BROOKS CLOTHING STORE, CATHARINE STREET, NY, 1845: The firm of Brooks Brothers, so long familiar to New Yorkers for its flagship store on Madison Avenue, and now many other locations nationally, began life modestly in 1818 at these quarters in Catherine (Catharine) Street. At that time it was known as Brooks Clothing Store. After the death of founder Henry Sands Brooks in 1833, control passed to his son Henry, then in 1850 to his sons Daniel, John, and Elisha—the Brooks Brothers for whom the firm was then renamed. The clothier, the nation's oldest, found new quarters several times before settling into 346 Madison Avenue in 1915. LITHOGRAPH BY GEORGE HAYWARD. PUBLISHED IN *VALENTINE'S MANUAL*, 1864.

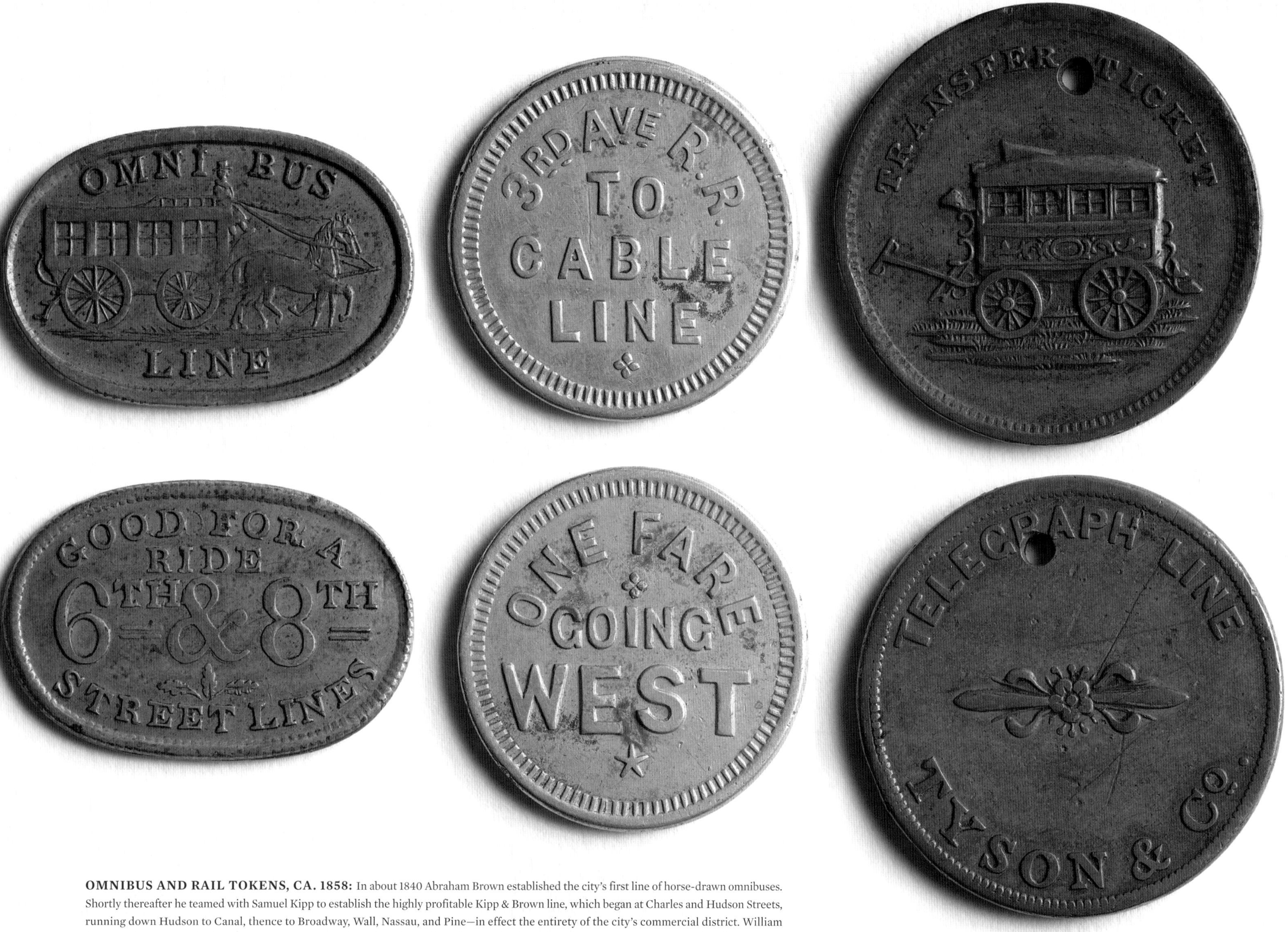

OMNIBUS AND RAIL TOKENS, CA. 1858: In about 1840 Abraham Brown established the city's first line of horse-drawn omnibuses. Shortly thereafter he teamed with Samuel Kipp to establish the highly profitable Kipp & Brown line, which began at Charles and Hudson Streets, running down Hudson to Canal, thence to Broadway, Wall, Nassau, and Pine—in effect the entirety of the city's commercial district. William Tyson & Co.'s Telegraph Line ran twenty-nine stages from the Williamsburg ferry to the foot of Cortlandt Street. In the 1890s the Third Avenue Railroad, a horsecar operator since 1858, built the city's first street-running cable line, in Harlem. MANUSCRIPT COLLECTION.

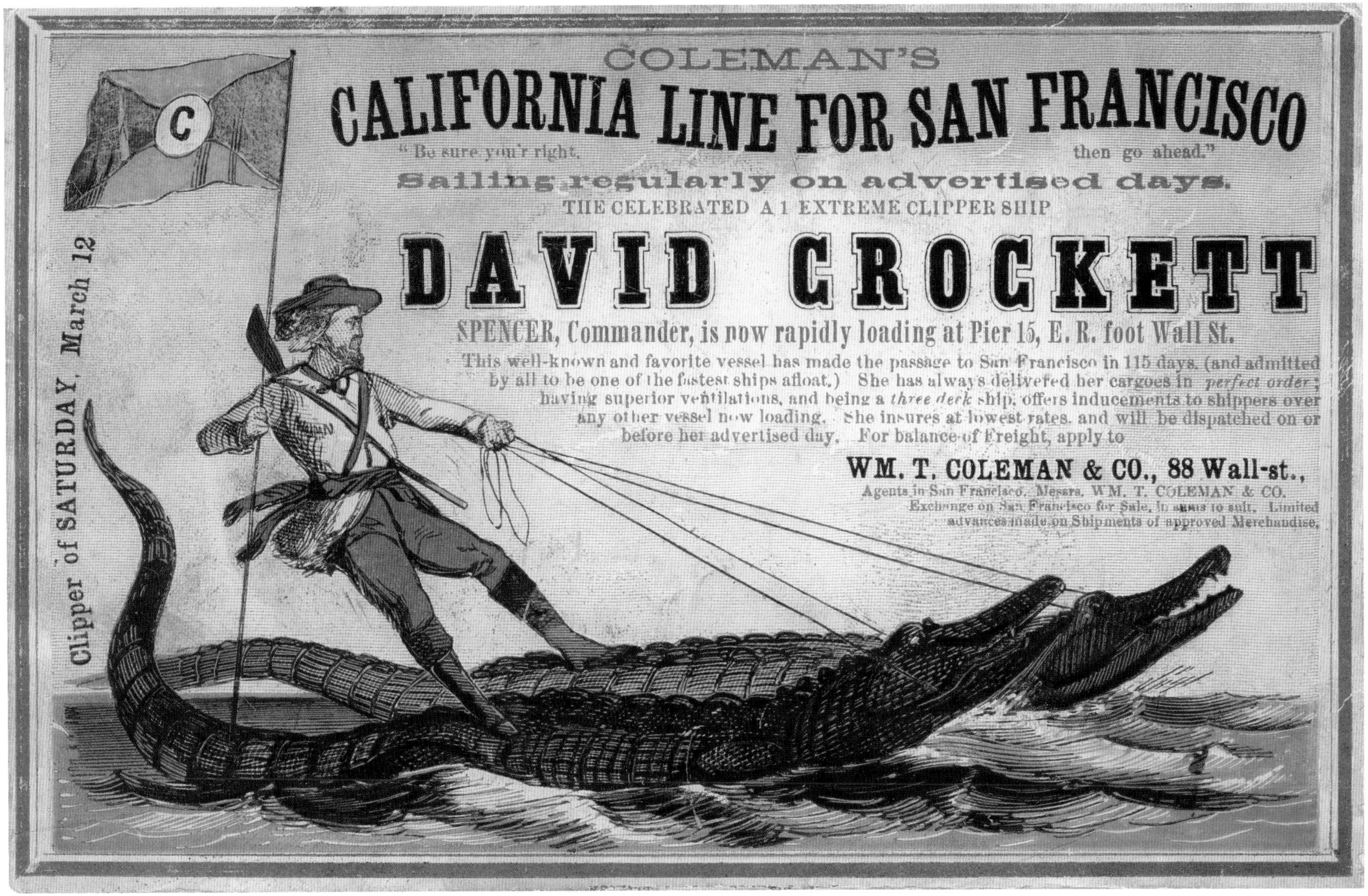

CARD FOR CLIPPER SHIP "DAVID CROCKETT," CA. 1850: In their brief heyday, approximately 1845–55, the big sailing ships pursued speed at almost any cost; a purportedly fast one would be deemed a "clipper." Prospective gold prospectors wanted to get to California fast; freight charges to San Francisco shot up from $10 to $60 a ton; and a profitable run home might include a stop in China. Along New York's South Street, urchins passed out advertising cards like this one, which reads: "Coleman's California line for San Francisco/Sailing regularly on advertised days/The celebrated A1 extreme clipper ship David Crockett/ . . . is now rapidly loading at pier 15 E[ast]. R[iver]. foot Wall St." Note the printing on the card of Davy Crockett's famous motto, "Be always sure you are right, then go ahead." The alligator vignette is echoed in another of Crockett's sayings: "I'm that same David Crockett, fresh from the backwoods, half-horse, half-alligator, a little touched with the snapping turtle; can wade the Mississippi, leap the Ohio, ride upon a streak of lightning, and slip without a scratch down a honey locust [tree]." MANUSCRIPT COLLECTION.

Dr. RICH'S

INSTITUTE

FOR

PHYSICAL EDUCATION.

No. 159 Crosby, near Bleeker St. New York.

ESTABLISHED FOR THE PROMOTION OF HEALTH

BY MEANS OF SYSTEMATIC PHYSICAL TRAINING

JOHN B. RICH, M. D. PRINCIPAL.

LITH. OF WM. ENDICOTT & CO. N. YORK.

(LEFT) DR. RICH'S INSTITUTE FOR PHYSICAL EDUCATION, C. 1850: "There are several things in the first impression of New York which ought to be mentioned: amongst these, the dull complexion and expressionless physiognomy of the common people. Whether their sallow hue and the languor of their looks, so strikingly different from the fresh and ruddy animation of the English, are the effects of a local climate, and of influences peculiar to the situation of the city, I shall not undertake to determine; but unquestionably both the figure and countenance of the Americans improve as you proceed into the interior" (*New Monthly Magazine*, London, 1828). To remedy this situation—and to emulate not only the British but also the German New Yorkers, with their athletic turnvereins, gymnasia began to open in New York. John B. Rich, M.D., founded this austere hall at 159 Crosby Street in the late 1840s, offering red-cheeked health to spindly clerks and sallow drudges like Edgar Allan Poe, who in his last year enrolled as one of Rich's clients. LITHOGRAPHED BY WILLIAM ENDICOTT & CO. THE J. CLARENCE DAVIES COLLECTION. 29.100.2583.

PEYTONA AND FASHION IN THEIR GREAT MATCH FOR $20,000, 1845: The national pastime in 1845 was not yet baseball, or even cricket—it was horse racing and, to a lesser extent, any other contest on which one might lay a bet. The $20,000 purse for this race between the northern horse Fashion and the southern steed Peytona was indeed impressive for a time when "a dollar a day was very good pay"; but the truly staggering figure was the size of the crowd in attendance, estimated at between 70,000 and 100,000. The race was conducted, according to the information in the border, "Over the Union Course L.I. May 13th, 1845. Won by Peytona. Time 7:39 ¾ [and, in the second heat] 7:45 ¼." Charles Severin created this lithograph for Nathaniel Currier in 1845. But when was the work published? No one knows for sure, yet because one other lithograph of the event was copyrighted (by J. Baillie) in June of that year, we might assume that from a commercial standpoint, the image would have been published within months of the race. THE HARRY T. PETERS COLLECTION, 58.300.52.

VIEW OF MURRAY STREET, NEW-YORK, FROM BROADWAY, TO CHURCH STREET, NORTH SIDE, 1855: The photographic street scene was not yet state of the art in 1855, when W. Stephenson issued this print, for long exposures were still required to obtain good effect; the blurry ghosts so often seen in outdoor views before 1860 were testimony to the still primitive nature of the camera. The stop-motion "reality" so brilliantly captured here would, for a little while longer, be the specialty of the artist and lithographer. PUBLISHED BY STEPHENSON & CO. GIFT SARAH F. DE LUZE IN MEMORY OF HER UNCLE JOHN SCHUYLER, C.E. 39.253.3.

VIEW OF LIBERTY-STREET, NEW-YORK, FROM BROADWAY TO GREENWICH STREET, SOUTH SIDE, 1855: This orderly array of buildings and commerce gives no hint of the chaos into which the street had been thrown only two years earlier, thanks to the corporation of the city having permitted the widening of the street and the demolition of the street's last Dutch-gabled buildings. *Putnam's Monthly* had given credit, in 1853, to the spirit of modernization, asserting that "the citizen who remembers this thoroughfare before its alterations . . . would hardly recognize in the handsome, fresh, and almost palatial Liberty-street of 1853, the dusky, tumble-down, and seedy lane, which bore that title in the spring of 1852. . . . One after another the old tenements have disappeared, the bricks painted and unpainted have gone the way of all clay, the narrow windows have been looked out of for the last time, and the small doors have followed the high steps to oblivion, and that 'undiscovered bourne' to which all the rubbish of this great city is carried." PUBLISHED BY STEPHENSON & CO. GIFT OF SARAH F. DE LUZE IN MEMORY OF HER UNCLE JOHN SCHUYLER, C.E. 39.253.2.

BROADWAY, NEW-YORK, FROM CANAL TO GRAND STREET, WEST SIDE, 1856: Of the several incredibly detailed views of New York thoroughfares issued by W. Stephenson & Co., this is one of the two rarest. One was sold at auction in 1913, by the estate of M. C. D. Borden, and its buyer may well have been J. Clarence Davies, a real estate dealer and formidable antiquarian who bequeathed his unequaled collection of prints to the Museum of the City of New York. At the time of the auction only one other example of this view was known to exist.
PUBLISHED BY STEPHENSON & CO. THE J. CLARENCE DAVIES COLLECTION. 29.100.2309.

447
HEWS' PIANOS,
N.P.B.Curtiss.
Glass Wareroom for French Lamps.
Imported French Gas Fixtures.
445
DEPOT of
French Mechanical Lamps.
Warerooms.
H. DARDONVILLE.
ABRAMS & JOHNSON
CROCKERY WARE.
PIANO FORTES.
PIANOS to let.
447
DAVIS COLLAMORE
China & Glass.
LONDON & PARIS FANCY GOODS
Steam Refined Candy.
H.N.WILD.
453
BURNS TRAINQUE & Co
Cabinet Ware House.
453 BURNS TRAINQUE & Co 453
Mc GRAW & ALLENDORPH
Cabinet & Upholstery Ware House
455 McGRAW & ALLENDORPH 455
J. BOWLES
French Corsets
Wholesale & Retail.
Mrs BOWLES.
Sweet Chocolate
FACTORY.
FELIX EFFRAY 457
Gentlements
Furnishing Goods
JAS W. FAULK
PLYMOUTH HOUSE
BROADWAY 6th AVENUE

CHAPTER VII | 1861–1875

STREET FIGHT

THE DRAFT RIOTS OF 1863

OWEN GUTFREUND

THE NEW YORK CITY DRAFT RIOTS OF 1863 WERE THE DEADLIEST RIOTS IN THE HISTORY OF THE UNITED STATES. THEY CONTINUED UNCONTROLLED FOR FOUR DAYS, INVOLVING TENS OF THOUSANDS OF RIOTERS. BY THE TIME UNION TROOPS BROUGHT IN FROM GETTYSBURG RESTORED ORDER, THERE WERE MORE THAN A HUNDRED DEATHS AND COUNTLESS INJURIES.* THE LIST OF DECEASED INCLUDED MANY AFRICAN-AMERICANS BEATEN TO DEATH BY MOBS, AS WELL AS BY POLICEMEN, SOLDIERS, AND RIOTERS WHO HAD FOUGHT THROUGHOUT THE CITY, FROM RIVER TO RIVER. THE VIOLENCE STARTED ON THE MORNING OF MONDAY, JULY 13—BUT TENSIONS HAD BEEN MOUNTING SINCE THE BEGINNING OF THE CIVIL WAR, MORE THAN TWO YEARS EARLIER. MANY NEW YORKERS VIEWED THE WAR AS A POLITICAL BATTLE UNRELATED TO THEIR OWN CONCERNS. TO BE CERTAIN, THERE WERE NUMEROUS ABOLITIONISTS AND OTHER ENTHUSIASTIC SUPPORTERS OF THE UNION CAUSE IN THE CITY, BUT THERE WERE ALSO MANY—INCLUDING LARGE CONTINGENTS OF IRISH IMMIGRANTS—WHO WERE ALREADY ENGAGED IN THEIR OWN DAILY BATTLE TO EARN A LIVING, AND WERE UNINTERESTED IN SETTING ASIDE THESE STRUGGLES TO FIGHT A WAR THAT WOULD ENABLE FREED SLAVES TO COMPETE WITH THEM IN THE LABOR MARKET. EARLY IN THE WAR, MAYOR FERNANDO WOOD RESPONDED TO THESE SENTIMENTS BY SUGGESTING, IN A SPEECH TO THE COMMON COUNCIL, THAT NEW YORK CITY SHOULD ITSELF SECEDE AND BECOME A free-trade republic. This came to naught, but opposition to the war continued to fester in the city. Labor strife also grew throughout the war, as real wages for many immigrant laborers declined, and there were periodic strikes across the city, affecting many different trades and industries. In some instances, free blacks stepped forward as replacement workers, exacerbating racial hostility.

Politicians and newspaper editors, with increasing frequency, gave voice to these mounting tensions. Manton Marble, editor of the *World*, published an editorial in early June proclaiming that the recently enacted Conscription Act—the first-ever federal military draft—was a violation of fundamental civil rights. The law required all men between the ages of twenty and thirty-five to register as potential draftees, as well as all single men between thirty-six and forty-five. The draft itself would then be decided by lottery drawings held throughout the country, district by district. The measure sparked fierce opposition, not just from partisan Democratic politicians, but also from the many struggling immigrants uncommitted to the Union cause. Just days before the first draft lottery, Democratic Governor Horatio Seymour, in a speech that was reprinted in sympathetic newspapers such as the *Daily News*, fanned the flames by warning that President Abraham Lincoln's policies could lead to mob resistance. At a well-attended rally, speakers denounced the war and the draft, drawing particular attention to the provision that allowed for draftees to purchase exemptions for $300 (a year's wages for many immigrants). This was, they argued, becoming a war fought by poor immigrants, at the behest of abolitionists and rich businessmen, to allow blacks to take their jobs for lower wages.

On the morning of Saturday, July 11, federal officials convened the first lottery at the Ninth District Provost Marshall's Office, on Third Avenue between 46th and 47th Streets. As the name of each selected draftee was called out, the assembled crowd of registrants and family members murmured and groaned. By the end of the day, 1,236 names had been called, and plans were announced to resume on Monday morning to fill the district's quota of 2,000 draftees. The names of the drafted men were published in the Sunday newspapers, and throughout the city groups of grumbling New Yorkers gathered to discuss the draft. As a sign of things to come, one angry gang tried to set fire to several homes in an African-American neighborhood on Carmine Street. Tensions that had been simmering now rose to a boil, ready to unleash a furious torrent of violence targeted at the city's free blacks, abolitionists, and Republican elites.

Violence erupted Monday morning. Gangs of angry men began to march down the streets in groups, gathering others as they passed. As these mobs passed factories and businesses across the city, laborers stopped working to join. One large group of protesters converged on the Ninth District Provost Marshall's Office, where officials were preparing to resume the lottery drawings. On their way, marchers destroyed telegraph poles to delay calls for help, raided hardware stores to steal axes and crowbars, and disrupted streetcar service by derailing a car on one line and pulling up the tracks on another. By 8 AM, the angry crowd already numbered in the thousands.

Draft officials sent soldiers to protect the Ninth District office, and also to the Eighth, where a second lottery was scheduled to begin. Police Superintendent John Kennedy dispatched sixty policemen to the Ninth and seventy to the Eighth. The assembled crowd, though, was not going to give way easily before uniformed forces. The fiery resistance first became apparent when James Crowley, a police telegraph system manager who had been riding the now derailed streetcar, attempted to repair damaged telegraph wires. Rioters attacked him, and he was barely able to escape and contact the central office. Kennedy sent out more police officers as reinforcements and called out all available reserves from both New York City and Brooklyn. He himself went to investigate the scene at the Ninth District draft office. However, before he could even get there, a crowd swarmed his buggy, beating, stripping, and robbing the driver. Kennedy himself was also beaten badly, so that his second in command, Commissioner Thomas Acton, had to take control of the police force. It was only mid-morning of the first day of a riot that would go on for more than four days and already the police were overwhelmed. Mayor George Opdyke turned to the state militia for help.

The draft still proceeded at the Ninth District, under the watchful protection of police. Then a group of incensed volunteer firemen arrived, upset because one of their members had been selected on Saturday—they thought that firemen ought to have been exempted. The firemen set the building on fire, and were joined by the mob in sacking the place. The assembled policemen were barely able to save the draft officials and their documents from the blaze. When militiamen arrived to help restore order, they too were attacked and pelted with rocks. A melee ensued and shots were fired. Several rioters were killed and many more were injured, but the mob successfully disarmed the soldiers, killing three of them and wounding others in the process. One of the soldiers was chased down, several blocks away, then kicked and beaten until his skull was fractured and his arm broken. As additional police reinforcements arrived, the crowd chased them away, too.

The draft offices were not the only target—because the unrest was not just about the draft; it was also about the war, about race, and about labor strife. Throughout the city, mobs gathered to voice their displeasure and to enumerate their complaints. One such location was the home of General George B. McClellan, the former top Union commander who would soon run for president as the Democratic candidate opposing Abraham Lincoln. Here, they only called for McClellan's endorsement, whereas when crowds gathered at the homes of well-known Republicans, they would chase out the inhabitants, vandalizing the homes and stealing possessions. Some rioters gathered at Printing House Square, where the city's newspapers were published. They cheered in front of Democratic newspapers such as the *Daily News*, and booed Republican dailies such as the *Tribune*. They called for Horace Greeley, the famous abolitionist editor of the *Tribune*, and threatened to kill him. Other mobs marauded along the waterfronts, calling themselves "longshoremen's association committees," searching for black men working on the piers.

Mob targets also included strategic military facilities. One group of protesters assembled to attack the Union Steam Works, an arms factory owned by a well-known Republican related to Mayor Opdyke. Here a large group of policemen, two hundred strong, successfully fought off repeated attacks from rioters. One block away, another mob—estimated by one observer to include several thousand rioters—surrounded the state armory. They threw rocks, broke the windows, tried to break down the doors, and attempted to burn down the brick building. The police stationed inside opened fire, killing some of the attackers. But, by mid-afternoon, as the angry mob grew, the guards fled; first to a local precinct house, until a crowd threatened this location, too. The mob finally forced its way into the now unguarded armory and started to steal the weapons. Fortunately, though, reinforcing police arrived just at that moment and retook the building, beating escaping looters.

City officials were in a panic. Mayor Opdyke asked for help from all directions, sending urgent requests to the governors of New Jersey, Connecticut, and Rhode Island, as well as city officials in Newark, Albany, Utica, and Rochester. He put out a public call asking for all able-bodied men to either return to work or to volunteer as "special police." Officials reacted with alarm in Washington as well. They decided to suspend the draft, but opted not to publicize this decision, lest it look as though they had capitulated. All available federal troops near the city were sent to help, but few were close enough to arrive quickly.

Throughout the day, the authorities were unable to restore order. There were too many mobs spread across the city, assaulting widely dispersed targets. Small gangs roamed Manhattan, attacking homes, shops, bars, brothels, and tenements suspected of harboring blacks or being congenial to them. These bands beat black men they encountered, in some instances hanging them from trees or lampposts. Landlords evicted black tenants to prevent arson or other violence. Rioters set fire to a house owned by Postmaster Abram Wakeman, a Republican. Late Monday afternoon, about five hundred men attacked an orphanage that cared for African-American children. They broke down the front door with an ax and set fire to the building. Within just a few minutes, the entire building was engulfed but, fortunately, the 237 children living there escaped by a rear exit.

Neither the police nor the militia were equipped or trained for this situation. Militia under the command of Colonel Henry O'Brien fired a howitzer to disperse a mob on Second Avenue, and in the process killed an innocent bystander and her child. Later that night, angry rioters found O'Brien's home and burned it down. In many instances, mobs would disperse or run away when confronted, only to return after the militia or police had moved on to another conflict. The Eighth District Provost Marshall's Office was a casualty of this tactic, set ablaze after military defenders were called away. Similarly, rioters attacking the offices of the *Tribune* returned soon after being dispersed by police, and then besieged the building again. The owners of *The New York Times* took matters into their own hands, scaring away attackers with two Gatling guns borrowed from the Army.

The rioting continued on Tuesday, with more violent and deadly clashes as both sides became more numerous, better armed, and more aggressive. In one instance, three hundred police were dispatched to respond to a particularly large crowd that had set fire to a number of buildings at 34th Street and Second Avenue. Rioters assailed the police as they arrived, throwing bricks and stones from rooftops. The police retaliated by opening fire and engaging the protesters in hand-to-hand combat in the street. The militia arrived, armed, to reinforce the police. By mid-morning, Second Avenue was littered with dead bodies. Another throng, also numbering in the thousands, gathered near the Lower East Side and clashed with federal troops, which responded by opening fire, killing fourteen rioters and wounding seven. The increased willingness of the authorities to use their weapons prompted rioters to seek their own firearms, looting gun shops or trying to raid armories. Meanwhile, even as big battles occurred across the city, small gangs continued to roam the city, still burning businesses in black neighborhoods, destroying railroad and streetcar tracks, vandalizing and sometimes burning the homes of well-known Republicans, and beating and killing any black men they could find. One mob set upon a black church and hacked at it with axes.

Colonel O'Brien (the officer who had fired the howitzer at a crowd the day before) was badly beaten by a mob when he returned to inspect his burned and looted home. Later, when O'Brien went to a drugstore to purchase medical supplies to tend to his injuries, he carried a gun to ward off another attack. A woman recognized him, and threw a rock at him; he responded by shooting near her feet to warn her away; the bullet ricocheted and wounded someone else nearby on the street. The crowd rushed in on O'Brien, beating him for hours before finally hanging him from a lamppost.

At noon a big crowd returned to the Union Steam Works, the Republican-owned arms factory. For a short while, rioters were able to take control of the building and the surrounding area. Using weapons taken from inside, they repelled at least one attempt by the police to remove them. A concerted effort by police and a company of the Twelfth U.S. Infantry regained access to the building long enough to take all the remaining munitions—including about a thousand rifles—before retreating, under attack along the way. Troops from the Twelfth Infantry were also involved in another battle on Fifth Avenue, where a mob had gathered to burn mansions. Along with sixty policemen, the soldiers engaged the crowd, and within minutes more than forty rioters were dead or severely injured. The rest fled.

While policemen and soldiers battled to restore order in the streets, some politicians and city leaders were also at work responding to the tumult. Secretary of War Edwin Stanton, in response to a plea from Mayor Opdyke, ordered five regiments of Union soldiers to march to the city to put down the riots. On Wall Street, leading bankers and merchants met and made plans to recruit volunteers to reinforce the police force, and also called for the imposition of martial law. Church leaders, though, were notably silent. A few priests and ministers spoke to some of the crowds, but when they did so their calls for an end to the violence were tempered by outspoken opposition to the draft and demands that the mayor pay the commutation fees of all draftees. Governor Seymour traveled around the city with an entourage of other recognizable Democratic politicians, including "Boss" William Marcy Tweed. He called for an end to the draft, and promised to protect the rights of any men who stopped rioting. These speeches elicited cheers from assembled crowds but did little to quell the violence. Meanwhile, behind closed doors, Seymour argued against martial law, which would bring the biggest city in his state under federal, and therefore Republican, control.

The riots showed no signs of abating. At sunset Tuesday, mobs tried to erect fortified barricades across Ninth Avenue to prevent the authorities from using the thoroughfare. A company of soldiers and policemen stormed the barricades, eventually scattering the crowd. Later that evening, armed rioters returned to the Union Steam Works, and to the 18th Precinct Police Station, setting both buildings ablaze again.

Marauding gangs continued to hunt down more black men on Wednesday. Rob Costello, a shoemaker, was beaten, stoned, and hanged—then his body was dragged through the streets. Abraham Franklin, a coachman, was dragged out of his house and hanged. Charles Jackson, a hotel waiter caught trying to escape by boat across the Hudson River, was beaten, stripped naked, and thrown into the river to drown. White men who helped blacks were also targeted. A mob burned the house of Josiah Porter, an Irish Protestant Republican. Another group targeted a German abattoir-owner who had prevented the burning of a black family's home. Yet another gang hunted a white woman married to a black man. In at least one instance, racially motivated incidents extended beyond blacks; downtown rioters targeted Chinese men suspected of having relations with white women.

Although more soldiers arrived in the city to put down the riots on Wednesday and Thursday, armed conflicts with crowds of rioters continued. Even as the authorities became more organized and effective in combating the mobs, so too were the rioters increasingly better armed and strategic, successfully establishing strongholds and armories of their own (an early-morning Army raid on a house on 32nd Street and Broadway yielded a horde of seventy-three rifles). The mobs laid traps for soldiers and police, pelting them from rooftops with bricks, stones, and gunfire. These encounters typically resulted in bloodshed, with both rioters and soldiers dead and wounded. Near Gramercy Park, patrolling soldiers were shot by snipers. The surviving troops retreated—but they returned with reinforcements to retrieve the dead body of a comrade. After snipers again shot at them from nearby rooftops, they systematically entered buildings and killed or captured the shooters. There were numerous casualties, on both sides. Jackson's Iron foundry, on Second Avenue at 28th Street, became the site of an extended conflict that started Wednesday morning and lasted until Friday morning. Two companies of the National Guard, buttressed by police and army reinforcements, defended the plant from a large and determined crowd, 4,000 strong. When newly arrived Union troops arrived to reinforce the plant Thursday morning, they found it besieged and had to shoot their way through the crowd using howitzers. Rioters who repeatedly tried to take control of the building or to set fire to it were repelled by gunfire.

Some city leaders tried to calm the rioters by responding to their concerns. On Wednesday morning, the Board of Alderman and Common Council approved a $2.5 million Draft Exemption Fund, to cover the $300 commutation fee for every draftee from the city. The city would raise the money by issuing "Conscription Exemption Bonds." The costly measure was vetoed by Mayor Opdyke, who supported a limited effort to relieve isolated hardship cases.

The riots finally began to wind down late on Thursday when Governor Seymour sent word to the crowd that the draft had been suspended, after he learned of rioters' intention to attack the state arsenal at the Seventh Regiment Armory. The undertaking was planned despite the growing presence of heavily armed, battle-hardened federal troops, many of which came straight from Gettysburg, now defending such sites. The crowd cheered when they heard news of the suspended draft, and then dispersed. By the next morning, Friday, Union soldiers had firmly secured all of the strategic targets in the city and patrolled the main thoroughfares. Only then, after the riots had lost steam, did Archbishop John Hughes speak out publicly, at last advising the public not to riot, but rather to resist the draft through legal and constitutional protest. That same afternoon, a group of Republicans created the "Committee of Merchants for the Relief of Colored People," to help the African-American community that had been so devastated by the riots.

Thus ended one of the darkest moments in New York City's history. For the better part of a week in the summer of 1863, the nation's greatest city was ravaged by uncontrolled violence. What had started as an anti-draft protest quickly grew into a complex mix of deadly anti-war protest, working class upheaval, partisan political battle, and brutally violent race riot.

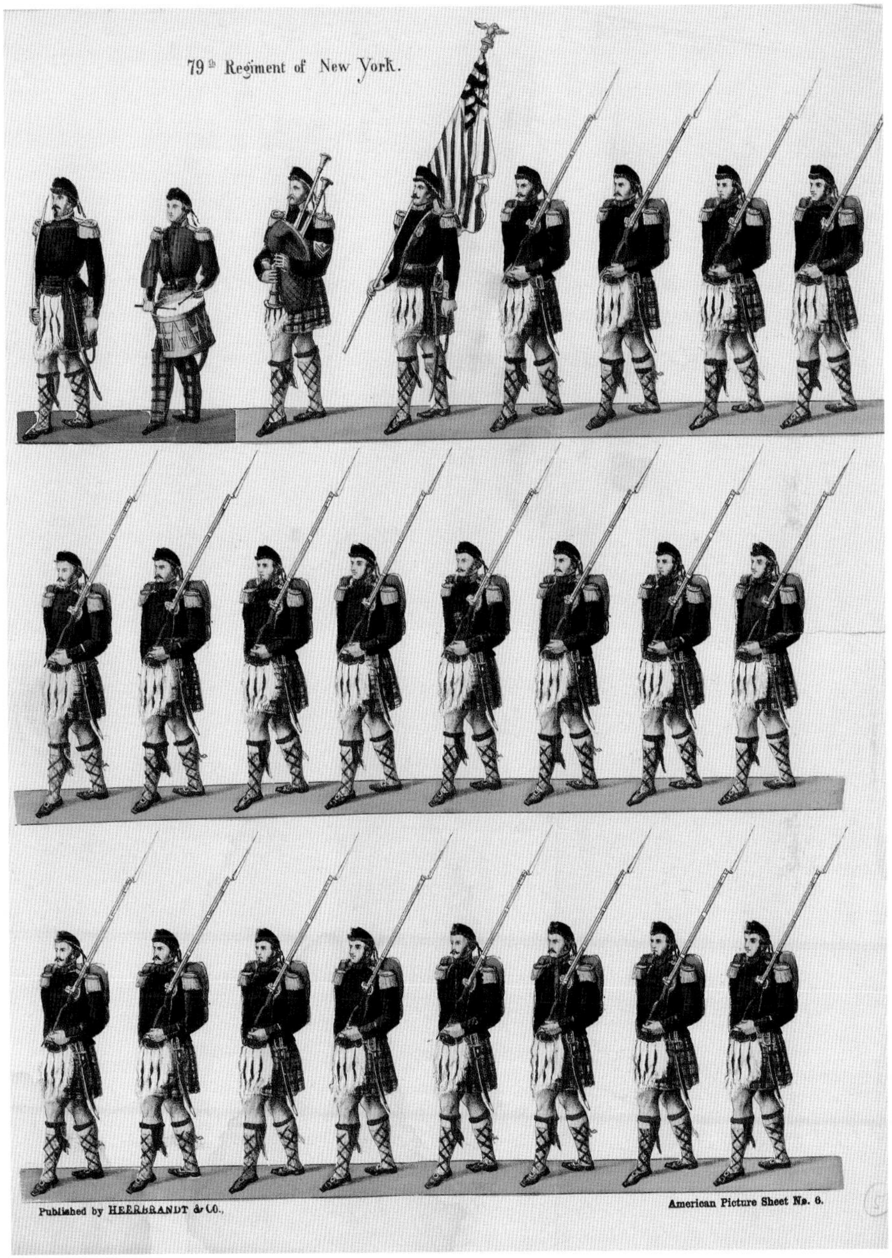

79TH REGIMENT OF NEW YORK "PAPER DOLLS," CA. 1862: In the years before the Confederates fired upon Fort Sumter, when war still seemed a grand and glorious game, regiments of the New York State Militia adopted thematic costuming, as if they were marching off to a parade. The era produced the ballooning Zouave trousers adopted by many regiments of the North and the South, the tasseled Corsican cap, and, for the 79th New York Volunteers, full Scottish regalia as they called themselves the "Cameron Highlanders." Once war was declared, however, the 79th turned serious and distinguished itself by being the first New York regiment to answer President Lincoln's call for volunteers. A small province of the voluminous ephemera of the Civil War embraces these paper-doll cutouts of the jaunty Highlanders, published by Gustav Heerbrandt of William Street. During the war he and the McLoughlin Brothers issued more than a dozen such picture sheets depicting different New York regiments. THE HARRY T. PETERS COLLECTION. 57.300.550.

OWEN GUTFREUND IS A PROFESSOR OF HISTORY AND URBAN STUDIES AT COLUMBIA UNIVERSITY. IN ADDITION TO HIS WORK ON THE NEW YORK CITY DRAFT RIOTS, HIS RECENT PUBLICATIONS INCLUDE *TWENTIETH CENTURY SPRAWL: HIGHWAYS AND THE RESHAPING OF THE AMERICAN LANDSCAPE* (OXFORD UNIVERSITY PRESS, 2005) AND "REBUILDING NEW YORK IN THE AUTO AGE: ROBERT MOSES AND HIS HIGHWAYS" IN *ROBERT MOSES AND THE MODERN CITY* (W.W. NORTON, 2007). HE IS CURRENTLY WORKING ON *CITIES TAKE FLIGHT*, A BOOK ABOUT CITIES AND THEIR AIRPORTS WHICH WILL BE PUBLISHED BY UNIVERSITY OF CHICAGO PRESS.

DEPARTURE OF THE 69TH REGIMENT, NEW YORK STATE MILITIA, 1861: On April 23, 1861, the 69th Regiment set off for war in the South amid the cheers of the Irish contingent around St. Patrick's Cathedral, at that time located at the corner of Prince and Mott Streets. One carriage for dignitaries bears the sign, "No North, No South, No East, No West, But One Whole Union." Three months later, on July 21, "The Fighting Irish," as the Regiment was called, distinguished themselves at the First Battle of Bull Run (Manassas). Their commander, Michael Corcoran, was captured and kept in Confederate prisons for thirteen months until exchanged in August, 1862. LITHOGRAPH BY SARONY, MAJOR & KNAPP FOR *VALENTINE'S MANUAL*, 1862.

FIFTH AVENUE HOTEL, CA. 1861: In 1859 Amos R. Eno built this six-story marble palace on Fifth Avenue between 23rd and 24th Streets, fronting Madison Square on the site of an old favorite roadhouse, Colonel Thompson's Madison Cottage. Eno's Folly, as it was called, offered its clientele "more than one hundred suites of apartments, each combining the convenience and luxury of parlor, chamber, dressing, and bathing rooms." The grand hotel was one of the targets in the Confederate arson plot of November 25, 1864, in which the city's noblest buildings were to be torched in a terrorist attempt to extort a favorable end to the Civil War. The Fifth Avenue Hotel also added a "perpendicular railway intersecting each story"—in other words, an elevator. Often referred to as the city's first, the hotel's lift was at best the second, for Elisha Graves Otis had installed one at the Haughwout department store at Broadway and Broome (still standing) two years earlier. He had also demonstrated an elevator at the 1853 Crystal Palace, and in the same year a steam elevator took visitors to the first and second landings of the Latting Observatory. The view in this extremely rare lithograph by John Henry Bufford, published by C. Brothers, was nearly the same as one used in 1859 for a song sheet, "The Fifth Avenue Hotel Polka Brilliant." THE J. CLARENCE DAVIES COLLECTION. 29.100.2282.

MARTEL'S NEW YORK CENTRAL PARK.

RESPECTFULLY DEDICATED TO THE PARK COMMISSIONERS.

(LEFT) MARTEL'S NEW YORK CENTRAL PARK, RESPECTFULLY DEDICATED TO THE PARK COMMISSIONERS, 1864: At the time this print was published, New York's great experiment to bring Arcadian vistas and fresh air to the toiling masses had barely begun. Phelps Stokes noted that this aerial view of the park from 59th Street looking north was "interesting especially for its depiction of the park six years after the work of improvement was begun, and also as showing Fifth Avenue in its undeveloped state. . . ." The lithograph depicts the only building then in the entire park below 105th Street, the Arsenal, today at 64th Street. Yet when the entrepreneurs of the Central Park Publishing Company took "Martel's Great Picture of Central Park" on the road, it was a national event. Selling by subscription having begun on December 12, 1864, the firm's agents exhibited the picture not only in New York but also in Boston, Philadelphia, Washington D.C., Cincinnati, Chicago, and San Francisco. Particularly telling was an advertisement in San Francisco's *Daily Evening Bulletin*: "The model from which the outline drawings were made cost over two years of patient toil, and a corps of artists have been many months engaged in reproducing, with life-like fidelity, a perfect and accurate facsimile of this the most beautiful Park in the world. . . . Our efforts to produce a picture of which every American may be proud, as representing this, 'The Eden of America,' have been most kindly noticed by the Press throughout the country." The first name of the artist Martel is unknown. The lithographer is Joseph C. Geissler. Henry C. Eno is the printer, and William H. Shields the publisher. THE J. CLARENCE DAVIES COLLECTION. 29.100.2568.

THE OLD PEAR-TREE PLANTED BY PETRUS STUYVESANT, 1861: Upon his return from Holland after the surrender to the English, Petrus Stuyvesant settled into the life of a gentleman farmer on his Great Bowery estate. A pear tree he had reportedly (there is no contemporary documentation) brought over from Holland in 1667 stood at the northeast corner of Third Avenue and 13th Street, bearing fruit for nearly two centuries. In 1856 Henry Webb Dunshee penned: "The forests dense that graced the land ere Hudson ploug'd the wave,/ Which once were travers'd fearlessly, by the Manhattan brave; The orchard trees, around whose base, such golden fruits were strewn,/Are gone—all gone—forevermore;—and thou art left alone." In 1867 the old pear tree was overthrown in a collision with a truck. LITHOGRAPH BY SARONY, MAJOR & KNAPP, ILLUSTRATION FOR *VALENTINE'S MANUAL*, 1861.

Lith. of Sarony, Major & Knapp, 449 Broadway, N.Y.
for D.T. Valentine's Manual 1861
THE OLD PEAR-TREE PLANTED BY GOVERNOR STUYVESANT,
Cor 3d Ave & 13th St.

STATE ARSENAL IN CENTRAL PARK, 57TH STREET, TROOPS LEAVING FOR THE WAR, 1861: This arsenal at 64th Street was already outmoded as a military facility when the Civil War broke out in 1861. Built by Martin Euclid Thompson, it had been an auxiliary headquarters for the Seventh "Silk Stocking" Regiment since 1848. Although it was vacated by them in 1857 when the city claimed the building for its new Central Park, the arsenal continued as a military storage center in the early years of the war. It subsequently became a museum (precursor to the American Museum of Natural History), a weather bureau, and an art gallery. It also served as a makeshift zoo until 1870, when the Central Park Menagerie was given more permanent grounds behind the Arsenal. Today it serves as headquarters for the Parks Department. LITHOGRAPH BY SARONY, MAJOR & KNAPP FOR *VALENTINE'S MANUAL*, 1862.

HARLEM-LANE, FROM CENTRAL PARK TO MANHATTANVILLE, 1865: Printed on border is "the old landmarks on Manhattan Island." While the title featured the brand new Central Park, the view depicts the ancient road that had been a favorite with New Yorkers since 1707, when the old Native American trail was formally laid out by the city. Extending from the northern boundary of Central Park to 145th Street along what is today St. Nicholas Avenue, the rural roadway let the trotters of such sportsmen as Commodore Vanderbilt and Robert Bonner really "open up" as they exited the Park. At 168th Street, the Harlem Lane racecourse met with another carriage track that ran along the Harlem River up to the High Bridge at 174th Street. This offshoot of Harlem Lane became known as the Harlem River Speedway, and ultimately the Harlem River Drive. LITHOGRAPH BY MAJOR & KNAPP FOR *VALENTINE'S MANUAL*, 1865.

VIEW OF THE BREVOORT ESTATE AND VICINITY, BETWEEN 54TH AND 55TH STREETS, NEAR FIRST AVENUE, 1866: John Flavel Mines wrote in 1893, "The old shot-tower yet looms up hard by the foot of Fifty-third Street, and people who wish to speak of the neighborhood begin as of yore with the preface: 'You know where the old shot-tower is,' as if everybody had known it from infancy [it dated to 1821]. Close by . . . stands a house that is a perfect specimen of the Dutch architecture of two centuries ago, and is probably the oldest building in the city [it dated to 1712]. Long before the War of the Revolution it was known as the Spring Valley farm-house. Outside, the walls are clapboarded, but an inside view discloses the massive stone and the huge cross-beams hewed out of solid oak." The tower survived into the twentieth century but the farmhouse did not. LITHOGRAPH BY MAJOR & KNAPP FOR *VALENTINE'S MANUAL*, 1866.

PROPOSED ARCADE RAILWAY UNDER BROADWAY; VIEW NEAR WALL STREET, 1869: Plans for elevated railways in New York go back as far as John Stevens's plan of 1832. In 1867, however, a New York State Senate special commission recommended "underground railroads" as the best way to reduce New York City's congestion. "Projected" by Melville C. Smith, a member of the State Senate, and approved by the legislature on four occasions, it was vetoed by the governor each time. By 1888 Melville had launched a company for which $25 million in capital was pledged, but again for naught. His plan was never implemented, and he died a frustrated visionary in 1898. Two years later, construction commenced for a subway that would run under Broadway. DRAWING BY JOHN M. AUGUST WILL. LITHOGRAPH BY FERDINAND MAYER & SONS. THE J. CLARENCE DAVIES COLLECTION. 29.100.2400.

SKATING IN CENTRAL PARK, 1865: In 1863, only five years after adopting the Greensward Plan of Frederick Law Olmsted and Calvert Vaux, Central Park's commissioners noted the aesthetic consonance between skating and the park's landscaping: "The movements of a throng of skaters, on a clear day, chasing each other over the crystal ceiling of the imprisoned lake, & the dusky foliage of the fir and pine on the adjacent heights, wrapped with wreathes of fleecy white; leafless branches strung with a fairy network of icy pearls & form in our midst a winter scene unmatched by that of any capital or country of modern times." OIL ON CANVAS BY JOHANN MENGELS CULVERHOUSE, 33 x 47. THE J. CLARENCE DAVIES COLLECTION. 29.100.1301.

W. C. ROGERS

FOR JOS. SHANNON'S M

Interior View of Tammany Hall Decorated for the National Convention July 4th 1868.

(LEFT) **INTERIOR VIEW OF TAMMANY HALL DECORATED FOR THE NATIONAL CONVENTION, JULY 4TH, 1868:** The Democrats of Tammany Hall went all out for the national ticket in 1868, supporting favorite son Horatio Seymour hopelessly against Republican Ulysses S. Grant. And the locals had a grand new hall to show off—on the north side of 14th Street, between Third Avenue and Irving Place. The new Tammany Hall was so grand that it was able to accommodate a theater within its confines—Tony Pastor's, which operated there beginning in 1877. This lavish room was demolished in 1928 along with the rest of the block to make way for Consolidated Edison's office expansion. This lithograph is by W. C. Rogers for *Joseph Shannon's Manual*, 1868. David Thomas Valentine fell ill in 1866, so no manual was issued for the following year, but in 1868 new city clerk Shannon picked up the baton and issued a large-format successor to the long-running *Valentine's Manual* (1841–66). PRINT ARCHIVES.

PLAYBILL FOR THE FIRST PERFORMANCE OF *THE BLACK CROOK*, 1866: Many historians cite *The Black Crook* as the progenitor of both the Broadway musical and the burlesque hall. The *New York Times* dismissed the play's melodramatic aspects as "rubbish" but added that "Scenic art has never, within our knowledge, been so amply and splendidly exemplified." Unclear is whether the unnamed reviewer was referring to the painted backdrops or the scantily clad ballet troupe, whose bare legs created both a scandal and a smash hit: *The Black Crook* ran for sixteen months. The *New York Clipper* (forerunner of *Variety*), versified its praise for the play's star: "O, who could be better,/ Than Marie Bonifanti?/ Tho' her clothing is scanty,/ She's the card to a letter/ For any establishment./ Ah, who could withstand her/ Light foot and white hand, her/ Every soft blandishment?" *The Black Crook* became a warhorse road show, frequently revived over the decades to follow. This historic playbill is for the play's opening night, at Niblo's Garden on September 12, 1866. ANONYMOUS GIFT. 42.471.

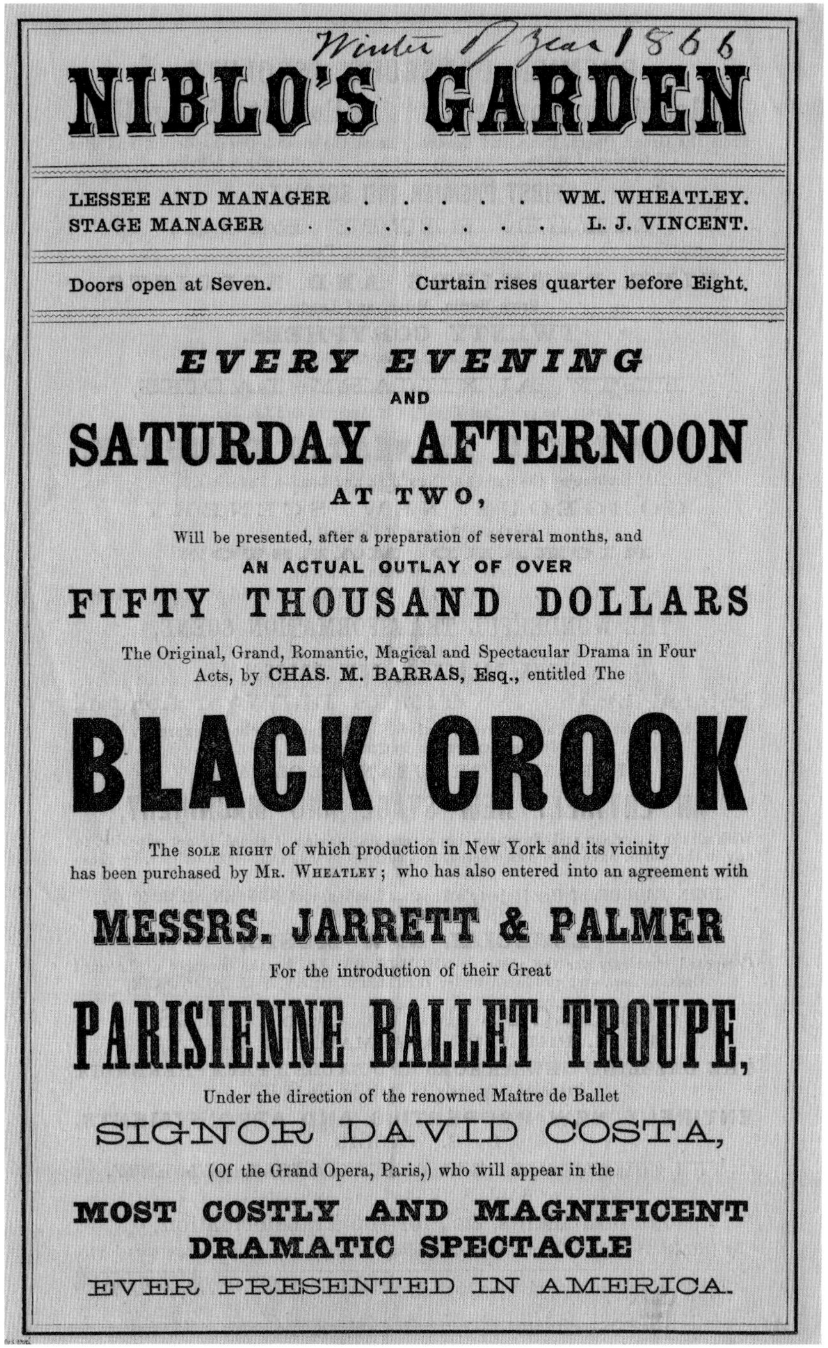

BEACH'S PNEUMATIC SUBWAY, 1870: This woodcut depicts one of the more romantic experiments in New York City history. In 1867, at the American Institute Fair at the 14th Street Armory, Alfred Ely Beach, co-publisher with his brother of the *New York Sun*, demonstrated the principles of his proposed pneumatic railway system—the propulsion of a subway car by the pneumatic pressure and vacuum created by a huge steam-powered blower. In the following year clandestine digging commenced in the basement of Devlin's Clothing Store on Warren Street, under the guise of creating small tubes for moving mail pneumatically. (Beach had not been able to win approval for his project without paying a bribe to the Tweed Ring. It defies reason to think that the entire tunnel could be constructed in secrecy, so perhaps at some point an accommodation with the city was reached.) On February 26, 1870 a working subway was inaugurated. It consisted of a single car that, for five cents, would transport up to twenty-two passengers underneath Broadway from Warren Street to Murray Street. The Warren Street station was rather lavish, featuring a goldfish fountain, grand piano, and zircon lighting. The Murray Street terminus was decidedly Spartan: only a ladder up the shaft to the street. By 1873 Beach's Pneumatic Railway was closed for lack of patronage and was more or less forgotten. In 1912, however, workers digging the BMT (Brooklyn–Manhattan Transit) subway tunnel under Broadway came upon Beach's tunnel with its underground fountain and candelabra—and his original pneumatic car, still on its tracks. PRINT ARCHIVES.

CHARLES T. HARVEY, FIRST ELEVATED TRAIN, 1867: In this year Charles T. Harvey built the prototype of the West Side and Yonkers Patent Railway Company, an experimental elevated line over which cars were propelled by a cable passing around huge pulleys. The founder is here portrayed taking the inaugural spin. In 1871 the line, which ran along Greenwich Street and Ninth Avenue, was replaced by the New York Elevated Railroad Company, which introduced steam locomotives. PRINT ARCHIVES.

WOODRUFF STABLES, 1861: Hiram Woodruff (1817–67) came from a family of trotting professionals—both his father and uncle were notable drivers and trainers—and young Hiram won his first race under saddle at age fourteen. In the remaining years of his life he was associated with nearly all of the great horses of his day—Topgallant, Ajax, Washington, Ripton, Gray Eagle, Kemble, Jackson, Lady Suffolk, Flora Temple, and Dexter. From his stables on Jerome Avenue in the Bronx he sold horses to Commodore Vanderbilt, August Belmont, Jay Gould, and other high fliers of the period, at prices as high as $30,000. Jerome Avenue was laid out to give access to the Jerome Park Racetrack, which opened only months after his death in 1867. OIL ON CANVAS BY JOHANNES A. OERTEL (1823–1909), 24½ x 40. GIFT OF HARRIS FAHNESTOCK. 34.340.

MADISON AVENUE STAGE LINE, CA. 1870: The proprietors of this venerable line from 1865 into the 1880s, when it gave way to surface rail, were Jesse A. Marshall and William H. Wilkins. In 1849 the latter bought into the Fourth Avenue Stage Line, and before long he succeeded its proprietors. After a decade-long sojourn in farming on Long Island, he returned to the carriage business and in 1870, with Marshall, he purchased the Madison Avenue Stage Line, running from 42nd Street to South Ferry. In 1884 the line's stables and carbarn were replaced by the long fashionable Murray Hill Hotel at 112 Park Avenue and 40th Street. MANUSCRIPT COLLECTION.

PASSENGER TICKET, BROOKLYN CITY RAILROAD COMPANY, CA. 1870: The Brooklyn City Rail Road (BCRR), incorporated in 1853, was Brooklyn's first and largest operator of horsecars and later trolleys. If Brooklyn was famous as the city of churches, it also became known as the city of trolleys, with so many lines intersecting that the hazard to life and limb made Brooklyn's citizens into "trolley dodgers"—which, when shortened, became the name of its beloved baseball team. After convoluted leases, bankruptcies, and mergers, the BCRR somehow reemerged under its old name in 1919 before finally disappearing as a corporate entity ten years later. MANUSCRIPT COLLECTION.

THE BATTERY, 1869: The landfill operations at the Battery, which had the effect of bringing Castle Garden onto the mainland, commenced in the mid 1850s and, as one may see here, were still in process by 1869. By this time the old Castle Clinton was no longer an entertainment venue. Only five years after the Swedish singing sensation Jenny Lind had debuted there in 1850, it became the Emigrant Landing Depot, continuing as the New York State immigrant processing facility until 1890, when its role was briefly assumed by another building in Battery Park, the Barge Office. In 1892 the Federal Government opened Ellis Island for that purpose. ARTIST F. A. LIEBLER. *SHANNON'S MANUAL*, 1869. THE J. CLARENCE DAVIES COLLECTION.

SARONY'S PHOTOGRAPH STUDIES NO. 3, 1867: By the time of this charming advertisement for his photographic services and supplies—*cartes de visite*, eight to the plate!—Napoleon Sarony (1821–1896) had left his lithographic partners Major and Knapp to devote full time to photography and to flamboyant associations and garb. Between 1870 and 1876 the little giant was at his zenith, occupying an entire building at Union Square except the storefront, with a rental of $8,000 per annum. He charged $14 for a dozen cabinet cards from a single negative and he made from thirty to forty sittings per day. If not the greatest photographer of the age, surely he was the most successful. THE HARRY T. PETERS COLLECTION. 57.300.591.

ADVERTISEMENT FOR ROCKWOOD & CO. STUDIO, CA. 1870: George Gardner Rockwood reportedly produced the first *carte de visite* in the United States, while running a photographic studio in St. Louis. He brought his bent for innovation to New York City in 1859, and by 1870 *Scientific American* noted, "We are indebted to Messrs. Rockwood &. Co., 839 Broadway, mechanical photographers, for a series of stereoscopic and other photographs illustrating the Pneumatic Railway under Broadway (see page 184). As the works are entirely below the surface of the street, artificial light was employed, in the use of which the photographers have been very successful. The illumination was obtained by means of two large and powerful oxyhydrogen calcium lights. Photography has been brought to such perfection that even the bowels of the earth yield to it their mysteries, and Broadway has proved no exception. The pictures were taken with the entire travel of the street, omnibus, cars, carriages, and steam fire-engines, all trotting directly over the head of the artist." 5 x 4. GIFT OF ROOSEVELT MEMORIAL ASSOCIATION. 41.366.94.

1. Chauncey Smith
2. Nicholas McGraw.
3. William H. Morris,
4. Miller & Kimpton, Coal and Lumber Yard
5. Joseph S. Ives,
6. Stewart & Blauvelt, Sash and Blind M'f'rs.
7. McGraw or Morrisania Hall,
8. Judge Silas D. Gifford,
9. Joseph Ives,
10. Baptist Church,
11. James L. Parshall,
12. Austin Carr,
13. A. Rice,
14. John S. Lyons Coal and Wood Yard,
15. J. Anderson,
16. St. Augustine,

HISTORICAL MORRISANIA.

(VILLAGE.)

1861.

17. J. B. Ayers,
18. F. Cordes,
19. Andrew Attendorph,
20. } J. Webb,
21. }
22. R. H. Elton,
23. Charles Snyder.
24. A. Folmar,
25. Wm. R. Collins.
26. T. Wicks,
27. Chas. L. Georgi,
28. Oliver Tilden Shop,
29. C. L. Georgi's Old Homestead,
30. Geo. Hand,
31. Caspar Markat,
32. Old Mill Brook.

(LEFT) **HISTORICAL MORRISANIA, 1861:** In this anonymous lithograph a train heads north on tracks parallel to the Boston Road. The horse and wagon head west along what today is 169th Street. The thirty-two reference points in the border's legend are to individual homes and civic and religious edifices that were the landmarks of their day. Number 16, St. Augustine's Catholic Church, still stands at Franklin Avenue. THE J. CLARENCE DAVIES COLLECTION. 29.100.2182.

THE NEW YORK YACHT CLUB REGATTA, 1869: The New York Yacht Club (NYYC) had been staging its annual regatta since 1846, two years after its founding in New York City and one year after the location of its clubhouse at the Elysian Fields of Hoboken. While the NYYC clubhouse has been located in Newport, Rhode Island since 1988, its headquarters are in Manhattan, on 44th Street between Fifth and Sixth Avenues. In 1869, however, as the subtitle in the lithograph's border attests—"The Start from the Stake Boat in the Narrows, off the New Club House and Grounds, Staten Island, New York Harbor"—the NYYC was based on Staten Island. The now decrepit but still standing structure, known as the Henry McFarlane House, at 30 Hylan Boulevard in the Clifton section, was designated a city landmark in 1969, but still awaits restoration. CHROMOLITHOGRAPH WITH SOME HAND-COLORING BY CHARLES R. PARSONS AND LYMAN W. ATWATER, PUBLISHED BY CURRIER & IVES. THE J. CLARENCE DAVIES COLLECTION. 29.100.2501.

ATLANTIC AVENUE, DRIVE AND PROMENADE, BROOKLYN, 1860: This tinted lithograph was published to promote the widening and improvement of Atlantic Avenue, from the terminus of which one could board the South Ferry and travel to Whitehall Street in Manhattan. An act "to provide for the widening of Atlantic avenue, in the city of Brooklyn, and to establish a public drive and promenade on said avenue" was indeed passed by the legislature in 1860 but the work was not completed for another decade. The beauty of the proposed enhanced drive and promenade served to advertise the prowess of Henry Seibert & Brothers. These "general lithographers and power press printers" were a coming force in financial printing. 29.100.3535.

W. D. WILSON & CO. PRINTING INK FACTORY, WEST AVENUE, LONG ISLAND CITY, CA. 1875: "Manufacturers of black and colored printing ink," the W. D. Wilson Company was founded in 1848 as Palmer & Co. It had its New York offices in the Harpers' Building at 325 Pearl Street but also constructed a state of the art plant in Long Island City, a burgeoning industrial region in the borough of Queens, in which the company's directors clearly took great pride. In the frankly promotional *History of Long Island City* (1896), compiler J. S. Kelsey writes: "The concern has facilities for the manufacture of printing ink of every known variety and in any quantity. All its goods are guaranteed and the house is characterized in all its dealings by honor and fairness." Lithographed by Endicott & Co. and sketched by Alfred R. Waud, the celebrated Civil War artist of *Harper's Weekly*. It was painted by Parsons and Atwater, so long associated with Currier & Ives. THE J. CLARENCE DAVIES COLLECTION. 29.100.3498.

VIEW OF THE HIGH BRIDGE, 1861: This interesting aerial view of the High Bridge testifies to its purpose: to bring water to the city without impeding boat traffic along the Harlem River below. The latter intent was increasingly foiled as boats became wider, so in 1927 the narrowly set stone arches were replaced by a broad steel span. A couple of the original stone arches survive on the Bronx side of the river. Built between 1839 and 1848, the High Bridge is the city's oldest span connecting Manhattan Island to the Highbridge neighborhood in the Bronx and the "Continent of America." The landmark High Bridge Tower was not constructed until 1872. LITHOGRAPH BY GEORGE HAYWARD FOR *VALENTINE'S MANUAL*, 1862.

BROADWAY, LOOKING NORTH FROM THE CORNER OF CANAL STREET, 1866: Anthony is one of the oldest names in the American photographic industry. Samuel Morse was one of the very first American daguerreotypists, and in 1840, Edward Anthony was one of his first students. In 1842, Edward opened his own daguerreotype studio, and founded the E. Anthony Company that dealt in daguerreian supplies. In 1852 Edward's brother, Henry, became a partner in the firm, and in 1862, the company name was changed to the famous E. & H. T. Anthony. (In their spare time the brothers played baseball with the Knickerbocker Base Ball Club from its earliest years, 1845–46.) In 1901, the Anthony firm merged with Scovill & Adams to become Anthony & Scovill, and in 1907, the name was shortened to Ansco—a name today familiar to photographers of a certain age. STEREOGRAPH PUBLISHED BY E. & H. T. ANTHONY AND CO. COLLECTION OF PRINTS AND PHOTOGRAPHS.

BARNUM'S MUSEUM AS IT APPEARED IMMEDIATELY AFTER THE FIRE OF MARCH 3RD, 1868: Upon being burned out of his great American Museum in 1865, P. T. Barnum leased the former "Chinese Building" at 539 and 541 Broadway and there unveiled "Barnum's New Museum." After initial experiments with classy fare, he soon reverted to the tried and true formula of soothsayers and giantesses, a "mammoth fat woman," and a "human skeleton," along with sundry human and animal oddities. He cut a circus ring underneath what had first been intended as a lecture hall and variety theater. Somehow it all worked—until half past the frigid midnight of March 3, 1868, when the whole enterprise went up in flames. Barnum was wiped out again, leaving only a picturesque ice sculpture behind, captured in an albumen print by Anthony & Co. COLLECTION OF PRINTS AND PHOTOGRAPHS.

LOOKING UP NASSAU STREET FROM THE CORNER OF WALL, SHOWING THE POST OFFICE, CA. 1865: In this "instantaneous view" the Anthony Brothers depict the old Middle Dutch Church, which in 1844 had been purchased by the Federal government and converted to the city's main post office, a role it fulfilled until 1875. In the following year the tablets bearing biblical inscriptions that had been embedded in the church until it was made a post office somehow made their way into the front wall of the Old Dutch Church in Kingston, New York, where they may be seen today. One of the city's oldest buildings at the time of depiction, the converted Middle Dutch Church dated to 1729–31. ALBUMEN STEREOGRAPH BY ANTHONY & CO. COLLECTION OF PRINTS AND PHOTOGRAPHS.

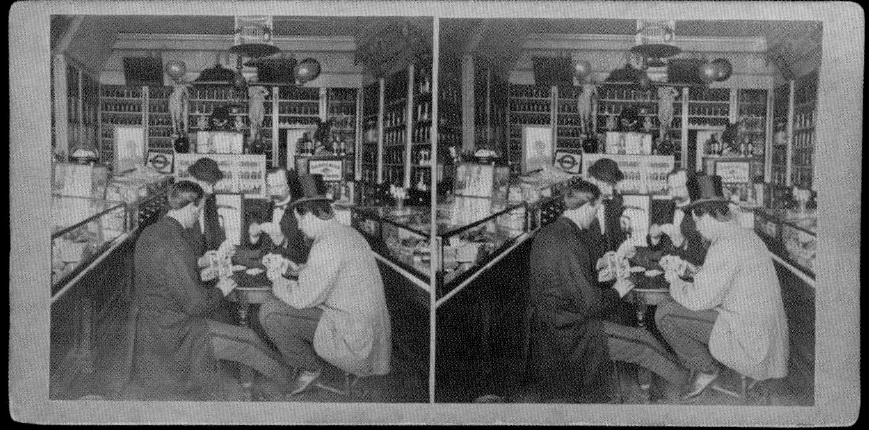

G. A. MARSH'S STORE, THIRD AVENUE AT 125TH STREET, 1865: Gambling and liquor were at the core of the masculine culture of this period. A sporting man was a hero, admired as one who could win or lose all at the turn of a card and retain his composure. The modest emulators depicted here at G. A. Marsh's uptown emporium included not only the proprietor, most likely the hatless gent at the rear, but also a Dr. Brookway, perhaps the fellow wearing the stovepipe hat, taking a break between house calls. STEREOGRAPH BY UNKNOWN PHOTOGRAPHER. COLLECTION OF PRINTS AND PHOTOGRAPHS.

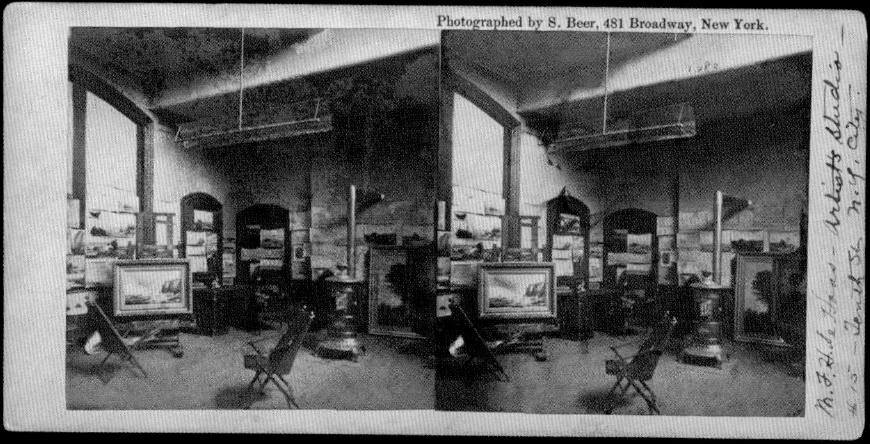

Photographed by S. Beer, 481 Broadway, New York.

10TH STREET ARTISTS STUDIOS, 1865: Depicted here is the artist's studio of Maurice Frederick Hendrick De Haas (1832–1895), a well-known painter of marine subjects. He was a resident of Brooklyn but for several decades maintained a studio in the celebrated building at West 10th Street, designed by Richard Morris Hunt, whose occupants included Winslow Homer, Frederic Church, Albert Bierstadt, Jervis McEntee, and William Merritt Chase. Though it ceased to be a center of the American art world by the turn of the century, the building continued in use as artists' space until its demolition in 1956. STEREOGRAPH BY S. BEER. COLLECTION OF PRINTS AND PHOTOGRAPHS.

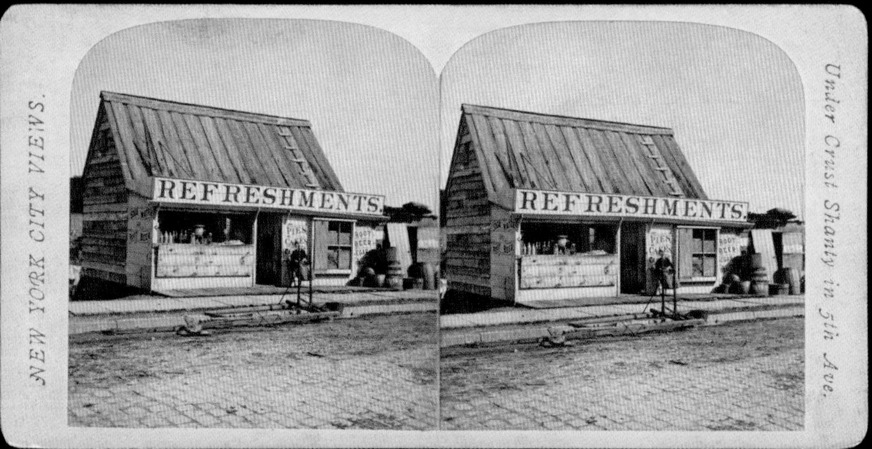

NEW YORK CITY VIEWS.
REFRESHMENTS.
Under Crust Shanty in 5th Ave.

UNDER CRUST SHANTY IN FIFTH AVENUE, CA. 1870: This fast-food eatery on a barren stretch of Fifth Avenue, north of the new Central Park, offered among its refreshments soda water, root beer, cigars, tobacco, sarsaparilla, cakes, and pies. But it was not the last-named that gave the shanty its name. Describing the lower classes of a generation earlier, George G. Foster had written: "The butcher-boy, the mechanic with his boisterous family—the b'hoy in red flannel shirt-sleeves and cone-shaped trousers—the shop-woman, the sewing and press-room girl, the straw-braider, the type-rubber, the map-colorer, the paper-box and flower maker, the g'hal, in short, in all her various aspects and phases—with a liberal sprinkling of under-crust blacklegs and fancy men—these make up the great staple of Bowery audiences." These, too, were the patrons of the Under Crust Shanty. STEREOGRAPH BY UNKNOWN PHOTOGRAPHER. COLLECTION OF PRINTS AND PHOTOGRAPHS.

INTERIOR VIEW OF THE GRAND CENTRAL DEPOT, 42ND STREET AND 4TH AVENUE, CA. 1871: Park Avenue was originally known as Fourth Avenue and carried the tracks of the New York and Harlem Railroad. The original Grand Central Depot was located at the northern edge of Madison Square and subsequently became P. T. Barnum's Hippodrome and then the first of the city's four Madison Square Gardens (handing down its name to today's sports arena). The next Grand Central, pictured in this stereo view, opened at 42nd Street and Fourth Avenue in 1871, a mansard-roof edifice that until 1910 served the New York Central; Harlem; Hudson River; and New York and New Haven Railroads. At that time work commenced on the Grand Central Station of today. PUBLISHED BY E. & H. T. ANTHONY & CO. COLLECTION OF PRINTS AND PHOTOGRAPHS.

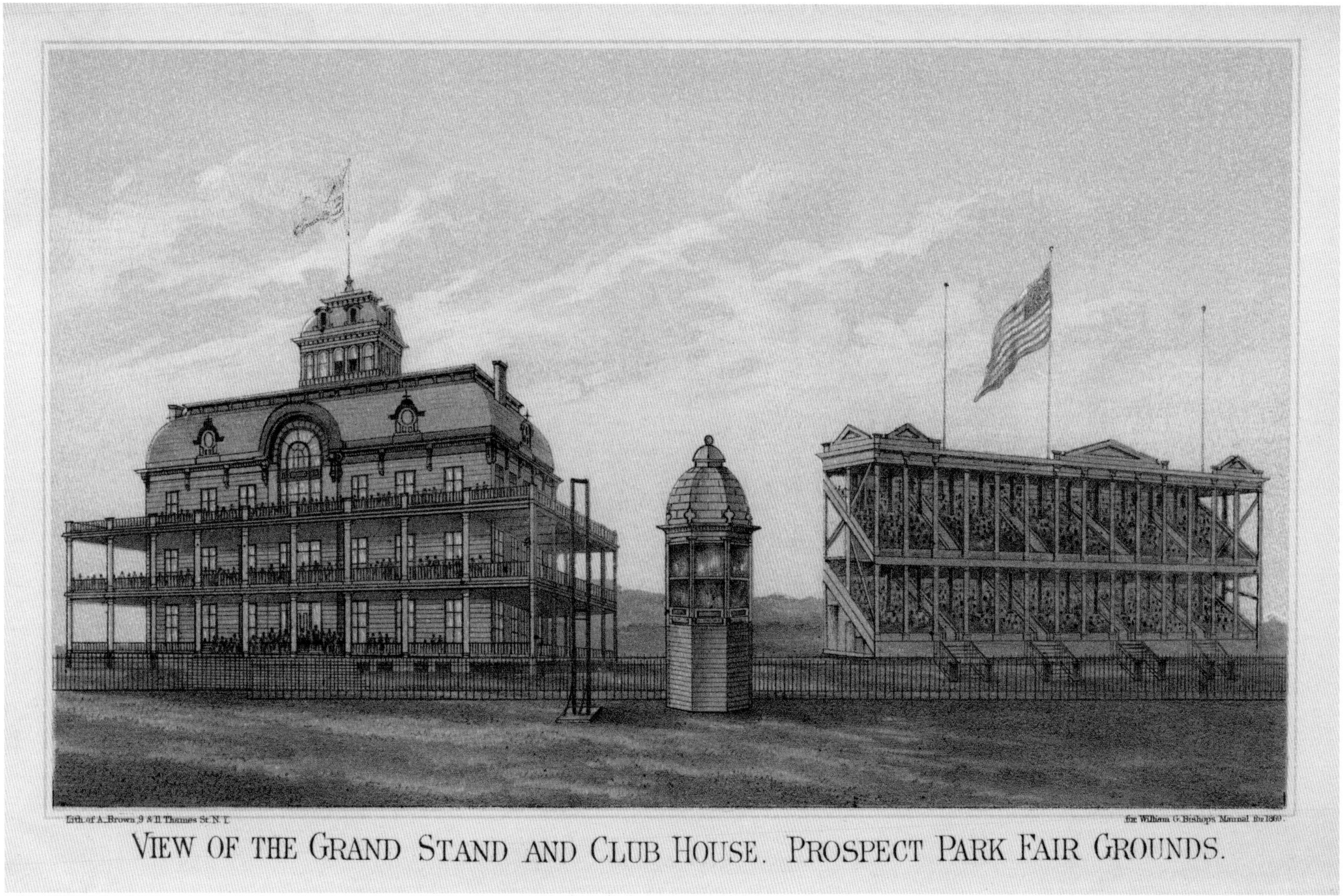

VIEW OF THE GRAND STAND AND CLUB HOUSE, PROSPECT PARK FAIR GROUNDS, 1869: Horse racing, long a favorite pastime in Brooklyn, came to the Prospect Park Grounds in Gravesend in 1868. The modest venue began sharing races with the Sheepshead Bay Race Track in 1884, and by 1887 it was only a memory, giving way to the more commodious Gravesend Race Track. Within just a few years that new Coney Island site became the racing capital of America. This lithograph appeared in the Manual of the Common Council of the City of Brooklyn, a publication deservedly less well known than the *Valentine's Manual* that was published for New York City. Although the credit on this image is to *William G. Bishop's Manual*, several other city clerks attached their name to the Brooklyn annual in its long life (1855–88). LITHOGRAPH BY A. BROWN.

(RIGHT) **AMERICAN NATIONAL GAME OF BASE BALL: GRAND MATCH FOR THE CHAMPIONSHIP AT THE ELYSIAN FIELDS, HOBOKEN, NJ, 1865:** This print is often misidentified as portraying the Knickerbocker Base Ball Club of New York in action at Manhattan's playground, the Elysian Fields of Hoboken, in the 1840s. The venue is correct, but the portrayed clubs are the Brooklyn Atlantics, at the bat, and the New York Mutuals in the field; the date of the match is August 3, 1865. Six members of the Atlantics can be clearly identified at the bottom right. They are Sid Smith, Joe Start, Dickey Pearce, Fred Crane, John Galvin, and Tom Pratt. In the crowd scene, facing the viewer, is Pete O' Brien. The advance of industry in New York City meant little open space for ballfields, so Gotham clubs leased their grounds and clubhouse from the Stevens family at Hoboken, or at the Red House Grounds in Harlem, or in Brooklyn. LITHOGRAPH BY CURRIER & IVES. THE HARRY T. PETERS COLLECTION. 58.300.34.

CURRIER & IVES. ENTERED ACCORDING TO ACT OF CONGRESS A.D. 1866, BY CURRIER & IVES, IN THE CLERKS OFFICE OF THE DISTRICT COURT OF THE UNITED STATES, FOR THE SOUTHERN DISTRICT OF N.Y. 152 NASSAU ST.

THE AMERICAN NATIONAL GAME OF BASE BALL.

GRAND MATCH FOR THE CHAMPIONSHIP AT THE ELYSIAN FIELDS, HOBOKEN, N. J.

LOEW'S BRIDGE, FULTON STREET, CA. 1868: Kenneth Dunshee writes of this short-lived structure, also known as the Fulton Street Bridge: "In the 1860s, the intersection of Broadway and Fulton Street was considered the busiest and most dangerous in the city. The Common Council was persuaded by Philip Genin, a hatter then occupying the southwest corner, to erect a pedestrian bridge over the crossing. Built in 1867 and known as the Loew Bridge, it immediately drew the wrath of Knox, a rival hatter on the northeast corner, whose shop was cast in constant gloom by the massive structure. The feud between the mad hatters of Manhattan ended in a victory for Knox and the eyesore was removed in 1868." TINTYPE. GIFT OF DR. ROBERT DRAPKIN. 84.180.3.

(RIGHT) **BROOKLYN BRIDGE TOWER, SEPTEMBER 1872:** John Roebling submitted drawings and specifications for his Brooklyn Bridge to the New York Bridge Company in 1865. He had already built a similar suspension bridge across the Ohio River at Cincinnati (which remains in heavy use). He was soon named chief engineer of the project and by 1869, with his estimated cost of $7 million approved, Roebling set to work. However, while he was standing on Fulton Street ferry slip, measuring to determine the precise location for the Brooklyn Tower, he had his foot crushed by an incoming ferry. Two weeks later he was dead of gangrene. His son, Washington Roebling, took over as chief engineer but two summers later, too long in an underwater caisson, he was afflicted with "the bends," a crippling ailment that compelled him to hand over day-to-day supervision of the project to his wife, Emily Warren Roebling. He oversaw the project for the next eleven years from an apartment in Brooklyn, watching progress on the towers through field glasses. This photo is credited to Talfor, Holmes & Pach, but it was Silas A. Holmes alone who received the commission to record the progress of work on the towers. Although the man labeled in the image as "No. 1" has often been identified in print as Washington Roebling, he was likely too ill in September to have been present; photographer Holmes identified the man as E. F. Farrington and supplied a key to the other numbered figures. PHOTOGRAPH BY S. A. HOLMES, GIFT OF MR. SHIRLEY C. BURDEN. 57.15.10.

1. E. F. Farrington, Head Carpenter — 2 W. C. Kingsley, Genl Superintendent — 3 O. P. Quintard, Book-Keeper. — 4 "Alex" McKinnon, foreman of masons on this pier. — 8 W. H. Paine, Asst Eng^r. — 5. F. Collingwood, Asst. Eng^r. — 6 G. W. McNulty, Asst. Eng^r. — 7 T. G. Douglass, Head Mason

Top of Brooklyn Pier at
5th Course above Roadway
Height above Tide 130 ft
Nov. 1872

CHAPTER VIII | 1876–1898

MYSTERIES OF THE CITY

RETHINKING CORRUPTION AND CRIME IN GILDED-AGE NYC

DANIEL CZITROM

IT WAS THE MOST POLITICALLY EXPLOSIVE SERMON IN THE CITY'S HISTORY. ON FEBRUARY 14, 1892 THE REVEREND DR. CHARLES H. PARKHURST, PASTOR OF THE MADISON SQUARE PRESBYTERIAN CHURCH, SHOCKED HIS ELITE CONGREGATION AND THE CITY BY DECLARING THE MUNICIPAL LIFE OF NEW YORK TO BE THOROUGHLY ROTTEN. THE CITY WAS CONTROLLED BY "POLLUTED HARPIES THAT, UNDER THE PRETENCE OF GOVERNING THIS CITY, ARE FEEDING DAY AND NIGHT ON ITS QUIVERING VITALS. THEY ARE A LYING, PERJURED, RUM-SOAKED, AND LIBIDINOUS LOT." HE RAILED AGAINST "THE OFFICIAL AND ADMINISTRATIVE CRIMINALITY THAT IS FILTHIFYING OUR ENTIRE MUNICIPAL LIFE, MAKING NEW YORK A VERY HOT-BED OF KNAVERY, DEBAUCHERY, AND BESTIALITY." EVERY BROTHEL, GAMBLING HALL, AND UNLICENSED SALOON, PARKHURST CLAIMED, "HAS AN IMMUNITY SECURED TO IT BY A SCALE OF POLICE TAXATION THAT IS AS CAREFULLY GRADED AND THOROUGHLY SYSTEMATIZED AS ANY THAT OBTAINS IN THE ASSESSMENT OF PERSONAL PROPERTY OR REAL ESTATE."[1] TWO YEARS LATER, IN THE SPRING OF 1894, A NEW YORK STATE SENATE COMMITTEE BEGAN A STARTLING INQUIRY into the inner workings of the New York City Police Department. Named for its chair, Republican senator Clarence Lexow, the committee began as a partisan examination of alleged police collusion in election frauds. But over the ten months of its hearings, the Lexow Committee turned into something larger and unprecedented: an astonishing exposure of how the city's police force acted as the manager of the city's lucrative vice economy. The long parade of nearly seven hundred witnesses included people from all walks of New York life: prostitutes and brothel keepers, police rank-and-file and top brass; theater owners and boxing promoters; obscure political operatives and well-known government officials; small businessmen and wealthy entrepreneurs; victims of police brutality and defenders of the force. By shining the harsh glare of publicity into the inner workings of the NYPD, the Lexow Committee produced the most in-depth study ever done of an American police force, as well as the prototype for sensational political investigations in the modern era. The investigation proved an electoral disaster for Tammany Hall in the 1894 mayoral contest, and reform Mayor William Strong appointed Theodore Roosevelt president of the Board of Police Commissioners. Dr. Parkhurst emerged as a hero for urban reformers around the nation.[2]

Most contemporary accounts framed the Lexow story as a simple morality play, a tale of noble crusaders cleaning up a corrupt police department and ousting its Tammany masters. But the further one gets from the 1890s, the more comic and cynical overtones creep into the historical chronicles, and the echo chamber of commercial culture. By the 1920s most Prohibition-era New Yorkers viewed Parkhurst (who died at age ninety-one in 1932) as a faintly ludicrous figure, his moral campaign against vice and corruption a quaint vestige of the Gay Nineties. In 1955 M. R. Werner published a multi-part *New Yorker* profile, "Dr. Parkhurst's Crusade," the first narrative account of Parkhurst's fight and its impact on city and state politics. Werner, a prolific journalist and a pioneering historian of Tammany Hall, was surprised that his series stirred more interest and praise than anything he had ever done. "Many people," he wrote to a friend, "have told me that strangers mentioned the pieces to them spontaneously as something they greatly enjoyed, not only here in New York but out of town." The 1960 Broadway musical comedy *Tenderloin*, with book and lyrics by Jerry Bock and Sheldon Harnick, starred the English Shakespearean actor Maurice Evans as Reverend Brock, an 1890s Parkhurst-like anti-vice crusader. But lukewarm reviewers complained there was too much rectitude in the Reverend Brock character and not enough sizzle on stage. The show closed on Broadway after a short run and then found a new home at The Dunes in Las Vegas, where it presumably played less righteous and more Rat Pack.[3]

But if we let go of the romantic model and the too-easy mockery, the Lexow story helps us understand the deeper structural realities of Gilded-Age New York. The history of the investigation illuminates a cluster of related themes: the growing political power of the urban underworld; the parallel "machines" of America's dominant political parties; the heavily contested nature and uses of police power; anti-urbanism as a force in American life; and New York's uneasy relationship with the larger republic at the dawn of the twentieth century. Sketching out just a few of the dramatic highlights of Lexow testimony offers a sense of how the investigation, stoked by fiercely competitive media coverage, evolved into a theatrical spectacle that forced a new openness about what Dr. Parkhurst had called New York's "subterranean mysteries."

For starters, consider a more sophisticated and dynamic understanding of the term "underworld." Beginning with the "penny-press" journalism of the early nineteenth century; continuing with the "sunshine and shadow" guidebooks of the post-Civil War years; and through the still-influential chronicles of twentieth-century writers such as Herbert Asbury and Luc Sante, and, more recently, Martin Scorsese in his film *Gangs of New York*, nearly all accounts of the city's underside have emphasized the sensational and the picaresque while ignoring its importance to the city's—and nation's—history. First popularized in the 1890s, the notion of an underworld evinced contradictory meanings in the metropolis. The underworld was simultaneously all of the following: the loose networks formed by professional criminals; a zone of pleasure for visiting businessmen, tourists, and slummers; raw material for journalists and guidebook writers; a potent political weapon for upstate Republicans; an economic and organizational resource for Tammany Hall Democrats; a lucrative path of mobility for skillful entrepreneurs, including many women; and a source of employment for immigrants and transients. The underworld was also the bailiwick of the New York Police Department, charged with its surveillance and control and, as revealed by Lexow, its management as well. Rather than thinking of it as a specific place or certain group of criminals, the underworld is best understood as a web of relationships, based on reciprocal services, whereby people gain power, profit, or pleasure from the city's vice economy. By the 1890s that vice economy, including prostitution, gambling, the saloon trade, blood sport, counterfeiting, theft, opium dens, bunco games, and entertainments, was as distinct a feature of New York City life as the opera, the museum, the department store, or the skyscraper. It had also matured into one of New York's most lucrative and popular tourist attractions.[4]

Charles Parkhurst was by no means the first city crusader against prostitution; nor was he the first minister to exploit sensational publicity with a Christian attack on the vice economy. But he was the first to politicize moral reform efforts by exposing links among the NYPD, the political power structure, and the lucrative vice economy. He coined the term "organized crime" and argued that there was "but one criminal practically, viz., the city government, whose very existence was a transgression, and its every act a felony." His startling charges quickly brought a summons to appear before the grand jury. Parkhurst at first could offer no proof of his allegations, but he resolved to get it. He hired Charles W. Gardner, a private detective with a shady past, to take him on a tour of the city's brothels. Details of what happened began leaking out to the city press within days. Newspaper coverage of two criminal trials involving brothels he visited was cryptic, including titillating specifics while leaving plenty of room for imagination. After a subsequent visit with the grand jury and a series of heavily publicized follow-up sermons, Parkhurst worked to create a movement that would transcend party politics, founding the City Vigilance League as a political arm for his crusade. He championed the idea of nonpartisan control of the police department and thus pioneered one of the bedrock principles of American Progressivism: the idea that city governance must be divorced from party politics. But the stubborn partisan realities of New York and the nation were greater obstacles than he realized.[5]

"The most serious question which faces the modern world today," argued E. L. Godkin in 1890, "is the question of the government of great cities under universal suffrage." Godkin, long-time editor of the *Evening Post* and founder of *The Nation* magazine, distilled the views of many propertied New Yorkers and elite opinion makers—the sort of people who made up Parkhurst's congregation—when he attacked the emergence of "criminal politics" in urban centers. Godkin's definition of the criminal class was capacious and explicitly political. He included not only thieves, burglars, fences, gamblers, and brothel keepers, "but all who associate with them in political work, and who share political spoils with them; . . . in other words, both the actual perpetrators of crimes and those who are not repelled by them and are willing to profit in politics by their activity." It included "the great army of those who shirk regular industry . . . who, though not, strictly speaking, part of the criminal population, live on it or through it, and readily descend into its ranks." Tammany Hall's strength—and that of every other urban political machine—lay, according to Godkin, "in the control it exerts over the ignorant, criminal, and vicious classes."[6]

For men like Godkin, what mattered most was the national political implications of all this, fueled by the fear of Tammany's burgeoning power. Tammany had been part of the city's political landscape since the early nineteenth century. But not until the late 1880s, under the hardnosed leadership of Richard Croker, did it emerge as the centralized, permanently dominant faction of the Democratic Party, the storied "machine" emblematic of big-city politics and the growing influence of the immigrant working-class vote. One key factor in its newfound strength was a successful drive to control hiring and (to a lesser extent) promotions in the NYPD.

In 1872 the state legislature had given the four-man Board of Police Commissioners a supervisory role over the city's election machinery, placing the Bureau of Elections under police department control. An unwritten agreement had kept the board bipartisan, with two Democratic and two Republican commissioners. But in 1888 Tammany Mayor Hugh J. Grant had upset the long-observed balance of power by appointing Tammany stalwart James J. Martin as commissioner and president, giving Tammany a clear majority. But the stakes were far larger than local patronage. Because the police Board of Commissioners supervised election machineries—selecting polling places, establishing election districts, verifying registry lists, and appointing inspectors and poll clerks—there were profound national implications in this situation.[7]

The strategic importance of New York State's electoral vote meant a reversal of the old political adage: in New York City, all politics was national. In an era when the two major parties were very closely matched and razor thin margins could determine presidential elections, New York was the ultimate swing state. Its thirty-six electoral votes were decisive in American politics. Grover Cleveland, one of only two Democrats elected president between the Civil War and the Great Depression, had carried the state by less than 1,200 votes in 1884. In 1888 Cleveland lost re-election to Benjamin Harrison, despite winning the popular vote. And when he returned to the White House in 1892, politicians of all persuasions duly noted that New York State gave him a 45,000-vote majority, with Democrats polling a record 80,000-vote majority in New York City. As Tammany subdued its intraparty rivals and looked to extend its influence, nervous Republicans had to confront the national implications of growing Democratic muscle in the city.

There have been few more widely accepted certainties than Tammany's reliance upon and genius for all manner of vote fraud. Yet the deeper reality was that machine politics in New York was a bipartisan affair, rooted in the peculiarities of an electoral system where the law made no provision for the printing and distribution of ballots. The mechanics of balloting had long been a private affair, the province of parties, rather than the legal business of the state. Partisan posturing about vote fraud was nothing new. Indeed, it was a defining feature of late nineteenth-century American politics. As Peter Argersinger has persuasively argued in the best recent overview of this subject, "election fraud was rooted in the political system. The interaction among the institutional framework, the competitive partisan balance of the party system, and an indulgent political culture encouraged and made possible election fraud in the Gilded Age."[8]

The controversies surrounding elections and the New York police require a consideration of what one might call the parallel machines in American politics. The familiar machine, the one whose power and influence has been endlessly attacked, demonized, satirized, and exaggerated, was Democratic—city based, with a largely ethnic and working-class clientele organized around municipal patronage. The other one was Republican—rural based, with a middle-class, Protestant (including African-American) clientele organized around federal patronage. An important, if largely forgotten, cog in the Republican machine was the Federal Election Commission, created in 1871 as part of the Reconstruction-era Enforcement Acts. Under the leadership of John I. Davenport, a Union Club attorney and stone partisan Republican, the commission monitored national elections only in cities with a population of more than 20,000 people and proved effective in tamping down voter turnout in the urban North. But it was New York that always attracted the bulk of Davenport's attention. During the 1892 presidential election, the city narrowly escaped a bloody confrontation between the New York police, alleged to be run by Tammany, and its Republican counterpart—some 8,000 deputy U.S. Marshals operating under the authority of the federal election inspectors. The election of 1892 thus raised a far more urgent question than how to deal with protected brothels and Sunday drinking: Could New York's underworld hold the balance of power in America's national elections?[9]

In fact, the Republican claim that Tammany controlled the NYPD was a myth. A Tammany "pull" might help a man get an appointment as patrolman. But although its influence in the rank and file had grown, the force—especially the captains and inspectors, where the real power lay—had remained a bipartisan institution. The political affiliations of police captains, roughly even in these years, were of great import to the political parties, making promotions (and dismissals) subject to intense partisan maneuvering. A contemporary survey of the political affiliations of the force's thirty-six captains found fifteen Republicans, nineteen Tammany Democrats, and two independents. The four inspectors were evenly divided between the parties.[10] Indeed, the deeper political importance of the NYPD lay elsewhere, driven by the hardening of class differences in the last third of the nineteenth century. Police interventions on the side of capital escalated over the last third of the nineteenth century, crushing strikes, protecting scab labor, and spying on unions. Here lay the source of the respect and confidence the NYPD enjoyed among the propertied and business classes—stockbrokers, bankers, real-estate developers, manufacturers, merchants, hotel and entertainment entrepreneurs, and many middle-class home owners. Police management of the vice economy seemed a small price to pay as long as NYPD brass kept the department's heel firmly dug into the neck of organized labor.

The careers of Gilded-Age NYPD leaders illustrate clearly that allegiance to big capital, along with a more militarized approach to policing, was far more important than allegiance to Tammany. Civil War veteran William Murray, who served as superintendent from 1885 to 1892, routinely mobilized the force to break strikes. During the tumultuous street car strike of March 1886, Murray personally commanded a phalanx of police as they drove a lone horse car across Grand Street, cracking the heads of strikers and their supporters along the way. His successor, Thomas Byrnes, had begun his reign as head of the Detective Bureau in 1881 by connecting every bank and brokerage house in lower Manhattan to police headquarters via telephone. Byrnes—a Democrat but not a Tammany man—maintained a tight surveillance over trade unions and radical groups by deploying detectives as spies and informers. And Inspector Alexander S. "Clubber" Williams, the city's most famous—and brutal—constable, was a prominent Republican who enjoyed enormous prestige among the real estate owners and businessmen in the "Tenderloin" district, which he had named and from which he had long profited. As patrolman, captain, and even inspector, Williams faced more police board trials for bribery and excessive violence than any officer in the history of the force. But his well-connected Republican lawyers, men such as Elihu Root, U.S. Attorney for the Southern District of New York and future Secretary of State, never failed to shield him from punishment. From this perspective, the crux of police power lay in maintaining "social order," preventing mob violence, and routing strikers. Routine police brutality against citizens and the protection of vice were thought a small cost of doing business.

Parkhurst's call for a state investigation of the NYPD went unheeded until the fall of 1893, when the state legislature returned to Republican control and GOP leaders pushed through legislation creating a special Senate committee. It was a shaky alliance from the start. While Parkhurst attacked the NYPD's failure to enforce the law, Republicans worried more about the rapid politicization of the police force under a resurgent and aggressive Tammany Hall. On March 9, 1894, two years after Parkhurst's famous sermon, the Lexow Committee began its hearings on the third floor of the county courthouse on Chambers Street, a building notorious as the most visible legacy of the corruption of the Boss Tweed years. The seven committee members, five upstate Republicans and two city Democrats, sat on a dais in front. For its first month the committee focused on allegations of vote fraud and the larger issue of the police role in elections. The star witness in these early sessions was Police Commissioner and Board President James J. Martin, a power in Tammany Hall, who calmly admitted that nearly all of his appointments to the force came from recommendations made by Tammany leaders. Several other witnesses offered first-hand testimony of police interference and intimidation at the voting booths during the 1892 election. Yet none of this early testimony offered much beyond familiar partisan charges and countercharges—and newspapers covered them through the filters of their own political leanings. The committee adjourned in mid-April to return to Albany business.

When it reassembled on May 21 it had a new chief counsel. He was John W. Goff, a tall, fiery white-bearded forty-five-year-old lawyer who had emigrated to New York as a boy from County Wexford, Ireland. Goff had worked his way through night classes at Cooper Union and had made a living as a journalist and telegraph operator while studying law. An independent Democrat, Goff had been active in the Clan-Na-Gael, a secret society dedicated to liberating Ireland from English rule by force. Goff would quickly become the dominant figure in the Lexow investigation, with his probing, carefully researched, often sarcastic questioning of witnesses.

Under Goff's lead, the Lexow inquiry redirected its agenda toward Parkhurst's concerns and began probing the vast extent of the vice economy and how it filled political coffers via informal taxation and blackmail. By the 1890s the city had some 9,000 licensed saloons and liquor sellers, and perhaps as many unlicensed ones. Prostitution and gambling thrived in more neighborhoods than ever before. Counterfeiting of greenbacks and a wide assortment of "bunco" games had also become lucrative business. The world of plebeian theater (including variety shows, burlesque, concert saloons, dime museums, and sporting events) had become a permanent fixture of the city's entertainment world. Goff had just begun calling a procession of madams, pimps, and low-level political fixers as witnesses when Democratic Governor Roswell P. Flower, sensing a partisan attempt to embarrass his party, vetoed the $25,000 legislative appropriation for the investigation. Republican leader Thomas Platt then turned to his patrician friends in the city's Chamber of Commerce for help, and they obliged by raising $25,000 in private funds to help bankroll the inquiry. By early June the accumulated weight of testimony had begun to turn public opinion.

In mid-June the committee heard from George Appo, a colorful, one-eyed "steerer" for the "green-goods" (or counterfeiting) racket. Appo's sensational testimony detailed the workings of this lucrative business, whereby printed circulars lured out-of-towners to the city with the promise of making easy money through the purchase of counterfeit greenbacks. The knowing cooperation of police was essential. Appo became a minor celebrity, touring the country in a play written for him, *In the Tenderloin*. Goff then steered the inquiry to police graft from saloons and other businesses. The star witness here proved to be Harry Hill, the old, gnarled, former proprietor of New York's most famous dance house. From the 1850s through the 1880s Hill had been one of the city's most famous personalities. He told a sad and sordid tale of how he had been forced out of business for resisting the rapacious kickback demands of the police. The press had a field day with this "ghost from the graveyard of old New York." "Old Harry Hill," the *New York World* reported in mock epic tone, "climbed into the witness chair. A dozen artists made pictures of him. A score of reporters watched and studied him for five million readers. . . . The committee behind him had dreamed of his place when they were boys, and now as great statesmen studied him carefully."[11]

John Goff resumed his attack on the NYPD from a variety of angles. The heavily covered testimony of Mrs. Caela Urchittel exemplified the widespread practice of police extortion and oppression of immigrant shopkeepers and small entrepreneurs. Urchittel had come to the city in 1891 from Russia, with her three children; her husband had died en route. She ran a boarding house for a time and then with her savings of $600 she opened a small cigar store on the Lower East Side. When she refused to pay cash tribute to the local police, they had her arrested and jailed on charges of running a disorderly house. She was unable to understand any of the proceedings against her. Upon being released, she discovered that her three children had been taken from her on the grounds that she was a prostitute. After a frantic five-week search she received a postcard from one of them from the Hebrew Orphan Asylum, where they had been committed by the Society for Prevention of Cruelty to Children. Her testimony before Lexow led to a tearful and highly publicized reunion with her children in the hearing room.

Goff also opened up the issue of police brutality when, on October 2, he subpoenaed all the police who had been accused of clubbing citizens over the past three years. Nearly one hundred cops, as well as many of their bandaged and bloodied victims, crowded into the hearing room. The testimony of both police and victims offered the most dramatic evidence ever of how routinely some cops used excessive force. In most of these cases, police took out their rage on ordinary citizens whose only crime was to refuse to pay off neighborhood beat cops. Perhaps the most chilling brutality case involved the well-known journalist Augustin Costello, who in 1885 had published *Our Police Protectors*, a highly celebratory history of the NYPD, with the full cooperation of the Police Commission. Part of the proceeds from Costello's book went to the Police Pension fund, and he at first enjoyed the confidence of Thomas Byrnes, Alexander Williams, and other top brass. But Costello fell out of favor, possibly because Byrnes saw Costello's book as a competitor to his own work, *Professional Criminals of America*. Costello told the grim tale of how he was lured to the First Precinct station house, only to be badly beaten on the orders of Inspector William McLaughlin. Costello's story raised a chilling question: If a writer who had been long identified as a friend of the force could receive such brutal treatment, was anyone safe?[12]

On November 7, a record number of New Yorkers went to the polls and, in a ringing rejection of Tammany, elected Fusion candidate William Strong as mayor. John Goff himself was elected city recorder, a judgeship with a term of fourteen years, as part of the Fusion ticket. The defeat of Tammany was widely viewed as a personal triumph for both Parkhurst and Goff, and many observers believed the election marked the beginning of the end for Tammany's grip on city politics. Goff and the committee were now under pressure to complete their work by the end of the year. Although Lexow had already caused a political earthquake in the mayoral election, it had still not heard from top officers on the force—and Goff believed that they would provide the most damning and compelling testimony yet heard. He was determined to show how the patterns of corruption, bribery, and brutality were nurtured and created at the top.

The issue of how police received promotions led to the most explosive testimony to date. On December 13, Goff called Captain Timothy Creeden to the stand and questioned him closely on how he had achieved his captaincy. Creeden at first denied under oath that he had paid anyone for the promotion. But after Goff elicited contrary testimony from a smalltime politico, Creeden returned to the stand the next day and recanted. In fact, he had had to come up with $15,000, to be paid to non-Tammany political associates of one of the police commissioners, before he could make captain. He had passed the civil service exam for captain several times, but was frustrated by his failure to receive promotion. The only way to raise the cash was with the help of saloonkeepers and local political fixers, who might then be repaid in a variety of ways. Creeden poignantly defended his original testimony, invoking his own background as an Irish revolutionary and his deep aversion to informing. His testimony proved that police promotions

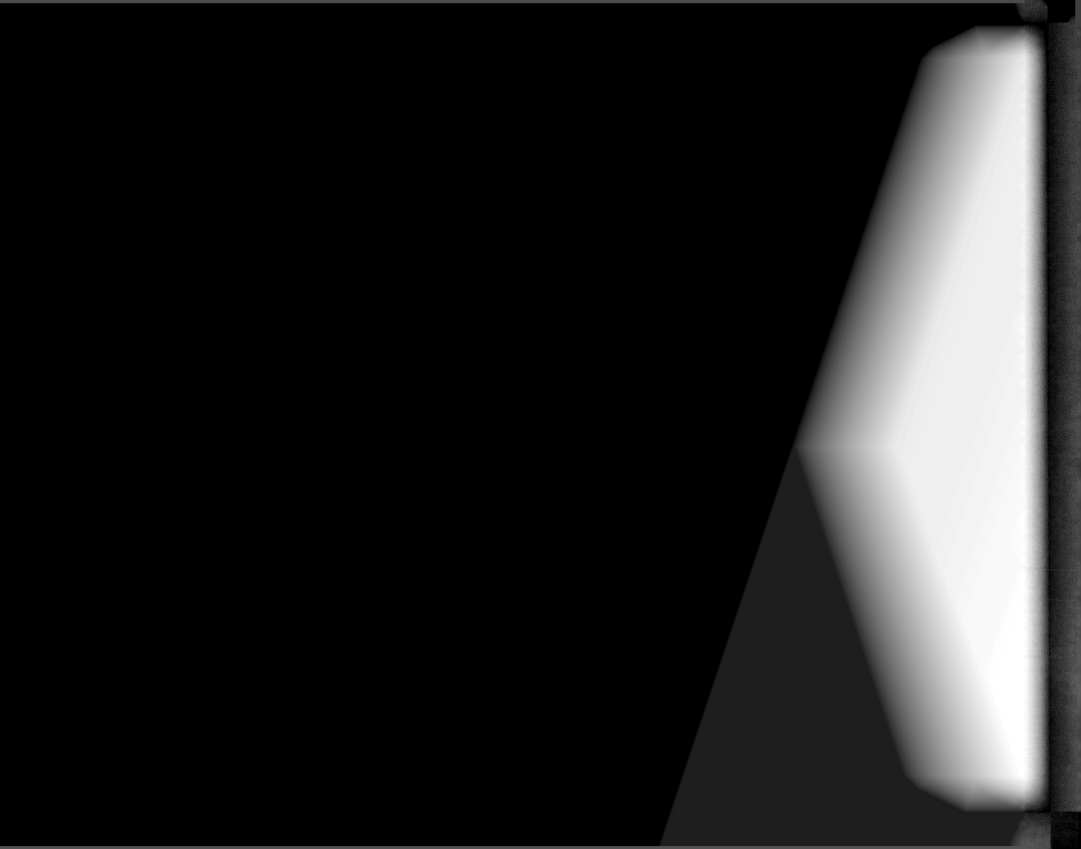

(LEFT) BOWERY AT NIGHT, CA. 1895: The fashionable Bowery of the 1860s, when the old Dutch lane reigned as the city's prime theatrical district, declined by the 1890s as saloons, dime museums, salacious tableaux, and freak shows took over. The unwitting were doped and robbed, while the smart set enjoyed the frisson of perambulating through the district. Chuck Connors, dubbed the "Mayor of Chinatown," would stage paid tours for the curious, including phony opium dens. Saloonkeeper Steve Brodie was Connors' rival for the title of the most famous man on the Bowery. His claim to have survived a leap off the Brooklyn Bridge in 1886 led him to the boards and the footlights, where in a stage vehicle titled *On the Bowery* he sang, "The Bowery, the Bowery! I'll never go there any more!" In 1933 Connors and Brodie were portrayed by Wallace Beery and George Raft, respectively, in a film titled *The Bowery*. The fame of these larger than life characters, the glitter of the shops, the roar of the Third Avenue elevated train, and the echo of more elegant times still held an allure for a depression-era audience. This watercolor by William Louis Sonntag, Jr. (1869–98) shares the spirit of the painting on the following two pages. 13 x 17¾. GIFT OF MRS. WILLIAM B. MILES. 32.275.2.

STATUE OF LIBERTY ENLIGHTENING THE WORLD, 1886: Also exhibited as *The Unveiling of the Statue of Liberty*, this painting depicts the grand festivities of October 28, 1886, when this enduring symbol of freedom from oppression was dedicated. Frédéric-Auguste Bartholdi's massive copper-clad statue, an engineering marvel as well as an artistic one, had been a decade in the planning. A gift from the people of France to the people of the United States, it seemed constantly to be underfunded and in jeopardy of being scrapped. Yet the backing trickled in from a variety of sources, which allowed the epic project to be completed, only three years after a similarly star-crossed venture, the Brooklyn Bridge, made its debut. The moment depicted in this painting is when a twenty-one-gun salute was fired to welcome President Grover Cleveland onto Bedloe's Island. OIL ON CANVAS BY EDWARD P. MORAN, 49½ x 39. THE J. CLARENCE DAVIES COLLECTION. 34.100.260.

(LEFT) **BROOKLYN BRIDGE, CA. 1895:** In 1882, when William Louis Sonntag, Jr., was only thirteen, he exhibited at the National Academy of Design a watercolor of the nearly completed Brooklyn Bridge. He came by his talent naturally, his father being a distinguished landscape painter of the Hudson River School. The night view depicted here was executed when the young artist's abilities were just beginning to be recognized. His paintings graced the pages of *Harper's Weekly*, *Scribners*, and Theodore Dreiser's *Ev'ry Month*. Twenty years after Sonntag's sudden death in 1898 at age twenty-nine, Dreiser wrote, in a profile of his friend in *Twelve Men*: "His name was in the perfunctory death lists of the papers the next morning. No other notice of any sort. Only a half-dozen seemed to know that he had ever lived. . . . " This painting says otherwise. GIFT OF MRS. FREDERICK A. MOORE (THE ARTIST'S WIDOW). WATERCOLOR AND GOUACHE ON PAPER, 15½ x 13. 54.63.

MADISON SQUARE GARDEN, CA. 1895: This building was the second on the site of 26th Street and Madison Avenue to bear the name Madison Square Garden. The first, built on the site of the Harlem River Railroad Depot, was known originally as "Barnum's Monster Classical and Geological Hippodrome," then as Gilmore's Garden, and finally in 1879 as Madison Square Garden. Its successor, built in 1888–89, was an opulent Moorish fantasy designed by architect Stanford White of the renowned firm of McKim, Mead, and White. He would meet his end on its roof garden in 1906, shot by Harry Thaw for having seduced, when he was forty-seven, the sixteen-year-old showgirl who had subsequently become Thaw's wife, Evelyn Nesbit. This Garden was demolished in 1925 and moved uptown to Eighth Avenue—first at 50th Street and next the current Garden at 33rd. WATERCOLOR BY WILLIAM LOUIS SONNTAG JR, 22½ x 15. 49.14.

THE BYRON COMPANY is bountifully represented in these pages for the years when it conducted business in New York City, 1888-1942. Although the firm began as a specialty studio for theatrical work, by the turn of the century, its range had extended to the interiors of elegant mansions, demotic street scenes, fancy-dress soirees, outdoor recreation, hotels and restaurants . . . anything that reflected the life of the city that Joseph Byron and his family had come to know since leaving their native England. In the 1920s ship photographs, particularly transatlantic liners, became a mainstay of the company's business. Photographer Edward Steichen wrote of the Byrons in 1958: "Their only specialty was making photographs, photographs without opinion, comment, slant, or emotion. If the word objective has any meaning in relation to photography here it is. There is no pretense or artifice, no willful accent or suppression. . . . These photographs are objective because the places, the things and the people photographed have a chance to speak for themselves without interference." When Joseph's son, Percy Byron, closed the firm in 1942 he presented to the Museum of the City of New York all 22,000 of its prints and negatives.

(LEFT) **THE EVENING TELEGRAM CYCLE PARADE, RIVERSIDE DRIVE, JUNE 6, 1896:** In a May 31, 1893 editorial in the *New York Times*, a writer sniffed, "With the cheapening in the cost of bicycle riding in the public streets has come the abuse of that privilege by thousands of ignorant loaferish individuals. Many of the bicyclists who swarm along the smooth asphalt of the Boulevard [Broadway north of 59th Street], particularly at night and on Sunday, are irresponsible and reckless young men to whom a stable keeper would not entrust a saddle horse." New York's other newspapers, however, sponsored races and parades as they competed for circulation. Here, the day's winners pose after traversing the course up the Boulevard from 65th Street to 108th Street, then on to Riverside Drive and around Grant's Tomb and the Claremont Inn. THE BYRON COLLECTION. 93.1.1.1501.

OLD WELL-WELL, 1897: Zane Grey's short story "Old Well-Well" appeared in the July 1910 issue of *Success*. In it the author went to New York's Polo Grounds in search of the man who was "famous from Boston to Baltimore as the greatest baseball fan in the East." Old Well-Well was no invention. Grey had been a Polo Grounds regular from 1892 to the middle of the following decade, and many times must he have heard the booming cry "Well! Well!! WELL!!!" with which Giants rooter Frank B. Wood annotated the tensest moments of a game. When the sixty-nine-year-old Wood died in 1914, Heywood Broun observed in his obituary: "Wood was a Giant rooter at a time when the fortunes of the team were at their lowest. Nothing could dampen his optimism. . . . The sudden and ear piercing shout of 'Well, Well, Well!' did not always please strangers who sat close at hand. In fact, complaints were made and Wood was barred from the park for many years." This is the only photograph of Old Well-Well known to exist. THE BYRON COLLECTION. 93.1.1.18315.

BASEBALL, NEW YORK'S POLO GROUNDS, 1896: A New York club had been a charter member of the National League in its first year, 1876, but the absence of a suitable park in Manhattan forced the New York Mutuals to play all their home games in Brooklyn. After a hiatus of six years, New York fielded a League entry once more in 1883, and this time they had a place to play: the original Polo Grounds at Fifth Avenue between 110th and 112th Streets. However, baseball at that location ended when the city built 111th Street through center and right fields in the fall of 1888. The field upon which this New York Giant is shown cavorting in practice was located uptown, between West 157th and 159th Streets, in the shadow of Coogan's Bluff, site of glory and heartbreak for Giants fans of ensuing generations. THE BYRON COLLECTION. 93.1.1.14858.

(RIGHT) **NONPAYING FANS, COOGAN'S BLUFF, OVERLOOKING POLO GROUNDS, 1895:** The Polo Grounds hosted college football games in the fall and baseball from April through October. Baseball players were a superstitious lot back in the day. "Find a hairpin," said Frank Chance of the famous double-play combination of Tinker to Evers to Chance, "and you'll get a hit that day." Joe Tinker believed that if he saw a wagon hauling a load of barrels he wouldn't get a hit for a week. Maybe these fans were trying to put a jinx on the Giants' opponents. THE BYRON COLLECTION. 93.1.1.15098.

OPPOSITE MULBERRY BEND [30 EAST BROADWAY], 1898: Mulberry Bend had been a notorious slum, of which Jacob Riis had written in *How the Other Half Lives* (1890): "Where Mulberry Street crooks like an elbow within hail of the old depravity of the Five Points, is 'the Bend,' foul core of New York's slums. . . . The city authorities, moved by the angry protests of ten years of sanitary reform effort, have decided that it is too much and must come down. Another Paradise Park will take its place and let in sunlight and air to work such transformation as at the Five Points, around the corner of the next block. Never was change more urgently needed." Two years later the tenements of the Bend were torn down and by the year of this photograph, respectable life had begun to take a hold, as Jewish residents strolled before the closed shops of the Sabbath. THE BYRON COLLECTION. 93.1.1.17141.

LITTLE ITALY, 1898: On the Lower East Side, Little Italy was informally bounded by Houston Street on the north, Canal Street on the south, and Broadway and Mulberry Street to the west and east, respectively. Today the Italian population of this area has dwindled as residents moved to other boroughs or the suburbs, and Chinatown has enlarged to fill much of the former enclave. THE BYRON COLLECTION. 93.1.1.3170.

BELLEVUE AMBULANCE, 1896: Bellevue, the oldest public hospital in the United States, began as an infirmary in 1736, located where City Hall now stands. In 1816, it opened its new establishment at 26th Street and the East River, where it launched the nation's first ambulance service in 1869 (until then hospitals waited for the sick to come to them). In 1892 alone, nine horse-drawn ambulances answered 4,858 calls. Here another stands ready to leave the hospital yard by the 26th Street gate. THE BYRON COLLECTION. 93.1.1.18388.

NEW YORK TELEPHONE CO. EXCHANGES, 1896: The first telephone exchange in the city was opened in October 1878 at 518 Broadway, with a makeshift switchboard that doubled as a burglar alarm system. Eighteen years later, as depicted here, the Cortlandt Street Exchange, one of twelve such in the city, boasted a row of "Hello Girls" staffing its 250-foot-long switchboard. In the "Woman's Special Supplement" of the New York *Daily Tribune* of October 2, 1898 a company spokesman declared that its early studies had revealed that males lacked the essential attributes of civility and accuracy, "leaving only one other sex to try." THE BYRON COLLECTION. 93.1.1.15998.

(LEFT) SKATING IN CENTRAL PARK, 1895: When Olmsted and Vaux planned Central Park in the 1850s they envisioned a park in the city with no intrusions of urban life. But in 1880 Edward Clark, who had made his fortune with Singer Sewing Machines, commissioned Henry J. Hardenbergh to create a massive apartment building out in the wild territories—at Eighth Avenue (what is now termed Central Park West) and 72nd Street—hence the name for the structure, the Dakota. Surrounded by other skyscrapers today, it still stands out. THE BYRON COLLECTION. 93.1.1.18321.

BATHING, MIDLAND BEACH, 1898: At the time depicted Midland Beach, Staten Island, was a vibrant resort community, attracting tourists who came by trolley or excursion boats from Manhattan and Newark. But the resonance of the photo is not in the locale, which is less vibrant today, but in its depiction of the eternal vibrancy of youth, even if copiously garbed. THE BYRON COLLECTION. 93.1.1.17474.

(LEFT) **BROOKLYN BRIDGE UNDER CONSTRUCTION, 1881:** Perhaps no image of the Brooklyn Bridge better illustrates its suspension construction than this taken by an unknown photographer. The catwalks, necessary for the cable-spinning operations, were a marvel and a caution to all New Yorkers, including the bridge engineers, who feared a calamity beyond the construction accidents that killed perhaps as many as thirty between 1865 and 1883. A sign at the head of one of the catwalks read, "Safe for only 25 men at a time. Do not walk close together, nor run, jump, or trot, break step!"—W. A. Roebling, *Eng'r in Chief.*" PRINT ARCHIVES.

THE HARBOR OF NEW YORK FROM THE BROOKLYN BRIDGE TOWER, LOOKING SOUTH-WEST, CA. 1883: From the traffic on the bridge we may date this splendid perspective view from the Brooklyn tower as post-1883, unless the artist was anticipating reality. Nine unnumbered references are offered in the border: Red Hook Point, Staten Island, Governors Island, Ellis Island, Bedloe's Island, East River, Hudson River, Jersey City, Hoboken. LITHOGRAPH PUBLISHED BY CURRIER & IVES. THE GERALD LEVINO COLLECTION. 57.100.24.

BROOKLYN BRIDGE CELEBRATION, MAY 1883: Eighteen years after it was originally proposed, the Brooklyn Bridge was formally dedicated on May 24, 1883, with President Chester Arthur and New York Governor Grover Cleveland participating. Business had shut down at noon, and few children attended school; they had positions to secure along the river banks for the grand fireworks display. At its opening it was the longest suspension bridge in the world, an engineering and aesthetic marvel. Since surpassed for length, it remains unequaled for achievement and beauty. Oil on canvas is by Warren Sheppard (1858–1937), who had studied with M. F. de Haas. 24 x 40. ON DEPOSIT FROM EDWARD C. GUDE. L779.

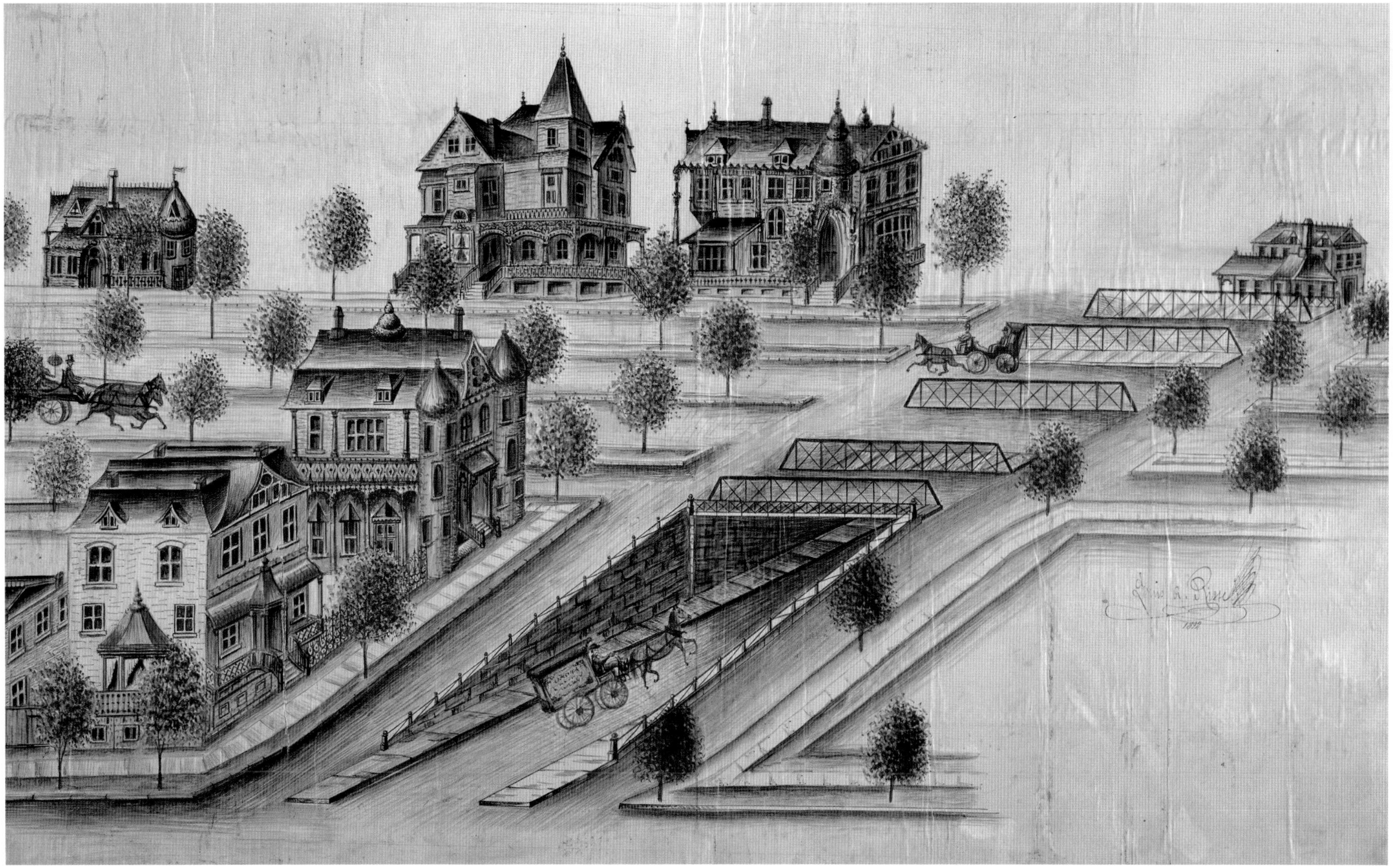

PLANNING THE GRAND CONCOURSE, 1892: Louis Aloys Risse, an Alsatian immigrant who became chief topographical engineer for New York City, first conceived of this plan for the Grand Boulevard and Concourse in the Bronx in 1870. It would connect the growing borough with Manhattan via a parkway modeled on the Champs Elysées of Paris—only larger, stretching four miles in length and separated into three roadways by tree-lined dividers. The roadway was opened to traffic in 1909. As Gloria Déak wrote in *Picturing New York*, "The Grand Concourse gave rise to elegant apartment houses where residency became a symbol of economic success for the thousands of immigrants . . . who sought a new life in this northern borough." WATERCOLOR ON PAPER, 19¾ x 29¾. GIFT OF MRS. F. L. BUNNELL. 69.111.2.

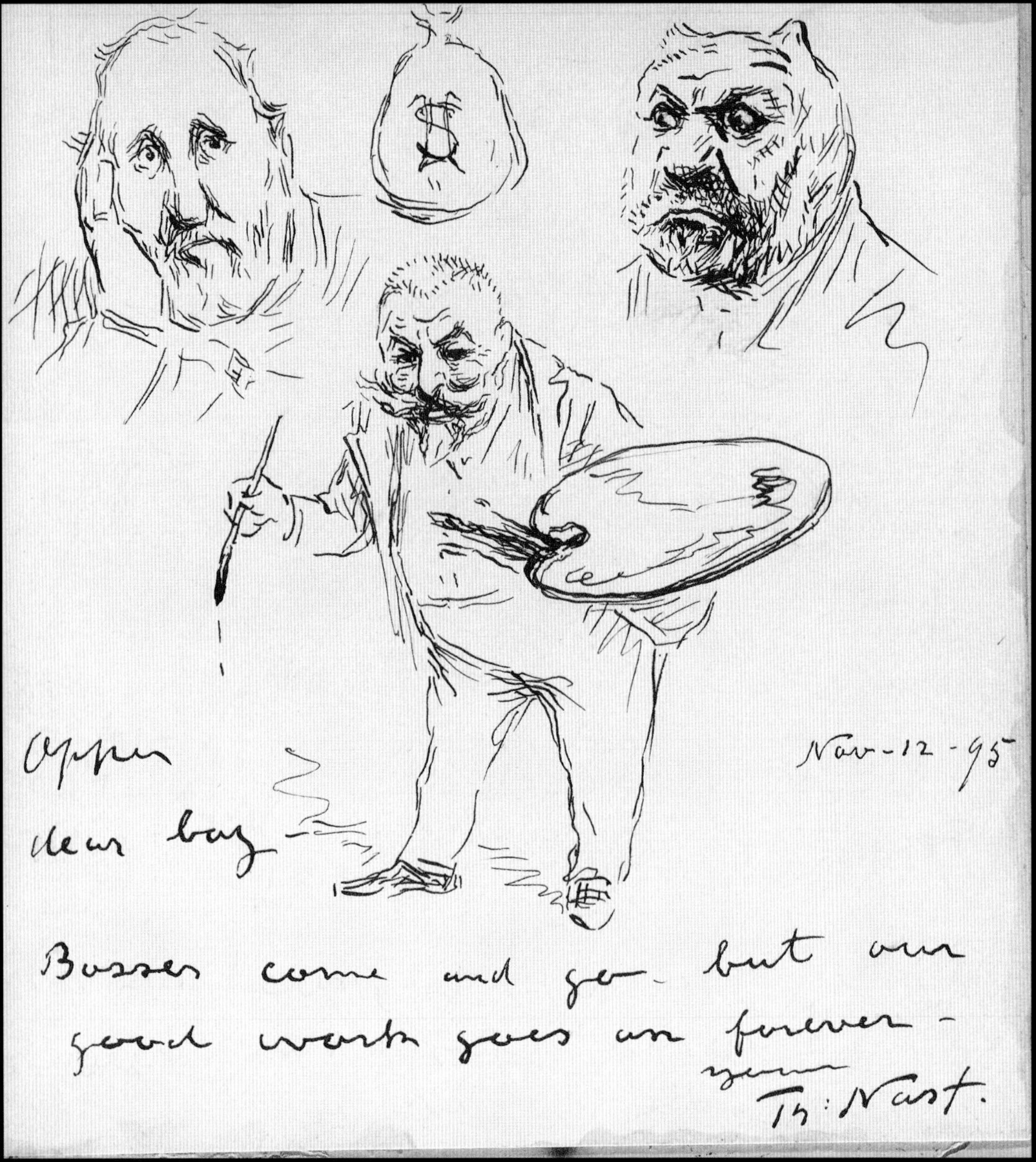
Opper
dear boy –
Nov-12-95
Bosses come and go – but our
good work goes on forever –
yours
Th: Nast.

SELF-PORTRAIT, THOMAS NAST, WITH VIGNETTES OF BOSS TWEED, 1895: "Bosses come and go," Nast wrote to fellow cartoonist Frederick Burr Opper (Happy Hooligan, Maud the Mule, Alphonse & Gaston), "but our good work goes on forever." By this time Opper was a rising star in the business and Nast, who had helped to bring down the Tweed Ring, had reason to rue his voluntary departure from *Harper's Weekly* a decade earlier. INK ON PAPER. GIFT OF CYRIL NAST. 43.239.2.

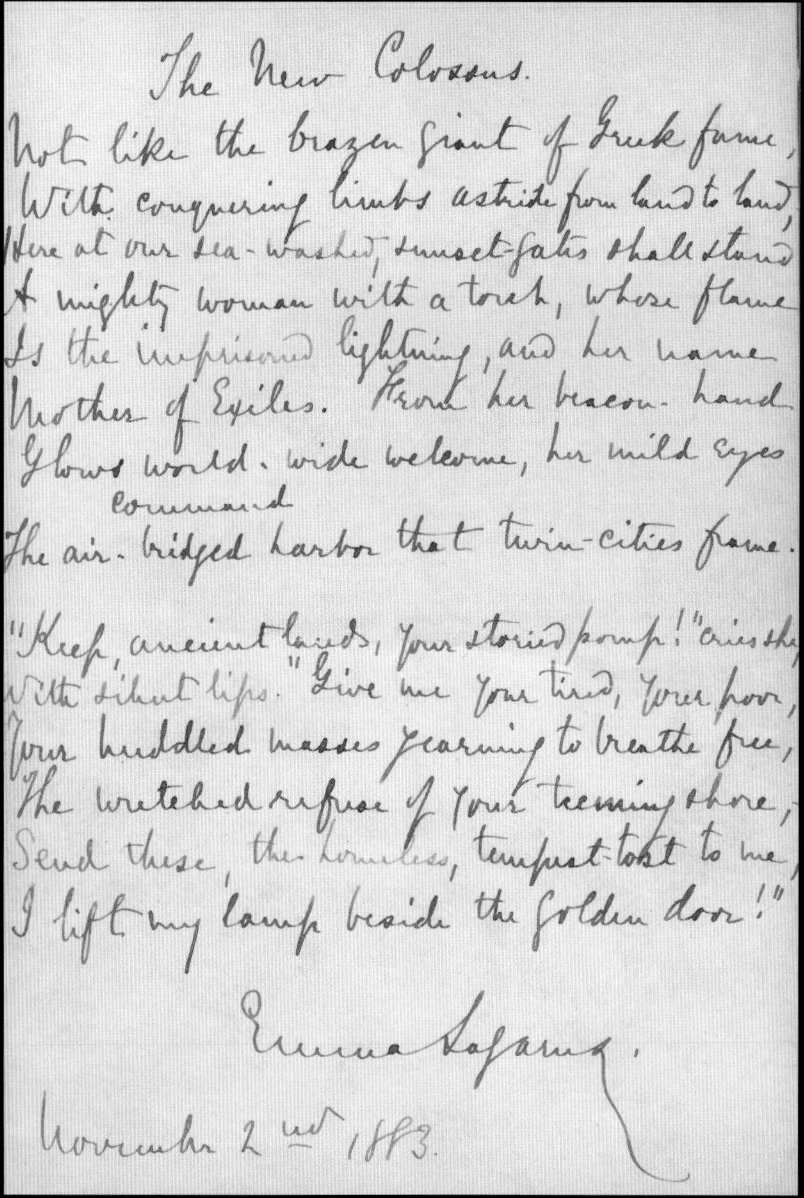
The New Colossus.

Not like the brazen giant of Greek fame,
With conquering limbs astride from land to land;
Here at our sea-washed, sunset-gates shall stand
A mighty woman with a torch, whose flame
Is the imprisoned lightning, and her name
Mother of Exiles. From her beacon-hand
Glows world-wide welcome, her mild eyes
command
The air-bridged harbor that twin-cities frame.

"Keep, ancient lands, your storied pomp!" cries she
With silent lips. "Give me your tired, your poor,
Your huddled masses yearning to breathe free,
The wretched refuse of your teeming shore,
Send these, the homeless, tempest-tost to me,
I lift my lamp beside the golden door!"

Emma Lazarus.

November 2nd 1883.

"THE NEW COLOSSUS," ORIGINAL MANUSCRIPT BY EMMA LAZARUS, NOVEMBER 2, 1883: Emma Lazarus (1849–87) wrote this celebrated sonnet for the benefit of the American campaign to raise funds for the pedestal of the Statue of Liberty. It was first read a month after she wrote it, on the opening night (December 3) of the Bartholdi Statue Pedestal Art Loan Exhibition at the National Academy of Design. Twenty years later the immortal words were inscribed on a bronze tablet within the monument. GIFT OF GEORGE S. HELLMAN. 36.319.

RAINY LATE AFTERNOON, UNION SQUARE, 1890: Union Square evolved from a fashionable northern neighborhood for the affluent of the 1840s into what *King's Handbook of New York City* described in 1893 as "a favored place for large outdoor mass-meetings." In 1882 a peaceable demonstration for an eight-hour workday had taken place here. In the next century the plaza would be known for political gatherings of a more confrontational character. Yet when Fredrick Childe Hassam (1859–1935) painted this lovely view it was still a fashionable place for a stroll. The above title is the one the artist inscribed on the back of the canvas, but the work has also been exhibited as *Rain Storm, Union Square*. OIL ON CANVAS, 28 x 36. GIFT OF MISS MARY WHITNEY BANGS. 69.121.1.

PANORAMIC VIEW OF LOWER MANHATTAN FROM BROOKLYN BRIDGE TOWER, 1876: By 1876 both towers of the Brooklyn Bridge had been constructed. Joshua H. Beal mounted the Brooklyn tower to create this five-plate panorama ending at Pier 39, around Houston Street, providing New Yorkers with an astonishing view of their city, dominated by a structure still seven years from completion. GIFT OF P. M. WHITMAN 42.410.

VIEW FROM THE ROOF OF GEORGE EHRET'S HOME, 1882: In 1879, brewer George Ehret bought a lot on Park Avenue between 93rd and 94ths Streets, not far from his Hellgate (Hell Gate) Brewery between Second and Third Avenues and one block south of his home. This dramatic view from the cupola of his brownstone, built on the north end of his lot, was part of a 360-degree series of eight photographs by Peter Baab executed in 1882. GIFT OF MRS. CARL EGGERS. 03.26.2.

(RIGHT) **THE WILLIAMSBURG WHEELMEN, 1896:** On July 4, 1895, 10,000 cyclists paraded in Brooklyn for the opening of the new bicycle path from Prospect Park to Coney Island. The Williamsburg Wheelmen, to which the three men pictured here—A. Smith, C. W. Hadley and A. Devenne—belonged, took part in the event. Only three weeks earlier, a contingent of the Williamsburg Wheelmen attended the Ainslie Street Presbyterian Church to hear a sermon by Rev. Roland S. Dawson on "The Bicycle as a Means of Grace." Hadley was a Brooklyn Consul of the nationwide League of American Wheelmen, a group more than 100,000 strong by the mid 1890s. It had been founded in 1880 to protest the rutted roads that made it hard for devotees of the "silent steed" to ride in a style befitting their fancy duds and extravagant vehicles. PHOTOGRAPHER UNKNOWN. GIFT OF CHARLES W. HADLEY. 49.300.7.

PRAYER-TIME IN THE NURSERY, FIVE POINTS HOUSE OF INDUSTRY, CA. 1889: Jacob Riis wrote in his classic *How the Other Half Lives* (1890), "The Five Points Mission and the Five Points House of Industry [at 155 Worth Street] have accomplished what no machinery of government availed to do. Sixty thousand children have been rescued by them from the streets and had their little feet set in the better way. Their work still goes on, increasing and gathering in the waifs, instructing and feeding them, and helping their parents with advice and more substantial aid. Their charity knows not creed or nationality. The House of Industry is an enormous nursery-school with an average of more than four hundred day scholars and constant boarders—'outsiders' and 'insiders.' Its influence is felt for many blocks around in that crowded part of the city. It is one of the most touching sights in the world to see a score of babies, rescued from homes of brutality and desolation, where no other blessing than a drunken curse was ever heard, saying their prayers in the nursery at bedtime. Too often their white night-gowns hide tortured little bodies and limbs cruelly bruised by inhuman hands. In the shelter of this fold they are safe, and a happier little group one may seek long and far in vain." THE JACOB A. RIIS COLLECTION. 90.13.1.127.

EASTER PARADE, FIFTH AVENUE NORTH FROM BELOW 41ST STREET, APRIL 10, 1897: Describing an earlier Easter Parade (1883), *Frank Leslie's Illustrated* had noted how Fifth Avenue "had blossomed into a splendor of elegantly clad men, women, and children, and of prancing horses, glittering harness, and shining carriages." The same might be said of the Byron Company's view fourteen years later of New Yorkers promenading alongside the Croton Distributing Reservoir, in its final year of service. In 1899–1901 it would be scuttled to make way for the New York Public Library. THE BYRON COLLECTION. 93.1.1.18453.

FIFTH AVENUE AND 23RD STREET, CA. 1898: One may no longer book a room at the grand Fifth Avenue Hotel (1859–1908) but the vista seen here is otherwise recognizable. The office building that took the place of the hotel long hosted the International Toy Center. The Worth Monument—the fifty-one-foot-high obelisk in the distance at Broadway and 24th Street, erected in 1857—still celebrates the achievements of Mexican War General William Jenkins Worth and stands above his burial place. The clock on the sidewalk still keeps time. THE BYRON COLLECTION. 93.1.1.18002.

STREET SCENE, LONG ISLAND CITY, 1897: If the view of Manhattan from the Queensboro Bridge, as F. Scott Fitzgerald wrote in *The Great Gatsby*, seemed to promise "all the mystery and the beauty in the world," the view of Queens Plaza was less gauzy. But at the turn of the century, as this view demonstrates, street life under "the El" was busy. THE BYRON COLLECTION. 93.1.1.15416.

(RIGHT) **ORCHARD STREET, LOOKING SOUTH FROM HESTER STREET, 1898:** Signs in Yiddish and English reflect the ethnic constitution of the Lower East Side, if not the variety of goods. "Bandannas and tin cups at two cents," wrote Jacob Riis in *How the Other Half Lives*, "peaches at a cent a quart, 'damaged' eggs for a song, hats for a quarter. . . . Here is a woman churning horseradish on a machine she has chained and padlocked to a tree on the sidewalk, lest someone steal it. Beside her a butcher's stand with cuts at prices the avenues never dreamed of. Old coats are hawked for fifty cents . . . and 'pants' at anything that can be got." THE BYRON COLLECTION. 93.1.1.18293.

ROSE & CO.

Byron N.Y.
9249

(LEFT) **MIDLAND BEACH, 1899:** Bathers at this Staten Island resort revealed little skin, whether on the boardwalk or on the beach. If anything, this image is a testament to a time when all men wore hats, all the time: fedoras, homburgs, bowlers, or, from "Straw Hat Day" (May 15) until summer's end, the boater. THE BYRON COLLECTION. 93.1.1.17837.

TANDEM BICYCLING, LONG BRANCH, NJ, 1898: Fleeing the heat of the city, New Yorkers would not have to travel far to find sun and surf—whether Coney Island, Midland Beach, or the Jersey Shore. Long Branch was a favorite of the middle classes; note the bathing pavilion in the background. THE BYRON COLLECTION. 93.1.1.14621.

SIXTH AVENUE NORTH, FROM 15TH STREET, 1895: It is seven decades since the IRT Sixth Avenue Elevated—the "El"—was razed in 1939 and replaced in 1940 by the IND Sixth Avenue Line. By the time of this view Sixth Avenue had become the city's major shopping district. The B. Altman store at 19th Street was faced across the avenue by Siegel-Cooper's ("The Big Store"). Simpson, Crawford & Simpson's was, as of 1900, one block north and O'Neill's occupied the next block. The stores anchored the district but the street vendors supplied its flavor, from popcorn to gum drops and peanuts, "extra fine and super roasted." THE BYRON COLLECTION. 93.1.1.18071.

A GAME OF CAT-STICK, 1898: Homeless or wayward boys of the era were known as Street Arabs. They smoked cigarettes, sold newspapers, shined shoes, and on occasion picked pockets. Yet still they were boys, with an instinct for play. The chalked scoreboard testifies to the serious nature of their game, more ancient than any American or English game of ball. Cat-stick involves striking a wooden spindle with a bat so that it pops in the air to be struck again. This image tellingly depicts the hardscrabble life of the children of the poor. THE BYRON COLLECTION. 93.1.1.18298.

RECENT VISION OF JOLLITY IN CENTRAL PARK, FEBRUARY 1895: The lucky children of the Gilded Age knew hills and fields and warmth, even in the snow. In 1974 one Jeffrey S. Granger wrote a letter to the Museum of the City of New York because he had received a Christmas card imprinted with this image. He recognized that the children in the photograph, taken nearly eighty years ago, were himself and his cousin Jewel Loebinger.
THE BYRON COLLECTION. 93.1.1.18319.

GOING TO THE RACES AT CONEY ISLAND, 1897: There is not a woman in sight as sportsmen board cars of the Smith Street-Coney Island Avenue Line of the Coney Island to Brooklyn Railroad (1890–1955). Their destination is the new Brighton Beach Racetrack, dismissed in the *Daily Tribune* as "certain to be a failure. Brighton will always be scorned by wealth and fashion . . . and beef and beans and sinkers and beer will always be the suitable bill of fare at this track." THE BYRON COLLECTION. 93.1.1.18365.

STEERAGE, S.S. *PENNLAND* RED STAR LINE, 1893: Passengers who came to this country with little more than the clothes on their backs occupied the steerage compartment of the ship—the lowest decks, with the fewest amenities. Many of the "passengers ships" were converted cargo vessels, so the steerage clientele were in fact riding in the former cargo hold. This image may be compared interestingly with Alfred Stieglitz's 1907 photograph of the same name. THE BYRON COLLECTION. 93.1.1.18432.

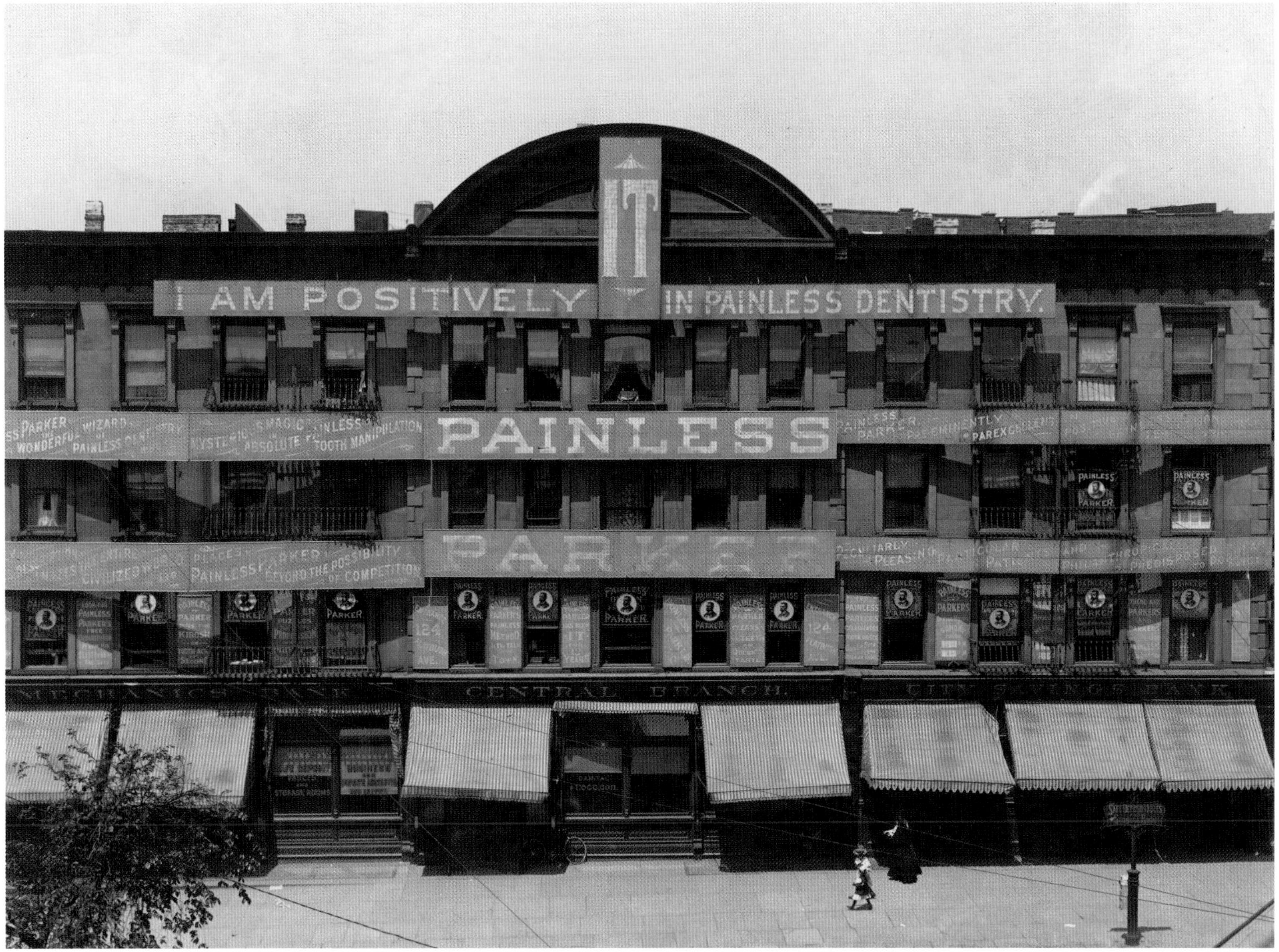

PAINLESS PARKER, 124 FLATBUSH AVENUE, BROOKLYN 1895: Edgar R. R. "Painless" Parker, "the wonderful wizard of painless dentistry," was the most flamboyant if not the best of all dentists. He employed dancing girls, a brass band, performing tigers and walruses, and a general circus setting to calm the masses frightened by dentistry. He arranged for a bugler to stand behind the patient and let fly with a mighty blast at the precise moment that Parker extracted the tooth . . . "painlessly." His enduring contribution may be that he pioneered the concept of group dental practice: at his height Parker operated thirty West Coast dental offices, employed seventy-five dentists and grossed $3 million annually. When he died in 1952 the obituaries labeled him a "chain-store dentist." But he is remembered today principally for his stunts. After some years as a street dentist, extracting teeth at fifty cents per, he established spectacular headquarters in Brooklyn. He extracted 357 teeth in one day—on a vaudeville stage—and then had a necklace made of them which he wore while practicing his trade. THE BYRON COLLECTION. 93.1.1.18393.

WEST END ROUTE
COPYRIGHT 1894
BY J.S. JOHNSTON, N.Y.
(GOVERNOR'S I.)
3010.
EL.R.R. AT SOUTH FERRY, N.Y.

(LEFT) **ELEVATED RAILROAD AT SOUTH FERRY, 1894:** J. S. Johnston is famous for his yachting views, including America's Cup participants. But he also photographed many cityscapes, including a series of elevated railway vistas in New York, where he made his home. Note the sign for Buffalo Bill's Wild West and Congress of Rough Riders of the World. During this summer's series of exhibitions, Thomas Edison filmed *Buffalo Dance*, the first time Native Americans had been depicted in the new medium. PHOTOGRAPH BY JOHN S. JOHNSTON. THE J. CLARENCE DAVIES COLLECTION.

[AMATEUR PHOTOGRAPHER, BRONX], 1886: Robert L. Bracklow (1849–1919) was a legal stationer and bookseller in Manhattan's financial district who sold his albumen prints in his shop, pasted on mounts and inscribed on the verso "Glimpses through the Camera." He was also a member of Stieglitz's Camera Club. He never thought of his straightforward style as art—yet artistic he certainly was. Neglected in his own day, Bracklow was "adopted" by Alexander Alland, who in the 1940s acquired 2,000 of his negatives for the Museum of the City of New York and printed them out, as he had previously done for Jacob Riis before Riis was recognized for his contributions to documentary photography. NEGATIVE BY ROBERT BRACKLOW, PHOTOGRAPH PRINTED BY ALEXANDER ALLAND. 93.91.260.

MAUDE ADAMS AND JESSIE MACKAYE IN *THE LITTLE MINISTER*, 1897: The evening of September 27, 1897 marked the Broadway opening of James M. Barrie's theatrical adaptation of his novel *The Little Minister* at the Empire Theatre. Reaching the heights in a role written for her (as Lady Babbie) was Maude Adams, who would surpass herself eight years later as the lead in another Barrie vehicle, *Peter Pan*. Following that great success, she remained for some time the top-grossing theatrical performer of her day. Jessie Mackaye never attained such heights, but she was admired for her way with light comedy and toured with DeWolf Hopper's company. PHOTOGRAPH BY NAPOLEON SARONY. GIFT OF EDWIN BOOTH GROSSMAN. 36.347.2.

ICE HOUSES ON BRONX RIVER, 1890: The ice supply to New York City derived from sources as far north as Troy and as near as Van Cortlandt Lake and the Bronx River which, dammed at Tuckahoe, furnished power for a local rubber mill in warm weather and the so called "Croton Lake Ice" for the city in the winter. The Museum of the City of New York owns several accomplished watercolors by John M. Slaney but little is known of him other than his consecutive listing as an engineer in the New York City directories of 1889–92. WATERCOLOR, 10½ x 14. THE J. CLARENCE DAVIES COLLECTION. 34.100.798.

(RIGHT) **STARIN'S EXCURSIONS, 1878:** John Henry Starin's specialty was day excursions—picnics to nearby garden spots more or less under his control; these locations included Glen Island on Long Island Sound and Islandwild, reserved for Sunday school parties. He won enormous good will (and election to the State Legislature) by providing annual complimentary excursions to members of the Grand Army of the Republic, the Metropolitan Police, and the New York Newsboys Home. A September 1876 trip for the newsboys featured, according to the *Herald*, "a collation of beef and ham sandwiches, bread and butter, pressed beef, red herrings, cheese, crackers, ginger snaps, sponge cakes, lemonade and milk . . . . the lads returned to New York, enlivened by one day's brightness that will, doubtless, be remembered with joy." LITHOGRAPH PUBLISHED BY DONALDSON BROS. THE J. CLARENCE DAVIES COLLECTION. 29.100.3525.

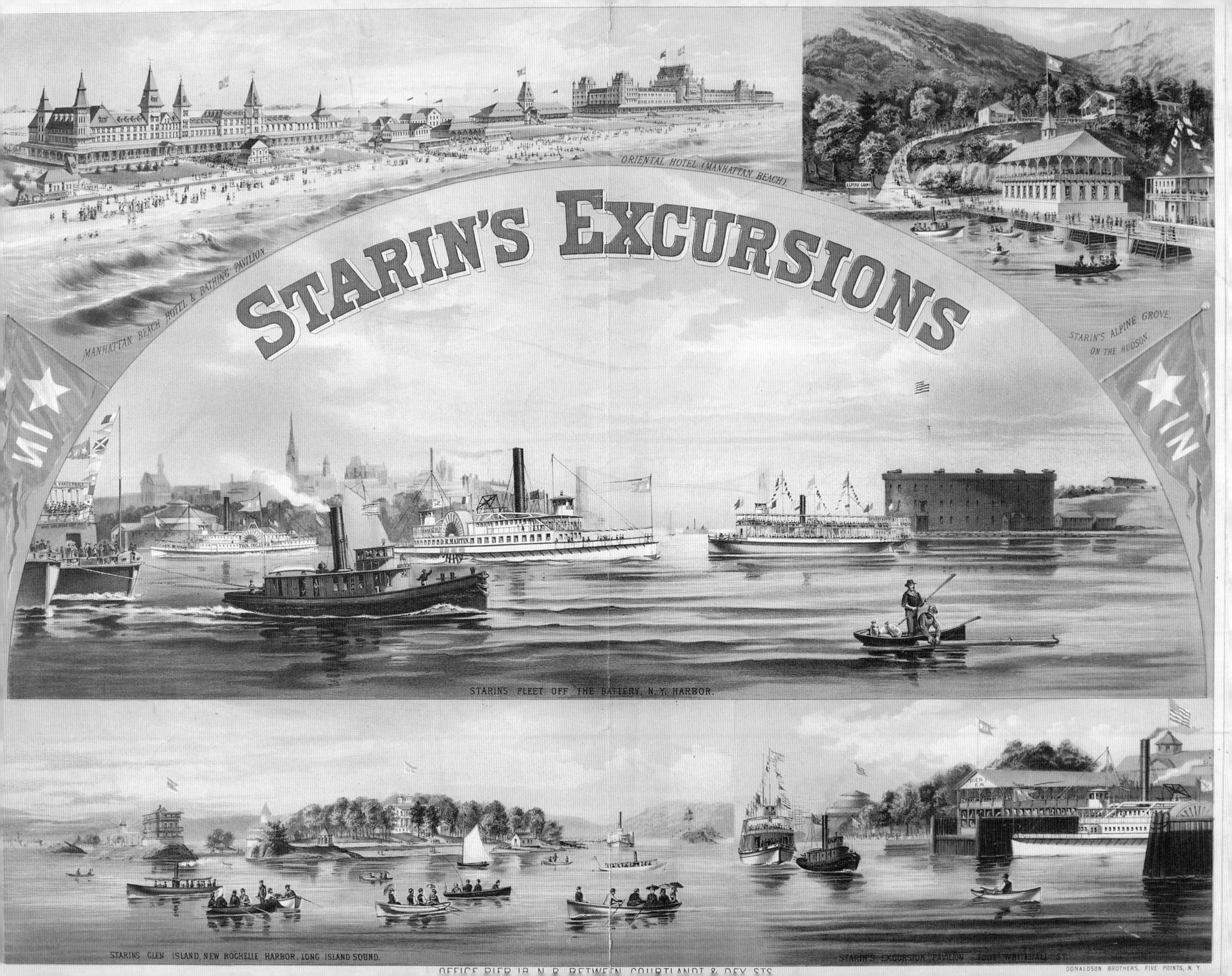
STARIN'S EXCURSIONS
ORIENTAL HOTEL (MANHATTAN BEACH)
MANHATTAN BEACH HOTEL & BATHING PAVILION
STARIN'S ALPINE GROVE, ON THE HUDSON
STARIN'S FLEET OFF THE BATTERY, N. Y. HARBOR.
STARINS GLEN ISLAND, NEW ROCHELLE HARBOR, LONG ISLAND SOUND.
STARIN'S EXCURSION PAVILION, FOOT WHITEHALL ST.
OFFICE PIER 18 N.R. BETWEEN COURTLANDT & DEY STS
DONALDSON BROTHERS, FIVE POINTS, N.Y.

THALIA THEATER (FORMERLY THE BOWERY THEATRE), CA. 1880: This is an undated exemplar of changing New York. The Bowery Theatre was a stalwart at 46–48 Bowery through four fires and many changes in ownership in the years 1826–1929. It was renamed the Thalia in 1879 when it converted to a Yiddish playhouse. The Atlantic Garden next door, which had begun life in 1858 as a German musical and vaudeville venue, had stood almost unchanged on its site until October 3, 1910, when its famous old sign was plastered over with billboards in Yiddish announcing a Hebrew variety program. These theatrical landmarks had long been obscured by the Third Avenue Elevated Railway, which outlived both of them, ending its long run in 1956. PHOTOGRAPHER UNKNOWN. THE J. CLARENCE DAVIES COLLECTION.

CENTRAL PARK BOAT HOUSE, CA. 1880: The cyanotype was already an antique process at the time of this serene image. Invented in 1842 by John Herschel, the photographic printing process that creates a cyan-blue print had a brief vogue as English botanist Anna Atkins published a book in the following year illustrated with cyanotypes of algae. When Augustus Hepp, a landscape gardener for Central Park and one of the entrants in the 1857 design competition for the park, was commissioned in 1879 by the U.S. Secretary of State, William Evarts, to make photographs of the park to be presented as a gift to the French government, he chose the cyanotype method. In the year he captured this image, however, he was dismissed from his job in a contretemps over his alleged removal of exotic plants from the park department greenhouses to his home. CYANOTYPE BY AUGUSTUS HEPP. GIFT OF RUTH A. HEPP.

NATIVE AMERICAN MAN, CA. 1898: This haunting image of intersecting cultures does not depict a visiting Native American accompanying Buffalo Bill's Wild West Show; this gentleman is a New Yorker, residing in an apartment and making his way in the workaday of urban life. FROM 6 x 9 GLASS PLATE NEGATIVE BY WILLIAM M. VAN DER WEYDE. THE VAN DER WEYDE COLLECTION.

NATIVE AMERICAN WOMAN, CA. 1898: This is no piecework assignment taken home for later delivery to the sweatshop. This young woman is beading in the traditional manner, most likely for later sale to curiosity seekers. FROM 6 x 9 GLASS PLATE NEGATIVE. BY WILLIAM M. VAN DER WEYDE. THE VAN DER WEYDE COLLECTION.

ITALIAN MOTHER, 1889: Of the rag trade, Jacob Riis wrote in *How the Other Half Lives* (1890): "Only a few years ago, when rag-picking was carried on in a desultory and irresponsible sort of way, the city hired gangs of men to trim the ash-scows before they were sent out to sea. . . . The men were paid a dollar and a half a day, kept what they found that was worth having, and allowed the swarms of Italians who hung about the dumps to do the heavy work for them, letting them have their pick of the loads for their trouble." In the original edition of Jacob Riis's book, this image was rendered as a drawing, signed "Kenyon Cox, 1889, after photograph." Of the book's thirty-six images, seventeen were reproduced in crude halftone, the other nineteen, including this one, as woodcuts. Thus Riis was remembered primarily as a social reformer and not a photojournalist and the images he and his colleagues produced were largely overlooked until 1947, when Alexander Alland made enlargements from the glass negatives that he had acquired for the Museum of the City of New York. JACOB A. RIIS

LODGERS IN A CROWDED BAYARD STREET TENEMENT—"FIVE CENTS A SPOT," 1889: This shocking photograph, one of the most famous in Riis's book, was shot at night with the aid of magnesium flash powder. Although he displayed the photograph in his lectures and lantern-slide shows, readers of *How the Other Half Lives* saw it only in woodcut. Riis wrote of the squalid apartment: "In a room not thirteen feet either way slept twelve men and women, two or three in bunks set in a sort of alcove, the rest on the floor. A kerosene lamp burned dimly in the fearful atmosphere, probably to guide other and later arrivals to their 'beds,' for it was only just past midnight. . . . Most of the men were lodgers, who slept there for five cents a spot." JACOB A. RIIS COLLECTION. 90.13.2.89.

TRAMP IN A MULBERRY STREET YARD, 1887–88: Riis writes of this scenic gentleman: "On one of my visits to 'the Bend' I came across a particularly ragged and disreputable tramp, who sat smoking his pipe on the rung of a ladder with such evident philosophic contentment in the busy labor of a score of rag-pickers all about him, that I bade him sit for a picture, offering him ten cents for the job. He accepted the offer with hardly a nod, and sat patiently watching me from his perch until I got ready for work. Then he took the pipe out of his mouth and put it in his pocket, calmly declaring that it was not included in the contract, and that it was worth a quarter to have it go in the picture." PHOTOGRAPH BY RICHARD HOE LAWRENCE. JACOB A. RIIS COLLECTION. 90.13.2.50.

MULBERRY STREET, 1890: Jacob Riis may well have used this colored lantern slide of a street scene to accompany his own more intimate images; Riis was not a master technician and this street scene was almost surely outside his range. Here Mulberry Street seems positively cheerful, in contrast with the menace that characterized his photographs of the Mulberry Bend a decade earlier. HAND COLORED LANTERN SLIDE. THE JACOB A. RIIS COLLECTION. 90.13.2.215.

BANDITS' ROOST, 1887–88: The location is the alley at 59½ Mulberry Street, at the heart of Mulberry Bend, notorious as the most crime-ridden district of the city. (This posed scene was reenacted precisely in Martin Scorsese's 2002 film *Gangs of New York*.) Of "the Bend" Riis wrote: "Abuse is the normal condition of 'the Bend,' murder its everyday crop, with the tenants not always the criminals. In this block between Bayard, Park, Mulberry, and Baxter Streets, 'the Bend' proper, the late Tenement House Commission counted 155 deaths of children in a specimen year (1882)." PHOTOGRAPH BY RICHARD HOE LAWRENCE. HAND COLORED LANTERN SLIDE. JACOB A. RIIS COLLECTION. 90.13.2.59.

WILLIAM MERRITT CHASE IN HIS 10TH STREET STUDIO, CA. 1885: Though he painted conventional subjects, Chase (1849–1916) was a nonconformist. A leader of the younger painters who challenged the supremacy of the National Academy of Design, he was a founding member of the Society of American Artists. He cultivated a flamboyance in dress and manner that was matched by the calculated disarray, exoticism, and excess of his 10th Street studio, which was the subject of one of his more celebrated paintings. By 1895 constrained means forced Chase to close his studio and auction his possessions. PHOTOGRAPH BY GEORGE COLLINS COX. GIFT OF ROSAMOND GILDER AND MRS. WALTER W. PALMER. 58.74.1.

CHAPTER IX | 1899–1929

BITING THE APPLE

NEW YORK NIGHTLIFE IN THE ROARING TWENTIES —— LEW ERENBERG

When nightclubs first developed as an affluent pastime in the 1910s and 1920s, they signaled the emergence of a new urban culture. Although many cities had a vibrant nightlife, New York stood out as the "Paris" of America. Cabarets helped form an image of the city as a place to be enjoyed, for they combined the entertainment of the cafés of Paris with that of lower-class American vice districts and marketed the blend as the height of urban life. In its restaurants, nightclubs and hotels, New York City offered to its well-off residents and visitors alike a nightly menu of excitement, sexual experimentation, pleasure, and fantasy. As a result, in novels and films of the era, New York was often depicted as the pleasure capital of the nation. Nightclubs helped form the mystique of the big city, and Broadway cafés were at the center of the excitement. They provided settings for the fantasies money might buy in an urban place where Victorian mores no longer reigned. In the same club could be found socialites, wealthy gamblers, ethnic entertainers, college students, and business couples. But above all, two features gave the cabaret its unique character. First, it offered informal and intimate entertainment in a public setting. A key aspect of the cabaret, which first emerged in the 1910s in Broadway's big lobster palace restaurants—Shanley's, Rector's, Churchill's, Louis Martin's—was the elimination of the stage and the placement of the action on the floor. Doing turns on the "floor" and among the tables, entertainers broke down the age-old barrier between performer and audience. To attract the attention of patrons amid all the clatter and distraction of a drinking environment, successful performers relied on personal appeal as much as their acts.

The second defining characteristic of the cabaret was that it provided a place where the public could eat, drink, and dance under one roof. Its anonymity gave New Yorkers a chance to experience and display public intimacy through new forms of dance. The dances were informal, based on the shuffle-walk step of black musical culture, and intimate, featuring close holds and tight embraces as in the well-named animal dances, the bunny hug, turkey trot, grizzly bear, and fox trot. That dancing patrons shared the floor with entertainers suggests that audiences were exploring their own "performing selves."

Much of the cabaret's appeal lay in the opportunity for men and women to engage in self-expression and sexual experimentation in fast heterosexual social environments, a sharp contrast to the all-male saloons and Tenderloin-district dance halls that marked the previous century. The dance craze of 1912–16 had made stars of ballroom dancers such as Vernon and Irene Castle, and drew men and women to Broadway cafés to dance from afternoon until the morning. The new steps, danced to James Reese Europe's ragtime music or the popular strains of Tin Pan Alley songwriters, encouraged couples to get on the floor and shake their shoulders, snap their fingers, and hug each other in public. After Florenz

Ziegfeld introduced his own "Midnight Frolic" atop the New Amsterdam Theater, cafés also turned to chorus girls who interacted with the men in the audience through ritualized flirting. Nightclubs thus became associated with action, experience, and possibility as new alternatives to the structured roles of home, job, and college. Alcohol contributed to this informality by helping people to "get loose." By permitting both sexes to enjoy a playful rebellion against the self-denying traditions of the past, New York nightclubs over the course of the twentieth century became symbols of the modern era.

The new urban culture associated with nightclubs flowered during the 1920s, fostered by prosperity, a middle-class youth culture bent on "going out" in the modern system of dating, and the desire for personal escape and liberation. Consumer capitalism was in the ascendant and "big spenders" fueled the surge in nightclubs. Yet as nightlife expanded in the Prohibition era, it rose outside the domain of acceptable middle-class morality. The war against alcohol expressed a larger hostility toward big cities, but it focused on New York as the capital of the new sexual and entertainment culture. Besides drink, moralists attacked movies, jazz, and cigarette smoking by women as un-American emanations of a mongrelized culture. Prohibition thus represented an attempt by small-town, rural, and urban Protestant citizens to establish the hegemony of their producer and familial values over the new, expansive consumption values associated with a more cosmopolitan urban life. Such moral opposition changed the face of nightlife by driving the older cabarets out of business because they could no longer sell liquor legally. "We can't go on at a profit on soft drinks," explained Shanley's owner. "We obey the law and lose money, and we can't afford that." Those who continued selling liquor were padlocked, fined, and lost considerable income. Many sold out to dancehalls or Chinese restaurants.

While nightclubs flourished during the 1920s in New York, they were driven underground as speakeasies. As their numbers grew, so too did the legion of bootleggers who profited from untaxed liquor sales. By 1925, when New York City, under the protection of Mayor Jimmy Walker, ceased enforcement of Prohibition, criminals dominated the nightclub business. For urbanites at a variety of social levels, criminals provided alcohol, entertainment, and prostitution. Most bootleggers, who came from the city's many ethnic gangs, saw Broadway as a splashy entryway onto a larger American stage. Welsh-born Owney Madden, former leader of the largely Irish Hell's Kitchen Gophers gang, left prison in 1923 to run the Phoenix Cereal Beverage Company, which supplied beer to West side and Harlem clubs. With several partners, Madden owned numerous clubs, including Broadway's Silver Slipper and Harlem's famed Cotton Club, while Irish-American Larry Fay ran Club Napoleon, El Fey Club, Del Fay, and several other spots with entertainer Texas Guinan. Jewish mobsters also played a large role. Gambler Arnold Rothstein lent money to bootleggers and owned pieces of many Broadway and Harlem clubs, while gambler Connie Immerman ran Connie's Inn in Harlem; Lou Schwartz ran spots with singer Harry Richman, including the Club Richman. Tommy Guinan's Playground, the Club Rendezvous, Les Ambassadeurs, Frivolity, Fifty Fifty, Parody, and the Plantation also had gangster ownership.

As liquor dealers and gamblers, the new owners were less attuned than the restaurant men to "civility" and more to primal audience demands. Under their direction clubs became exclusively drinking environments and food was of minor interest. People came to drink, dance, and be entertained, and illegal liquor and a $2–$5 cover charge provided the profits. Prohibition brought other changes too. The threat of raids made expensive décor unwise, and many clubs sought the relative anonymity of cellars, basements, and back rooms in the brownstones of the Forties and Fifties. As a result, Broadway-area clubs became more intimate. El Fay's on 46th Street, east of Broadway, on the second floor above a restaurant, for example, seated eighty people. Customers climbed a narrow stairway to a door with a peephole. Everything was portable. Membership cards, peepholes, silk on the walls, and a tent effect over the dance floor made the club into what entertainer Jimmy Durante called "more like an intimate party." Liquor fueled the profits. Clubs were supposed to supply set-ups only, but Durante estimated that 90 percent of the clubs sold illegal alcohol, while the owners paid protection to local and federal officials. Removed from the public eye, people pursued personal freedom in a more private atmosphere. Gangster club owners were tolerated because they challenged restrictions on personal choice.

Part of an ethnic gambling and male sporting subculture, the new gangsters viewed life from a rough male perspective. They sought "action" outside established social hierarchies and operated between social worlds. Indeed, the Broadway clubs offered gamblers and other mobsters the opportunity to dress up and mix with businessmen, athletes, and entertainers. The attractions of risk, danger, public intimacy, and the chance to see a good show and rub elbows with celebrities out to play appealed to enough of the public to make the clubs profitable. Moreover, the new bootleggers and club owners welcomed lower-class entertainers and gave them freer rein than had the earlier cabarets. In the smaller clubs, they featured chorus girls and innovative entertainers who engaged in lively exchanges with patrons and were rougher in tone and "more popular" than pre-World War I performers. Led by such stars as Ted Lewis at the Parody; Clayton, Jackson, and Durante at the Silver Slipper; Helen Morgan at the House of Morgan; Sophie Tucker at her Playground; Harry Richman at Club Richman; and Texas Guinan all over the Broadway area, the nightclub merged people of varying status to create a new vernacular culture. And in that culture, spending and consumption seemed to expand the realm of the personal, promising to free people from authority, hierarchy, and the demands of social position. As a well-known opponent of Prohibition, Texas Guinan glorified the new personal freedom as a part of the public's private rights.

Unregulated by law and protected by politicians, nightclubs were not above unscrupulous activities. As investigations made clear, club owners often operated "clip" joints barely a step above whorehouses. These "closed-door" spots relied on out-of-town buyers and cheating husbands looking for a good time. Often run by lower-level criminals, they paid cab drivers and waiters at other clubs to steer unsuspecting customers to their cafés, where anything could happen. The club owners might change the sums on the checks of drunken patrons or, in extreme cases, use "knock-out" drops so that they could rob customers. While clip joints continued to give all nightclubs an unsavory reputation, other nightclubs expanded the space available for hetero-social entertainment. Around Broadway and on the East Side, the Club Richman, the Montmartre, Terrace, Villa Vallee, and the Silver Slipper appealed to younger audiences. The *New Yorker*'s nightlife columnist, Lipstick, often focused on clubs where young daters could find "Tables for Two" suitable for fun and romance. Public nightlife offered the young a greater range of dances, drinks, and friends without the direct supervision of parents, as well as a privacy that their familial homes and more genteel ballrooms could not.

The increased emphasis on personal impulses contributed to the development of exotic activities outside the downtown amusement zones. During the 1920s, adventurous pleasure seekers traveled to "bohemian" Greenwich Village tosspots like Don Dickerman's Pirate's Den or Barney Gallant's Greenwich Village Inn, which merchandised the atmosphere of New York's Latin Quarter. Village club owners commercialized the "free love" atmosphere and homosexual aura of the area for uptown tourists who could indulge in more adventurous forms of sensuality. The Village's overtones of free sexuality attracted people from many backgrounds because they could see artists and free-thinkers apparently uninterested in success or money, desirous only of living the good life. Moreover, the Village had a reputation for homosexuality, and conventional whites went there to see "long-haired men and short-haired women" at play. Uptowners may have desired this same lack of responsibility in leisure, but in their normal lives they remained committed to a world of success and respectability. Consequently, the Village's many cabarets and tea rooms existed as an area of fantasy, where visitors could easily buy an experience and vicariously take part in a world of a wilder imaginary. Some of the clubs capitalized on this penchant for slumming by creating atmospheres steeped in fantasy. Don Dickerman's Pirate's Den, for example, reproduced a pirate's ship replete with pirate-dressed doormen, dimly lit tunnels, ship balconies, and netting—all lit with ships' lanterns.

Broadway clubs also exploited the potentials of fantasy. The Rendezvous on Broadway featured a South Sea Island décor, which alternated with Russian trappings. In its all-black recreation of *Shuffle Along*, Lew Leslie's Plantation Club created a plantation atmosphere with log cabins, black Mammies, a picket fence around the dance floor, and even Aunt Jemima flipping flapjacks. The Plantation anticipated the rise of Harlem as a nightlife zone for whites. Just as whites had looked to the Village for real life while keeping it at a distance, they did the same in Harlem.

By the 20s, Harlem had become a segregated neighborhood, but one that took great pride in its artistic and entertainment contributions to American life. Praised for their natural freedom and expressiveness but restricted by racial fears, African Americans created their own places of amusement where they could enjoy the benefits of Northern urban life and freedom from Southern segregation. In exploring their pasts, blacks created a new urban slang, a host of vernacular dances such as the Charleston, and the music that gave the decade its name—jazz. By 1925, whites began going to Harlem, attracted by the wide open atmosphere, the free flow of alcohol, and the opportunity to enjoy the sensuality and free expression of the "New Negro," who conformed to a white vision.

From the mid-1920s to the early 1930s, Harlem clubs represented the epitome of slumming. Originally intended for black patronage, these clubs began opening their doors to whites. The Cotton Club, Connie's Inn, and Ed Smalls' Paradise were the most famous, but there were also innumerable small clubs, some of which operated only after hours and featured mixed-sex heterosexual and homosexual entertainment. Most of the bigger clubs were white owned and appealed to white fantasies of Harlem life. Blacks comprised the entertainment, but the business talent was usually white. While many of the big clubs presented revues that were variants of Broadway, whites had the image that black men and women were natural performers—this was the real thing. Black performers were presented as natural, childlike, and uninhibited because unlike whites, they were not confined by civilization. Guidebooks advised whites to go late, when all things forbidden during the day were available in those few hours stolen from conventional life. Out for the evening, whites created a city that never slept.

The Cotton Club and Connie's Inn created a cosmopolitan entertainment world linked to Broadway and high society. Geared to downtown whites, the bigger clubs welcomed ethnically mixed Broadway entertainers and the wealthy in a sensual but safe environment. The sensual was supplied by the African décor and primitive themes in the entertainment, while safety emerged from the segregation of blacks from the audience and the overlay of plantation settings. With liquor money at their disposal, the owners assembled the greatest talents available. This led to the creation of a vernacular musical culture based on the mixing of two outsiders to American life—black and Jewish entertainers. Harold Arlen, Dorothy Fields, Irving Berlin, and George Gershwin, for example, wrote popular music for black performers in Harlem or else took the dance steps and jazz styles for use downtown. Meanwhile, Ethel Waters, Lena Horne, Buck and Bubbles, and a vast array of other black talents performed popular songs written especially for them by Jewish songwriters. In the clubs of Harlem, black and Jewish entertainers, songwriters, and performers created a new style of American culture.

Jazz bands heightened the exotic image of the clubs. The bigger clubs paid the highest salaries to the best bands, offering national exposure over the live radio programs that emanated from the club floors. Duke Ellington, Jimmy Lunceford, and Cab Calloway, along with singers such as Ethel Waters and dancers such as Snake Hips Tucker, for instance, attracted white dancers and listeners eager to get loose. Moreover, black musicians and performers gained Broadway show experience, while white Broadway composers created hits with black-inspired material written especially for black artists. As these black bands became household names, Harlem clubs became the pinnacle of black musical hopes. Indeed, the Harlem clubs often supplied the money to bring black revues, such as *Connie's Hot Chocolates*, to Broadway. Given the segregated nature of the experience, the bands were marketed as "exotic" and sensual, suitable for the Harlem night but problematic for the day. As he watched whites dancing in a Harlem café, James Weldon Johnson was amazed as whites tried to throw off the inhibitions of civilization and strived to become "colored." Segregation notwithstanding, Harlem clubs provided a space where jazz became an essential part of American culture.

The Depression temporarily devastated nightlife. Along with every other type of entertainment, by 1932 nightclubs were in grave trouble. The association with illegal alcohol and crime, sexual looseness, a decadent upper class, an inattentive city administration, and "mongrelized" entertainment made nightclubs representative of corruption of American values and contributed to their decline. The decline was short lived. By 1935, fueled by Repeal and New Deal spending, nightclubs reemerged in new and altered form, and New York resumed its role as the nation's amusement capital. Though Harlem's nightlife declined, huge clubs appeared on Broadway, Café Society emerged along the East Side, and Fifty-Second Street became the swing capital of the world. New York was the Big Apple.

(RIGHT) STEEPLECHASE PARK, CONEY ISLAND, CA. 1903: George C. Tilyou's Steeplechase Park was both naughty and nice. Opening in 1897 at Ocean and Surf Avenues and West 16th Street, it was named for its signature ride: a mechanical racecourse (right, center) that sped "horse" riders along a half mile of curving tracks in less than thirty-five seconds. The ride concluded indoors, where jets of air blew up women's skirts. Today the site of Steeplechase Park, shuttered in 1964, is occupied by a minor-league baseball club named for the old rollercoaster, the Brooklyn Cyclones. Information about the unsigned painting was provided by the donor, Mrs. George C. Tilyou. She believed the artist was named McKay—Leo, she thought—a scenic painter in her husband's employ. A search of the 1900 census for New York reveals, however, that Leo McKay was then the eight-year-old son of forty-four-year-old painter Peter McKay. OIL ON CANVAS, 51 x 80. GIFT OF MRS. GEORGE C. TILYOU. 54.167.

LEW ERENBERG IS PROFESSOR OF HISTORY AT LOYOLA UNIVERSITY CHICAGO. HE IS THE AUTHOR OF *STEPPIN' OUT: NEW YORK NIGHTLIFE AND THE TRANSFORMATION OF AMERICAN CULTURE, 1890-1930* (UNIVERSITY OF CHICAGO REPRINT, 1984); *SWINGIN' THE DREAM: BIG BAND JAZZ AND THE REBIRTH OF AMERICAN CULTURE* (UNIVERSITY OF CHICAGO, 1998); *THE GREATEST FIGHT OF OUR GENERATION: LOUIS VS. SCHMELING* (OXFORD UNIVERSITY PRESS, 2005); AND CO-EDITOR OF *THE WAR IN AMERICAN CULTURE: SOCIETY AND CONSCIOUSNESS DURING WORLD WAR II* (UNIVERSITY OF CHICAGO PRESS, 1996).

STADIUM

LUNA PARK, CONEY ISLAND, 1906: In 1901 Elmer "Skip" Dundy and Frederic Thompson created a twenty-minute ride called "A Trip to the Moon" and exhibited it at the Pan-American International Exposition in Buffalo. George C. Tilyou saw it and convinced the proprietors to install it at Steeplechase Park for the following year. After a dispute with Tilyou over profit splits led to a rupture, Dundy and Thompson bought out the ramshackle Sea Lion Park, the first of Coney's clustered amusement centers, and on May 16, 1903 opened Luna Park at night. As Albert Bigelow Paine wrote, "A long festoon of electric light leaped from one side of the park to the other, and was followed by a second and a third. Then there was a perfect maze of them. Tall towers that had grown dim suddenly broke forth in electric outlines and gay rosettes of color, as the living spark of light traveled hither and thither, until the place was transformed into an enchanted garden, of such Aladdin never dreamed." Luna Park fell victim to several fires in 1944 and was not rebuilt. PHOTOGRAPH BY SAMUEL H. GOTTSCHO. THE GOTTSCHO-SCHLEISNER COLLECTION. 54.77.6.

CHEF LEONI EXERCISING HIS COOKS ON THE ROOF OF THE COMMODORE HOTEL, 1920: This vision in fluttering white shows perhaps a hundred cooks atop the Commodore Hotel. Located at 42nd Street and Lexington Avenue, the mammoth building containing 1,956 guest rooms within its twenty-eight floors had just been completed in 1919. The Byrons shot a series depicting the flamboyant chef's daily routine. THE BYRON COLLECTION. 93.1.1.6074.

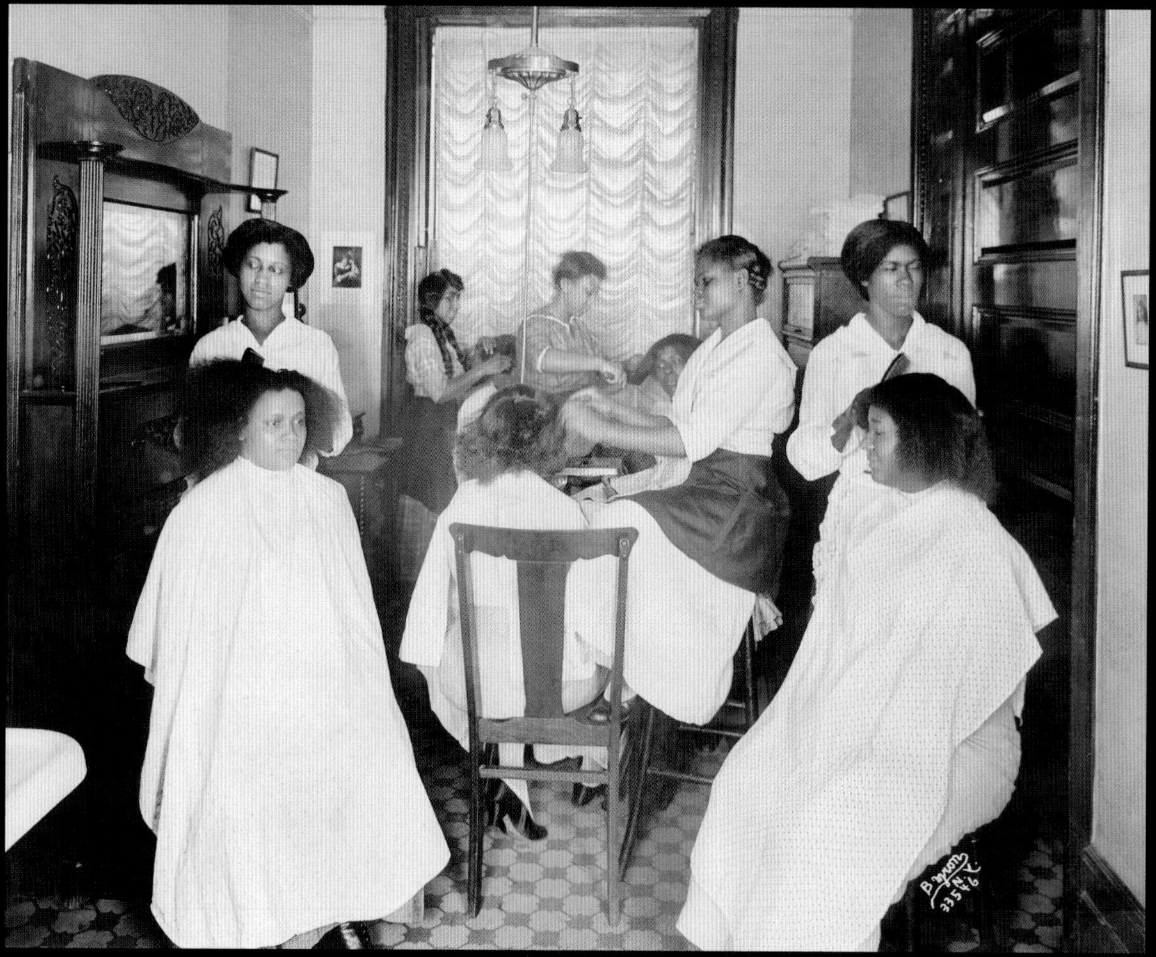

MRS. ROBINSON'S BEAUTY PARLOR, 1915: Madame C. J. Walker (née Sarah Breedlove) developed a line of hair care products and methods for African-American women that made her America's first self-made female millionaire. Her daughter and business partner, A'lelia Walker Robinson, invited the Byron photographer to document her extensive business in beauty at West 136th Street. THE BYRON COLLECTION. 93.1.1.10837.

C. K. G. BILLINGS' HORSEBACK DINNER AT SHERRY'S RESTAURANT, 1903: In an event that has come to symbolize the wretched excess of the Gilded Age, "American Horse King" C. K. G. (Cornelius Kingsley Garrison) Billings threw quite a dinner party. At Louis Sherry's Restaurant, at the southwest corner of Fifth Avenue and 44th Street, he gathered thirty-six guests to celebrate with him the opening on the morrow of his new capacious stable at 196th Street and Fort Washington Road. Each guest was given a calm riding-academy horse whose saddle carried a dining tray. Champagne was supplied in saddle bags with a rubber tube for imbibing. Waiters were dressed as grooms. At the conclusion of the dinner, oat-filled troughs were set before the patient equines. THE BYRON COLLECTION. 93.1.1.3940.

AUTOMATIC VAUDEVILLE, 46 EAST 14TH STREET, 1905: Beginning life in March 1904, this penny arcade of wonders occupied an ornate building at the south end of Union Square. Under the management of former furriers and future movie magnates Adolph Zukor and Marcus Loew, New York's Automatic Vaudeville (and others like it in Boston, Newark, and Philadelphia) offered to dazzled patrons penny-operated peeps, phonographs with individual listening devices, stationary bicycles, punching bags, and a basement shooting gallery. Among the mutoscope offerings were such alluring titles as *My Cosey Corner Girl*; *Hannah, Won't You Open that Door*; *An Affair of Honor*; and *South African Warriors*. Several years later a movie theater was added on the floor above the arcade, which showed two-reelers at a nickel a head (thus a "nickel-odeon," or five-cent theater). At some point in the 1910s the whole operation was renamed Crystal Hall. THE BYRON COLLECTION. 93.1.1.1839.

(RIGHT) **T. E. FITZGERALD'S BAR, SIXTH AVENUE AND 44TH STREET, 1912:** The time is six minutes after noon, and men of all social classes place a foot on the brass rail for the preamble to the businessman's lunch. THE BYRON COLLECTION. 93.1.1.17847.

Byron
N.Y.
31413

AJEEB, THE CHESS-PLAYING AUTOMOTON, EDEN MUSEE, 1907: The Eden Musee at 599 West 23rd Street, "was a funny old institution," wrote Henry Collins Brown, "and it ought never to have gone out of business [which it did, in 1915]. It was originally built by a group of titled Frenchmen, with the idea of duplicating Mme. Tussaud's Wax Works in London, and for many years they were successful. The change in the shopping district caused their demise." "Ajeeb," who mystified generations with his uncanny chess skill, first appeared at the gloriously seedy Eden in 1884–85. "Some of the most brilliant players in the world essayed to beat Ajeeb, but all were defeated and retired in disgust." O. Henry frequently dropped in to challenge him to a game; so did French actress Sara Bernhardt each time she came to this country. Christy Mathewson, the baseball player, liked to puzzle with him; as did Harry Houdini and Teddy Roosevelt. What they did not know was that skilled chess players including Henry Pillsbury and Peter J. Hill were the men in the machine. THE BYRON COLLECTION. 93.1.1.15517.

MUTUAL FILM CORPORATION, 1600 BROADWAY, 1918: New York was the country's film capital in the first decade of the twentieth century, but by the time the country entered the First World War, much of the business had gone west to Hollywood. The Mutual Film Corporation, originally a Midwest concern, had swallowed up competitors large and small—Keystone, Thanhouser, Reliance-Majestic, and more—in an attempt to corner distribution. Thwarted by court decisions, Mutual next went after monopoly control of the rising star in the industry—Charlie Chaplin—and signed him to a landmark two-year contract at an annual salary of $670,000, making him the world's highest-paid entertainer. During his Mutual years he produced twelve two-reel comedies that defined the era. THE BYRON COLLECTION. 93.1.1.4188.

KEITH'S BICYCLE TRACK, UNION SQUARE THEATRE, 1902: Showman Benjamin Franklin Keith and his business partner Edward F. Albee (grandfather of the modern playwright of that name) were giants of vaudeville. Together they built the Keith-Albee circuit of theaters and movie palaces, several of which survive under the original syndicate names as the original pair linked with the Orpheum, Proctor, and other theater circuits. In addition to movies, these houses offered (anywhere from two to six times a day) monologists, ventriloquists, animal acts, acrobats, jugglers, contortionists, and trick bicyclists. THE BYRON COLLECTION. 93.1.1.1461.

DAY AND NIGHT, CA. 1924: This Yiddish drama was written by Shloyme Zanvl Rappoport (1863–1920), better known by the pseudonym S. Ansky, under which he also wrote *The Dybbuk*. A posthumously gathered work, it was produced as the first drama at the Unser Theatre in the Bronx in 1924. Lazar Weiner composed the music, and new immigrant Boris Aronson created the sets. Aronson became famous on Broadway as designer for the original productions of such plays as *The Crucible*, *The Diary of Anne Frank*, *Fiddler on the Roof*, and *Cabaret*; yet in a 1961 interview, Aronson recalled, "I did my most experimental work [at Unser], which I haven't topped yet." BELLA BELLARINA COLLECTION. GIFT OF HENRY RUBINLICHT. 69.132.

(RIGHT) **AMERICAN THEATRE, TED MARKS' BIG SUNDAY NIGHT CONCERT, 1902:** Designed by architect Charles C. Haight, the American Theatre opened at the southeast corner of Eighth Avenue and 42nd Street on May 22, 1893 with a production of *The Prodigal Daughter*. Later renamed the American Music Hall, it was demolished in 1932. In the theater's heyday, vaudeville promoter Ted Marks was known for his regular Sunday afternoon and evening "sacred concerts," as he termed them. They were such an attraction, he said, that "people go to the Sunday concert when they might go to saloons." THE BYRON COLLECTION. 93.1.1.274.

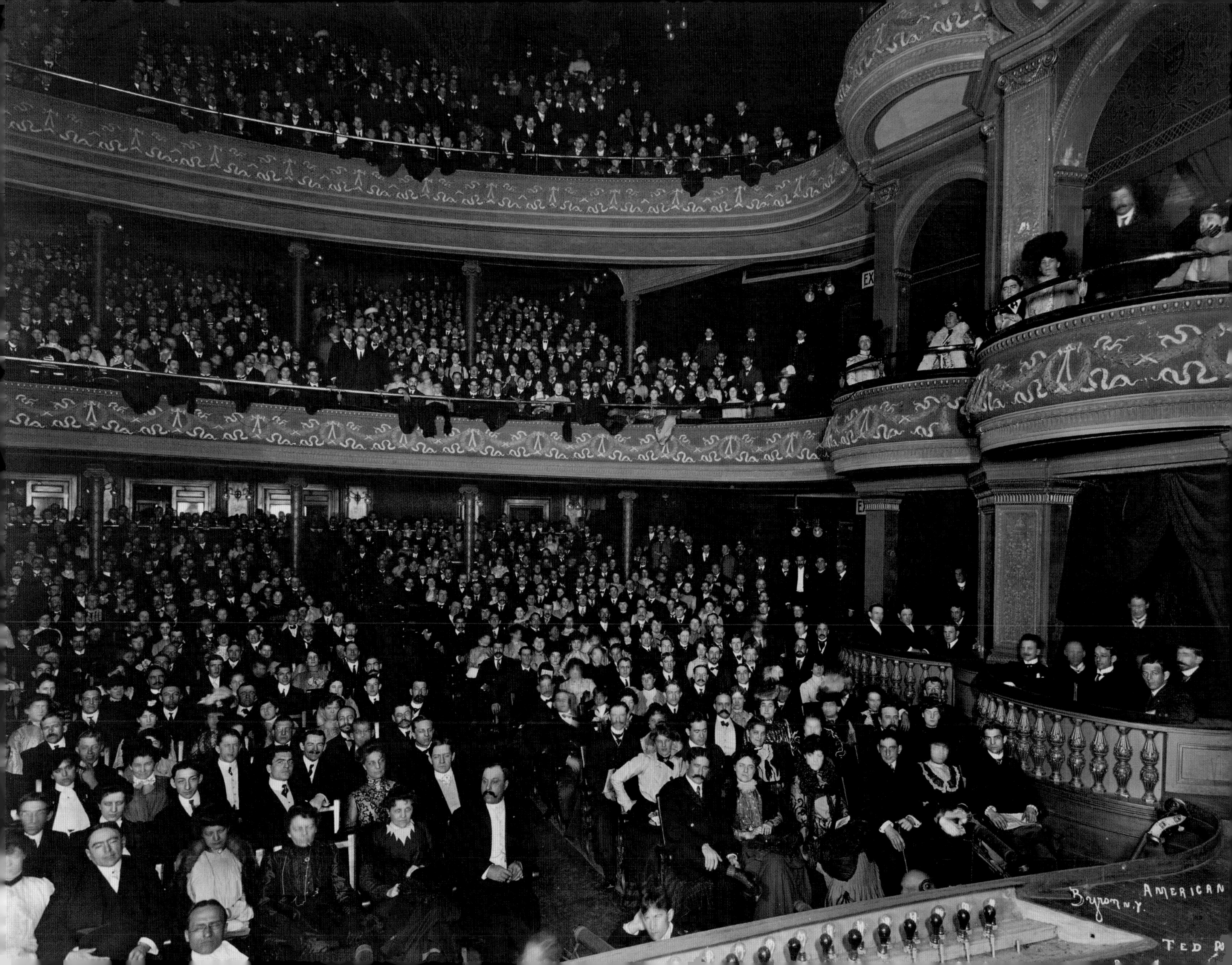
AMERICAN
Byron N.Y.
TED

(LEFT) PORTRAIT OF ETHEL BARRYMORE AT AGE TWENTY-ONE, 1901: Miss Barrymore (1879–1959) is depicted here in her first starring role, as Madame Trentoni in Clyde Fitch's play, *Captain Jinks of the Horse Marines*, which had a good run at the Garrick Theatre. Ethel was the sister of John and Lionel Barrymore, and as highly regarded a thespian. *Captain Jinks* was one of four plays Fitch had running simultaneously on Broadway in 1901. OIL ON CANVAS BY SIGISMUND DE IVANOWSKI. GIFT OF MISS ETHEL BARRYMORE. 53.205.

JOHN BARRYMORE IN *HAMLET*, 1922: If John Barrymore (1882–1942) was the consummate actor of his age—breaking Edwin Booth's record with 101 performances as Hamlet in 1922—James Montgomery Flagg (1877–1960) occupied the same rank among illustrators. He produced illustrations for books, magazines, and posters. His most famous poster, created in 1917, showed Uncle Sam pointing at the viewer and saying, "I Want YOU for U. S. Army." OIL ON CANVAS BY JAMES MONTGOMERY FLAGG. GIFT OF MR. FLAGG. 46.214.1.

VOLUNTEER HOSPITAL
24246

(LEFT) WALL STREET EXPLOSION, 1920: One minute after noon on Thursday, September 16, 1920, a horse-drawn wagon stopped across the street from the headquarters of the J. P. Morgan and Company bank at 23 Wall Street. The one hundred pounds of dynamite it held exploded in a timer-set detonation. Thirty-eight were killed and four hundred people were injured by the blast. Italian anarchists were suspected, but after three years of active investigation, no charges were brought. The facade of 23 Wall Street bears visible scars of the 1920 explosion to this day. PHOTOGRAPH BY BROWN BROTHERS, MUSEUM PURCHASE WITH THE NEW YORK STOCK EXCHANGE FUND. 38.299.12.

ATTEMPTED ASSASSINATION OF MAYOR WILLIAM JAY GAYNOR, AUGUST 9, 1910: The photographer, William Warnecke of the *New York World*, captured this horrific image while snapping what he thought would be a typical photograph of the new mayor, in his first year in office. Instead, Warnecke captured the very moment that James J. Gallagher, a discharged city employee, shot a bullet through Gaynor's throat at point-blank range. Before the assailant could be wrestled to the ground he got off two more shots, neither of which struck Gaynor or seriously injured others. The incident happened on board the Europe-bound S.S. *Kaiser Wilhelm der Grosse*, docked at Hoboken. Although the mayor quickly recovered, the bullet remained in his throat until he died, three years later. GIFT OF CORNELIUS O'CONNOR. 43.119.

WASHINGTON SQUARE, 1900: In 1837, New York University established itself in a Gothic building on the square's east border. To Henry James, born on nearby Washington Place, Washington Square had "a riper, richer, more honorable look than any of the other ramifications of the great longitudinal thoroughfare—the look of having something of a social history." But the Square as we know it today is not truly old. The plan of the park was not settled until 1880, the Stanford White arch was not dedicated until 1895, and of course the folkies and hippies and reggae enthusiasts did not follow until much later on. This impressionistic view of the Square in 1900 exudes the warmth of Paris. OIL ON CANVAS BY PAUL CORNOYER (1864–1923). GIFT OF MISS HARROW FARROW. 49.299.

GREEN-WOOD CEMETERY, BROOKLYN, FIFTH AVENUE AND 25TH STREET, MAY 30, 1899: George Templeton Strong had written in his diary in 1839, ". . . in this city of all cities some place is needed where a man may lay down to his last nap without the anticipation of being turned out of his bed in the course of a year or so to make way for a street or a big store or something of that kind." Chartered in 1838, Brooklyn's Green-Wood Cemetery followed the models of Boston's Mt. Auburn (1831) and Philadelphia's Laurel Hill (1836) in giving to New York a serene, dignified burial spot—indeed, one so beautiful that it became a favorite destination for strollers and picnickers, especially in the years before Central Park and Prospect Park. THE BYRON COLLECTION. 93.1.1.18440.

GRANT'S TOMB, CA. 1900: At his death the illustrious General Ulysses S. Grant stood atop the pantheon of revered heroes with Washington and Lincoln. A huge public subscription enabled the completion of John Duncan's design in 1897, and the mausoleum in Riverside Park instantly became a favored destination for Sunday strollers. PHOTOGRAPH BY ROBERT BRACKLOW. 93.91.138.

A BUNCH OF RAGS
19
6141

(LEFT) SHEET MUSIC DEPARTMENT, SIEGEL-COOPER STORE, 1899: Henry Siegel and Frank Cooper opened a vast department store at Broadway between 18th and 19th Streets on September 12, 1896, featuring an ornate waterworks that launched the saying, "Meet me at the fountain." This dry-goods emporium was the first on Ladies' Mile to have an extensive range of merchandise under one roof. Its robust sheet-music department boasted special prices to push featured items, such as "She Was Happy Till She Met You" and "Bunch of Rags." The portrait is of Irish tenor Andrew Mack, whose big hit was "The Picture That is Turned Toward the Wall." THE BYRON COLLECTION. 93.1.1.14373.

BILL POSTERS, 1904: The lithographic poster craze began to sweep Paris in the late 1880s but it did not hit New York until Edward Penfield began his poster campaign for *Harper's Weekly* in 1895. After that came the deluge, and the ubiquitous admonition to "Post No Bills" was observed only in the breach. Wells Hawks wrote in *Theatre Magazine* in June 1904, "As soon as a play is placed in rehearsal, its manager orders the 'wall printing.' This is in various sizes, from the large stands (printed in sheets and put together by the posters) down to the smaller half sheets used on boxes and barrels and the narrow slips, or 'snipes,' that are pasted on fences or anything along a thoroughfare." THE BYRON COLLECTION. 93.1.1.15908.

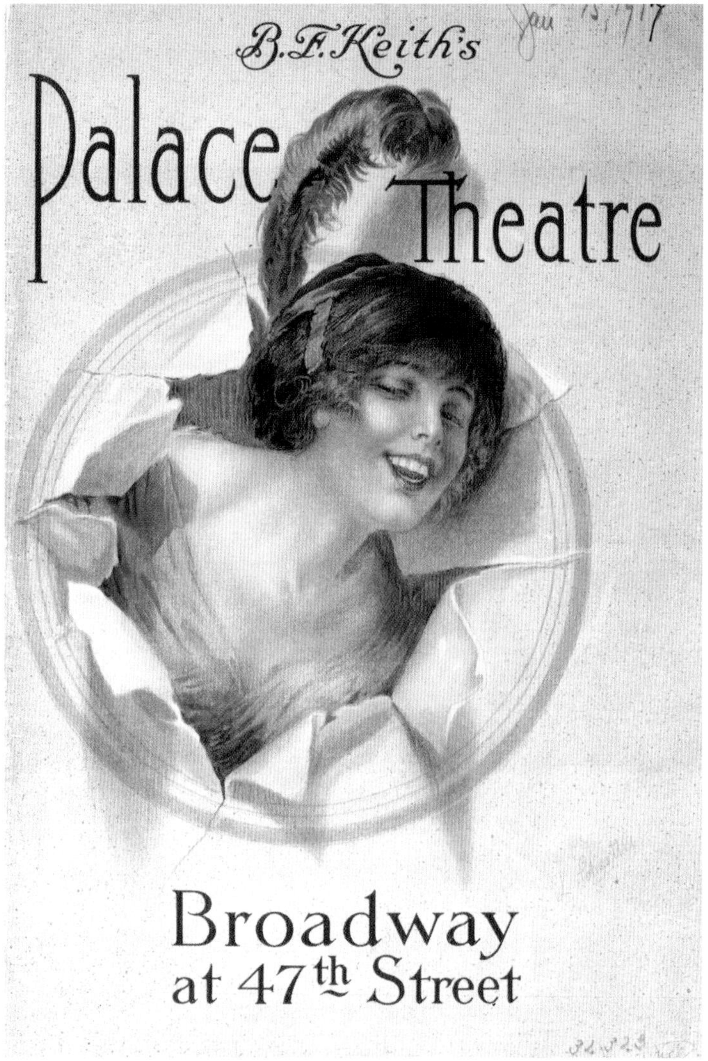

KEITH'S PALACE THEATRE, 1913: For an individual or an act to play the Palace at Broadway and 47th Street was to reach the pinnacle of the vaudeville profession. Among the illustrious performers that trod the boards here were Fanny Brice, Harry Houdini, Eddie Cantor, Weber and Fields, Sophie Tucker, and Ed Wynn. As the premier theater of the Keith-Albee circuit, the Palace ran two shows a day at two dollars per show until 1932 when, after many years of incursion by film, the house policy became movies only. After an extensive renovation the Palace, which had opened in 1913, reopened as a musical comedy venue in 1966. THEATER COLLECTION.

"GIVE MY REGARDS TO BROADWAY," SHEET MUSIC, 1905: This was the enduring song from George M. Cohan's *Little Johnny Jones*, a musical play which stirred, according to the publicists, "a commotion from ocean to ocean." This was not only because the play was a hit, but also because of the jingoistic sentiments expressed by its male lead ("You think I'd marry an heiress and live off her money? What do you take me for? An Englishman?"). The character of Little Johnny Jones was a brash American jockey based on the diminutive rider Tod Sloan, who had gone to England to ride the ponies in 1903 but came to disgrace, perhaps unfairly, for fixing a race. PUBLISHED BY F. A. MILLS. GIFT OF THE EDWARD B. MARKS MUSIC CORPORATION. 68.127.59.

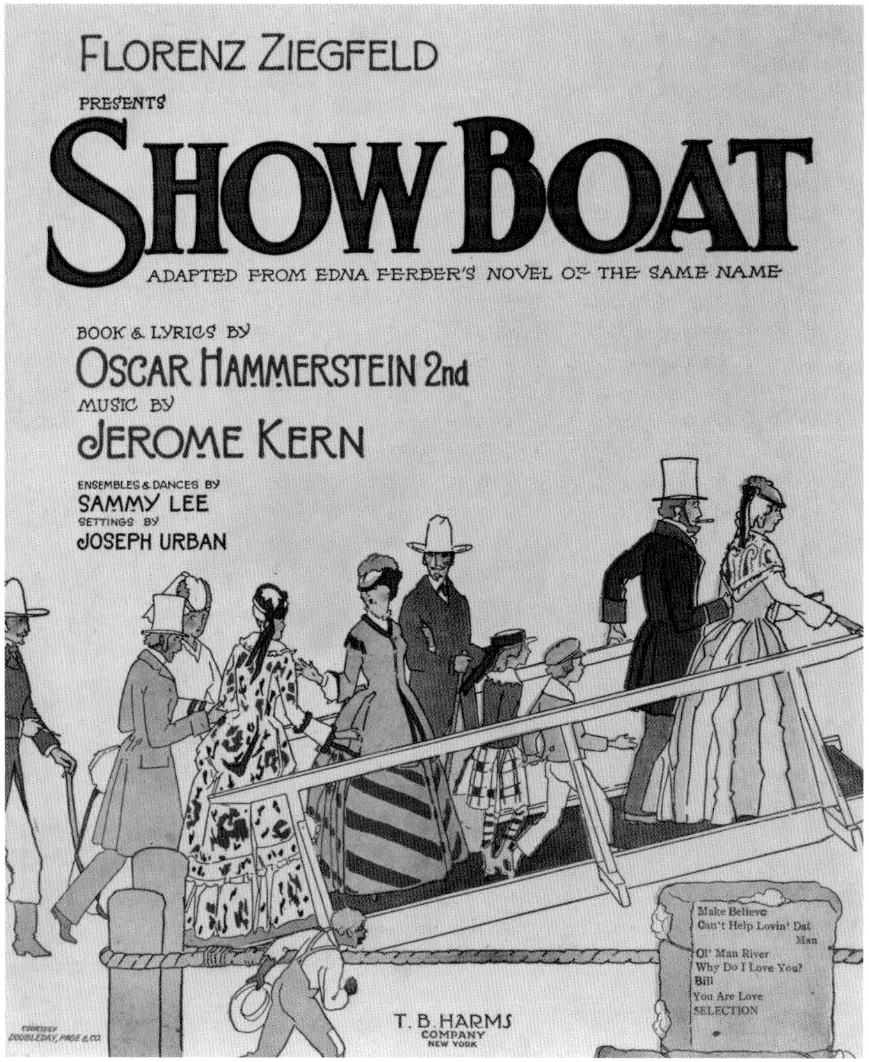

WINDOW CARD FOR *SHOW BOAT*, CA. 1927: This play, unique at the time for its intertwined story lines and daring for its theme of racial prejudice, was a testament to the courage of composer Jerome Kern, lyricist and librettist Oscar Hammerstein 2nd, and producer Florenz Ziegfeld. In the minds of many theater historians, *Show Boat* is considered the first modern Broadway musical. It opened at the Ziegfeld Theater on December 27, 1927 and featured such beloved songs as "Ol' Man River," "Can't Help Lovin' Dat Man," and "Bill." The original cast included Norma Terris as Magnolia Hawks Ravenal, Howard Marsh as Gaylord Ravenal, Charles Winninger as Cap'n Andy, Helen Morgan as Julie La Verne, and Jules Bledsoe—not Paul Robeson—as Joe. THEATER COLLECTION.

ZIEGFELD 9 O'CLOCK REVUE AND MID NIGHT FROLIC, 1920: In addition to his *Follies*, the celebrated revue which commenced in 1907 and ran annually until 1931, impresario Florenz Ziegfeld (1867–1932) initiated a series of cabaret shows on the roof of his New Amsterdam Theater in 1919. Depicted is the playbill for the second annual event, starring Fannie Brice and W. C. Fields. In the following year Ziegfeld ended his roof-garden frolics, citing Prohibition as the spoilsport. "The best class of people from all over the world have been in the habit of coming up on the roof," he said in May 1921, "and when they are subjected to the humiliation of having policemen stand by their tables [as authorized by the new state law] and watch what they are drinking, then I do not care to keep open any longer." THEATER COLLECTION.

KINGS COUNTY ALMSHOUSE, CLARKSON STREET, FLATBUSH, 1900: Byron did a series at this home "for infirm adult persons entirely destitute" that stands out for its stark pathos. The female section of this sixty-five-acre refuge dated from 1850; the male from 1869. A report in 1898 estimated the weekly expense per inmate at $2.71. With rose-colored glasses, an official report stated, "The entire grounds about the buildings have been beautifully laid out, and ample walks built and shrubbery of various kinds planted. A large number of settees have been provided, and the old women of the almshouse are permitted to roam about in the park or rest themselves as they choose." THE BYRON COLLECTION. 93.1.1.18394.

SUBWAY CONSTRUCTION, FOURTEENTH STREET CUT, JULY 29, 1921: Two workers are visible on the beams of the ring as they extend the reach of the Brooklyn Rapid Transit Company (BRT, later renamed the Brooklyn–Manhattan Transit Company, or BMT). The Independent (IND) line was proposed as a municipally owned project in 1925. THE BYRON COLLECTION. 93.1.1.17086.

NEW YORK SUBWAY, FIRST TICKET SOLD, OCTOBER 27, 1904: William Barclay Parsons (1859–1932), Chief Engineer of the New York Rapid Transit Commission, was responsible for construction of New York's first subway line, the Interborough Rapid Transit (IRT). Parsons Boulevard in Queens is named for him. When the IRT opened to the public at Grand Central Station on October 27, 1904, the first ticket sold went to his eighteen-year-old daughter, Sylvia. This is that ticket. GIFT OF MRS. RUDOLPH WELD. 35.51.1.

READING ROOM, SAILORS' SNUG HARBOR, STATEN ISLAND, 1899: Retired from the active world, these worn-out old seafarers still devour the news of the day in their Staten Island retreat. THE BYRON COLLECTION. 93.1.1.14191.

***MCCALL'S* MAGAZINE, ART DEPARTMENT, 1912:** More than a dozen illustrators (a few of them female) are poised at their easels to execute the fashion drawings that were the staple of this long-lived magazine. From its offices at 236 West 37th Street, *McCall's*—which reached a peak circulation of six million—influenced what women wore all over America. THE BYRON COLLECTION. 93.1.1.17750.

(RIGHT) **CHILDS UNIQUE DAIRY LUNCH ROOM, 1900:** The Childs chain of restaurants is fondly remembered, especially by those who dined there as children back in the day. The walls were clad in glass tile and mosaic, the floors of vitrified tiling were noisy. The kitchen was visible and the cleanliness of the place was a strong selling point at a time when food poisoning was a real fear. Dinner in 1900 was thirty-five cents (fifty years later a ten-course dinner at Childs would set you back $1.99) and was served by a waitress, a Childs innovation. THE BYRON COLLECTION. 93.1.1.18413.

Cold Fresh
BUTTERMILK
Byron N.Y.

QUEENSBORO BRIDGE UNDER CONSTRUCTION, 1908: Also known as the 59th Street Bridge, this East River span links Long Island City in the borough of Queens with Manhattan. At its ceremonial grand opening in June 1909 it was known as the Blackwell's Island Bridge, named after the island over which it passes. Blackwell's Island was later to be renamed Welfare Island and ultimately Roosevelt Island. THE BYRON COLLECTION. 93.1.1.17877.

(RIGHT) **ROLLER SKATING AT THE CLAREMONT AVENUE RINK, BROOKLYN, 1906:** This vast hall accommodated religious revivals, political speeches, dog shows, automobile fairs, labor rallies, roller polo, and, as depicted here, roller skating. Invented in the mid-eighteenth century, roller skating boomed in this country in the 1880s after the introduction of steel ball bearings permitted skaters more maneuverability than a leisurely linear stroll. THE BYRON COLLECTION. 93.1.1.17513.

EXIT

BARBER SHOP, 1903: The location of this tonsorial parlor is unknown. However, we may assume from its seven white-jacketed barbers, two lady manicurists, and absence of the *Police Gazette*, that this was a high-toned establishment of the sort usually placed within hotels. THE BYRON COLLECTION. 93.1.1.18149.

POULTRY AND GAME TRADE, AUGUST SILZ MARKET, 267 WASHINGTON STREET, 1906: Wild Boar, French Lamb, Boston Gosling, and Imported Hare—these signs speak to the broad trade of August Silz, an immigrant from France who became the world's largest poultry and game dealer. Later in the year depicted, Silz left Washington Street for larger quarters at 14th Street and established branches in Baltimore, Pittsburgh, Albany, and Havana. THE BYRON COLLECTION. 93.1.1.18150.

(RIGHT) **WORKMAN AT MARTINKA'S "PALACE OF MAGIC," 493 SIXTH AVENUE, 1906:** The brothers Martinka—Antonio and Francis—were born in Prague but came to New York in 1872, with a wealth of magic experience, and established a shop on Broadway near Duane Street. In 1885 they moved uptown and truly became the "Magicians' Mecca" thereafter. In 1902 the Society of American Magicians formed in the "Little Back Shop" at Martinka's. Shown in this photograph, a workman puts the finishing touches on a stock trick called the "Talking Skull." Francis Martinka retired in 1917, and the store later passed through many hands, including, in 1919, those of Harry Houdini. THE BYRON COLLECTION. 93.1.1.18346.

21266

EWYORK
BURLESQUE
ALLET AND VARIETIES
HOTEL
ADILLAC
CRITERION
THE
PABST
HOTEL
GRAND OPENING
AND FRUITS.
Byron N.Y.
10688

(LEFT) **WHITE WINGS AT LONGACRE SQUARE (NOW TIMES SQUARE), 1900:** The city's entertainment rialto had been drifting north for a century when it crept up to the intersection of Broadway and 42nd Street. First the Empire Theatre arrived at 40th and Broadway in 1893; then Oscar Hammerstein's Olympia opened at 44th Street two years later. The New York Theatre, shown at left, is in fact the renamed Olympia. In this view looking south from 45th Street, toward what would become the Times Building in 1904, what draws our attention is the fellow sweeping the streets. At this dawn of the automobile age, Colonel George Waring was still the talk of the town, as his "white wings" made the streets passable. Before his day, "street cleaner" was a term of degradation. Waring put his men in uniform, gave them pride in their necessary work, and ever after his men were known as "Waring's White Wings." THE BYRON COLLECTION. 93.1.1.17932.

EUSTACE TILLEY, 1925: This drawing was the basis of the first cover of *The New Yorker*, for the issue of February 21, 1925. The comic figure, revived for use on the cover every February, is the work of Rea Irvin, the magazine's first art director and creator of its distinctive typeface. REA IRVIN/*THE NEW YORKER*, © CONDE NAST. GIFT OF MR. AND MRS. REA IRVIN. 67.100.73.

SPEAKEASY CARD, COTTON CLUB, CA. 1927: The first Prohibition-era night club at 142nd Street and Lenox Avenue was the Club De Luxe, operated by former heavyweight champion boxer Jack Johnson. In 1922 bootlegger Owney Madden, despite having an address at a Sing Sing cellblock, took over the De Luxe and renamed it the Cotton Club. Black entertainers and "tall, tan, and terrific" showgirls entertained an all-white clientele, with Sunday nights marked by a white celebrity audience. After the 1935 race riots in Harlem, the area was considered unsafe for whites and the club closed, only to reopen downtown, at Broadway and 48th Street. It closed its doors for good in 1940. MANUSCRIPT COLLECTION.

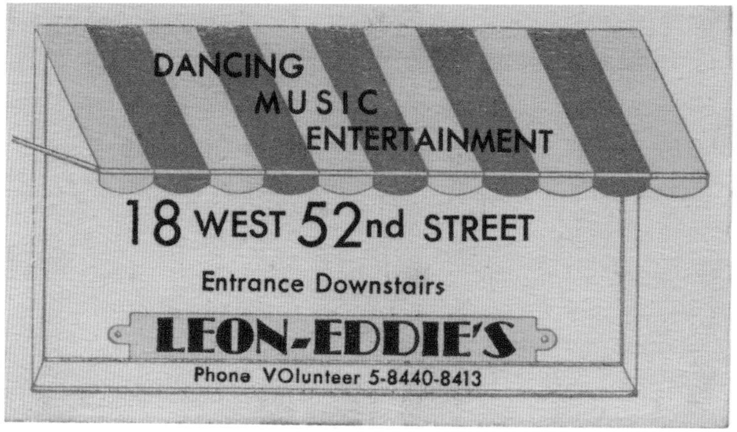

SPEAKEASY CARD, LEON-EDDIE'S, CA. 1929: Prohibition wiped out nearly all of the city's great restaurants and cafes—Bustanoby's, Delmonico's, Reisenweber's, Rector's, Maxim's, Churchill's—because, as it is today, their profit margin was in the drinks, not in the food. Speakeasies sprang up like weeds to fill the void. Leon Enken and Eddie Davis opened Leon-Eddie's as a speakeasy in a brownstone basement at 18 West 52nd Street. When Prohibition was repealed in 1933, the club moved across the street to 33 West 52nd Street and remained a famous watering hole into the 1940s. Apprenticing at the latter address as a daytime manager was Toots Shor, who would operate his own restaurant and bar in years to come. MANUSCRIPT COLLECTION.

BILLBOARDS, 1904: Even the genteel English-born actress Julia Marlowe (1866–1950) was given the rough treatment of being plastered wherever bill posters found space. In May 1904 she was appearing as Mary Tudor at the Empire Theatre production of *When Knighthood Was in Flower*. Also posted for passersby amid the rubble is a notice for Virginia Harned, playing in *Camille* at the Garrick. THE BYRON COLLECTION. 93.1.1.1665.

NED WAYBURN'S, REHEARSAL FOR *TOWN TOPICS*, 1915: Born Edward Claudius Weyburn (1874–1942), Wayburn was the most influential choreographer of his day, extending from the small-group patterns and formation symmetry of minstrelsy toward the coordinated dance lines that still characterize the Broadway musical. In September 1915 he opened *Ned Wayburn's Town Topics* at the capacious Century Theatre, located at Central Park West and 62nd Street. Its twenty-one scenes were outpaced by its gargantuan cast: thirty principals, sixty-five chorus girls, and twenty-six male singers and dancers. Will Rogers performed a lariat dance, and Trixie Fraganza, Blossom Seeley, and Clifton Webb added further star power, but the show proved a financial disaster. THE BYRON COLLECTION. 93.1.1.15956.

BRIGHTON BEACH PANORAMA, 1919: Today known as "Little Odessa" for its large population of Ukrainian emigrants, Brighton Beach started out as a resort spot in the 1870s, then settled into a dense residential community by the 1920s. In the aftermath of World War II the community welcomed many tempest-tossed survivors, Jews in particular. PHOTOGRAPH BY WILLIAM DAVIS HASSLER (1877–1921). 01.35.2.37.

OPEN AIR PLAYGROUND, FOOT OF WEST 50TH STREET, CA. 1901: In 1835, Davy Crockett said, "In my part of the country, when you meet an Irishman, you find a first-rate gentleman; but these are worse than savages; they are too mean to swab hell's kitchen." He was referring to denizens of the Five Points neighborhood in present-day Chinatown, but it is the area from Eighth Avenue to the Hudson, from 42nd Street to 59th, that for over a century has borne the name Hell's Kitchen. Seeking to belie the notion that disease-ridden slums were the cauldron in which tomorrow's criminal class was forged, the city sought to encourage open-air athleticism. PHOTOGRAPH BY WILLIAM M. VAN DER WEYDE. THE VAN DER WEYDE COLLECTION.

TRINITY CHURCH AND VIEW OF BROADWAY, CA. 1909: The parish received its charter from King William III of England in 1697 and built its first church at this site, the intersection of Broadway and Wall Street, in the following year. That church burned in the great fire of 1776, and its successor was taken down for structural inadequacies. The present Episcopalian church was built in 1846 from a design by architect Richard Upjohn, pioneer of the Gothic Revival style. PHOTOGRAPH BY GEORGE P. HALL & SON. 92.53.50.

WHEN LIFE IS VERY STRENUOUS AND SPIRITS ARE WAY DOWN
YOU'D BETTER GO TO POLLY'S IN LITTLE GREENWICH TOWN
FOR THERE THE CLANS ARE GATHERED - ITS THERE YOU'LL FIND 'EM ALL
THE ARTISTS AND THE WRITERS RANGED ALONG THE WALL.
MISS POLLY TAKES THE MONEY AND MIKE SAYS HE JUST CAN'T
WAIT ANY FASTER ON THE FOLKS IN POLLY'S RES-TAU-RANT
J.T.B.
24
GREENWICH VILLAGE - NEW YORK
© JESSIE TARBOX BEALS

POLLY'S RESTAURANT, 137 MACDOUGAL STREET, CA. 1915: Artist and writer tearooms and restaurants were all the rage in Greenwich Village in the 1910s and 1920s. Beginning in 1914 Polly Holladay ran an eatery in the basement below the rooms of the Liberal Club. Her lover Hippolyte Havel, who had formerly played that role with anarchist Emma Goldman, was the cook. Polly's won citywide fame when morals czar Anthony Comstock yanked the decorations off the walls. Next door was the Provincetown Playhouse, which opened in 1916. Photographer Jessie Tarbox Beals (1870–1942) drew upon her intimate knowledge of the neighborhood to depict the tearooms, garrets, and shops in a series that she sold from her studio at 6½ Sheridan Square. PHOTOGRAPH BY JESSIE TARBOX BEALS. MUSEUM PURCHASE WITH FUNDS DONATED BY LISA AND ERIC GREEN. 95.127.21.

(LEFT) LOWER MANHATTAN, 1921: Soaring into the sky at left are two buildings that in turn claimed the title of world's tallest. At 612 feet high, the Singer Building at Liberty Street and Broadway was the tallest upon its completion in 1908, a distinction it held for only one year, when the Metropolitan Life Insurance Company Tower went up on Madison Avenue. In 1913 the neo-Gothic Woolworth Building topped out at 792 feet, and was the tallest building until the Bank of Manhattan Company Building at 40 Wall Street surpassed it in 1929. For all the verticality of this unsigned aerial view, the eye is drawn to old Castle Clinton at the Battery. After many reincarnations since 1811, it would have been serving as the city's aquarium when this photograph was taken. PRINT ARCHIVES.

HERALD SQUARE, CA. 1904: Macy's Department Store, whose Sixth Avenue front is visible at left, had gone up on the block between 34th and 35th Streets in 1901–02. The New York Times Building, the second tallest building in the world when it opened on January 1, 1905, may be seen in an incomplete state at center. Herald Square was named for the *New York Herald*, a newspaper founded in 1835 by James Gordon Bennett that since 1893 had been headquartered on 35th Street. Its arcaded two story Italianate building designed by McKim, Mead, and White was demolished in 1921. Three years later, after Bennett Jr.'s death, the *Herald* was merged with its hated rival, the *New York Tribune*. PHOTOGRAPH BY GEORGE P. HALL & SON. 92.53.72.

THE TREASURE BOX, 7 SHERIDAN SQUARE, CA. 1917: According to the *New York Times* of December 23, 1917, "There has been a shift in the centre of gravity of Greenwich Village, if Greenwich Village may be said to have any gravity. Washington Square has been replaced by Sheridan Square . . . now the centre of population of New York's Latin quarter." The studio of photographer Jessie Tarbox Beals at 6½ Sheridan Square stood next door to Teddy Peck's Treasure Box gift shop, "its sign a frieze of seven black pirates marching across the yellow front of a one-story converted stable." PHOTOGRAPH BY JESSIE TARBOX BEALS, NO. 23 IN HER GREENWICH VILLAGE SERIES. MUSEUM PURCHASE WITH FUNDS DONATED BY LISA AND ERIC GREEN. 95.127.20.

AMY MALI HICKS STUDIO, 158 WEST 11TH STREET, CA. 1917: Interior decorator and textile artist Amy Mali Hicks, a descendant of Hicksite Quakers, was also a thoroughgoing radical and a proponent of Henry George's single-tax theory. An expert in dyeing techniques, she anticipated Village residents' adoption of batik by half a century. PHOTOGRAPH BY JESSIE TARBOX BEALS, NO. 39 IN HER GREENWICH VILLAGE SERIES. MUSEUM PURCHASE WITH FUNDS FROM LISA AND ERIC GREEN. 95.127.25.

(RIGHT) FIFTH AVENUE AT 25TH STREET, CA. 1920: Fog, mist, and the Flatiron Building have made for an irresistible combination to legions of photographers ever since the unusual building went up at 175 Fifth Avenue in 1902. The skyscraper designed by Chicago architect Daniel Burnham was officially named the Fuller Building after George A. Fuller, founder of the company that financed its construction. But the odd triangular shape—conforming to the nexus of Fifth Avenue and Broadway at 23rd Street—led to the informal name by which it has been known almost since its inception. In the foreground is the General Worth Monument. PHOTOGRAPH BY JESSIE TARBOX BEALS. MUSEUM PURCHASE WITH FUNDS FROM LISA AND ERIC GREEN. 95.127.55.

FRAUNCES TAVERN, CA. 1907: In the Long Room at Fraunces Tavern on December 4, 1783, George Washington bade farewell to his officers. The site continued to function as a tavern throughout the next century but several serious fires resulted in substantial changes to the structure, to the extent that architects today do not truly know what the 1783 tavern looked like. In 1890, the first floor exterior was remodeled and the original timbers sold as souvenirs. Threatened with demolition at the turn of the century, Fraunces Tavern was rescued by New York State's Sons of the Revolution, who purchased the building in 1904. Extensive reconstruction over the next three years created this multipart building, constituting not only the original tavern site but also four nineteenth-century buildings. PHOTOGRAPH BY GEORGE P. HALL & SON. 92.53.12.

KINGSBRIDGE ARMORY, CA. 1917: Built between 1912 and 1917, the armory was once the pride of the West Bronx. The nine-story Romanesque building on Kingsbridge Road at Jerome Avenue—noted for its vaulted ceilings, decorative brick and terra cotta, and twin battlement towers—had been home to the National Guard's Eighth Coastal Artillery Regiment since 1917. Designated a city landmark in 1974, it was nonetheless abandoned in disrepair by the National Guard twenty years later. Recent efforts toward bringing the Kingsbridge Armory back to life have focused on making it a shopping center. PHOTOGRAPH BY WILLIAM DAVIS HASSLER (1877–1921). GIFT OF MRS. W. G. HASSLER. 01.35.1.192.

BRONX ZOO, SNAKE HANDLING, CA. 1900: The largest metropolitan zoo in the United States, the Bronx Zoo comprises 265 acres of parklands and naturalistic habitats—and is home to more than 4,000 animals. The Bronx Zoo's department of herpetology, as old as the zoo itself (1899), is unlikely to have guided these attendants in their today unfathomable aims. Perhaps they were returning the escaped snake to the House of Reptiles? COLLECTION OF PRINTS AND PHOTOGRAPHS.

BLACK HORSE TAVERN, AMBOY AND RICHMOND ROADS, NEW DORP, CA. 1915: New Dorp, or New Town, was founded about 1671, ten years after an earlier town founded by the British called Dover. At that time the Black Horse Tavern was already six years old. In 1776, when the British established themselves on Staten Island, General Howe resided here. The oldest such establishment in New York at the time depicted in this postcard, it was run by Patrick Curry, who had purchased it in 1876. Curry took great pride in maintaining the original hanging sign, hundreds of years old, and the three rooms preserved from the original tavern. When the Black Horse was demolished in 1934 to widen Richmond Road for automobiles, the widowed Mrs. Curry refused to part with the sign. COLLECTION OF PRINTS AND PHOTOGRAPHS.

EBBETS FIELD UNDER CONSTRUCTION, FLATBUSH, 1913: The Brooklyn National League Base Ball Club had come to be known as the Trolley Dodgers, or Dodgers for short, in the 1880s, when multiple trolley lines crisscrossed in front of their Washington Park grounds near the Gowanus Canal. Owner Charles Hercules Ebbets bought up lots in the unglamorous section of what was called Pigtown to build a new ballpark. Opening in time for the start of the league season in 1913, Ebbets Field played host to the Dodgers through 1957. The next year, the team was moved to Los Angeles and Ebbets Field was left empty until the time it was demolished in 1960. PHOTOGRAPH BY GEORGE P. HALL & SONS.

PLAYING GOLF, JACKSON HEIGHTS, 1921: Although the Wurts Brothers Lionel and Norman specialized in commercial and especially architectural photography, the occasional vista was added to the firm's repertoire when Lionel's son Robert joined the company in the 1920s. The company produced many thousands of views for architects, developers, contractors, and manufacturers in its long history (1894–1979). THE WURTS COLLECTION.

FOOTBALL IN CENTRAL PARK, CA. 1925: When Frederick Law Olmsted and Calvert Vaux designed Central Park, they envisioned it as a place for silent contemplation and genteel pastimes, where working people could go to catch a glimpse of the rural serenity available to the upper classes. They underestimated the need for vigorous play like baseball or football. Olmsted wrote, "It seems difficult for them [the ball players] to realize that the large open surface of turf that, to the cultivated taste is among the most attractive features of the Park, can have any other use than that of a playground, and nothing is more certain than that the beauty of these lawns would soon be lost, and that they would be rendered disagreeable objects, if these games were to be constantly played upon them . . . ." PRINT ARCHIVES.

SNOWSTORM IN THE "VILLAGE," 1925: Born in Lock Haven, Pennsylvania, and growing up in Philadelphia, John French Sloan (1871–1951) came to New York's Greenwich Village in 1904 and became associated with several artists who became known as "The Eight" or, more derisively, as the "Ashcan School." From his studios in Chelsea and later at Washington Square he painted several enduring works—*McSorley's Bar*, *Wake of the Ferry*, and *Sixth Avenue Elevated at Third Street*. Like the last named painting, this view looking north along Sixth Avenue shows the Jefferson Market Court tower and the elevated tracks on Sixth Avenue. MUSEUM PURCHASE. ETCHING. 82.200.2.

TRIANGLE SHIRTWAIST FIRE, MARCH 25, 1911: One hundred forty-eight garment workers lost their lives in the fire at what was then called the Asch Building, at the intersection of Greene Street and Washington Place. Some perished in the flames, others leapt to their deaths. Seven of the total died later from injuries. The company occupied the top three floors of the ten-story building. Of two exit doors on the eighth floor, where the fire started, one was locked and the other led to a stairwell that soon became impassable. The lone fire escape twisted and broke under the weight of fleeing workers. The site survives as the Brown Building, which has been designated a national landmark. The event helped build support for the International Ladies Garment Workers' Union and for workplace safety regulations. PHOTOGRAPH BY GEORGE GRANTHAM BAIN AGENCY. IMAGE COURTESY OF THE LIBRARY OF CONGRESS.

CHAPTER X | 1930-1940

THE NEW DEAL

AND NEW YORK CITY'S HOMELESS

ELLA HOWARD

The arrival of the Great Depression in the late 1920s brought a dramatic increase in the number of impoverished people living in New York City. Thousands of working-class and middle-class New Yorkers fell on hard times and were joined by new arrivals flooding in from outlying towns and neighboring states. Unable to provide for themselves, these groups appealed to the city's social services divisions and private charities for assistance. When those organizations proved unable to meet the unprecedented demand, city, state, and later federal officials developed new aid programs. Many of the impoverished had no fixed address. Homeless people were not a new sight for New Yorkers in the 1930s. The hobo or tramp, who traveled the country in search of employment and adventure, had long been a familiar image. Since the 1880s, homeless men, many of whom were temporary workers, had congregated along the Bowery. A thriving entertainment district in the mid-nineteenth century, the area had gradually transformed into a skid row. By the turn of the century, few women who were not involved in prostitution ventured to the Bowery. The area continued to serve as home to the city's down and out throughout the early decades of the twentieth century. As the Depression began, early forecasts predicted the economic crisis would be brief. It appeared that the city's traditional resources and systems would suffice to meet the needs of the poor. Indeed, during the nineteenth and early twentieth centuries, New York City had developed an elaborate system of assistance for its poorest residents. The Bowery itself proved one of the most important forms of aid. Dingy restaurants offered affordable meals to area residents. In commercial lodging houses, the homeless could find meager accommodations useful for enduring periods of harsh weather. During the late 1920s, skid-row speakeasies provided not only access to alcohol but also a place to socialize. Some allowed men who purchased alcohol to stay overnight, crowded onto chairs or sprawled on the floors. These "flops" in the back rooms of Bowery bars had housed a stream of homeless men for decades.

Locally funded public assistance was available from the Municipal Shelter. Since 1896, the facility had offered temporary lodging and basic meals to indigent applicants. The city's private charities also played a substantial role in this relief structure. The Bowery Mission and the Salvation Army, both of which had begun operations in New York City in the nineteenth century, continued to provide shelter, meals, and spiritual comfort to homeless clients. As the crisis mounted, the Salvation Army and other organizations expanded, in an effort to meet the community's need for assistance. The Army's Gold Dust Lodge, a warehouse converted to a temporary shelter, lodged more than 2,000 men by 1931, while staff served nearly 5,000 meals each day. The Bowery Y.M.C.A. also expanded its operations during the Depression, sponsoring thirty-two city locations by 1930, including a branch in Harlem.

Jewish homeless individuals and families received aid from two established charitable organizations, the Jewish Social Service Association and the Hebrew Sheltering and Immigrant Aid Society. The JSSA, rooted in German-American traditions of charity, carefully screened applicants through interviews and background checks. The Eastern European HIAS espoused a very different approach, offering aid to applicants with no questions asked; in 1932, HIAS served more than 438,000 meals.

Some assistance was provided on a less formal basis. Charitable institutions and private individuals sponsored breadlines, distributing food and sometimes clothing or vouchers for medical care to those who endured the line. Breadlines distributed a substantial amount of food; by early 1931, 70,000 breadline meals were served each day, at seventy-nine city locations. But the sight of impoverished individuals lining the streets disturbed many city officials and residents. Some worried about the system's potentially damaging psychological effects on relief recipients, especially children, who might be scarred by the seemingly degrading experience. Others feared that word of the lines would circulate and publicize the city's generosity, attracting additional impoverished people to the area. Some charity reformers also worried that such assistance was too easily obtained, and might lead the poor to prefer lives of leisure to ones of work. These reformers struggled to regulate the lines and access to meals.

Some homeless individuals shunned many of the available aid programs. They cherished their independence, either fearing or resenting institutional situations and controls. Rather than apply for lodging, many slept in abandoned buildings, or in their own "Hooverville" shantytowns. New York City's best-known shantytown was constructed by unemployed skilled laborers in Central Park's recently drained lower reservoir. Foraging lumber, tar paper, and bricks from construction sites, the residents built remarkably sturdy homes and maintained them carefully, until a 1932 police raid shut down the community.

City officials and charity reformers also frowned on panhandling: Several campaigns were launched to ban it on the subway and on city streets. One campaign brought 5,000 repeat panhandlers to the city's Night Court. Coupled with police crackdowns, these campaigns intimidated many city homeless out of the practice.

Women experienced homelessness differently than their male counterparts. Few organizations offered help to homeless women, who confronted social norms relegating them to the domestic sphere. As a result, they risked personal violence on the city streets, as well as social judgment. Widows accounted for more than one-third of the city's homeless female population.

The Depression proved especially devastating for the city's African-American population. Families who had attained only marginal economic stability prior to the crisis rapidly found themselves destitute. Those individuals and families who had arrived in the city only recently from the South and mid-Atlantic region often lacked resources and access to support networks. Compounding these problems, many of the skid-row facilities barred the entry of African Americans, who instead stayed in public parks and on the margins of Harlem.

In the face of this mounting need, New York Governor Franklin Delano Roosevelt implemented state funding of local relief. By 1931, the Temporary Emergency Relief Administration, led by social worker Harry Hopkins, funneled $20 million to the state's home and work relief programs. Two years later, the Federal Transient Program (FTP) initiated a similar, federal approach to homelessness. Launched during the Roosevelt administration's ambitious first hundred days in the White House, the program sorted the homeless into three categories: local homeless, state homeless, and the transient homeless, i.e., those who lacked one year of state residence. The FTP allocated $15 million for the funding of state plans to aid transient homeless. Shelter, meals, clothing, and medical treatment were among the assistance funded by the program, which soon encompassed nearly five hundred transient centers and camps nationwide.

This influx of state and federal funding sponsored new facilities in New York; by 1935, camps throughout the state lodged more than 3,000 men. In Chester, federal funds led to the 1934 launch of the residential Camp Greycourt. More than two-thirds of the camp's six hundred residents hailed from New York City. Residents worked thirty hours per week on road building and maintenance or farming. Camp administrators helped nearly one-third of the participants find employment, primarily as agricultural workers, during the facility's first year of operation.

Several of the programs initiated under state and federal funding were remarkably innovative. One of the few urban FTP facilities was Hartford House in midtown Manhattan. Operated by the Temporary Emergency Relief Administration's State Transient Division, the program aided educators and professionals who had become homeless. Program participants included accountants, pilots, industrial scientists, and architects.

As these transient camps, residential facilities, and work programs drew many younger, employable homeless individuals away from skid row and outside the city, the Bowery remained home primarily to older, sick, and unemployable homeless men. FTP-funded vouchers for lodging houses and restaurants ensured that even those men unsuited for the large programs received some assistance. As a result, the cheap hotels, restaurants, thrift shops, pawnshops, and barbershops that had been Bowery landmarks for decades continued to thrive.

The publicly funded homeless programs of the 1930s paralleled the broader patterns of public aid for the poor during the Depression. By 1934, Mayor Fiorello La Guardia reported 400,000 city families relying on relief for survival. By 1935, the Roosevelt administration sought to end its relief programs, in favor of a work-based system of aid. Roosevelt announced the establishment of a two-tiered welfare system based in the Social Security program, which would include old-age pensions, and the launch of the Works Progress Administration (WPA), a large-scale, federally funded program of public building.

As the FTP was rapidly phased out, social service providers hoped the city's homeless would find employment on WPA projects. Many homeless applicants, however, after enduring extended periods of unemployment, lacked the physical fitness to work, or the interpersonal skills required to overcome the prejudices of hiring coordinators. Instead, local governmental programs and private charities resumed their roles as the principal caretakers of the city's homeless population.

One Depression-era homeless institution that long outlasted its initial New Deal origins was Camp La Guardia. Originally Camp Greycourt, the facility reopened after World War II, and housed elderly homeless men until 2006. As homelessness became a local affair again, the Bowery largely returned to its pre-Depression state. Flophouses, bars, restaurants, missions, and the Municipal Shelter again became the only institutions invested in the care of the city's homeless population, and they retained that role for much of the postwar era.

CONSTRUCTION WORKER, EMPIRE STATE BUILDING, 1931: Heroic poses were part of the public relations campaign to endear the new Empire State Building not only to capitalists and prospective tenants but also to the common man. The "hero of labor" figure whose precursor in this country was the legendary miner John Henry came to be identified by 1935 with Alexey Stakhanov of the Soviet Union, a miner whose exploits landed him on the cover of *Time*. PHOTOGRAPH BY LEWIS W. HINE. PERMANENT DEPOSIT OF THE EMPIRE STATE BUILDING CORPORATION. L638.9.

ELLA HOWARD IS ASSISTANT PROFESSOR OF HISTORY AT ARMSTRONG ATLANTIC STATE UNIVERSITY IN SAVANNAH, GEORGIA, WHERE SHE TEACHES AMERICAN URBAN HISTORY, PUBLIC HISTORY, AND MATERIAL CULTURE STUDIES. SHE IS REVISING FOR PUBLICATION HER BOSTON UNIVERSITY DISSERTATION, *SKID ROW: HOMELESSNESS ON THE BOWERY IN THE TWENTIETH CENTURY*.

PARIS
BWAY-7TH AVE
242ST VANCORT
James W. Kerr
July 1931

(LEFT) SEVENTH AVENUE SUBWAY, 1931: Straphanger democracy, as portrayed on the IRT Seventh Avenue Line. Fur collars and cuffs sit beside plain cloth coats; races and classes mingle, oblivious to each other in the straight-ahead gaze that is *de rigueur* in the crowded subway car. OIL ON PANEL BY JAMES WILFRED KERR, 22 x 36. GIFT OF THE ARTIST. 77.16.4.

SULLIVAN STREET, 1936: Sullivan Street in Greenwich Village was largely Italian at the time of this vigorous depiction of a bustling crossing. But the neighborhood attractions were cosmopolitan, as they remain today. Of the restaurant "El Gaucho" at 245 Sullivan, which features prominently in this painting, Rian James noted in his 1934 guide *Dining in New York*, "El Gaucho means 'the cowboy,' and you'll find lots of them, of the drug-store variety, at this Argentine–Spanish club." One such, perhaps, may be seen at far left. WATERCOLOR BY ESTHER BECKER GOETZ, 7⅞ X 12. GIFT OF GEORGE C. MCCOY IN MEMORY OF HIS WIFE, ESTHER GOETZ MCCOY. 71.154.

ALFRED E. SMITH LAYS CORNERSTONE OF EMPIRE STATE BUILDING, SEPTEMBER 9, 1930: The razing of the Waldorf-Astoria Hotel, which had occupied the southwest corner of Fifth Avenue and 34th Street, began on the first of October, 1929 and continued despite the shock waves of October 24, Wall Street's Black Thursday. Though brief consideration was given to canceling the project, in December, Alfred E. Smith, head of Empire State, Inc., announced a loan of $27.5 million from the Metropolitan Life Insurance Company and the project moved on. Here Smith is shown with silver trowel in hand to cement the cornerstone into place. PHOTOGRAPH BY ROBERT A. KNUDTSEN. GIFT OF THE PHOTOGRAPHER. 95.56.24.

(RIGHT) **EMPIRE STATE BUILDING CONSTRUCTION, CA. 1931:** Belle Moskowitz, former aide to Governor Al Smith, opened a private public relations firm, Publicity Associates, when both retired from public life. Smith became the president of the Empire State Building Corporation, which built and operated the Empire State Building; Moskowitz won the contract to promote the new champion skyscraper, slated to open in 1931 filled with tenants despite the crushing economics of the time (it became known as the Empty State Building—when it opened with only one-quarter rented). One of Moskowitz's first moves was to secure the services of photographer Lewis Wickes Hine (1874–1940), a former sociologist and muckraking photographer of child labor conditions. This time, however, Hine was charged with glorifying the workers and their task. PERMANENT DEPOSIT OF THE EMPIRE STATE BUILDING CORPORATION. L638.8.

LEWIS W. HINE
HASTINGS-ON-HUDSON, N.Y.

DRUGS
LUNCH
LAUNDRY

(LEFT) **SUICIDE CURVE, NINTH AVENUE EL, 110TH STREET STATION, 1940:** The curve at this point was so drastic that the motorman had to slow to a crawl—hence the name "Suicide Curve" or "Dead Man's Curve." Although the line was constructed in 1879, not until 1903 did the authorities place a station here. From that point on the location became a favorite for would-be suicides until this section of the elevated line was demolished. PHOTOGRAPH BY ROBERT A. KNUDTSEN. GIFT OF THE PHOTOGRAPHER. 95.56.12.

ELEVATED TRAIN, SOUTH FROM 42ND STREET AND SIXTH AVENUE, 1932: Dominating the skyline rising above the platform of the Sixth Avenue El is the newly erected Empire State Building, but also of interest at left is the American Radiator Building at 40 West 40th Street. The Gothic Art Deco masterpiece, with a façade featuring a powerful array of black and gold bricks, was conceived by the architects Raymond Hood and John Howells in 1924 for the American Radiator and Standard Sanitary Company. The building was later renamed the American Standard Building and today it is the Bryant Park Hotel. THE BYRON COLLECTION. 93.1.1.17087.

25
Behold He Is Coming
ACCIDENT-HEALTH INSURANCE
PILGRIM PENTECOSTAL
CHURCH OF GOD
SERVICES
SUNDAYS 11 AM. & 8 P.M.
SUNDAY SCHOOL 2 P.M.
MID-WEEK
WED. THUR. & FRI. 8½ P.M.
ALL ARE WELCOME
Missionary
Service at 3. PM
Subject How Shall
We work Out Our Soul
Salvation
Sister Huggins
President

(LEFT) **CHURCH OF GOD, 25 EAST 132ND STREET, 1936:** The Pilgrim Pentecostal Church of God was typical of Harlem's many storefront churches. Despite its small size, the church held services five days a week and supported a Sunday school. During the Depression the congregation could not pay the Reverend Elder Johnson (here portrayed) a salary, but he lodged rent-free in the church study and supported himself selling insurance. On the ground floor was the Pentecostal Barber Shop, run cooperatively by the brethren. PHOTOGRAPH BY BERENICE ABBOTT. GIFT OF THE FEDERAL ART PROJECT, WORK PROJECTS ADMINISTRATION. 43.131.1.309.

SEWING, 10TH AVENUE & 36TH STREET, CA. 1938: The contrast between this Garment District loft and the older tenement sweatshops of lower Manhattan is striking. Photographer Andrew Herman was one of several to be assigned series under the auspices of the Federal Art Project, documenting the needle trades, Harlem street scenes, East Side market scenes, a Coney Island set, and more. PHOTOGRAPH BY ANDREW HERMAN. GIFT OF THE FEDERAL ART PROJECT, WORK PROJECTS ADMINISTRATION. 43.131.4.4.

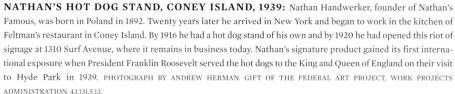

NATHAN'S HOT DOG STAND, CONEY ISLAND, 1939: Nathan Handwerker, founder of Nathan's Famous, was born in Poland in 1892. Twenty years later he arrived in New York and began to work in the kitchen of Feltman's restaurant in Coney Island. By 1916 he had a hot dog stand of his own and by 1920 he had opened this riot of signage at 1310 Surf Avenue, where it remains in business today. Nathan's signature product gained its first international exposure when President Franklin Roosevelt served the hot dogs to the King and Queen of England on their visit to Hyde Park in 1939. PHOTOGRAPH BY ANDREW HERMAN. GIFT OF THE FEDERAL ART PROJECT, WORK PROJECTS ADMINISTRATION. 43.131.5.13.

CONEY ISLAND GALLERY, 1939: "Test your skill and win a prize! Impress your girlfriend!" These were the sorts of cries one heard called by carnies while walking down the sidewalks and alleys of Coney Island. Three balls for a nickel, or a hot dog for the same amount . . . tough choice. PHOTOGRAPH BY ANDREW HERMAN. GIFT OF THE FEDERAL ART PROJECT, WORK PROJECTS ADMINISTRATION. 43.131.5.12.

(RIGHT) STEEPLECHASE PARK—THE BARREL, 1939: At George C. Tilyou's "Steeplechase—the Funny Place," admission to the fifteen-acre pavilion cost a dollar but then all the rides were free. Mystery and joy, light and shadow, all for a buck! PHOTOGRAPH BY ANDREW HERMAN. GIFT OF THE FEDERAL ART PROJECT, WORK PROJECTS ADMINISTRATION. 43.131.5.74.

FIRST AVENUE AND 10TH STREET MARKET OPENING, MAYOR FIORELLO LA GUARDIA, 1938: The "Little Flower" was mayor of New York for three terms from 1934 to 1945 and became as much a symbol of the city in those hard years as President Roosevelt was for the nation at large. Here he performs a typical ceremonial function in opening what became known as the First Avenue Retail Market. What is iconic in the image is the radio microphone of station WNYC. As soon as he was in office La Guardia (1882–1947) used it to go after the mob, urging his constituents over the radio, "Let's drive the bums out of town." In his last year in office, he read the funnies over the air during the newspaper strike. PHOTOGRAPH BY SOL LIBSOHN. GIFT OF THE FEDERAL ART PROJECT, WORK PROJECTS ADMINISTRATION. 43.131.6.20.

133RD STREET BETWEEN LENOX AND FIFTH AVENUES, 1939: This image is part of an extensive Harlem series photographed by Sid Grossman (1913–55) between May and July 1939. Like Andrew Herman, Arnold Eagle, David Robbins, and others, he was attached to the New York City Federal Art Project. GIFT OF THE FEDERAL ART PROJECT, WORK PROJECTS ADMINISTRATION. 43.131.9.34.

FRANKFURTERS, CA. 1940: Dining *al fresco* was not necessarily a matter of choice for those on the prowl for a job or a home. But for most New Yorkers the outdoor carts offered good fast food at bargain prices. PHOTOGRAPH BY ANDREW HERMAN. GIFT OF THE FEDERAL ART PROJECT, WORK PROJECTS ADMINISTRATION. 43.131.7.183.

PENNSYLVANIA RAILROAD PARK: BIDDING AT A FRUIT AUCTION, 1938: "Despise not the pushcart men," wrote Gilson Willets in his assessment of the city's fruit markets in *Workers of the Nation* (1903). "At the fruit auction sales they buy ten per cent of all the fruit that comes into New York. At an ordinary sale $40,000 worth of fruit is sold, and for their share the pushcart men pay $4,000 in cash. The boss pushcart men run from ten to fifty carts and corner stands, and some of them, in Naples or Genoa, would be deemed millionaires." PHOTOGRAPH BY SOL LIBSOHN. GIFT OF THE FEDERAL ART PROJECT, WORK PROJECTS ADMINISTRATION. 43.131.6.201.

FULTON FISH MARKET: UNLOADING FISH, 1938: In 1936 Sol Libsohn (1914–2001) founded the Photo League, an organization of photographers committed to the documentary style of depicting urban subjects. It was shut down by blacklisting in 1947. The dignity of labor was a recurring theme in the work of a whole legion of likeminded artists of the decade. PHOTOGRAPH BY SOL LIBSOHN. GIFT OF THE FEDERAL ART PROJECT, WORK PROJECTS ADMINISTRATION. 43.131.6.90.

SEA FOOD BAR & CLAM HOUSE, 1938: "If it swims, we have it." And New Yorkers will eat it. New York has had a long and omnivorous relationship with the fruit of the sea—especially the local bivalves. PHOTOGRAPH BY SOL LIBSOHN. GIFT OF THE FEDERAL ART PROJECT, WORK PROJECTS ADMINISTRATION. 43.131.6.168.

(RIGHT) **SIXTH AVENUE SUBWAY RECONSTRUCTION, 42ND STREET, CA. 1939:** The IND Sixth Avenue Line opened gradually, beginning in 1936 with a portion of roadway from West Fourth Street (where it splits from the Eighth Avenue Line) to East Broadway. By 1940 the old elevated railway of the IRT Sixth Avenue Line was gone and the new line was entirely underground except for a brief stretch over the Gowanus Canal. PHOTOGRAPH BY ANDREW HERMAN. GIFT OF THE FEDERAL ART PROJECT, WORK PROJECTS ADMINISTRATION. 43.131.13.28.

[FROM THE SERIES *WATERFRONT*], 1938: In some cases with funding in place before the stock market crash, a tall-building boom marked the 1930s with the Chrysler Building, the Empire State Building, Rockefeller Center, and more. PHOTOGRAPH BY DAVID ROBBINS. GIFT OF THE FEDERAL ART PROJECT, WORK PROJECTS ADMINISTRATION. 43.131.10.102.

[FROM THE SERIES *WATERFRONT*], 1938: Photographers Arnold Eagle and David Robbins joined forces in May to August 1938 to create the landmark "One-Third of a Nation" series, putting a human face on hard times. The title came from a line in President Franklin D. Roosevelt's second inaugural address: "I see one-third of a nation ill-housed, ill-clad, ill-nourished." PHOTOGRAPH BY DAVID ROBBINS. GIFT OF THE FEDERAL ART PROJECT, WORK PROJECTS ADMINISTRATION. 43.131.10.61.

JITTERBUGGING IN HARLEM, 1939: The gaiety of the image aside, the Great Depression was felt hardest in Harlem and other largely African-American enclaves of the city. The nightclub business that had accompanied the Harlem Renaissance was decimated, even though the quality of the art and the dance and the jazz only continued to soar. PHOTOGRAPH BY SID GROSSMAN. GIFT OF THE FEDERAL ART PROJECT, WORK PROJECTS ADMINISTRATION. 43.131.9.69.

MERRY GO ROUND ON A TRUCK, 1935: Well into the 1950s children playing on the street would be alert for the jolly music accompanying the truck with the ride (could be the Whip or the Trip to the Moon or the Merry Go Round) or the ice cream truck. Or the kids would yell to an open window that the knife-and-scissor-sharpening man had pulled up to the curb. PHOTOGRAPH BY ARNOLD EAGLE. GIFT OF THE FEDERAL ART PROJECT, WORK PROJECTS ADMINISTRATION. 43.131.11.90.

MOHAWK CHILDREN, CA. 1939: These diligent children are learning the catechism as transcribed in *The Book of Common Prayer in Mohawk*. PHOTOGRAPH BY ALEXANDER ALLAND. 94.104.57.

CHINESE-AMERICAN GIRL SCOUTS, CA. 1939: Russian-born Alexander Alland (1902–89) arrived in this country in 1923. He became well-known as a documentary photographer of New York ethnic and religious groups in the 1930s, including the "Red Bandanna" Romany Gypsy group in the Bowery, a black Jewish congregation, Mohawk Indians in Brooklyn, and many others. Some were marked by separatist inclinations, but these smiling Girl Scouts spoke to successful assimilation. PHOTOGRAPH BY ALEXANDER ALLAND. GIFT OF HOWARD GREENBERG. 02.130.14.

BOY READING COMIC, 1940: Escapism has been the constant fare of youth and—in this grindingly difficult era—adults too. The golden age of comic books is considered by collectors to have begun in 1938 with the first issue of *Superman*. This young man, absorbed in *Champion Comics*, may have his feet on the pavement but his mind is in the stratosphere with the comic's hero, Duke O'Dowd, the Human Meteor. PHOTOGRAPH BY ANDREW HERMAN. GIFT OF THE FEDERAL ART PROJECT, WORK PROJECTS ADMINISTRATION. 43.131.8.1.

WILLOW PLACE, NOS. 43-49, BETWEEN JORALEMON AND STATE STREETS, BROOKLYN, 1936: This Greek Revival residential row, dating back to perhaps the mid 1840s, had a single occupant in each, all of Irish descent. No 43, Meehan; No. 45, Sullivan; No. 47, McKenna; and No. 49, Dowling. In a decrepit state at the time of Abbott's photograph, all have been rehabilitated and survive today. PHOTOGRAPH BY BERENICE ABBOTT. GIFT OF THE FEDERAL ART PROJECT, WORK PROJECTS ADMINISTRATION. 43.131.1.177.

(RIGHT) **[HOOVERVILLE, CENTRAL PARK], CA. 1932:** In late 1929 the large rectangular reservoir in Central Park was being taken out of service. In early 1930 it was drained but with land fill scarce, it remained an open field for some time. By September 1932 there were seventeen shacks along "Depression Street" in what even the Parks Department termed "Hoover Valley." PHOTOGRAPH BY NAT NORMAN. GIFT OF THE PHOTOGRAPHER 81.114.49.

"DAWN OF A NEW DAY" (SONG OF THE NEW YORK WORLD'S FAIR), 1939: The dreary "Official March of the World's Fair" urged visitors to cast off their gloom and "live and laugh the American way." Released after George Gershwin's death and thought to have been pieced together from his notebooks, the tune was recorded by Horace Heidt and His Musical Knights. THEATER COLLECTION.

WORLD'S FAIR, NEW YORK, 1939–40: The Trylon and the Perisphere were two of the three design symbols of the futuristic fair, whose theme was "The World of Tomorrow." The third symbol, less prominent in the iconography of the fair and only dimly visible here, was the Helicline, a long spiral ramp that partially encircled the Perisphere. Among the several innovations debuted at the fair was television, including the launch of regularly scheduled broadcasts over NBC station W2XBS (now WNBC). President Roosevelt's opening day address was not only broadcast over radio but also televised. PHOTOGRAPHER UNKNOWN. GIFT OF BENJAMIN BLOM. 91.69.39.

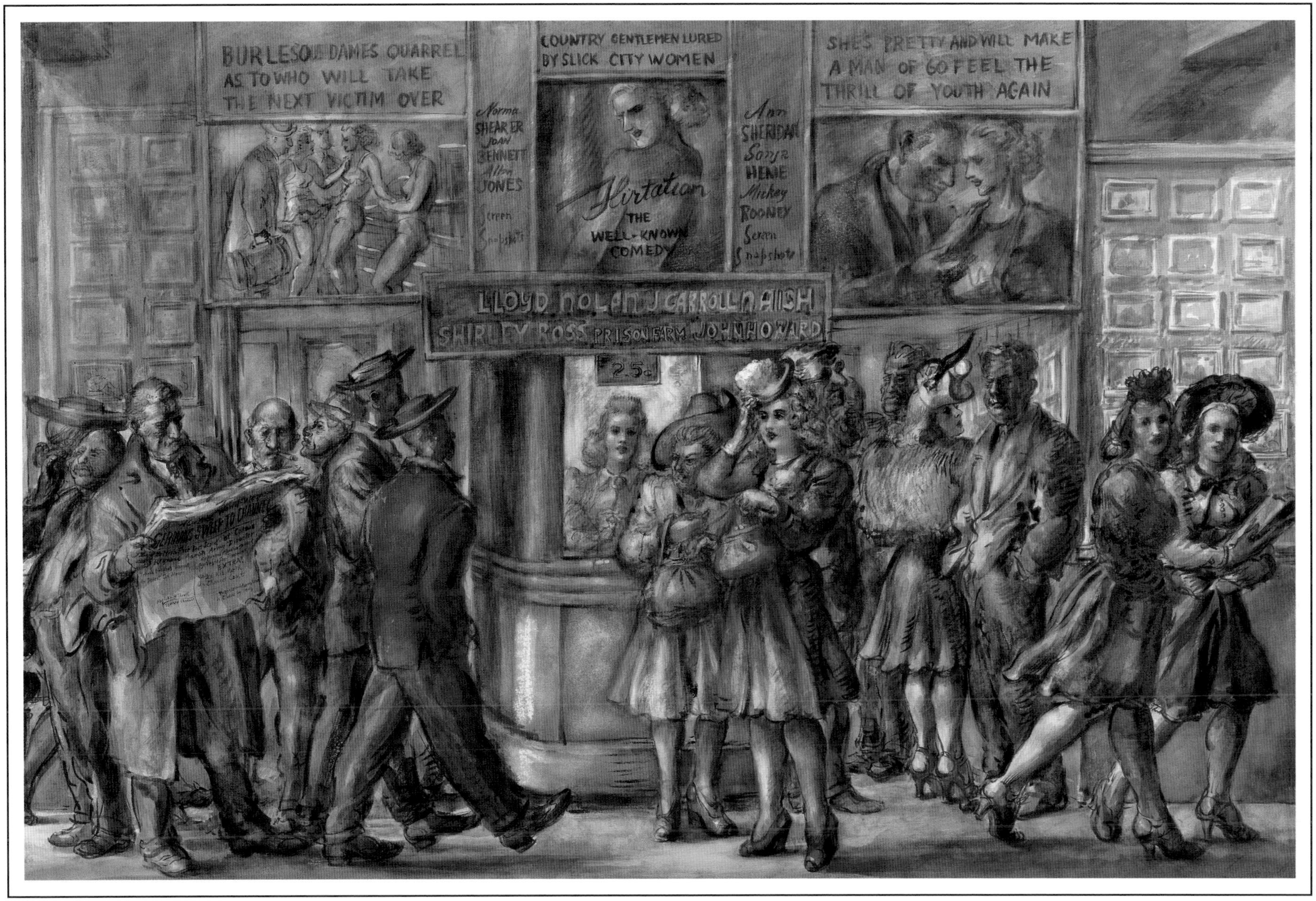

HARRIS THEATER, NEW YORK, 1940: In the words of Grace Mayer, the curator who founded the prints and photographs collection at the Museum of the City of New York, Reginald Marsh was the "unofficial Artist Laureate" of the city. He would walk around the city, sketchbook and camera at the ready to capture impressions that he would later develop in his studio overlooking Union Square. This busy watercolor depicts the sidewalk spectacle outside the entrance to the Harris Theater at 226 West 42nd Street. Formerly managed by George M. Cohan's partner Sam Harris, the musical venue had long since abandoned live entertainment for the celluloid variety. WATERCOLOR AND INK ON PAPER BY REGINALD MARSH, 27 x 40⅜. GIFT OF THE ARTIST. 53.107.3.

[FROM THE "SABBATH STUDIES" SERIES], 1937: Arnold Eagle began work in 1934 on a photographic series about Orthodox Jewish life on the Lower East Side. He continued it in the following year under the auspices of the new Works Progress Administration (WPA, called the Work Projects Administration from 1938 until its shuttering in 1943). He was one of millions employed by this largest of all New Deal agencies. PHOTOGRAPH BY ARNOLD EAGLE. GIFT OF THE FEDERAL ART PROJECT, WORK PROJECTS ADMINISTRATION. 43.131.12.19.

COMMUNIST PARTY HEADQUARTERS, 1930: In the summer of 1930, when the depths of the economic depression could be envisioned, social unrest simmered in the city, and the Communist Party gained considerable traction for its championing of the rights of the unemployed, the evicted, and the victims of racial discrimination. The Communist Party Headquarters trumpeted its 1930 slate for state office, headed by William Z. Foster. The shabby walkup at 16 Union Square also housed the offices of the Communist newspaper *The Daily Worker* and, at street level, the Co-Operative Cafeteria, which writer Maxwell Bodenheim described as "a pathetic and humorous hive, crowded with courage and inhibition throwing noise at each other." PHOTOGRAPH BY CHARLES RIVERS. GIFT OF THE PHOTOGRAPHER. PRINT ARCHIVES.

BONWIT TELLER WINDOW, 1936: This display designed by surrealist artist Salvador Dalí puzzled onlookers but was nothing compared to the ruckus raised by his next round of window settings for the Fifth Avenue department store, in March 1939. Outraged customers convinced the Fifth Avenue department store's managers to alter the display, which infuriated Dalí to such an extent that he smashed the plate glass window. Dalí asserted that it was all an accident, and night court Magistrate Louis B. Brodsky awarded him a suspended sentence. PHOTOGRAPHER UNKNOWN. GIFT OF BONWIT TELLER, INC. 37.67.8.

CAB CALLOWAY, 1933: In the 1920s, novelist, critic, and photographer Carl Van Vechten became interested in promoting black artists and writers. A frequent visitor to Harlem, he conducted a photo shoot on January 12, 1933 with the high priest of jive, the "hi-de-ho man," Cab Calloway, who had moved from the Cotton Club onto the national scene with "Minnie the Moocher," which he performed not only on vinyl but also for a Betty Boop cartoon of that name. PHOTOGRAPH BY CARL VAN VECHTEN. 42.316.255.

SET DESIGN FOR *AH, WILDERNESS!* BY EUGENE O'NEILL, 1933: Eugene O'Neill's only comedy, *Ah, Wilderness!*, debuted on Broadway on October 2, 1933 at the Guild Theatre, where it ran for 289 performances. Robert Edmond Jones designed the set for this play and many others produced by the Theatre Guild, including several by his friend O'Neill. His realistic approach, in which the sets were integral parts of the action rather than mere backdrops, represented a departure from tradition. SET DESIGN BY ROBERT EDMOND JONES, 7 x 18. GIFT OF MRS. EUGENE O'NEILL. 34.35.1C.

SAILING OF *NORMANDIE* FROM PIER 88, 1936: Photographing the great ocean liners, those of the French Line in particular, was a dependable source of work for the Byron Company. The S.S. *Normandie*, for which Percy Byron was official photographer, was set to depart New York in this image taken one year after its maiden voyage. Requisitioned for military use in 1941, she was gutted by fire in 1942 and never put into service. To modern eyes the subject of the image is not the famed ship but the enormous crowd, so typical of *bon voyage* occasions in the golden age of passenger ships. THE BYRON COLLECTION. 93.1.1.12197.

NEWSSTAND, 1940: Charlie Chaplin looks out at us as "The Great Dictator" from the September 24, 1940 cover of *Look* magazine. Even though the advent of picture magazines *Life* and *Look* had thinned the playing field of the former Golden Age of magazines, the general reading public of 1940 still also had *The Saturday Evening Post* and *Collier's* to complete the Big Four (with *Life* and *Look*) among general interest weeklies. Now they are all long gone. In 1940 New York City had eight major daily newspapers, down from twenty at the turn of the century. Today there are four. PHOTOGRAPH BY ANDREW HERMAN. GIFT OF THE FEDERAL ART PROJECT, WORK PROJECTS ADMINISTRATION. 43.131.8.33.

LAMP CLEANER, 42ND STREET AND FIFTH AVENUE, 1940: "Where the underworld can meet the elite"—that's how lyricist Al Dubin described "naughty, bawdy, gaudy, spawty Fawty Second Street" (thus pronounced in the 1933 musical film *42nd Street*). This corner of 42nd Street, two blocks east of Times Square, is more sedate than sexy. PHOTOGRAPH BY ANDREW HERMAN. GIFT OF THE FEDERAL ART PROJECT, WORK PROJECTS ADMINISTRATION. 43.131.8.6.

JAY STREET, NO. 115, 1936: In 1918 Berenice Abbott (1898–1991) left Ohio for New York and came under the wing of Hippolyte Havel, the Greenwich Village anarchist and *bon vivant*. In Paris during the 1920s she worked for Man Ray and came under the influence of Eugene Atget. Returning to New York in 1929, she saw the city with the new eyes of a documentarian. After six years of photographing a city in transition—with a handheld Kurt-Bentzin camera that produced 8 x 10-inch negatives—she finally won support from the Federal Art Project to complete her series, *Changing New York*, for the collections of the Museum of the City of New York. The Museum holds seven hundred negatives from the project, along with 353 proof prints, 941 unmounted prints, the documentary files completed by the project's researchers, and two sets of 305 mounted exhibition prints. This image, one of the few in the entire project that is not about the built environment, is a portrait of an African-American family headed by James Sullivan living in "Irishtown." Abbott later recalled that the family told her "a dog shouldn't live in this place."

PHOTOGRAPH BY BERENICE ABBOTT. GIFT OF THE FEDERAL ART PROJECT, WORK PROJECTS ADMINISTRATION, 43.131.1.122.

GARIBALDI MEMORIAL, 1937: After the failure of Giuseppe Mazzini's Roman Republic, established briefly in the Revolutionary movement of 1848, Italian military leader Giuseppe Garibaldi came to Staten Island on July 30, 1850. Hosted by inventor Antonio Meucci, Garibaldi tried his hand at candle making with little satisfaction. He left New York in 1853, but the wooden cottage where he stayed at Tompkins Avenue and Chestnut Street in Staten Island was preserved within a cement pantheon as the Garibaldi Memorial. Note that a column of the structure designed to preserve the original home pierces it instead. This "pantheon" was taken down in 1952, but the house is maintained as the Garibaldi-Meucci Museum. PHOTOGRAPH BY BERENICE ABBOTT. GIFT OF THE FEDERAL ART PROJECT, WORK PROJECTS ADMINISTRATION. 43.131.1.478.

GASOLINE STATION, 1936: During Abbott's years in Europe, gas stations became a common feature of the American landscape, and when she returned in 1929, they fascinated her. She considered them "truly American," reminding her of totem poles, as she told Jim McQuaid and David Tait in a 1975 interview. PHOTOGRAPH BY BERENICE ABBOTT. GIFT OF THE FEDERAL ART PROJECT, WORK PROJECTS ADMINISTRATION. 43.131.1.209.

TRAVELING TIN SHOP, BROOKLYN, 1936: Horsedrawn emporia were on their way out when Abbott captured this itinerant dealer in tinware. A research report accompanying this Works Projects Administration image reports, "Carts like one shown here may carry as many as 100 different items, and does an average of from four to seven dollars worth of business in an average day. The cart and stock represents an investment of $200-300." PHOTOGRAPH BY BERENICE ABBOTT. GIFT OF THE FEDERAL ART PROJECT, WORK PROJECTS ADMINISTRATION, 43.131.128.

HUNGARIAN PICNIC, LONG ISLAND CITY, 1937: Hungarian immigrant photographer John Albok (1894–1982) is known for his street scenes, people at leisure, and political rallies. This is one of his many Great Depression-era views of his countrymen expressing their heritage in New York. PHOTOGRAPH BY JOHN ALBOK. GIFT OF ILONA ALBOK PARKER. 82.68.45.

[PROTESTOR], 1935: Voluntarily chained to the post in the garment center at 38th and Broadway, nineteen-year-old Mary Slate shouted "don't work for scabs" until she was hoarse, while perspiring police worked with files and hacksaws and chains to free her. A sympathizer of striking shop clerks, she kept up a running patter for nearly half an hour while the strike was brought to an end by a compromise agreement on wages and hours between nine employers associations and the Ladies Apparel Shipping Clerks Union. This union had been formed out of an earlier protest in which approximately 150 women, including Ethel Rosenberg of later spy notoriety, lay down in the middle of West 36th Street, blockading the entrance to the shipping company's warehouse and preventing company trucks from making deliveries. PHOTOGRAPHER UNKNOWN. PRINT ARCHIVES.

FROM 27TH FLOOR, RIVER HOUSE, SUN AND CLOUD STUDY LOOKING SOUTH, CA. 1930: River House at 435 East 52nd Street was regarded as the city's finest apartment house when it was erected in 1931, arising from the dead-end slum of the East Side docks. The title given to this spectacular view reflects that it was taken from the parapet, as the tower contains only twenty-six residential stories. PHOTOGRAPH BY SAMUEL H. GOTTSCHO. THE GOTTSCHO-SCHLEISNER COLLECTION. 88.1.5.2.

VIEW EAST FROM TUDOR CITY TO HUNTERS POINT, CA. 1930: Tudor City, a complex of a dozen apartment buildings that went up in the late 1920s between 40th and 43rd Streets between First and Second Avenues, provided this dramatic view of Hunter's Point. Then a bustling industrial peninsula of Queens, Hunter's Point fell upon hard times after World War II, with the erosion of industrial plants and warehouses. It is a neighborhood on the upswing today. PHOTOGRAPH BY SAMUEL H. GOTTSCHO. THE GOTTSCHO-SCHLEISNER COLLECTION. 88.1.5.26.

(LEFT) **FLAGPOLE PAINTER OPPOSITE CHRYSLER BUILDING, CA. 1937:** The eye goes to the flagpole painter, so evocative of the flagpole-sitting stunts that marked an era in which a man might make a buck in strange ways. But of no less interest is the Art Deco masterpiece Chrysler Building. Designed by architect William Van Alen, it was briefly the world's tallest building. In his race to exceed the height of the Bank of Manhattan Building at 40 Wall Street, also under construction, the architect kept his plans secret: "Van Alen planned a dramatic moment of revelation," wrote Peter Gossel and Gabriele Leuthauser. "The entire seven-story pinnacle, complete with special-steel facing, was first assembled inside the building, and then hoisted into position through the roof opening and anchored on top in just one and a half hours. All of a sudden it was there—a sensational *fait accompli*." PHOTOGRAPH BY JOHN ALBOK. GIFT OF ILONA ALBOK PARKER. 82.68.66.

VIEW FROM CHRYSLER BUILDING, CA. 1930: Like some contemporaneous European photographers, Sherril Schell (1877–1964) saw beyond photography's documentary function, employing unconventional perspectives to create striking compositions, often with strong diagonal elements that stressed the abstract qualities of the city's built environment. PHOTOGRAPH BY SHERRIL SCHELL. GIFT OF THE PHOTOGRAPHER. 56.51.4.

EDNA ST. VINCENT MILLAY, 1933: The first woman to receive the Pulitzer Prize for Poetry, Edna St. Vincent Millay was equally famous for her bohemian lifestyle and her dedication to her adopted city. Her best-known poem may be "First Fig," published in 1920: "My candle burns at both ends;/ It will not last the night; But ah, my foes, and oh, my friends—/ It gives a lovely light!" This image by writer-turned-photographer Carl Van Vechten is one of his many portraits documenting the creative milieu of the time. His sitters included such subjects as F. Scott Fitzgerald, Langston Hughes, Alfred A. Knopf, Bessie Smith, and Gertrude Stein. PHOTOGRAPH BY CARL VAN VECHTEN. GIFT OF THE PHOTOGRAPHER. 42.316.370.

ENTRANCE TO EL, SIXTH AVENUE, CA. 1930: A reviewer for the *New York Times* wrote of a 2006 Museum of the City New York exhibition of Sherril Schell's work that the photographer's closely cropped views of Manhattan monuments "emphasize compositional order, structure, pattern, light and shadow." PHOTOGRAPH BY SHERRIL SCHELL. GIFT OF THE PHOTOGRAPHER. 56.51.2.

(RIGHT) **CITY ARABESQUE, 1938:** Berenice Abbott took this celebrated shot from 60 Wall Tower at 70 Pine Street, a faux address that resulted from a bridge connecting a low building at 60 Wall Street to the Cities Service Building at 70 Pine Street. Looking west from the Art Deco balcony she framed a view of skyscrapers, which remain, and of tenements, long gone. PHOTOGRAPH BY BERENICE ABBOTT. GIFT OF THE FEDERAL ART PROJECT, WORK PROJECTS ADMINISTRATION. 43.131.2.246.

[CHINATOWN], CA. 1939: The matter of fact air with which these men approached their trade might give way, in the presence of customers, to animation. New York's Chinatown, like those of other cities, was a tourist destination, but it was also, and primarily, a vital neighborhood in which the residents could extend their ethnic and national traditions while embracing their new home. PHOTOGRAPH BY ALEXANDER ALLAND. 94.104.181.

(NEAR RIGHT) **[CHINESE PRESSMEN], CA. 1939:** New York has long welcomed foreign-language newspapers, and even today, as the large newspapers struggle to maintain circulation and advertising revenue, as many as eighty foreign-language papers, daily and weekly, are circulated in the five boroughs. PHOTOGRAPH BY ALEXANDER ALLAND. 94.104.216.

(FAR RIGHT) **[ARMENIAN LINOTYPIST], CA. 1939:** In a *New York Times* review of "The Committed Eye: Alexander Alland's Photography," a 1991 exhibition at the Museum of the City of New York, Charles Hagen commented: "The issues Mr. Alland dealt with in his work echo with special resonance today. His belief that a chief strength of the United States is its ethnic diversity foreshadowed current debates over multiculturalism." PHOTOGRAPH BY ALEXANDER ALLAND. 94.104.97.

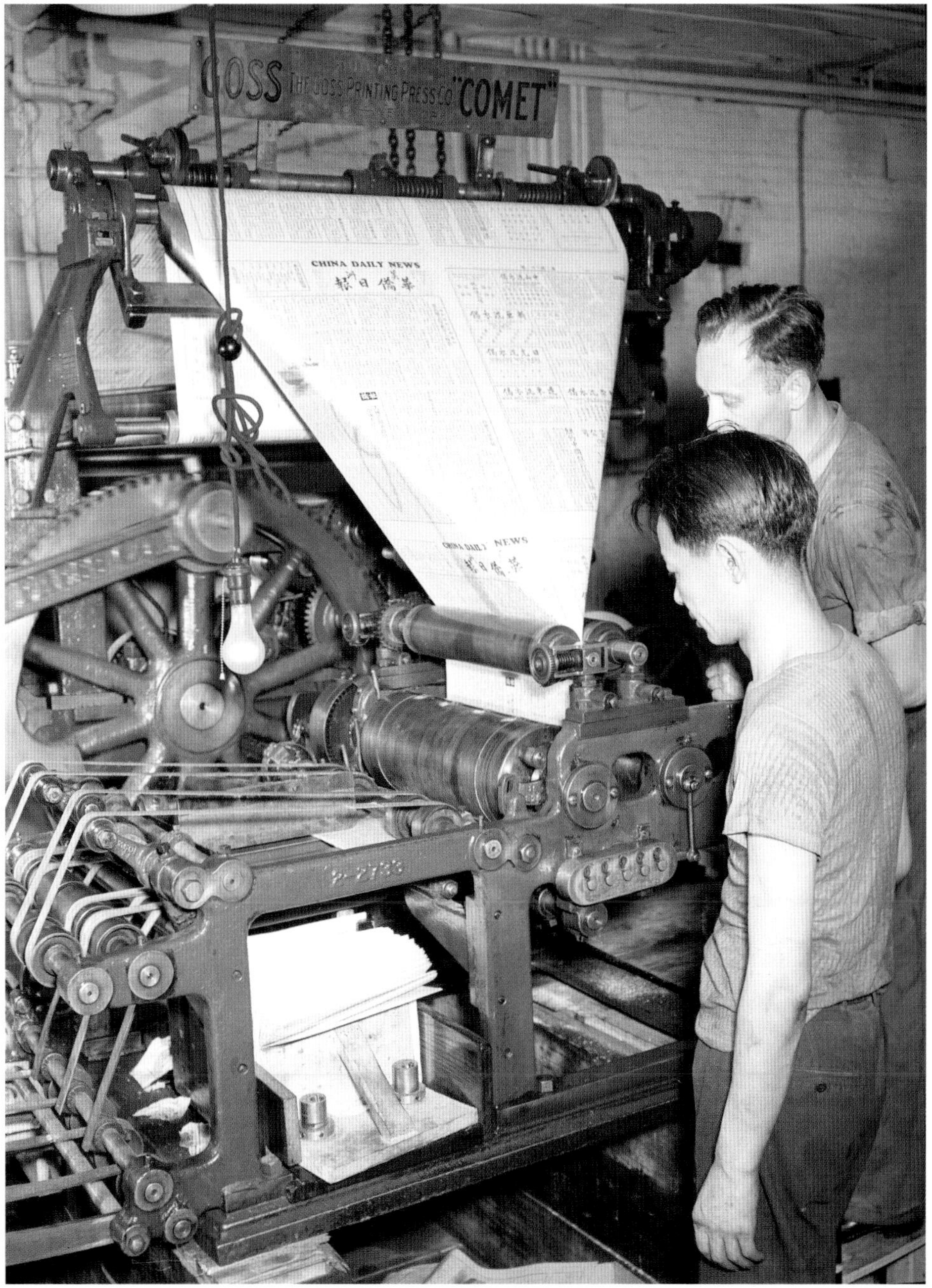
GOSS THE GOSS PRINTING PRESS CO. "COMET"
CHINA DAILY NEWS

ՀՐԱՊԱՐԱԿԱՅԻՆ ՄԵԾ ՄԻԹԻՆԿ
Manhattan Center

CHAPTER XI | 1941-1945

GOTHAM GIRDS FOR WAR

THE RIGHT TO FIGHT

MIKE WALLACE

NEW YORK'S HARBOR WAS THRONGED WITH MARITIME TRAFFIC IN THE FALL OF 1941, AS FOOD AND WAR MATÉRIEL POURED INTO GOTHAM FOR TRANS-SHIPMENT TO BRITAIN. WHEAT FROM THE MIDWEST—BARGED ACROSS THE ERIE CANAL AND DOWN THE HUDSON—WAS TRANSFERRED DIRECTLY TO OCEANGOING VESSELS BY FLOATING GRAIN ELEVATORS THAT COULD OFFLOAD TONS IN MINUTES FLAT. OIL WAS PIPELINED IN FROM PENNSYLVANIA TO AREA REFINERIES AND STORAGE TANKS, WHERE IT WAS PICKED UP BY AN ENDLESS STREAM OF TANKERS, LINED UP OFF STATEN ISLAND LIKE CABS AT A TAXI STAND, WAITING TO FILL UP AND CARRY THEIR CARGO OUT INTO THE NORTH ATLANTIC TO FUEL ENGLAND'S BOMBERS AND WAR SHIPS. MUNITIONS AND MANUFACTURED GOODS, ROLLED IN ON THE NATIONAL RAIL NETWORK, WERE TRANSFERRED TO FREIGHT-CAR LIGHTERS AND THEN WERE TOWED BY TUGS TO ONE OR ANOTHER OF THE PORT'S ROUGHLY NINE HUNDRED PIERS, WHERE THEY WERE TRANSFERRED TO DEEP-SEA TRANSPORTS. ALL NIGHT LONG THE BUSTLE CONTINUED, AS SHADOWY HULLS, BARGES, LIGHTERS, AND TUGS CRISSCROSSED THE GREAT BOWL OF THE UPPER BAY, ITS DARK WATERS RIMMED WITH SHORE LIGHTS, DOTTED WITH WINKING GAS BUOYS, AND PIERCED BY BEAMS FROM FIXED AND REVOLVING LIGHTHOUSES. THIS SURGE IN TRAFFIC WAS UNDERWRITTEN BY A TORRENT OF MONEY, FIRST LARGELY BRITISH, then increasingly American, as preparedness expenditures by the U.S. government rocketed upward. These monies also underwrote a host of collateral manufacturing enterprises in Gotham itself.

Federal funding put shipbuilding back on the city's agenda big time, the long doldrums of the 1920s and '30s having been terminated by Japan's abrogation of the Naval Limitation Treaty in 1936, which triggered a naval arms race. Almost immediately, President Franklin Delano Roosevelt had launched a construction program, in which Brooklyn's facilities figured prominently, especially the Navy Yard. All this activity generated jobs—by 1939 there were 9,000 men employed at the Yard; by mid-1941, more than 20,000.

In addition to maritime projects, a plethora of federal contracts were issued to produce the wide range of manufactured goods demanded by the military buildup. Some of the most substantial funding went to the cluster of high-tech firms that had, since World War I, dominated the nation's output of gyroscopic and mechanical analog computer equipment—bombsights, compasses, fire control systems, automatic pilots. The Big Four companies, whose genealogies were intricately intertwined, were: Sperry Gyroscope (whose three plants in Brooklyn and one in Long Island City expanded employment from 5,500 in 1940 to 8,000 in 1941); Ford Instruments (whose William H. Newell, having mastered engineering at the City College of New York in the evenings, produced scores of inventions critical to naval gunnery); Carl L. Norden, Inc. (whose famous bombsight, produced at 80 Lafayette Street in

Manhattan, was reserved for U.S. planes—the British having to settle for Sperry's somewhat lesser version); and Arma Corporation (whose gyrocompass, produced since 1924 at 254 36th Street in Brooklyn, was the preferred device for navigation and fire control on U.S. submarines and battleships).

City manufacturers also received contracts for more conventional arms or accessories such as gun mounts, searchlights, anti-aircraft apparatus, and artillery material (R. Hoe and Company—the venerable printing firm—received an accessories contract). But New York businesses were also showered with orders for non-combat related items, notably uniforms. In addition to orders for arms and clothing, contracts were issued for a vast panoply of miscellaneous items, including dental operating chairs, feather pillows, goggles, trunk lockers, printing equipment, surgical instruments, flashlight batteries, drugs, aero-photo enlargers, electrical capstans, canteen covers, blood lancets, cap insignia, stopwatches, tar oil, optical goods, machine parts, and canned spinach (for which Kemp, Day & Company, at 73 Hudson Street, received a contract in 1941 valued at $191,602.30).

For all this, New Yorkers did not benefit nearly as much from defense spending as did other industrial areas. When the fifteen largest recipient cities were ranked by the dollar volume per capita of contracts awarded between June 1940 and March 1942, New York came in dead last, with Newark, San Francisco, Cleveland, and Los Angeles each garnering roughly four times what Gotham did, and Detroit pulling down approximately six times New York's take.

In part this was because Gotham, though long the nation's manufacturing powerhouse, seemed too geared (in the estimation of defense chiefs in Washington) toward small-scale production of consumer goods by small-scale outfits. And in part New York's last place finish was because politics affected the allocation of funds. Contracts from agencies such as the Defense Plant Corporation, which channeled vast sums into building shipyards or airplane factories from scratch, became the new pork barrel, and senators and congressmen deluged the White House in 1941 with pleas to build something military in their states and districts. Southern clout helped ensure that by May 1941, the Gulf Coast from Tampa to Galveston, where oceangoing ships had not previously been built, now boasted four shipyards working round the clock, with another four under construction.

The enormous amount of federal funds flowing into the country's economic arteries was, with amazing dispatch, erasing the Depression across the continent. In 1939, 17.2 percent of the U.S. work force had been unemployed; by 1941 that figure was cut in half. By mid 1941, national retail sales were up 16 percent over the previous year; by autumn, sales had jumped 40 percent, with radios, refrigerators, washing machines, and furniture flying out the door.

But in New York, overall, the Depression dragged on. A year after the Crash, 46 percent of the total population had been gainfully employed; by 1940, the figure had dropped to 38 percent; and in 1941, unemployment actually increased in Gotham, even as it was evaporating elsewhere. More than 10 percent of the population still received some form of government assistance that year. An estimated 6,000 beggars walked the streets, undeterred by a message posted in the subway from Mayor Fiorello La Guardia saying: "BEGGING IS UNNECESSARY. The City Provides for Its Destitute and Homeless. DO NOT GIVE TO BEGGARS! Refer Begging Men and Women to the Department of Welfare."

As always, how you made out depended largely on who you were. Some New Yorkers—by skill and experience and connections—benefited from the defense program, and many more would have, had it been larger in scope. But others were actually precluded from participation by law and/or custom. In 1940, Congress, feverish with concern about possible Fifth-Columnist spies and saboteurs, had barred resident aliens from holding certain defense jobs. The exclusion was based solely on their country of origin, not their politics: All German aliens were *verboten*, whether Nazis or antifascist refugees. Many businesses, moreover, wishing to take no chances on violating federal guidelines, went farther and banned not only aliens, but Americans with "alien" (e.g., Italian) names. The Carl L. Norden Company sought "Christian, not Italian" applicants; the personnel director explained that a large number of the firm's employees were Germans who didn't like to work with Italians (or Jews). Help-wanted ads were festooned with qualifiers such as "American parents" or "Native (or American) born," though some stipulated more broadly that "Nordic" would be acceptable.

There was yet another constellation of New Yorkers in the "need not apply" category—men and women who though they were in fact citizens (often of very long standing), nevertheless confronted their own exclusionary qualifiers on the help-wanted page, terms like "White Only" or "Anglo-Saxon." But now, with the looming likelihood of war against racial-supremacists abroad, Gotham's African Americans would take unprecedentedly dramatic steps toward overcoming local varieties of racial discrimination at home.

In the winter of 1941, more than 120,000 New Yorkers held defense-related jobs. Fewer than 3 percent of them were black—the lowest rate of any of the major defense-production regions—and the jobs they held were the least attractive, worst paid, and most dead-end. A 1941 survey of 202 New York City defense firms found that 32.7 percent of their positions classified as "white required," 36.6 percent as "white preferred," and 30.7 percent as "open." Another study that year—a detailed scrutiny of ten New York-area defense plants—discovered that African Americans held 142 of the 29,215 positions.

Black applicants found themselves up against an interlocking and all but impervious system of discrimination, comprising employers, unions, and training schools, each of which shifted responsibility to the other. Businesses with closed-shop agreements turned down black applicants on the grounds that they were not in a union, a catch-22 situation, because many unions refused to admit blacks, notably the Boilermakers and the International Association of Machinists, which dominated the shipyard and aircraft industries. One reason employers rejected black job seekers was that they were deemed unqualified, but industrial training schools restricted their intake of black candidates to less than 5 percent, arguing that it was pointless to train them because they had no job prospects.

When it came to the military—an escape route from unemployment open to whites of whatever background—blacks faced a similar set of barriers. New York's Senator Robert F. Wagner had won an amendment to the 1940 Selective Service Act that forbade racial discrimination in drafting men into the armed forces, but the law did not bar the armed forces from segregating their ranks. The Army had four separate Negro units, only one of which trained its members for combat, with the others assigned to support duties—digging ditches, building roads, cooking and serving meals. Draft picks were indeed made on a *de jure* nondiscriminatory basis: Names were selected by a color-blind lottery and assigned a number. But inductions proceeded on a *de facto* racial basis, skipping over the next draftee in line if he was black, when filling white units, and reaching into the black community only when necessary to bring one of the four black outfits up to strength. This meant that some 300,000 single black men who were in the 1-A (prime) eligibility pool went undrafted, even though this forced draft boards to call up married white men to meet their overall quotas. As a result, by fall 1941, an Army of half a million included only 4,700 African-Americans. This was, to be sure, a better percentage than the Navy attained—it accepted blacks only as mess men (to cook, make up officers' beds, shine their shoes)—much less the Marines, which refused black enlistments altogether. One Harlemite summed up the situation: "We can become no more than flunkies in the army and kitchen boys in the navy."

This limit on access to defense jobs and to the military—coupled with ongoing everyday civilian racism—was one reason that in November 1941 Welfare Department statistics showed blacks constituting 26 percent of New York's total relief roll. They also accounted for 20–23 percent of the 63,500 still in WPA positions, though in 1937 they had been only 13 percent. Their percentage had risen in four years as whites moved on to positions from which blacks were barred.

In the face of such Jim Crow practices the country's black leadership began to protest. In June 1940, the annual convention of the National Association for the Advancement of Colored People (NAACP) resolved to campaign against racial exclusions. In September of that year, the Brotherhood of Sleeping Car Porters (BSCP), assembled at the Harlem YMCA, argued for the same strategy. But when BSCP leader A. Philip Randolph and NAACP leader William White asked for an appointment with President Roosevelt to argue their case, they were rebuffed by his deeply racist secretary, Steve Early. First Lady Eleanor Roosevelt had been in attendance at the BSCP's Harlem gathering. After learning of the snub by Early, she wrote her husband a letter advising him to take the meeting and address the issues; not to do so, she added pointedly (the presidential election season being in full swing) would be "bad politically besides being intrinsically wrong."

Thus began a remarkable dialogue/confrontation between the nation's black leadership, almost without exception from New York City, and the nation's highest elected and appointed military command, almost without exception from New York City.

On September 27, the president, Assistant Secretary of War Robert P. Patterson, and Secretary of the Navy Frank Knox met with White, Randolph, and T. Arnold Hill of the National Urban League. The visitors related the rebuffs their people were experiencing in trying to get jobs, entering unions, and joining the military. Roosevelt listened intently and asked questions. When Knox explained that integrating the Navy was almost impossible because the different races would be confined together on a ship, Roosevelt suggested—without irony or intended disrespect—that perhaps Negro bands might be put on board so white sailors could get accustomed to a black presence. At meeting's end, he thanked the leaders for coming and promised to confer with other officials about the issues.

Secretary of War Henry Stimson was not of the same mind as the Roosevelts. Indeed, he groused in his diary about "Mrs. Roosevelt's intrusive and impulsive folly" and deplored the "tremendous drive going on by the Negroes" to take "advantage of the last weeks of the campaign in order to force the Army and the Navy into doing things for their race which would not otherwise be done and which are certainly not in the interest of sound national defense." Were the Army to "mix the white and the colored troops together in the same units," Stimson insisted, then "we shall certainly have trouble." He flatly opposed any concessions "to satisfy the Negro politicians."

Patterson, though less prejudiced than Stimson, believed radical shifts in the Army's racial policies would impede preparedness and weaken public (white) support for the military. Accordingly, he drafted an official statement of War Department policy for Roosevelt's consideration, which proclaimed that separating colored and white enlisted personnel in different regimental organizations had "been proved satisfactory over a long period of years, and to make changes now would produce situations destructive to morale and detrimental to the preparation for national defense." The statement was approved by Roosevelt on October 9. Steve Early, who also acted as Roosevelt's press secretary, not only promulgated this document to the public—a slap in the face to the leaders who had been awaiting FDR's response—but managed to convey the utterly false impression that they had agreed to this perpetuation of segregation.

Randolph was stunned. Harlem was enraged: thousands attended a mass protest meeting. FDR, having noted polls showing Wendell Willkie gaining ground (the Republican presidential candidate was far stronger on civil rights), publicly regretted Early's remarks and insisted blacks would be treated on a "nondiscriminatory basis." On October 25, three days before his final campaign swing through Gotham, the president announced he was promoting to brigadier general Colonel Benjamin Davis, commander of New York State's 369th National Guard Infantry Regiment. Privately, Stimson snickered with Knox about his "colored Brigadier General" and said the Navy secretary would now have to come up with a matching "colored Admiral."

Three days later in New York, Secretary Early managed to pour accelerant on the flames Roosevelt had tried to douse. After FDR's Madison Square Garden speech winding up his Gotham visit, the presidential party was boarding a train back to Washington when James Sloan, a black New York Police Department officer, unwittingly blocked Early's access to the presidential compartment. The choleric Early hauled off and kicked Sloan in the *cojones*. This triggered headlines across the country, massive outrage among blacks, and yet another apology from FDR. But once the election was safely past, and black leaders asked for another conference with the president, they were again rebuffed.

Randolph now concluded that African Americans

were up against a system that could not be changed politely from within but had to be frontally assaulted from without. He decided, accordingly, on a drastic change in tactics. In early January 1941 Randolph published an article in the black press arguing that "only power can effect the enforcement and adoption of a given policy." The requisite degree of power, moreover, could never be mustered by quiet backstage diplomacy, but only by mobilizing the Negro masses for direct and highly public action. "I think we ought to get 10,000 Negroes and march down Pennsylvania Avenue asking for jobs in defense plants and integration of the armed forces," he declared. Only this "would shake up Washington" and embarrass the administration into reversing discriminatory policies that Randolph branded as "undemocratic, un-American, and pro-Hitler." On January 15, he formally issued a press release calling for a march on Washington, under the slogan, "WE LOYAL NEGRO AMERICAN CITIZENS DEMAND THE RIGHT TO WORK AND FIGHT FOR OUR COUNTRY." If blacks were to get anything out of the federal government, he asserted, "WE MUST FIGHT FOR IT AND FIGHT FOR IT WITH THE GLOVES OFF."

Randolph's unabashed militancy attracted rapid and widespread support from blacks in New York. Some were already well versed in direct action—notably the members of his union, the largest organization of black workers in the United States, for whom picket lines were *modus operandi* of labor struggle. Activist Adam Clayton Powell's "Don't Buy Where You Can't Work" campaign had accustomed thousands of Harlemites to taking to the streets to overcome discrimination. But even middle-class moderates like William White and the NAACP's rank and file had been impressed by the tangible benefits of New Deal interventions and were now prepared to push for federal political action to increase local economic opportunity. The notion that fighting for jobs and expanding civil rights were complementary projects was born, like the New Deal itself, on the sidewalks of New York.

The unprecedented unity of African Americans across the political spectrum became apparent when a conclave at Harlem's Hotel Theresa issued the official call for a March on Washington, to be held on July 1, 1941. It would be followed by a rally at the Lincoln Memorial. The call was signed by Randolph, White, Powell, Lester Granger of the National Urban League, Layle Lane of the American Federation of Teachers, Frank Crosswaith of the Harlem Labor Committee, and Channing Tobias of the YMCA, among others.

One victory came almost immediately. In March 1941, New York Governor Herbert H. Lehman appointed a Temporary Committee on Discrimination in Employment and gave it the task of exposing job discrimination and encouraging its voluntary elimination via persuasion and conciliation. A month later the New York state legislature gave the committee some teeth by making discrimination by public officials or defense contractors on grounds of race, color, or creed a misdemeanor punishable by fines of up to $500—hardly a crippling sum, but nonetheless a step toward enforceability.

Meanwhile, Randolph pushed ahead on the federal front, even raising the stakes by deciding to summon not 10,000 but 100,000 blacks to D.C. Pullman porters carried the word to black communities throughout the country. The March on Washington Committee (MOWC) opened headquarters—two in Gotham and one in eighteen other cities. Randolph himself pounded the pavement in New York, talking up the project in beauty parlors, barber shops, and taverns. Thousands of "March on Washington" buttons were sold.

FDR's placid facade began to crack. "I want you to go to New York," he commanded Aubrey Williams (National Youth Administration head), "and get White and Randolph to call off the march. . . . Get the missus and Fiorello and Anna [Rosenberg, Regional Director of New York City's Social Security Board] and get it stopped."

On June 10, Eleanor told Randolph his plan was a "grave mistake" and might do more harm than good if, as seemed likely, it led to violence. On June 13, La Guardia, who Steve Early thought had "great influence with the New York negroes," dutifully tried to wield it at a meeting in City Hall. A hyperventilating Archibald MacLeish chimed in with his own reason for curtailing the March, stating that perhaps "American Fascists" out to "incite the Negro population" were behind it. Under intense pressure, some moderate blacks wavered, suggesting that perhaps FDR should just be trusted to do the right thing. Nonsense, White replied, noting that "the President's promises are not more than water, and soon forgotten because it is politically expedient." Randolph never budged an inch.

Finally, on June 18, FDR summoned White, Randolph, and others to a White House sit-down. Roosevelt turned on the charm, but Randolph was in no mood for banter. He bluntly told the president: "Our people are being turned away at factory gates because they are colored. They can't live with this thing. Now, what are you going to do about it?" Roosevelt offered to call up the heads of those plants and ask for equal opportunity. "We want you to do more than that," Randolph replied. "We want something concrete, something tangible, definite, positive, and affirmative." Specifically, "we want you to issue an executive order making it mandatory that Negroes be permitted to work in these plants." Roosevelt insisted nothing could be done until the march was called off. Randolph, equally insistent: "I'm sorry, Mr. President, the march cannot be called off." Roosevelt, probing: "How many people do you plan to bring?" Randolph, steely: "One hundred thousand, Mr. President." Roosevelt, turning to White, hoping for a better number: "Walter, how many people will really march?" White, steadfast: "One hundred thousand, Mr. President."

At which point La Guardia piped up: "Gentleman, it is clear that Mr. Randolph is not going to call off the march, and I suggest we all begin to seek a formula." FDR concurred, charged the mayor with hammering out an agreement, and the meeting adjourned. Five days later La Guardia proposed that FDR establish by executive order a Fair Employment Practice Committee (FEPC) that would have the power to withhold defense contracts from manufacturers that discriminated in hiring, and even to seize a plant should its owner prove refractory. Stimson, Patterson, and Under Secretary of the Navy James Forrestal objected. FDR overruled them, and Executive Order 8802 was issued the following day, June 25. It required all defense industries and training programs receiving government contracts to "provide for the full and equitable participation of all workers . . . without discrimination because of race, creed, color or national origin." A watchdog FEPC was authorized to investigate and act on reports of discrimination, making it the first federal agency since Reconstruction whose mandate was to promote equal opportunity for African-Americans.

The executive order, however, did not apply to the armed forces—Stimson had drawn the line at desegregation—but Randolph, calculating that he'd gotten as much as he was going to get, called off the march, just days before it was scheduled to get underway.

There was considerable grumbling among Randolph's troops, not only about the failure to win changes in military policy, but the limits on the FEPC's ability to alter industrial practice. On paper, the committee had tremendous power—it could cancel the contract of any firm that discriminated—but that very power was its greatest weakness. The FEPC had no small arms in its enforcement arsenal; it could not fine recalcitrant companies, or reduce their profits, or send their executives to jail; it was the big gun of termination, or nothing. And given the tremendous push for preparedness, cancellation of a major rearmament order was simply not in the political cards.

(RIGHT) **TIMES SQUARE DIM-OUT, 1944:** As a wartime precaution the "Great White Way" (actually, long since become the neon way) was dimmed. In the eerie amber glow the women come and go. OIL ON CANVAS BY JAMES WILFRID KERR, 18 x 20. GIFT OF THE ARTIST. 77.16.3.

MIKE WALLACE IS CO-AUTHOR OF THE PULITZER-PRIZE-WINNING *GOTHAM: A HISTORY OF NEW YORK CITY TO 1898*, AND IS, ON HIS OWN, WRITING *GOTHAM II*, FROM WHICH THIS MATERIAL IS DRAWN. HE IS ALSO AUTHOR OF *A NEW DEAL FOR NEW YORK*, WHICH EXAMINES THE FUTURE OF POST–SEPTEMBER 11 GOTHAM IN THE LIGHT OF ITS PAST. HE HAS PUBLISHED A SERIES OF ESSAYS THAT EXPLORE THE WAYS HISTORY IS USED AND ABUSED IN AMERICAN POPULAR CULTURE; THESE HAVE BEEN COLLECTED IN *MICKEY MOUSE HISTORY AND OTHER ESSAYS ON AMERICAN MEMORY* (1997). HE IS DISTINGUISHED PROFESSOR OF HISTORY AT JOHN JAY COLLEGE OF CRIMINAL JUSTICE. HE IS ALSO BOARD CHAIR OF THE GOTHAM CENTER FOR NEW YORK CITY HISTORY AT THE CUNY GRADUATE SCHOOL, DEVOTED TO THE STUDY AND POPULAR PROMOTION OF THE HISTORY OF NEW YORK CITY (WWW.GOTHAMCENTER.ORG). WALLACE GOT HIS UNDERGRADUATE AND GRADUATE DEGREES AT COLUMBIA UNIVERSITY, STUDYING WITH PULITZER PRIZE-WINNING HISTORIAN RICHARD HOFSTADTER, WITH WHOM HE COLLABORATED ON A HISTORY OF AMERICAN VIOLENCE PUBLISHED BY KNOPF IN 1970. WALLACE HAS TAUGHT HISTORY TO POLICE OFFICERS AND OTHERS AT JOHN JAY SINCE 1971. HIS COURSES INCLUDE THE HISTORY OF NEW YORK CITY AND THE HISTORY OF CRIME IN NEW YORK CITY.

DANCING
RIALTO
DANCING
HENRY YOUNGMAN
WALK

U.S. ARMY
U.S. ARMY
VACANCIES EXIST!
ENLIST NOW
U.S. ARMY
GO
UNITED STATES ARMY

(LEFT) [GOVERNORS ISLAND, RECRUITING, DEPARTMENT OF WAR], 1943: Even after Pearl Harbor transformed the case against the Axis powers into a universally acknowledged "good war," recruitment efforts still seemed worth the effort. PHOTOGRAPH BY BOB HANSEN. THE *LOOK* COLLECTION.

AIR RAID INSTRUCTIONS, CA. 1944: The lighthearted cartoons by Fred G. Cooper (1883–1962) belie the seriousness of the mood that necessitated publication. The prolific artist was long associated with *Life*, the humor magazine that preceded the Time Inc. pictorial, and his "bighead" characters gave rise to the clip-art style of the era. MANUSCRIPT COLLECTION.

READ THIS – IT MAY SAVE YOUR LIFE
AIR RAID INSTRUCTIONS
CD
BLUE SIGNAL
SUSTAINED NOTE ON SIREN
RED SIGNAL
WARBLING NOTE ON SIREN
BLUE SIGNAL (AFTER RED SIGNAL)
SUSTAINED NOTE ON SIREN
If at home
NO
If dark, obscure or turn out lights visible from outside. Keep RADIO on.
DON'T PHONE. Turn off gas burners. Windows partly open. Go to cover area of building. Keep RADIO on.
Home blackout remains. Activities otherwise normal. Keep RADIO on.
If in commercial or public building
By day, continue normal business activities. Same by night, if blackout equipment is used.
Seek cover area in building. Follow WARDEN'S instructions.
Same as first BLUE SIGNAL.
KEEP RADIO ON
If out walking
Continue your walk, prepared to take cover.
Take cover.
THE NEAREST COVER
Same as first BLUE SIGNAL.
If in car or truck
Continue driving, cautiously. At night use only low beam headlights.
Pull to curb and stop. Don't obstruct hydrants, hospitals, etc. Put out lights. Take cover.
Same as first BLUE SIGNAL.
PARENTS, if your children are at school
Stay at home. Teachers are trained and ready. DON'T PHONE!
NO, NO!
If on bus or trolley
Vehicles continue, at night using low beam headlights. Continue your trip.
Vehicle will stop. You take cover.
THE NEAREST COVER
Same as first BLUE SIGNAL.
If in subway
Transit facilities not interrupted.
Stay on train or platform.
Trains resume normal schedule.
If on el train or platform
Stay where you are. Transit facilities not interrupted.
Train stops at next station. Take cover in nearby building.
Trains resume normal schedule.
If you hear a RUMOR
Ignore it. Obey AIR WARDEN'S instructions.
PST! PST! PST!
If you want to SHOUT, SCREAM, or RUN
DON'T.
If bombs drop near you in the open
Lie down and protect the back of your head.
FRED COOPER
THE ALL-CLEAR WILL BE ANNOUNCED OVER THE RADIO AND BY POLICE AND WARDENS' WHISTLES
This card to be placed on elevator, kitchen, or other prominent wall for the duration of the war.
F. H. LaGuardia, Mayor
THIS PLACARD DISTRIBUTED BY COURTESY OF RADIO STATIONS WABC·WEAF·WHN·WJZ·WNEW·WNYC·WOR
New Era Litho. N. Y.

[BOYS COMING HOME, ITALIAN NEIGHBORHOOD], 1945: As seen earlier in this volume, photographer John Albok had the gift of making his presence invisible to his subjects. A mix of joy and sadness appropriate to a homecoming is evident on the faces in the crowd. PHOTOGRAPH BY JOHN ALBOK. GIFT OF ILONA ALBOK PARKER. 82.68.73.

[PENN STATION, MILITARY PERSONNEL], 1945: In July 1945 when this image was taken, victory in Europe had been achieved but matters in the Pacific were one month from being settled. These soldiers and sailor, on leave and waiting for a train at old Penn Station, betray no sign that they are headed home for good. PHOTOGRAPH BY HY PESKIN. THE *LOOK* COLLECTION.

[PENN STATION, CIVILIANS], 1945: The Old Penn Station, above ground with light streaming in, sat where today one may attend a basketball or hockey game at the fourth arena to be named Madison Square Garden. The enormous main waiting room, inspired by the Roman Baths of Caracalla, was the largest indoor space in New York City and, at seven acres, one of the largest public spaces in the world. Public outcry over the demolition of the pink granite masterpiece of McKim, Mead, and White beginning in 1963 led to the creation of the New York City Landmarks Preservation Commission. As an editorialist in the *New York Times* wrote in 1963, "Until the first blow fell, no one was convinced that Penn Station [erected in 1910] really would be demolished, or that New York would permit this monumental act of vandalism against one of the largest and finest landmarks of its age of Roman elegance." PHOTOGRAPH BY HY PESKIN. THE *LOOK* COLLECTION. 10513.

GRAND STREET, 1942: Perhaps for the elucidation of editors at the *Herald Tribune*, which published this image on June 21, 1942, the photographer wrote in the margin: "Only from the El Train was the family wash so noticeable—Grand St. 'El' station, lower east side, May 15, 1942." PHOTOGRAPH BY ROBERT A. KNUDTSEN. GIFT OF THE PHOTOGRAPHER. 95.56.27.

(RIGHT) **[BROADWAY ON SATURDAY NIGHT], 1945:** This northward view of the great thoroughfare of New York, which runs on the diagonal, east to west from the Battery, captures the excitement of a city ready to throw off wartime constraints. The Paramount Theater features a double bill of the sort found only at the city's largest theaters: the movie *You Came Along*, starring Robert Cummings and Lizbeth Scott, and a live stage show featuring the Stan Kenton Orchestra, the Wesson Brothers, and the inimitable Louis Jordan ("Caldonia! Caldonia! What makes your big head so hard?"). Gutted in 1965, the Paramount spirit survives in an office building. PHOTOGRAPH BY HY PESKIN. THE *LOOK* COLLECTION.

RENT THIS FLOOR
CAFETERIA
E'S OFFICE
Paramount
ROBERT CUMMINGS LIZABETH SCOTT
"YOU CAME ALONG"
IN PERSON
STAN KENTON AND HIS ORCH.
DICK & GENE WESSON
EXTRA LOUIS JORDAN AND HIS TYMPANY FIVE
W 43 ST
ONE-WAY
BOND
VAUDEVILLE
MAXWELL
CAFETERIA
FRESH FRUIT DRINKS
HYGRADE FRANKFURTERS
GIFTS-JEWELRY
SOUVENIRS
SOUVENIRS-GIFTS
fresh fruit DRINKS
HYGRADE
All beef
HACK STAND
2 TAXI CABS
NO PARKING

[BENNY GOODMAN], 1945: "The King of Swing," Goodman (1909–86) started as a session clarinetist in Chicago and New York in the 1920s, but by the mid 1930s he and his "hot" style—aided by charts from African-American jazz legend Fletcher Henderson—had broken through to launch the Big Band Era. His landmark concert at Carnegie Hall on June 16, 1938 ended with "Sing, Sing, Sing" and its memorable drumwork by Gene Krupa. Goodman integrated the personnel in his band in the 1930s, adding in African Americans Charlie Christian, Teddy Wilson, and Lionel Hampton, who said, "As far as I'm concerned, what he did in those days—and they were hard days, in 1937—made it possible for Negroes to have their chance in baseball and other fields." PHOTOGRAPH BY HAROLD RHODENBAUGH. THE *LOOK* COLLECTION.

[NAT KING COLE TRIO AT NBC STUDIOS], 1944: Then as now, the National Broadcasting Company was headquartered at New York's Rockefeller Center. In the last decade before radio began to yield audience share to television, regional stars could be developed into national headliners over the air. When Nathaniel Adams Coles, better known as Nat King Cole, formed his trio of piano, guitar, and bass, big bands were all the rage. By the end of World War II other jazz troikas followed and Cole's career as a solo recording act took off. PHOTOGRAPH BY HAROLD RHODENBAUGH. THE *LOOK* COLLECTION.

[NEW YORK YANKEES CLUBHOUSE], 1945: Lou Gehrig's locker and that of Babe Ruth stood alongside those of active Yankees players for several years after their retirement and premature deaths—Gehrig in 1941 at age thirty-seven, Ruth in 1948 at age fifty-three. Today both lockers may be seen in Cooperstown at the Baseball Hall of Fame and Museum. PHOTOGRAPH BY HY PESKIN. THE *LOOK* COLLECTION.

(LEFT) [EMPIRE STATE BUILDING OBSERVATION DECK], CA. 1944: The city's signature skyscraper has two observation decks: one on the 86th floor, where these "New York City vacationers," as *Look* dubbed them, are peering out over the city; and another on the 102nd floor, which was originally designed as a landing platform and gangplank for passing dirigibles. This latter notion proved unwise. Only once did a dirigible dock at the mast, in September 1931, and it was able to stay moored for only three minutes due to high winds. Architects and engineers had not factored in the drafts created by the very height of the building. World War II came to the Empire State Building in an unexpected way on July 28, 1945, when a B-25 bomber flying a routine mission became fogbound and struck the building at its 79th floor, killing three on the plane and eleven inside. PHOTOGRAPH BY BOB HANSEN AND FRANK BAUMAN. THE *LOOK* COLLECTION.

[ITALIAN FAMILY], 1941: In November 1941, when peace still seemed possible, *Look* commissioned a series following the life of the Rossis, a family of Neapolitan immigrants who lived on the Upper East Side and were adjusting to American life while maintaining their Italian heritage. Here is a sidewalk scene in front of the six-story tenement owned by Mother Rossi (left), which serves as the social center for the forty-four-strong Rossi clan therein. She looks on while her sons play pinochle. PHOTOGRAPHER UNKNOWN. THE *LOOK* COLLECTION.

COSTUME SKETCH, *ZIEGFELD FOLLIES*, 1943: In a career spanning more than sixty years, Miles White (1914–2000) designed costumes in Rodgers and Hammerstein's first two Broadway hits, *Oklahoma!* and *Carousel*. The sketch shown here was for the *Follies*, produced at the Winter Garden in 1943, the same year that *Oklahoma!* opened at the St. James. WATERCOLOR, PENCIL, AND PEN ON PAPER, 15 x 18. THEATER COLLECTION. GIFT OF TOBIAS VAN RUUSUM DAUM. 03.108.24.

(RIGHT) "LONELY TOWN," FROM THE MUSICAL *ON THE TOWN*, 1944: This may have been a nice song, but the one that everyone today knows from this famous musical begins thus: "New York, New York, it's a helluva town./ The Bronx is up and the Battery's down./ The people ride in a hole in the ground./ New York, New York! It's a wonderful town!" If you have only seen the 1949 film based on this show, the lyrics will seem amiss, for in bowing to the film industry Production Code, lyricists Betty Comden and Adolph Green consented to change "helluva" to "wonderful." Leonard Bernstein suffered greater indignities, for most of his music—including "Lonely Town"—was dropped for new songs by Roger Edens. GIFT OF BETTY COMDEN AND ADOLPH GREEN. 70.22.31.

LONELY TOWN

Music by **LEONARD BERNSTEIN**
Lyric by **BETTY COMDEN & ADOLPH GREEN**

Oliver Smith and Paul Feigay present

ON THE TOWN

directed by **George Abbott**
book by **Betty Comden and Adolph Green**
from an idea by **Jerome Robbins**
music by **Leonard Bernstein**
choreography and
musical numbers staged by **Jerome Robbins**
settings by **Oliver Smith**
costumes by **Alvin Colt**

PRICE **60c** IN U.S.A.

LUCKY TO BE ME
I CAN COOK TOO
LONELY TOWN
SOME OTHER TIME
YA GOT ME
NEW YORK, NEW YORK

M. WITMARK & SONS
NEW YORK
PRINTED IN U.S.A.

[LORD & TAYLOR DEPARTMENT STORE, WINDOW DECORATION], 1943: The dresser and his mannequin partner appear to be executing a standard if somewhat stilted jitterbug move. Window shopping as a national pastime had begun along Ladies' Mile, roughly between Sixth Avenue and Broadway and 9th and 23rd Streets by the 1890s. *King's Handbook of New York City* in 1893 asked, "What are the Parisian boulevards, or even Regent Street, to this magnificent panorama of mercantile display?" The shopping district moved north of 32nd Street in the years that followed, with Lord & Taylor, Arnold Constable, B. Altman, Saks, Bergdorf Goodman, and Bonwit Teller lining Fifth Avenue, while Macy's, Gimbels, Ohrbach's, and Franklin Simon clustered near Herald Square. PHOTOGRAPH BY HAROLD RHODENBAUGH. THE *LOOK* COLLECTION.

[SUBWAY], 1944: The subway started out costing a nickel, and as of this writing the price of a fare has reached the two-dollar mark and one day soon will surpass it. Adjusted on a Consumer-Price-Index basis, however, the five-cent fare of 1904 has only doubled, in twenty-first-century terms, to ten cents. Permitting low-income workers to travel to and from their jobs inexpensively has been perhaps the city's greatest promoter of democracy and opportunity. PHOTOGRAPH BY HAROLD RHODENBAUGH. THE *LOOK* COLLECTION.

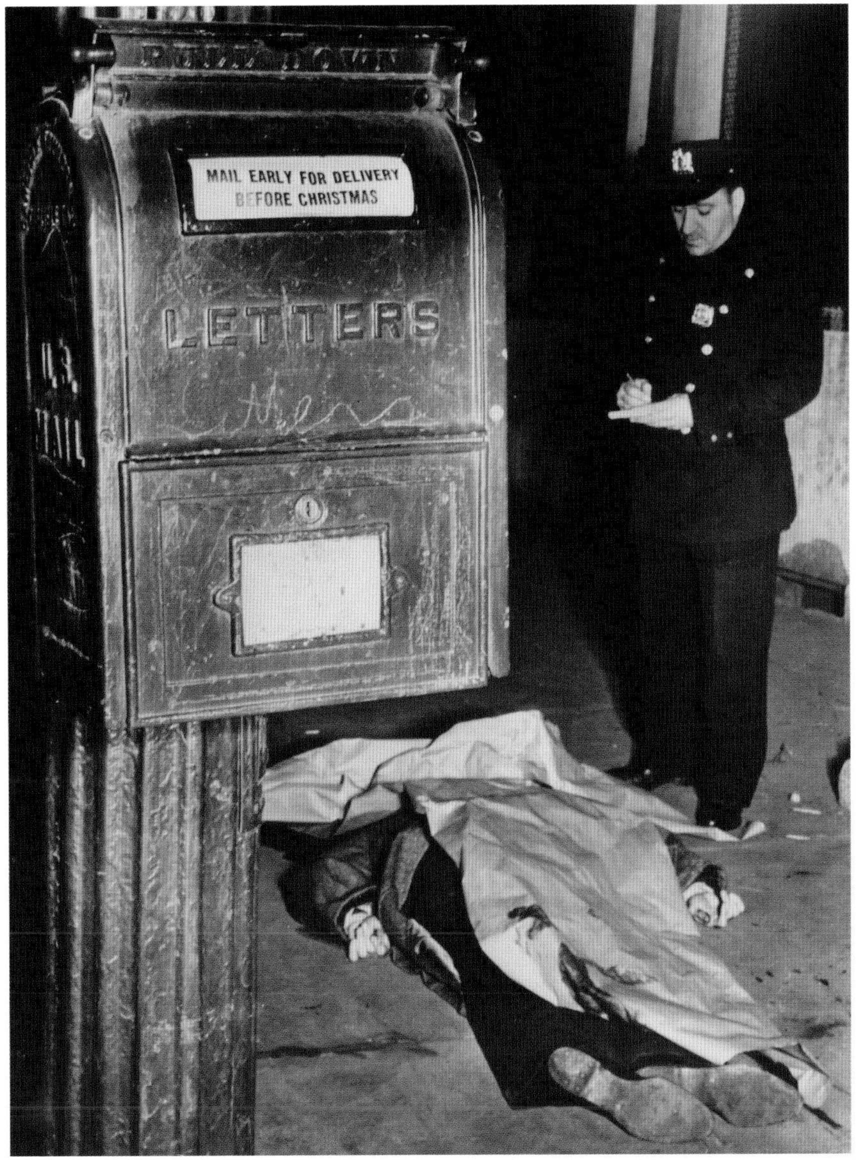

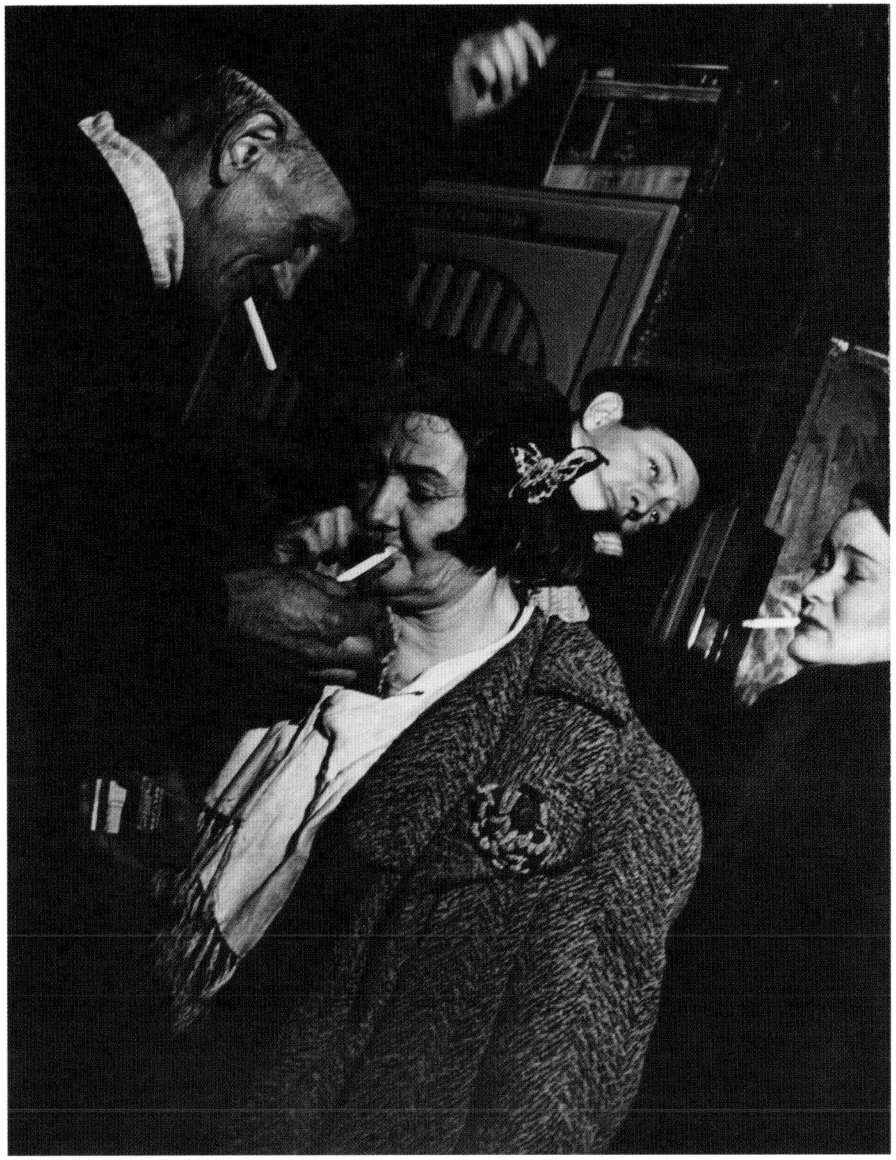

MURDER VICTIM, CA. 1945: Arthur Fellig (1899–1968) was a self-taught photographer who won his nickname (a phoneticized version of Ouija) for his uncanny ability to arrive at a crime scene minutes after the occurrence. It didn't hurt his efforts that he was the city's only newspaper reporter with a portable police-band shortwave radio. His first book collection of photographs, *Naked City* (1945), inspired a 1948 movie. PHOTOGRAPH BY ARTHUR FELLIG (WEEGEE). MUSEUM PURCHASE. 84.195.10.

SAMMY'S BAR, 1944: Viennese-born Lisette Model (1901–83) moved to New York with her husband in 1938. She was soon hired by *Harper's Bazaar*, which published the first of her two series of images from Sammy's on the Bowery, an especially picturesque bar known as the "poor man's Stork Club" because it was hard to get back into if you'd been tossed out once. Berenice Abbott wrote, "One of the first reactions when looking at Model's pictures is that they make you feel good. You recognize them as real because real people express a bit of the universal humanity in all of us." PHOTOGRAPH BY LISETTE MODEL. MUSEUM PURCHASE. 84.32.

[PAUL ROBESON], 1942: After graduating from Rutgers with All-America honors in football and earning a law degree from Columbia University, Paul Robeson (1898–1976) became a star of radio, theater, and film. Among his memorable roles before the New York footlights were performances in *The Emperor Jones*, *Othello*, *Porgy* (the dramatic precursor to the musical *Porgy and Bess*), and *Show Boat*. In this ironic photo Robeson is depicted joyously setting foot on American soil after travel, a right later denied to him for passage abroad. The U.S. government revoked his passport during his blacklist years of 1950–58. PHOTOGRAPH BY FRANK BAUMAN. THE *LOOK* COLLECTION.

[DUKE ELLINGTON WITH YOUNG FANS], 1942: The Duke is here depicted between two career landmarks important to New York City: the release of "Take the A Train" in 1941 (written with long-time "alter ego"—as Ellington termed him—Billy Strayhorn) and his Carnegie Hall debut in 1943 of "Black, Brown, and Beige." PHOTOGRAPH BY EARL THEISEN. THE *LOOK* COLLECTION.

(RIGHT) **[PHYSICS CLASS AT BRONX HIGH SCHOOL OF SCIENCE], 1944:** Text on the back of this image reads: "A physics classroom demonstration in molecular theory." This image is from an Office of War Information series, the martial utility of which is as unclear as what the intent young man sees in the beaker. PHOTOGRAPHER UNKNOWN. GIFT OF THE DEPARTMENT OF LOCAL GOVERNMENT, PUBLIC RECORD OFFICE OF SOUTH AUSTRALIA. 90.28.63.

CHAPTER XII | 1946–1959

POSTWAR NEW YORK

A SOCIO-CULTURAL SKETCH

PHILLIP LOPATE

IN ATTEMPTING TO UNDERSTAND ANY RECENT HISTORICAL PERIOD, IT IS NECESSARY TO LOWER THE VOLUME ON MEDIA STEREOTYPES AND SHORTCUTS, BEFORE SIFTING THROUGH THE EVIDENCE AND COMPETING MYTHOLOGIES. SAY THE FIFTIES, FOR INSTANCE, AND YOU ARE LIKELY TO BE PELTED WITH CONFORMITY, MCCARTHYISM, AND THE ORGANIZATION MAN, ON THE ONE HAND, AND THE STIRRINGS OF A REBEL COUNTERCULTURE, FROM THE BEATS TO PAUL BOWLES TO BOB DYLAN, ON THE OTHER. IT HELPS TO HAVE BEEN ALIVE AT THE TIME, THOUGH THE FACT THAT ONE MAY HAVE WITNESSED A VERY DIFFERENT ERA CAN PROVE EVEN MORE BAFFLING. I REMEMBER, FOR INSTANCE, THAT "GREASERS" OR "ROCKS," AS WE CALLED THEM GROWING UP, WERE MUCH FEARED BY THE AVERAGE TEENAGER AS VIOLENT, BORDERLINE-PSYCHOPATHIC TYPES, SO IT CAME AS A SHOCK WHEN THE FONZ WAS PACKAGED IN LATER DECADES AS A PARAGON OF FIFTIES YOUTH. THE FILM BIOGRAPHY *POLLOCK* SHOWS, AMONG OTHER THINGS, HOW DRENCHED IN LONGING OUR ERA IS FOR COLD-WATER FLAT BOHEMIAN HEROISM, WHICH WE SEE EXEMPLIFIED BY THE ABSTRACT EXPRESSIONISTS. HOW, THEN, TO FACTOR IN THE STUBBORN SOCIAL REALITY CAPTURED BY JOHN KOCH'S REALIST PAINTINGS, OF MEN IN SUITS AND WOMEN IN EVENING DRESS CALMLY LISTENING TO CHAMBER MUSIC? THAT A METROPOLIS OF NEW YORK'S SIZE SUSTAINS COUNTLESS, CONTRADICTORY SUBCULTURES AT ANY ONE TIME IS PART OF THE ANSWER AND IT IS UP TO US TO RETRIEVE THE MEMORY OF THOSE COMPLEX JUXTAPOSITIONS AND TRY TO PLACE THEM IN A MORE DOUBT-FRIENDLY CONTEXT.

- HAPPINESS IN '45 -

Let us start with that season of 1945 when victory was in the air, when the servicemen and women streamed into New York harbor at the end of World War II. It has come to be considered a peak moment in the city's fortunes. Jan Morris rhapsodizes in *Manhattan '45*: "Ask almost anyone who remembers Manhattan then, and they recall it with proud nostalgia, even if they were poor and lonely; and if their memories have been heightened or bowdlerized by the passage of time, much of the delight they remember was real—a Gallup poll taken at the time found that 90 percent of New Yorkers considered themselves happy. Few cities in the history of the world can have stood so consciously at a moment of fulfillment, looking into a future so full of reward." *New York Times* literary critic Anatole Broyard offered a similarly euphoric judgment: "New York City had never been so attractive. The postwar years were like a great smile in its sullen history. The Village was as close in 1946 as it would ever come to Paris in the Twenties. Rents were cheap, restaurants were cheap, and it seemed to me that happiness itself might be cheaply had."

New York was about to be chosen home of the United Nations, thus clinching the symbolic title of "world capital." The United States and its currency, the dollar, would dominate the global economy for the next quarter-century, which would see a great world boom. These were, according to historian Eric Hobsbawm, the Golden Years. "One must constantly bear in mind that in 1950 the U.S.A. alone contained 60 percent or so of all the capital stock of all the advanced capitalist countries, and produced 60 percent or so of all their output. . . ." he wrote in *The Age of Extremes*. New York, which then had the world's greatest port and most active stock exchange, was at the fulcrum of that expanding wealth.

Yet New Yorkers, then as now, were a nervous, moody people, strangers to contentment, and they imbibed with eagerness the darker side of the postwar mood. In every country around the world, *après-guerre* was a term signifying uneasiness, malaise, and disenchantment. How could it be otherwise after Hiroshima, Auschwitz, the battlefield carnage, and the massive task of rebuilding? Even if New York had escaped the physical war, it was still a city of immigrants, and took many of its mood cues from the other side, rather than the American hinterlands. If, as Broyard says, happiness might be cheaply had, it was also the period when *Kafka Was the Rage* (to use the title of his memoir). Nothing suited the cultivated New Yorker better than the Prague anxiety artist who said that certainly happiness is possible, but not for us. The Italian neorealist films, such as *Open City* and *Paisan*, exploded like revelations in Manhattan movie-houses, stimulating a thirst for harsh anti-glamour and stories about the acute suffering of ordinary people. Hollywood would turn out *film noir*, a genre largely the creation of European *émigrés* and East Coast ghetto exiles, to satisfy this taste. Even an elegant stylist of the old school like George Cukor would get off the studio lot and take to New York locations to film *The Marrying Kind* and *It Could Happen to You*. An appetite for the real, warts and all, was momentarily ascendant and the production of gritty images would become a New York specialty, à la Weegee's sidewalk murder photographs.

- STREET BALLET -

The city that the returning soldiers admired from their troopships, and which Broyard found so attractive, belonged—curiously, given New York's infamous, self-cannibalizing mutability—to an earlier era. Almost no construction had occurred since the early 1930s, having been halted first by the Great Depression and then by the wartime scarcity of building materials. The skyline was still fortuitously frozen in the ziggurat, step-back pattern dictated by the city's 1916 zoning resolution, still infused with art deco adornments and Babylonian-Mayan eclectic crowns that belonged more to that weird, hedonistic mélange Rem Koolhaas characterized as "Manhattanism" than to the more sober International Style. The significance of this architectural hibernation is that it gave people a chance to discover New York: It was as if during the war the city had grown lovably familiar and legible. Edwin Denby, dance critic and poet, characterized the New York aesthetic gestalt this way:

> Daily life is wonderfully full of things to see. Not only people's movements, but the objects around them, the shape of the rooms they live in, the ornaments architects make around windows and doors, the peculiar ways buildings end in the air, the water-tanks, the fantastic differences in their street facades on the first floor. A French composer who was here said to me, "I had expected the streets of New York to be monotonous, after looking at a map of all those rectangles; but now I see the heights between buildings, I find I have never seen streets so diverse one from another." But if you start looking at New York architecture, you will notice not only the sometimes extraordinary delicacy of the window framings, but also the standpipes, the grandiose plaques of granite and marble of ground floors of office buildings, the windowless side walls, the careful, though senseless, marble ornaments. . . .

What should be noted first, in this passage from *Dancers, Buildings and People in the Street*, is that Denby is talking about *prewar* architecture, with its tripartite structure of granite base, shaft, and pediment, and construing it as the eternal New York pattern. This prewar look must have been visual comfort food in the postwar years, even before it began appearing in real estate ads as shorthand for quality. Second, Denby hauls in a Frenchman to give the blessing to the city's diversity: New Yorkers were starting to look at their city from a fond distance, perhaps internalizing the enthusiasm of visiting Europeans. Third, Denby's pileup of simultaneous and serendipitous detail sums up the whole postwar New York school aesthetic. The very clashes of planned and unplanned, new and old, dignified and absurd, which had made the world formerly sneer at New York, suddenly began to seem, in the flush of America's imperial strength and New York's cultural centrality, harmonious, in an odd, unforced, collaged sort of way.

> ON
> TO TIMES SQUARE WHERE THE SIGN
> BLOWS SMOKE OVER MY HEAD, AND HIGHER
> THE WATERFALL POURS LIGHTLY. A
> NEGRO STANDS IN THE DOORWAY WITH A
> TOOTHPICK, LANGUOROUSLY AGITATING.
> A BLONDE CHORUS GIRL CLICKS: HE
> SMILES AND RUBS HIS CHIN. EVERYTHING
> SUDDENLY HONKS: IT IS 12:40 OF
> A THURSDAY.

In this stanza from "A Step Away from Them," Frank O'Hara's inventory of New York street sensations is both up to the minute and a revival of Whitman's sensual-democracy catalogs. These high-low dissonances of the city's daily life would turn up in the paintings of Robert Rauschenberg, Jasper Johns, and Larry Rivers, in the poems of O'Hara, Kenneth Koch, and John Ashbery, and in the dance performances of George Balanchine, Merce Cunningham, Yvonne Rainer, and the Judson Dance Theater. Dance is key because it became a repeated metaphor for what was happening in the streets. Jane Jacobs, in her extraordinarily influential 1961 book *Death and Life of Great American Cities*, spoke of daily life in her neighborhood as "an intricate sidewalk ballet. . . . Under the seeming disorder of the old city is a marvelous order for maintaining the safety of the streets and the freedom of the city. . . . This order is composed of movement and change, and though it is life, not art, we may call it the art form of the city, and liken it to the dance. . . . "

In the years 1964–65, there would be an accelerating appreciation of the historically layered architecture of New York and its lively pedestrian street-culture. This pro-urbanist consensus, theorized and expressed by artists in every field, including authors Nathan Silver (*Lost New York*), Ada Louise Huxtable (*Classic New York*), and Elliot Willensky and Norval White (*The AIA Guide to New York City*), occurred just at a moment when the city was being put under tremendous anti-urban strains and threats. Federal legislation after the war had done everything it could to support highway construction and single-family home ownership, which encouraged the flight of 1.2 million whites to the suburbs. Within the city, transportation czar Robert Moses' attempts to accommodate the automobile led to bulldozing old neighborhoods and severing people from the waterfront. The skyrocketing value of Manhattan real estate encouraged developers to tear down priceless landmarks such as Pennsylvania Station and the Singer Building, and replace them with mediocrities more instantly lucrative. The influential anti-street aesthetics of Swiss-born architect Le Corbusier in New York underpinned the 1960 zoning changes, which provided incentives to break the street-wall with public plazas; this, in turn, spawned dreary super-blocks and "towers in the park" (at the high end, glassy curtain-wall skyscrapers, at the low end, public housing done in incarcerative brick).

The story has been told many times since of the struggle for New York's soul, and of the often mistaken planning decisions made in the '50s and '60s, as the city, no longer restrained from construction, went through an enormous physical transformation. What is harder to recapture is the excitement of those first, pioneering glass towers. I can remember how my brother and I took the train in from Brooklyn for our weekly pilgrimages to East 53rd Street and Park Avenue, just for the privilege of staring at the ultramarine green, inverted T-square Lever House from the Seagram Building. After that we would cross the street to admire architect Ludwig Mies' whiskey-bronze masterpiece from the white stone planters in front of Lever House. At that moment in time its radical, aristocratic, Mondrian solitude was accentuated by the frou-frou, dowager masonry of older buildings up and down Park Avenue, but the street would soon become swamped by knock-offs. Every forward-thinking New Yorker seemed thrilled that the city was finally shedding its provincial ways and joining up with the best, the purest international expression of High Modernism.

- HEADQUARTERS TOWN -

In 1946 New York was the nation's largest manufacturing town. In the next twenty-five years it would lose, or divest itself of, more than a half-million manufacturing jobs, in the process being transformed from a working-class metropolis into a service-oriented, white-collar office center. In many ways, the working class had given the city its coloration: The New York type, as portrayed in the media, had been blue collar in argot and viewpoint, from the takes-no-guff Flatbush G.I. in war movies to the downtrodden Ralph Kramden type immortalized on *The Honeymooners*. The employment picture was about to change, as manufacturers were lured overseas or to the southern United States by cheaper wages and horizontal factories. Meanwhile, the great port quietly expired, done in by containerization and the lack of adjoining space. In future decades, the loss of these level-entry unskilled jobs in manufacturing and on the docks would have tragic consequences for inner-city youth, but for the moment, nobody seemed dismayed. Manhattan was about to be reconfigured as an upmarket residential and office center, where the messy production or transport of goods simply did not belong.

The United States' expanding role in the postwar world economy meant that every American company with eyes to expand overseas or become part of a multinational corporation needed to be in New York. A survey in 1960 "revealed that not only were 25 percent of the nation's five hundred largest corporations headquartered in the city, but of those that were not, more than 69 percent had sales offices there," according to the authors of *New York 1960*. The '50's and early '60s were to see the pinnacle of New York's life as a corporate town. Subsequently, many CEOs would move their headquarters to "office parks" in the suburbs, conveniently nearer their own residences, but for the moment, those glass towers sprouting everywhere in Midtown seemed just the ticket for the company logo.

Movies of the day brought to life the image-codes of corporate life: the uniform (*The Man in the Gray Flannel Suit*), the hierarchy (*Executive Suite*), the interiors that left nothing to chance (*How to Succeed in Business Without Really Trying*). The advertising man, split between creativity and abject servility, became a symbolic figure representing the tensions of the new corporate culture. The poet Weldon Kees's remarkable *Robinson* series captured just such a pointman's inner emptiness:

> ROBINSON AFRAID, DRUNK, SOBBING. ROBINSON
> IN BED WITH A MRS. MORSE. ROBINSON AT HOME;
> DECISIONS: TOYNBEE OR LUMINAL? WHERE THE SUN
> SHINES, ROBINSON IN FLOWERED TRUNKS, EYES TOWARD
> THE BREAKERS. WHERE THE NIGHT ENDS, ROBINSON IN EAST
> SIDE BARS.

Actually, despite the many sermons at the time about how amoral or sterile or soullessly greedy the New York corporate world was, it does seem to have resulted in the flowering of a very specialized, sophisticated design sense. Postwar industrial interior, and graphic design reached new heights of stylized confidence and mass communication. In the trademarks of Paul Rand and Raymond Loewy; in the posters of Lester Beall and Ben Shahn; in the office furniture produced by Herman Miller and Knoll; in the products designed by Herbert Bayer; in the magazines art-directed by Alexey Brodovitch and Leo Lionni; in the album covers of Milton Glaser and the advertisements of Ivan Chermayeff; in the Richard Avedon-designed title sequence for the film *Funny Face*; there was a canny synthesis of the best of the avant-garde modernism of Europe, tempered by American pragmatism. If a Willem de Kooning abstraction from the mid-fifties might be read as an expression of the impacted planes and drives of downtown loft life, so a *New Directions* paperback cover by Alvin Lustig might tell us as much about the dry-martini rhythms and cultural aspirations of postwar midtown. And the line between the Museum of Modern Art and Madison Avenue was about to get thinner: In 1957, Andy Warhol won the New York Art Directors Club Medal for exceptional achievement—before he had ever painted a Campbell's Soup can.

- THE CRY OF JAZZ -

Postwar New York was a great time for other forms of art, including jazz. Nothing caught the jangled energies, frustrated desires and downbeat chic of the *jolie-laide* city at night or early dawn better than modern jazz, one proof being that you could not show a New York street on film at the time (be it in *Shadows*, *Sweet Smell of Success*, *The Hustler*, etc.) without an accompanying jazz score. Newspaper editors, schoolteachers, students, admen, abstract painters, high-priced call girls—all could be found at the clubs on 52nd Street or downtown in the Village, united by a love of jazz such as would never again exist, just as you could never duplicate the miracle of that particular moment: to have the opportunity to hear live the giants of swing (Duke Ellington, Count Basie, Coleman Hawkins, Lester Young, Billie Holiday, Roy Eldridge, and even Louis Armstrong), coexisting with the masters of bebop (Charlie Parker, Dizzy Gillespie,

Thelonious Monk, Miles Davis, Sonny Rollins) and the new sound (John Coltrane, Eric Dolphy, Ornette Coleman, Charlie Mingus). At the same time, blues greats like John Lee Hooker, Muddy Waters, Lightning Hopkins, and Howling Wolf were doing their best work. All of that thrown in with the whole field of rhythm and blues, great gospel groups, and the sudden emergence of rock 'n' roll, added up to riches beyond riches. But jazz set the tone. As Norman Mailer somewhat embarrassingly announced in his essay "The White Negro," blacks had become inescapably the paragons of cool and existential grace under pressure and the black jazz musician was the central focus of that hero worship. His tastefully buttoned-down dress code, consisting of thin-lapel jackets, white shirts, and slender dark tie, were, in fact, not that far removed from the uniform of the gray flannel suit. But unlike your corporate cog, he could at any moment cut loose with thunder and fire.

As in the '20s, the high esteem in which many whites held black artists little affected the masses of African Americans, who still had a hard time finding jobs in Midtown. New York, with its postwar influx of Southern minorities looking for employment, had the largest black population of any city in the world. As expectations were crushed, the mood in the ghetto began to boil over with an unappeasable anger (articulated in very different ways by James Baldwin and Malcolm X). By the early '60s, issues of race had made it to the front burner of the city's consciousness. There was suddenly the sense that something had to give or the place would explode—that apocalyptic note, which darts in and out of the imagination of New York.

- THE EMPIRE OF GROWNUPS -

It was a good time for jazz, then, and baseball (the city had, for awhile, three great teams, two of which always seemed to reach the World Series), and abstract painting, of course, and literary quarterlies, and psychoanalysis, and Jewish-American fiction. Gore Vidal would note later how marginalized and overlooked he felt in those years, not as a gay but as a goy.

Moving from Midtown to the Upper West Side, the climate became more Freudian, the radios more tuned to classical music, the newsstands apt to sell out *Partisan Review* and *Aufbau* faster than *Time* or *Look*. Stretching from the sixties to Washington Heights, the Upper West Side contained a higher concentration of elderly people and European refugees from Fascism (often the same) than anywhere else in the country. The impact of European intellectuals on postwar New York could be felt in every discipline: political philosophy (Hannah Arendt, Max Horkheimer), psychology (Fritz Perls, Wilhelm Reich, Alfred Adler), sociology (Paul Lazarsfeld), theology (Paul Tillich), music (Kurt Weill, Lotte Lenya, Bela Bartok), photography (André Kertesz, Lisette Model, Robert Frank), painting (Marcel Duchamp, Arshile Gorky), literature (Hermann Broch, André Breton), aesthetics (Rudolph Arnheim, Siegfried Kracauer), physics (Albert Einstein, close by at Princeton). The analytical skepticism of the émigrés set the tone for New York culture. The immensely popular revival of Brecht-Weill's *The Threepenny Opera* in the late '50s demonstrated the perfect synchronicity of Berliner *Schnauzer* (lip) and New York sardonic.

The Europeans also lent a moral authority to the New York Intellectuals, a band more fearsome and combative in retrospect than Sid Vicious and the Sex Pistols. Mary McCarthy and Alfred Kazin, who looked up to few, could still take marching orders from Hannah Arendt. Of course, there had always been New York intellectuals, but they emerged as a self-conscious, interactive tribe that dominated the city's mental life from 1945 to 1965. Even more than by aesthetics, this New York intellectual community was fused by the heat of political events—first by the split in the Left between Stalinist and Trotskyite camps, later by the Rosenberg and Hiss cases, and then by the response to McCarthyism. It was an amazing period for critical prose, perhaps the most lush this country has ever seen: Lionel Trilling, Meyer Schapiro, Harold Rosenberg, Clement Greenberg, Mary McCarthy, Edmund Wilson, Robert Warshow, Irving Howe, Alfred Kazin, Sidney Hook, James Baldwin, Elizabeth Hardwick, Daniel Bell, Leslie Fiedler, and Seymour Krim produced an outpouring of passionately intelligent commentary.

The core of that commentary was qualification, an insistence on the complexity of social, political, and autobiographical entanglements. This stance was at opposite ends from what most people have come to regard as the hallmark of the Eisenhower Years—bland simplification and *Ozzie and Harriet* pieties. New York may have been out of step with the national mood: Here, for instance, the blacklist and anti-Communism had very personal ramifications, because everyone knew Communists, or had a Communist family-member, or had, conversely, fought against the party.

In Williamsburg, the Brooklyn ghetto where my

family lived, my mother wore a mouton coat just like Ethel Rosenberg's, and we all felt obscurely that the federal government was going after "our kind" (working-class, Jewish, outer-borough New Yorkers), just as we all felt obscurely that the Rosenbergs probably *were* guilty of something. Because Stalinists, such as Lillian Hellman in her book *Scoundrel Time*, have portrayed the blacklist period as purely and simply one of cowardice and unprincipled betrayal, we have lost the progressive nuances of that era: It tends to be forgotten how very liberal the liberal anti-Communists were. At the federal level, Eisenhower presided over a system of government planning and mixed economy that was really an extension of the New Deal, while at the city level, Mayor Robert F. Wagner, Jr. saw to massive construction of public housing and municipal hospitals. It was a mixed legacy and a very mixed political signal.

Be that as it may, New York intellectuals relished the era's gaudy contradictions, as well as their own temporarily glamorous status. Coeds clutched collections of literary criticism to their bosoms; Philip Rahv and Clement Greenberg were hot stuff. It was probably the last moment in Western society when middle-aged intellectuals still had erotic cachet. By 1964, the Beatles would arrive, and longhaired musicians would replace balding essayists as sex symbols. The discovery by merchandisers that American teenagers possessed more than a billion dollars in disposable income led to the institutionalization of youth culture. The young were to be flattered and sexualized, even as their lives as working adults were put on hold indefinitely by graduate school and the military, and a gerontocracy clung to the actual power.

Part of what is so shocking about John Koch's paintings is that, even into the '60s, they so refuse to honor the invasion of youth culture. He still portrays an empire of grownups, gathering for adult rituals like afternoon cocktail parties and dinner gatherings. These balding men and composed, thoughtful women bear the mark of maturity and psychotherapy: a self-scrutiny etched in their brows. Koch's willingness to expose his subjects' sagging flesh and wrinkles is the physical equivalent of the analysand's acceptance of his or her own sour, unruly psyche.

No one is trying to hold onto youth in Koch's paintings. The subjects inhabit graciously, if slump-shouldered, the grubby-elegant surroundings of New York's Upper West Side; they accept the dues of living in a society and sometimes playing the host and the responsibilities of money and high culture. Koch's marriage to Dora Zaslavsky had brought him into a world of European émigrés, complete with piano lessons and the never-flagging discipline that classical music requires. I like to think of them going to concerts together, maybe to hear the post-serial composers (Stefan Wolpe, Charles Wuorinen, Elliott Carter) who were then in vogue at Columbia University's MacMillan Theater, or the legendary performances by Glenn Gould of Bach's Goldberg Variations, as emblematic a sound of that era as Elvis Presley. All that rigor and severity, all that respect for formal tradition and insistence on the challenging nature of new art, as well as all the creature comforts of bourgeois life, should be taken into account when scrutinizing this striking juncture in the city's history.

(RIGHT) **TEENAGERS ON CONEY ISLAND BEACH, 1949:** Photographer Harold Feinstein was only eighteen when he captured this image of seemingly carefree teenagers at Coney Island on a fine summer day. PHOTOGRAPH BY HAROLD FEINSTEIN. MUSEUM PURCHASE WITH FUNDS FROM THE RICHARD FLORSHEIM ART FUND. 96.121.11.

PHILLIP LOPATE IS AN ESSAYIST, NOVELIST AND POET, WHOSE BOOKS INCLUDE ***WATERFRONT: JOURNEY AROUND MANHATTAN, BEING WITH CHILDREN, THE RUG MERCHANT, AGAINST JOIE DE VIVRE,*** AND ***PORTRAIT OF MY BODY.*** HE HAS EDITED SEVERAL ANTHOLOGIES, AMONG THEM ***THE ART OF THE PERSONAL ESSAY, WRITING NEW YORK,*** AND ***AMERICAN MOVIE CRITICS.*** HE IS THE RECIPIENT OF GUGGENHEIM, NEW YORK PUBLIC LIBRARY, AND NATIONAL ENDOWMENT FOR THE ARTS FELLOWSHIPS. A NATIVE OF BROOKLYN, WHERE HE CURRENTLY RESIDES WITH HIS WIFE AND DAUGHTER, HE IS A PROFESSOR IN THE GRADUATE DIVISION OF COLUMBIA UNIVERSITY.

(LEFT) **THIRD AVENUE EL, SATURDAY NIGHT DATE, 1953:** The Third Avenue Elevated rail was to have endured until a Second Avenue underground line came in to replace it—which was talked about as early as 1929—but instead underwent a slow demise, closing in sections from 1950 to 1973. PHOTOGRAPH BY ANN ZANE SHANKS. GIFT OF THE PHOTOGRAPHER. 94.32.50.

PAST AND PRESENT, EMPIRE STATE BUILDING AND GASHOUSE DISTRICT, 1946: Here the Empire State Building is framed by the final remaining wall of the Gas House District, looking northwest from 20th Street and First Avenue. The area was razed to make way for the residential developments of Stuyvesant Town and Peter Cooper Village. The Gashouse District, running from 14th to 27th Streets between the East River and Third Avenue, was named in the previous century for the "gas houses" or gas-generating plants located there, which provided the city with the fuel for gaslight in homes and in street lamps. It had been notorious for its foul odors of leaking gas and even more foul gangs of "Gashousers." PHOTOGRAPH BY ROBERT A. KNUDTSEN. GIFT OF THE PHOTOGRAPHER. 95.56.20.

FORDHAM ROAD, THE BRONX, 1951: This wide view of the billboards and storefronts of Fordham Road testifies that New York City's Jewish population had found a home in the Bronx of the 1950s. "Uptown—It's Alexander's" proclaims the massive sign atop the department store that in the following decades grew to a chain with fifteen locations including a midtown headquarters next to Bloomingdale's. All its stores are gone now, as is the x-ray foot-growth detector (officially, a "Shoe Fitting Fluoroscope") in Alexander's Fordham Road store, with its not-so-helpful caution that children ought to receive no more than twelve such exposures in a single year. PHOTOGRAPH BY WILLIAM GLOVER. THE GLOVER COLLECTION.

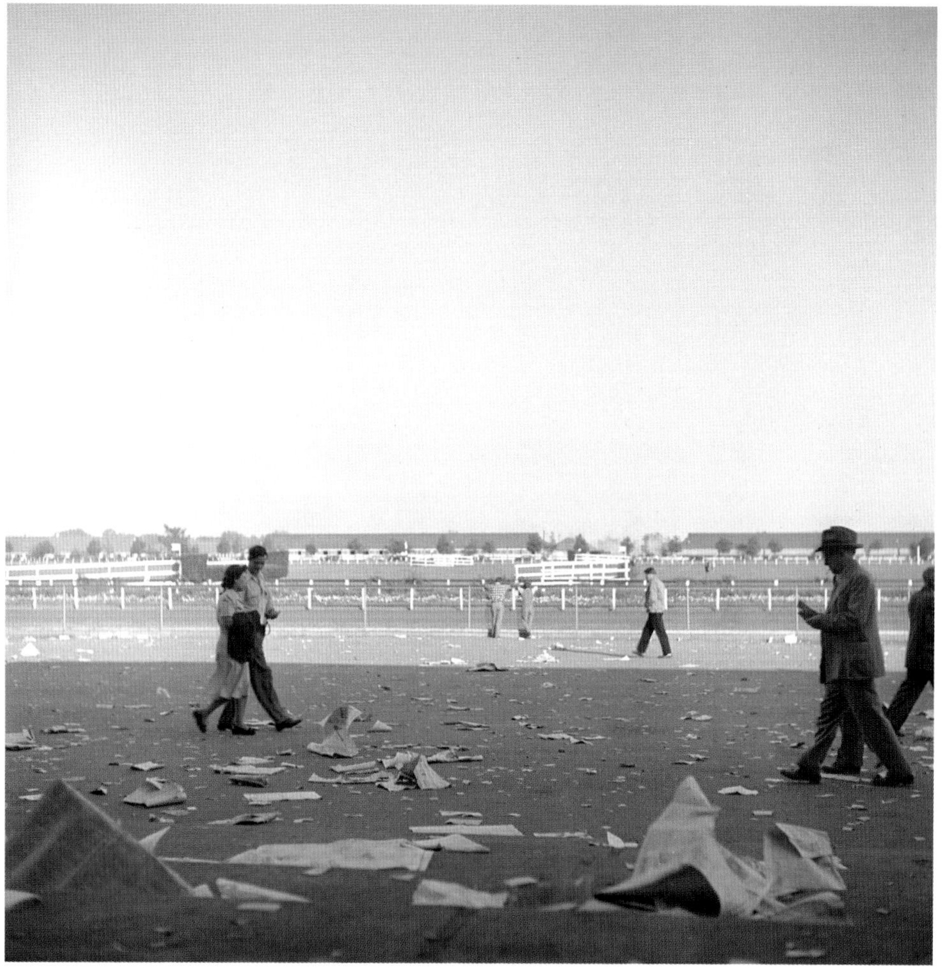

[AQUEDUCT RACETRACK], 1947: Working for *Look*, nineteen-year-old Stanley Kubrick (1928–99) shot a day's worth of images at Aqueduct Race Track in South Ozone Park, Queens, on September 19, 1947. In not a one do we see a horse, let alone a race. Like this image, the session was all about aftermath, with people drifting about as aimlessly as the swirling paper and ripped-up betting slips. Kubrick would again use this setting to advantage in his first full-length feature film, *The Killing* (1956), about a racetrack robbery gone wrong. THE *LOOK* COLLECTION.

[PALISADES AMUSEMENT PARK], 1946: One day, the young man may be explaining to his sister, she'll be big enough to ride the rollercoaster at Palisades Park, once located across the Hudson in Bergen County, New Jersey. The venue had opened as a picnic ground in 1898, becoming a modest amusement park by 1908. Two years later it was purchased by Nicholas and Joseph Schenck, brothers who were prominent in the nascent motion picture industry in nearby Fort Lee. All this may have augured large for Stanley Kubrick, who had just graduated high school and quickly exited City College when he took this assignment from *Look*. PHOTOGRAPH BY STANLEY KUBRICK. THE *LOOK* COLLECTION.

[THE POOL, PALISADES AMUSEMENT PARK], 1946: Palisades Park advertised its mammoth swimming pool not only as the world's largest, at 400 x 600 feet and containing 2.5 million gallons of water, but also as the world's largest salt-water pool, because it was filled from the tidal waters of the Hudson, saline below the George Washington Bridge. PHOTOGRAPH BY STANLEY KUBRICK. THE *LOOK* COLLECTION.

[WONDER WHEEL, CONEY ISLAND, FROM THE *YOUTH SQUAD* SERIES], 1958: Built in 1918 by Herald J. Garms and the Eccentric Ferris Wheel Company, the Wonder Wheel was the world's largest when it opened at Coney Island two years later. At 150 feet high, with a diameter of 135 feet and a passenger capacity of 144, it has thrilled customers ever since. PHOTOGRAPH BY JOHN VACHON. THE *LOOK* COLLECTION.

[CONEY ISLAND YOUTH, FROM THE SERIES *YOUTH SQUAD*], 1958: John Vachon (1914–75) began his long photographic career in 1937 with the Farm Security Administration, which took as its charge the documentation of the effects of the Depression on the common man, especially the poor. Included among the FSA photographers at various times were Walker Evans, Dorothea Lange, Gordon Parks, Arthur Rothstein, Ben Shahn, and Vachon. From the age of thirty-four, in 1948, Vachon was a staff photographer for twenty-one years at *Look* magazine, for whom he shot some seventy-five picture stories and saw more than 2,000 of his photographs in its pages. In this and the companion images of youth on the rise amid a Coney Island in decline (the magazine titled the series, "Youth Squad"), he captured the moment in a style that was uniquely his own. PHOTOGRAPH BY JOHN VACHON. THE *LOOK* COLLECTION.

[CONEY ISLAND, FROM THE SERIES *YOUTH SQUAD*], 1958: The motto of the souped-up Cyclone rollercoaster fit the age of rock 'n' roll and the teen preoccupations so worrisome to adults. The new cars had fins, the new clothing styles seemed provocative, and the whole city seemed obsessed with speed. PHOTOGRAPH BY JOHN VACHON. THE *LOOK* COLLECTION.

[OPEN HYDRANT, BROOKLYN, FROM THE SERIES *YOUTH SQUAD*], 1958: Another in the "Youth Squad" photo shoot of July 2, 1958, this scene was replicated in countless city neighborhoods in the sweltering heat that shimmered from the pavement and was held close by the tenement-lined streets. The policeman standing idly by testifies to the social and legal acceptability of opening the hydrants to provide a little relief. PHOTOGRAPH BY JOHN VACHON. THE *LOOK* COLLECTION.

FUR MARKET, SEVENTH AVENUE AT 33RD STREET, CA. 1953: At street level the Garment District, between 34th and 42nd Streets and Fifth and Ninth Avenues, is perhaps the city's busiest, noisiest, and most congested. But the fur district was different. It was smaller, slower, a relatively tranquil area of discreet signs and sleek pelts. PHOTOGRAPH BY ANN ZANE SHANKS. GIFT OF THE PHOTOGRAPHER. 94.32.27.

[PARK AVENUE AND 52ND STREET], 1957: When Lever House, not visible here but one block north on Park Avenue, was built in 1952 at 390 Park Avenue, it was the pioneer curtain-wall skyscraper in New York City. In 1956–58 the Seagram Building, a modernist masterwork in thirty-eight stories by architects Ludwig Mies van der Rohe and Philip Johnson, went up at 375 Park, and the International Style took hold on the city's new construction for a generation. Here the building is shown under construction. PHOTOGRAPH BY ARTHUR ROTHSTEIN. THE *LOOK* COLLECTION.

(NEAR RIGHT) **[CHILDREN WITH FLAGS, FROM THE SERIES *PUERTO RICANS*], 1953:** After 1917, when an act of Congress granted citizenship to residents of the former Spanish colony of Puerto Rico, travel from the island to the mainland was not classified as immigration. Puerto Ricans, who had come to the city since the nineteenth century, began to arrive in large numbers in the 1950s with the advances in air travel and changes in the economy on the island. Also, prosperity in New York increased the demand for low-cost labor to such an extent that Mayor Robert Wagner publicly stated in 1953 that he and all New Yorkers would welcome any Puerto Rican willing to work. In that same year, *Look* selected Phillip Harrington to document the lives of the newcomers and their neighborhoods. PHOTOGRAPH BY PHILLIP HARRINGTON. THE *LOOK* COLLECTION.

(FAR RIGHT) **[PUBLIC POOL, FROM THE SERIES *PUERTO RICANS*], 1953:** During the 1930s Parks Commissioner Robert Moses used federal money to construct eleven massive public swimming pools throughout the city, mostly in working class neighborhoods. The pools offer much needed respite from the sweltering New York City summers. All but one of the pools built by Moses are still in use today. PHOTOGRAPH BY PHILLIP HARRINGTON. THE *LOOK* COLLECTION.

[EL BARRIO AT NIGHT, FROM THE SERIES *PUERTO RICANS*], 1953: The great influx of Puerto Ricans in the 1950s—by some estimates nearing a million in the decade—made the newly arrived into New Yorkers, but it also brought the flavor of the island to New York. Early concentrations of "Nuyoricans" had settled in East Harlem and the Lower East Side in Manhattan, the South Bronx, and Atlantic Avenue in Brooklyn. Although Puerto Ricans are today dispersed over many states, New York and New Jersey still account for more than half the national total, exceeding two million. PHOTOGRAPH BY PHILLIP HARRINGTON. THE *LOOK* COLLECTION.

HOTEL ASTOR
CHEVROLET
PARK SHERATON HOTEL
KINSEY 40
LOEW'S STATE
HOTEL CLARIDGE
Pepsi-Cola
HOTEL ASTOR
BOND
TWO TROUSER SUITS
Camel
I'D WALK A MILE FOR A CAMEL
CAFETERIA
NEWMAN'S THEATRE TICKETS
Benhil SHOPS
SCHRAFFT'S
KLEE
ARTKRAFT STRAUSS

(LEFT) [BROADWAY AT NIGHT, LOOKING NORTH FROM TIMES SQUARE], 1952: You could get an ice cream soda at Schrafft's for thirty-five cents, or a rice pudding and coffee at Rector's for about the same. The Camel Cigarettes billboard would belch smoke at regular intervals, delighting any child out after dark. The Bond haberdashers could outfit a fellow with a two-trouser suit to make the sparse wardrobe seem robust. A larger than life Little Lulu was somehow the Kleenex Girl. A Broadway show or a first-run movie, maybe with a stage show besides, cost two dollars. PHOTOGRAPHER UNKNOWN. THE *LOOK* COLLECTION.

THIRD AVENUE EL, TAKEN FROM PLATFORM, CA. 1953: There are those who love the subway. Poet May Swenson was one. In "Riding the A," she complained, "The station is reached too soon." The subway cars of the 1950s were incredibly noisy, and rattled one's frame so thoroughly that chiropractors despaired of ever getting clients. The rattan seats were always split and spiky, and air conditioning was a dream in the gloaming. And yet there are those who love the subway. PHOTOGRAPH BY ANN ZANE SHANKS. GIFT OF THE PHOTOGRAPHER. 94.32.59.

97TH STREET AND COLUMBUS AVENUE, 1959: One might leap to the conclusion that this barren cityscape showed the South Bronx of the 1970s rather than the thriving Upper West Side of Manhattan. But what is depicted in this photograph is "slum clearance," paid for with federal money, to make way for "middle class" housing (in this case, Park West Village). PHOTOGRAPH BY FRANK PAULIN. GIFT OF THE PHOTOGRAPHER. 93.80.18.

RUSH HOUR, BATTERY TERMINAL, 1949: The ferry boat "Gold Star Mother" disgorges commuters from Staten Island at the Battery terminal in Manhattan. The ferry fare famously stayed stuck at a nickel from 1897 until 1972—even as the price of a subway ride increased to a dime in 1948, and then ratcheted up every few years. But today a nickel will no longer buy you a ride on the ferry—for foot passengers the passage across the bay is free. Andreas Feininger (1906–99), son of painter Lyonel Feininger, came to this country in 1939 and four years later joined the staff of *Life* magazine. He shot this view in 1949. GIFT OF THE PHOTOGRAPHER. 55.31.21.

BROOKLYN NAVY YARD, 1946: The Brooklyn Navy Yard (or New York Naval Shipyard) came under federal control in 1801 and turned out ships in prodigious quantity during World War II, when 70,000 people worked three shifts around the clock. The Navy decommissioned the yard in 1966 and sold it to the city, which today manages its industrial development. PHOTOGRAPH BY ANDREAS FEININGER. GIFT OF THE PHOTOGRAPHER. 55.31.143.

WEST 42ND STREET REFLECTIONS, 1953: This portion of the famous thoroughfare, between Seventh and Eighth Avenues, today is labeled the "New 42nd Street," to signify its return to legitimate theater and ostensibly high-toned values after many decades of hosting "grind house" theaters and petty crime. Of course, some folks liked this street just fine the way it was and mourned the passing of Hubert's Dime Museum and Flea Circus and the con artists, pickpockets, magicians, and burlesque entertainers. PHOTOGRAPH BY ALAN ROSENBERG. GIFT OF THE PHOTOGRAPHER. 83.65.4.

NEW YEAR'S EVE AT TIMES SQUARE, 1950–51: When the headquarters of the *New York Times* moved uptown to Longacre Square, so did the city's annual New Year's Eve celebration. Long conducted at Trinity Church on Broadway at Wall Street, the event multiplied in importance and attendees as the new building was the celebration's focal point for the more than 200,000 revelers. The *Times* moved to West 43rd Street in 1913 and in 2007 to Eighth Avenue between 40th and 41st Streets. Yet New Year's Eve has not moved with the paper, nor has the name Times Square. PHOTOGRAPH BY DAN WEINER. GIFT OF SANDRA WEINER. 99.127.8.

MAN IN RAIN, 1952: Ruth Orkin (1921–85) lived on West 88th Street in the mid-1950s and found the vantage point of her second-floor apartment pleasing. Much of her New York City imagery over the ensuing decades is also taken from on high, at arresting angles. PHOTOGRAPH BY RUTH ORKIN. GIFT OF THE ESTATE OF RUTH ORKIN. 97.162.

BRIGHTON BEACH, 1948: The purported health-giving properties of sea air constituted a great draw for Jewish immigrant families, especially those who had first settled on Manhattan's Lower East Side. The *Brooklyn Eagle* observed in 1925 that "the advantages of Brighton Beach as a health resort have long been well known. Almost every physical ailment is benefited by the fresh ocean air, freedom from dust, smoke, and pollen. Abundant ozone is especially beneficial in the case of neurotics." Neil Simon could not have improved on the punch line. PHOTOGRAPH BY DAN WEINER. GIFT OF SANDRA WEINER. 99.127.3.

SAILORS ON THE SUBWAY, 1947: These swabs were not much older than the man who photographed them, then sixteen-year-old Harold Feinstein. "When I was a young man," Feinstein writes today, "beyond my favorite haunt of Coney Island, my photographer's eye found delight in New York City street life in all its variety—the glittering lights of Times Square, the streets of Harlem, smoke-filled coffee shops, subways, city stoops, and shop windows." PHOTOGRAPH BY HAROLD FEINSTEIN. MUSEUM PURCHASE WITH FUNDS FROM THE RICHARD FLORSHEIM ART FUND. 96.121.4.

[STAGE DOOR, PUERTO RICO THEATER, 490 EAST 138TH STREET], BRONX, 1950: This New York showcase for Hispanic acts launched many Puerto Rican and Cuban stars, such as Perez Prado in 1951, as stateside performers. Cuban-born César Romero, however, had been a dancing star of the Broadway stage and in Hollywood was a romantic lead in comedies and musicals between turns as the Cisco Kid in a handful of westerns in the 1930s and '40s. PHOTOGRAPH BY JANET MEVI. THE *LOOK* COLLECTION.

CHAPTER XIII | 1960–1969

THE CIVIL RIGHTS MOVEMENT IN NEW YORK CITY

Clarence Taylor

As the most important social protest movement of the twentieth century, the civil rights movement seems a well documented part of our common heritage. It produced important national figures and moved countless numbers of Americans to participate in civil rights campaigns. The movement was responsible for two enduringly important pieces of legislation, the 1964 Civil Rights Act and the 1965 Voting Rights Act. The 1964 act required that voting rules be applied on a non-discriminatory basis; outlawed discrimination in places of public accommodation such as hotels, restaurants, and theaters; banned discrimination from municipal and state-operated facilities; and gave the U.S. Attorney General the authority to file suit against school systems that practiced racial, sexual, and ethnic discrimination. Title VII of the act banned employers from engaging in racial, ethnic, sex, and religious discrimination. The 1965 Voting Rights Act outlawed discriminatory practices such as the literacy test that had been used to exclude blacks from voting and gave the Federal Government oversight of elections in states that had a history of denying blacks the franchise. Thanks to the Voting Rights Act, even today the majority of black elected officials come from the South.

Until recently, monographs, documentaries, commercial films, and commemorations devoted to the Civil Rights Movement have paid little attention to the freedom struggle outside the South. A focus on the civil rights struggle in New York City, which had one of the largest black populations in the country, throws into question the popular view that the civil rights movement began soon after the Supreme Court's *Brown v. Board of Education* decision of 1954 and that the arena of change in the following decade was the South because racism was not a national problem. Scholars of the Northern civil rights movement, however, note that labor, the Communist Party, and others on the left were in the forefront of equal-opportunity campaigns well before then. The Southern wing of the movement fought for voting rights, school integration, and public accommodation. While Northern civil rights activists also struggled for school integration, they attempted to end police brutality and discrimination in hiring, housing, and city services as well.

As early as the 1920s, black people organized to challenge police brutality as a form of racial terror sanctioned by the state. The Brooklyn branch of the National Equal Rights League, an early civil rights organization headed by the Reverend Thomas Harten of Holy Trinity Baptist Church, led demonstrations against police assaults on blacks. In July 1925, 2,000 people attended a national equal rights rally at Holy Trinity protesting the "apparent propaganda of racial prejudice and oppression carried on by the police force in Brooklyn." Several black men had been picked up and brought in for questioning in regards to the murder of a white woman. The protesters at Holy Trinity created a committee to call upon the district attorney of Brooklyn and demand an end to police harassment of black men. The committee included Harten and the pastor of St. Augustine Protestant Episcopal Church, the Reverend George Frazier Miller.

Long before the Montgomery Bus Boycott of 1955, Harlem, the largest black community in the country, had a bus boycott. Harlem residents complained that New York City's Omnibus Corporation adopted a policy to exclude blacks from employment. In 1941 there were no black bus drivers or mechanics working for Omnibus. The Harlem Labor Union, an independent labor union that campaigned for jobs for Harlem residents, began demonstrating at bus stops. The Reverend Adam Clayton Powell, Jr., head of the Greater New York Coordinating Committee for Employment, teamed up with the Manhattan branch of the National Negro Congress and the Harlem Labor Union to launch the boycott. On one occasion he drew more than 1,500 people to his Abyssinian Baptist Church, who pledged to honor the boycott and donate funds to support it.

Labor supported the boycott when Powell managed to win the backing of Mike Quill, head of the Transport Workers Union. Quill also agreed to open membership of the TWU to blacks. Boycotters demonstrated at bus stops throughout Harlem as well as other places in the community. Those writing on the Montgomery Bus Boycott note that activists organized carpools to help transport boycotters. This strategy was used in the Harlem Bus Boycott to some extent, but in New York the boycotters were able to use taxis and the subway, which were affordable for working-class people. More than 60,000 people stayed off the Omnibus daily, causing great financial difficulty for the company.

After a boycott lasting one month, protesters were able to force Omnibus to the negotiating table. In the end, the company agreed to hire one hundred blacks as drivers and mechanics. In addition, the company agreed to assure that 17 percent of its workforce was black.

Much attention has been paid to the clergy and religious community in the movement in the 1950s and 1960s. However, labor and the left played a crucial role in civil rights campaigns before the Cold War decimated the forces of the left. A leading labor organization that championed civil rights in New York City was the New York Teachers' Union (TU). The communist-dominated leadership of the TU conducted a fierce school-wide effort for racial justice. Before the *Brown* decision and the battles over school integration in the South, the Teachers' Union launched a campaign to eliminate racist and biased textbooks in the public schools, hire more black teachers, and promote Negro History Week. The union's Harlem Committee, founded in 1935, was a racially diverse group that challenged racial stereotypes in books. A twenty-five-page pamphlet issued by the committee in 1950, "Bias and Prejudice in Textbooks in New York City Schools," explored how textbooks treated blacks, Jews, "Colonial Peoples," and other "minority groups." In fact, several of the texts, covering American history from the colonial period to World War II, were written by Board of Education administrators. The union and its allies argued that these books reinforced a sense of inferiority and distorted the truth about the role blacks and other minorities played in American history. Although it never recognized the TU's effort, the Board of Education eventually removed most of the offensive texts from its approved reading list.

As part of the push for racial equality, the Teachers Union campaigned for what it labeled Negro history. The union connected the promotion of black history to its textbook campaign by contending that it was not enough to remove negative images. Black history was necessary for corrective purposes, to highlight the contributions that African Americans had made to the nation. The union also contended that teaching black history was a way of documenting the systemic racism that was responsible for the inequality that existed. History, union members contended, also revealed lessons of how people struggled to eradicate inequality. The union declared that teachers were not opposed to teaching black history; they simply did not have the knowledge or resources. Thus, the union created and distributed to the schools educational kits on black involvement in the American Revolution, the Civil War and Reconstruction, World War I, and World War II. The TU also sponsored events featuring scholars on African-American history.

Except for the school integration campaign of the 1950s and 1960s, no other crusade drew as much controversy as the effort to persuade the city's Board of Education to increase the number of black teachers in the school system. By conducting surveys, the union revealed that a city with one of the largest black populations in the nation hired very few blacks. In the early 1950s, blacks made up less than 3 percent of licensed teachers. Moreover, most black teachers were assigned to schools with a predominantly black student body. The union informed board and city officials and the public of its studies' results, in an attempt to force the Board to recruit black teachers. The union's campaigns in fighting for the elimination of racist depictions of blacks in textbooks, its promotion of black history, and its push for more black teachers in the school system helped make it a leading voice in the New York City civil rights struggle. The effort of the TU demonstrates the broader civil rights agenda in New York City, not only to redress the abuses of the past but also to adopt a form of affirmative action.

All of the national civil rights organizations were active in New York City. One of the most active was the Congress of Racial Equality. Formed in 1942, CORE adopted the principles of nonviolent resistance as practiced by Gandhi. Its Brooklyn branch was considered its most radical—the first CORE chapter to use direct militant action such as picketing and sit-ins. The diverse membership consisted of both young blacks and whites and middle-aged militants who had been involved in radical politics since the 1940s. Starting in the summer of 1962, Brooklyn CORE initiated "Operation Clean Sweep," demanding that city officials end their discriminatory practice of providing unequal sanitation services to the predominantly black community of Bedford-Stuyvesant. In order to put pressure on the city to act, Brooklyn CORE organized the Bedford-Stuyvesant residents and dumped garbage on the steps of City Hall.

In the summer of 1963 Brooklyn CORE also launched a dual campaign against bias in the construction industry and unemployment in black communities, protesting for jobs for blacks and Puerto Ricans at the Downstate Medical Center project. Downstate was also chosen because of the racially discriminatory policies practiced by the numerous building and construction trade unions. CORE asked the black clergy of Brooklyn to assist in the campaign. The black ministers stepped to the forefront by organizing the Ministers' Committee for Job Opportunities. For two weeks, hundreds of protesters—many of them members of the black churches of Brooklyn—denied trucks entrance to the work site by lying down in the streets. Police arrested demonstrators, many of whom were carried away singing freedom songs. As one group of demonstrators was taken away by police, another group moved in and took its place. The police erected barricades to deny the protesters access to the entrances. However, that did not stop many of the demonstrators from running under the police barricades. By the end of the protest more than seven hundred people were arrested. The Downstate campaign helped focus attention on the construction industry, one of the most discriminatory in the country. The campaign forced state, city, and union officials to take action. In addition, it helped make people aware that racial discrimination was not simply a Southern problem.

The most important civil rights campaign in New York City was the attempt to integrate its public school system. Soon after the *Brown* decision, City College of New York's psychology professor Kenneth Clark accused the New York City Board of Education of segregating its schools. Although board officials publicly supported the *Brown* decision, they made little effort to desegregate the school system. Instead, the superintendent of schools, William Jansen, argued that segregation in New York was not due to any deliberate attempt on the board but because of housing segregation. While not supporting segregation, Jansen contended that he supported the neighborhood school concept, arguing that children should attend the schools in their neighborhood. The Brooklyn branch of the National Association for the Advancement of Colored People (NAACP), headed by the Reverend Milton Galamison, pastor of Siloam Presbyterian Church, became the most vocal critic of the New York City Board of Education for not ending segregation in the public schools. Galamison pointed out that even when black and white children lived near one another, the board zoned them to different schools.

In 1960, Galamison resigned the presidency of the Brooklyn NAACP and organized the Parents Workshop for Equality in New York City Schools. The organization consisted of parents across racial lines that pressured the Board to come up with a plan to integrate the schools. After years of the Board's refusal to present a citywide plan for integration, civil rights organizations threatened to take action. In 1963 Galamison became head of the City-Wide Committee for School Integration, a group that consisted of the New York branches of the NAACP, CORE, and the Harlem Parents Committee. On February 3, 1964 the City-Wide Committee launched a school boycott in an attempt to force the New York City Board of Education to come up with a timetable and a plan to integrate the public schools. More than 460,000 students, or about 45 percent of the student body, stayed out of school. There were demonstrations at hundreds of schools in the city and thousands marched to the Board of Education.

Despite the success of the boycott, the coalition soon fell apart, accusing Galamison of acting arbitrarily by calling for a second boycott. Although Galamison carried out a second boycott, it was half the size of the first. By 1965 it was clear to many activists and parents that the Board of Education was not coming up with a timetable and plan for citywide school integration. Many of these individuals instead began to demand community control of the schools. They reflected the new sentiment that was sweeping the black communities nationwide. Instead of calling for integration, blacks began to demand black empowerment. The Student Nonviolent Coordinating Committee and the Congress of Racial Equality switched from being proponents of the "beloved society" to advocates of Black Power. Moreover, new leaders emerged in the freedom struggle that were committed to Black Power objectives rather than goals advocated by civil rights leaders. Thus, by the late 1960s, the struggle to achieve civil rights had been supplanted by an assertion of Black Power.

(RIGHT) **MADISON AVENUE, 1969:** The medium is the message, and Madison Avenue brings it home. PHOTOGRAPH BY JOHN ALBOK. GIFT OF ILONA ALBOK PARKER. 82.68.12.

CLARENCE TAYLOR is Professor of History at Baruch College and the Graduate Center, CUNY. He has written several books and articles on the civil rights struggle in New York City. His books include *The Black Churches of Brooklyn* (Columbia University Press, 1994), *Knocking at our Door: Milton A. Galamison and the Struggle to Integrate New York City Schools* (Columbia University Press, 1997), *Black Religious Intellectuals: The Fight for Equality from Jim Crow to the 21st Century* (Routledge, 2002), and *Civil Rights in New York City* (Fordham University Press, forthcoming). Taylor is completing a book on the New York City Teachers Union.

6 out of 10 nonwhite children grow up poor.
2 5TH & 7TH AVENUES
Give a damn.
New York
Coalition.
"A TRIUMPH! SHOULD NOT BE MISSED!"
THE GREAT WHITE HOPE
PULITZER PRIZE · N.Y. DRAMA CRITICS AWARD · TONY AWARD
ALVIN THEATRE,

[THE DEMOLITION OF PENNSYLVANIA STATION], 1964–65: Beneath the imposing pink-granite façade of Penn Station, opened in 1910, lay the true glory of the building's underpinnings. The masonry and the colonnade referenced ancient Rome, but the steel and glass elements harkened back to the city's own Crystal Palace. This photograph is one from a series of 118 documenting the demolition. Because photographers were not allowed on the site, these images were made when there were no workers present, and thus no demolition activity is seen in the photographs. PHOTOGRAPH BY AARON ROSE. GIFT OF THE PHOTOGRAPHER. 01.30.37.

[THE DEMOLITION OF PENNSYLVANIA STATION], 1964–65: New York City, the *Times* opined in 1963, "will probably be judged not by the monuments we build but by those we have destroyed." Of the eight allegorical figures and twenty-two eagles that once adorned Penn Station, a few survive in locations from Brooklyn to Kansas City. The rest are buried in the landfill of the New Jersey Meadowlands. In 1999 plans were announced that would in part create a new train hall at the Farley Post Office and relocate Madison Square Garden. STONEWORK BY ADOLPH A. WEINMAN. PHOTOGRAPH BY AARON ROSE. GIFT OF THE PHOTOGRAPHER. 01.30.117.

[TIMES SQUARE], 1960: Amateur photographer Frederick Kelly (1905–99) was a Baltimore resident who brought a visitor's eye but a New Yorker's heart to his photographs of the city. Here he captures the assault upon the senses that compels walkers in the city constantly to look—not straight ahead but up, down, and all around. PHOTOGRAPH BY FREDERICK KELLY. GIFT OF RENA C. KELLY. 01.59.13.

[PATRONS AT HORN & HARDART AUTOMAT, EAST 14TH STREET NEAR IRVING PLACE], 1969: The automat was a self-service cafeteria in which the delights were displayed behind glass doors that would open upon deposit of the requisite number of nickels and a turn of the chrome-plated knob. After their debut in 1912 they proliferated in the city—at their height automats numbered 180 in New York and Philadelphia alone. At the time of this image they were in decline; however, the last automat hung on until 1991. Veteran patrons will recall the automat's simple specialties—creamed spinach, meat loaf, macaroni and cheese, baked beans with molasses served in little brown crocks, and a legendary cup of coffee. PHOTOGRAPH BY DAVID BERNSTEIN. GIFT OF THE PHOTOGRAPHER. 01.51.4.

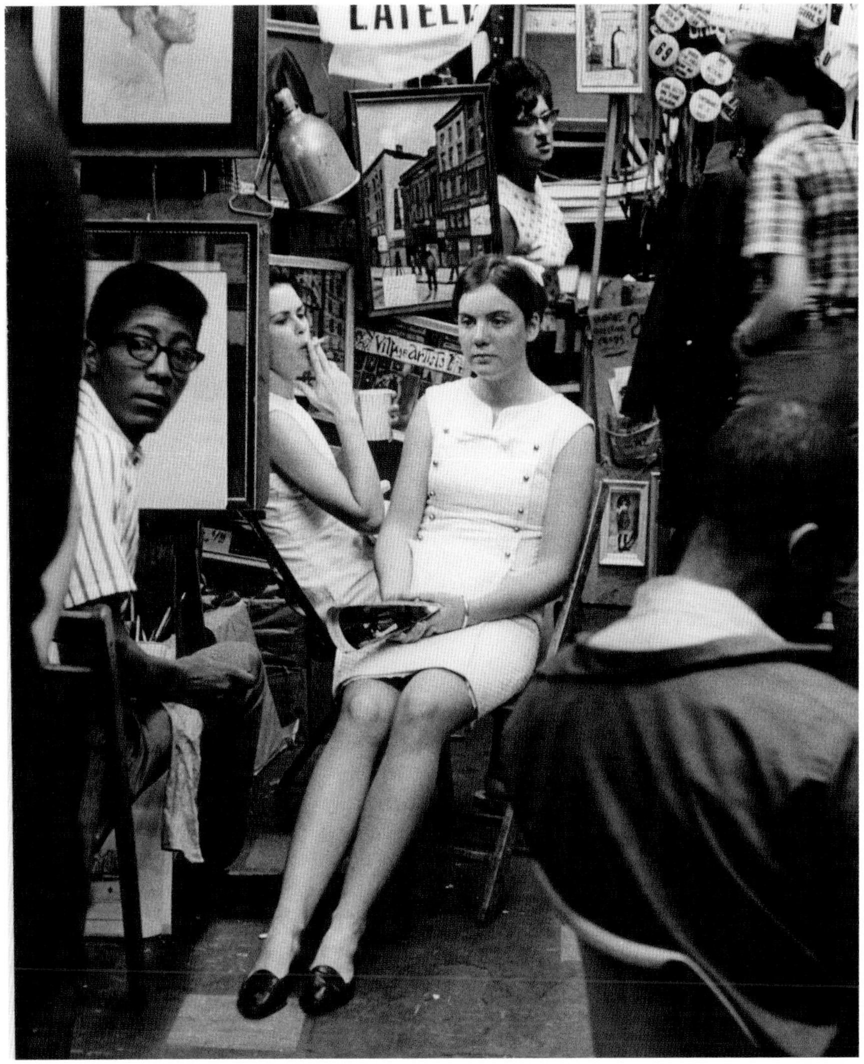

GREENWICH VILLAGE NIGHT, 1966: The purported license of Greenwich Village life had long been a lure to the straitlaced—and a profitable angle for producers of souvenirs, from the clever to the crass. Hang out with a hippie (formerly the beatnik)! See racy Swedish movies! Buy groovy clothes! Get your portrait painted by a "starving artist"! PHOTOGRAPH BY FREDERICK KELLY. GIFT OF RENA C. KELLY. 01.59.4.

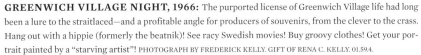

(LEFT) **FREEDOM AND ORDER: CHILDREN PLAYING, EAST 116TH STREET, 1968:** Neither inventiveness nor joy knows socioeconomic limits. PHOTOGRAPH BY DAVID BERNSTEIN. GIFT OF THE PHOTOGRAPHER. 01.51.5.

BROOKLYN, NEW YORK, 1968: One of America's worst years was no picnic in New York either. Tinderbox neighborhoods combusted in riots and looting. A decade-long rise in murders culminated in a rate in 1968 triple that of 1960. A subway strike, a sanitation strike, three separate teacher strikes, a rupture of the traditional comity between blacks and Jews, and so on—but for the most part New York avoided the kind of violence that devastated Watts and Newark. It was the worst of times, and yet it could be the best of times, as might have described much of the decade that followed. PHOTOGRAPH © BENEDICT J. FERNANDEZ. GIFT OF THE PHOTOGRAPHER.

MUSICIANS IN WASHINGTON SQUARE, 1962: Rock 'n' roll had fallen into the doldrums in the aftermath of the Twist, Elvis had gone Hollywood, and the Beatles were not yet on the scene. Into the void rushed that hardy perennial, folk music, made fresh and vital by the addition of Greenwich Village newcomers Bob Dylan, Phil Ochs, Joan Baez, and a legion of other notables to such MacDougal Street royalty as Dave Van Ronk and Ramblin' Jack Elliott. All stood on the shoulders, of course, of Woody Guthrie and Pete Seeger and Leadbelly. And in Washington Square an unpremeditated hootenanny might be struck up at any time. PHOTOGRAPH BY FREDERICK KELLY. GIFT OF RENA C. KELLY. 01.59.21.

CENTRAL PARK "BE-IN," 1967: By 1967 the city was by no means unique in its opposition to the Vietnam War, the military-industrial complex, the draft, racism, and most anything identified with the older generation—this was justly an age of counter-culture. While in previous decades Union Square had been the preferred place to register one's political protests, the flower-power movement found the Sheep Meadow of Central Park more congenial, despite Parks Department opposition. The "be-in" phenomenon continued until 1969. PHOTOGRAPH BY FREDERICK KELLY. GIFT OF RENA C. KELLY. 01.59.7.

DAY AFTER POLICE RAID ON COLUMBIA UNIVERSITY, 1968: On April 23, three hundred Columbia students, led by the campus branches of Students for a Democratic Society (SDS) and Student Afro-American Society (SAS) protested the university's plan to construct a gymnasium on public parkland in Morningside Park. The students barricaded the office of the college dean, holding him hostage. By April 30 the situation exploded, with police rushing the sit-in demonstrators, sending more than 150 to the hospital, and arresting more than 700. PHOTOGRAPH BY CATHERINE URSILLO. GIFT OF THE PHOTOGRAPHER. 03.104.5.

BURNING OF DRAFT CARDS, 1963: Lay Catholics, hardly hippies, took the lead in protesting United States involvement in the war in Vietnam. Tom Cornell, editor of the *Catholic Worker* newspaper, organized the very first demonstration against the war, in New York City in July 1963, and went to jail for burning his draft card. PHOTOGRAPH © BENEDICT J. FERNANDEZ. GIFT OF THE PHOTOGRAPHER.

BOCCE PLAYERS, FIRST AVENUE AND HOUSTON STREET, 1966: You can take the man from Italy, but you can't take Italy from the man. The month is March, the wind is whipping hard enough to justify the hats, coats, and gloves. But spring is just around the corner. PHOTOGRAPHIC LINE RENDERING BY SCOTT HYDE. 91.106.6.

[WORKER ON A WALL], 1966: Jan Lukas (1915–2006) was exiled from his native Czechoslovakia in 1965 and arrived in New York, where he continued his already notable photographic career. "He caught immediately the special qualities of New York," wrote William F. Buckley, "the circus of getting-and-spending and foolishness and gaiety and spirit; the love of country and tolerance of variety." In this image the worker seems, like Lukas himself, poised between the old world and the new. PHOTOGRAPH BY JAN LUKAS. 93.92.21.

MAIN POST OFFICE ON EIGHTH AVENUE, 1961: Designed by McKim, Mead, and White and opened in 1914, this massive edifice placed between 31st and 33rd Streets has since 1982 been called the James A. Farley Building, after the Postmaster General and New York political kingpin; at this writing plans are in the works to turn it into Moynihan Station. The building's colossal order of Corinthian columns is the world's largest. PHOTOGRAPH BY HORST SCHÄFER. GIFT OF THE PHOTOGRAPHER. 02.93.3.

ON 42ND STREET, WEST OF TIMES SQUARE, 1965: Life imitates art. A crowd of men, including policemen, swarm around a body lying on the street in front of the Harris Theatre. One of the movies promoted on the marquee is *The Killers*. The glittering city of *Breakfast at Tiffany's* was becoming the ungovernable city of *Midnight Cowboy*. Before the end of the decade New York's crime and drug problems would make a late night television joke of its nickname "Fun City." PHOTOGRAPH BY HORST SCHÄFER. GIFT OF THE PHOTOGRAPHER. 02.93.2.

SAN GENNARO FESTIVAL, MULBERRY STREET, 1962: New York hosts many ethnic and religious festivals that are celebrated diversely and ecumenically. The Feast of San Gennaro is the longest running of these, in two senses: it has been held in Little Italy annually since 1926, and it takes place over eleven days. Originally a single-day affair, the fair has as its centerpiece a religious procession that winds along the length of Mulberry and Mott Streets, between Canal and Houston Streets. But you don't have to be Catholic or Italian, to enjoy the food and entertainment. PHOTOGRAPH BY VICTOR LAREDO. GIFT OF THE PHOTOGRAPHER. 82.74.43.

TELEPHONE BOOTHS AT PENN STATION, CA. 1960: The wooden enclosure with a fan-fold glass door was originally designed not merely to provide privacy but more importantly, to magnify a signal that was too weak to be heard in the open-air setting of public phones today. In the age of mobile-phone ubiquity, public telephones are an endangered species and telephone booths of the sort depicted here are rare antiquarian delights. PHOTOGRAPH BY ALAN ROSENBERG. GIFT OF THE PHOTOGRAPHER. 83.65.3.

CHAPTER XIV | 1970–1979

SEEING IT THROUGH

NEW YORK IN THE 1970s

JOSHUA B. FREEMAN

DURING THE 1970S, NEW YORK CITY SUFFERED ECONOMIC AND SOCIAL DECLINE AND DIMINISHED NATIONAL REGARD. LONG THE NATION'S LARGEST CITY AND UNRIVALED CENTER OF ECONOMIC POWER, NEW YORK HAD HELPED SET THE POLITICAL COURSE OF THE NATION THROUGH THE INFLUENCE OF ITS CITIZENS IN THE FEDERAL GOVERNMENT AND BY ESTABLISHING A MODEL LIBERAL POLITY. THE CITY WAS THE NATIONAL CENTER OF THE HIGH ARTS—PAINTING, CLASSICAL MUSIC, AND LITERATURE—BUT IT ALSO FORGED POPULAR CULTURE THROUGH ITS BROADWAY MUSICALS, BRILL BUILDING SONGWRITERS, JAZZ MUSICIANS, STAND-UP COMEDIANS, AND LEGION OF AD WRITERS AND COMMERCIAL ILLUSTRATORS. FROM THE FOUNDING OF THE UNITED STATES THROUGH 1970, EVERY TEN YEARS THE BUREAU OF THE CENSUS REPORTED THAT THE POPULATION IN THE AREA THAT NOW CONSTITUTES THE CITY OF NEW YORK INCREASED, WITH THE EXCEPTION OF A MINOR DIP IN 1960. YEAR AFTER YEAR, THE CITY GOT RICHER, ITS SKYLINE BECAME MORE STUNNING, AND ITS CULTURAL REACH WENT FARTHER. NEW YORK WAS DIFFERENT FROM THE REST OF THE COUNTRY. WORLDLY AND INTENSE, IT WAS A PLACE MANY AMERICANS ADMIRED, LONGED FOR, AND IMITATED. AND THEN IT ALL CHANGED. IN A DEPARTURE FROM ITS HISTORICAL PATTERN, THE TRAJECTORY OF NEW YORK TURNED DOWNWARD BETWEEN 1970 AND 1980. THE POPULATION OF THE CITY FELL BY WELL OVER 800,000, A 10 PERCENT DECLINE, TO ITS SMALLEST SIZE since well before World War II. For most New Yorkers life became harsher, as their standard of living dropped and their sense of security eroded. For eight years in succession, the number of jobs in the city fell. Crime increased while the city government drastically cut back even the most basic services—education, police and fire protection, street paving, and bridge maintenance. Housing abandonment and arson in large parts of the city left behind a landscape of desolation and destruction that in places resembled the bombed-out cities of Europe at the end of World War II. New York came to be widely seen elsewhere in the country, especially in Washington, D.C., as a moral and political failure, an object lesson in what could be done wrong and what the nation should not be. Once a social laboratory for political liberalism, New York became a testing ground for an effort to deconstruct the welfare state.

The forces that brought New York to its knees—deindustrialization, suburbanization, and national economic recession—caused decline in cities all across the Northeast and Midwest. But their impact in New York proved unusually severe. Unlike most large cities, New York had not been in decline during the 1960s, so that the plummet that followed came unexpectedly. With unusually extensive public services and a large debt, the city found itself teetering on the brink of bankruptcy.

In the past, the diversity of the New York economy had given it resiliency. During the post-World War II decades, it had more manufacturing workers than any other city in the country. It also was the nation's busiest port, its preeminent location for corporate headquarters, and the most important financial center in the world. As automation and the movement of industry to areas with lower costs and more available land brought a drop in blue-collar employment, an increase in white-collar jobs kept the city work force growing. People wanted to live in New York City as well as work there. In an era when most older cities suffered significant population loss, New York's robust economy, tolerant culture, and rich urban fabric kept drawing a broad cross-section of people to its neighborhoods, stores, and places of entertainment.

But the national recession that began in 1969 hit New York especially hard, and the next downturn, in the mid-1970s, hit even harder. Between 1969 and 1977, New York lost more than 600,000 jobs, 16 percent of its total. The unemployment rate reached 12 percent by mid-1975. Manufacturing employment fell by more than a third in less than a decade, as national recessions accelerated what had once been a gradual process of deindustrialization, leaving displaced workers and abandoned factories and lofts all across the city. Meanwhile, construction all but ground to a halt in the face of a surplus of office space and a drastic drop in residential development.

With many fewer jobs to be had, workers flooded out of New York in search of employment elsewhere. People left for other reasons, too. Increased crime made the suburbs seem attractive to many families, as did the availability of more living space than could be had within the city itself. Some whites recoiled from the racial integration of their neighborhoods. Retirees moved to warmer parts of the country. Once seemingly immune from the depopulation of urban cores that had been common in the North and East, New York shed its exceptionalism.

Job and population loss and recession significantly affected the financial health of the New York City government, with more dire consequences than in most other cities because the government in New York did much more for its citizenry—at greater cost—than in the typical American city. Under the influence of liberal reformers, left-wing political groups, and strong labor unions, New York had adopted an expansive notion of government function, building its own version of a social democratic welfare state. In addition to such core municipal functions as police and fire protection, education, parks, road maintenance, and courts, the New York City government and various public agencies ran a vast, low-cost, mass transportation system; a large, free municipal college system; a sprawling hospital network; and public housing projects with more than half a million residents. The city even operated its own television and radio stations. All this, of course, cost a great deal of money, much of it for personnel. Municipal employees, traditionally poorly paid, had won major improvements in their salaries, benefits, and pensions during the 1960s and early 1970s through militant union action, including illegal but highly effective strikes. Welfare consumed another big piece of the city budget. New York had a large poor population and, because of the way the state structured welfare finances, had to pay a much larger proportion of the welfare outlay than most municipalities.

Even in good times, the city struggled to balance its budget, adding a city income tax in 1967 and raising other taxes and fees. Chronically short of cash, it turned to borrowing to cover not only capital expenses but also ongoing operating costs. As the economic downturn and population exodus cut into the city's tax base, and the city kept adding to its workforce to meet the increasing demand for social services, the borrowing became heavier and heavier and the need constantly to raise money to roll over debt more onerous.

During the winter of 1974–75, the large commercial banks and brokerage houses that marketed New York City notes and bonds and kept some of them for their own accounts became increasingly resistant to further sales. Investors feared that the city would be unable to repay its debt. Some banks, needing to shore up their own liquidity, quietly cashed out of the city paper they already held. Mayor Abraham Beame made some modest spending cuts to try to convince investors to lend the city money, but to no avail. By the start of the spring, New York found itself unable to sell its bonds. Without new borrowing, it would soon run out of cash to pay back the billions of dollars it owed to holders of maturing city securities.

With the city tottering on the edge of financial disaster, Governor Hugh Carey, working closely with finance and business leaders, set up a series of new institutions effectively to take over New York City's finances, impose austerity, and create mechanisms to refund its debt. First came the Municipal Assistance Corporation, or Big MAC as it became widely known, whose appointed leaders from the business community had the power to sell bonds on behalf of the city, but only had to if they approved its progress toward budget reform. Under pressure from MAC, the state government, and the banks, Mayor Beame laid off thousands of city workers and instituted sharp cutbacks in services beginning in July 1975. In spite of a wave of protest demonstrations, MAC pressured the city to make additional cuts, including deferring scheduled city worker pay increases and forcing the City University to end its historic policy of free tuition (which, after an effort at resistance, it did). The transit system raised the bus and subway fare largely as a demonstration to the financial community that municipal leaders now would be willing to lower the social wage even in the face of widespread popular opposition.

MAC temporarily staved off city bankruptcy by raising $2 billion through bond sales, but by the fall of 1975, investors wanted no more of its securities either, leading to the renewed possibility of default. Once again, the state stepped in, creating the Emergency Financial Control Board (EFCB), which it gave pervasive control over city finances (including labor contracts) and even the power to remove the mayor if he defied its policies. Still, private investors shunned New York City debt.

Desperate, city and state leaders turned to Washington, seeking federal loans to forestall bankruptcy. But in the capital they found mostly hostility. Secretary of Treasury William Simon, who as a bond trader had helped build up the New York City debt, now saw an opportunity to launch an attack on liberal notions of governance, exemplified by New York's rent control system, free university, and powerful municipal unions. While some financiers simply wanted to make sure that they got back the money the city owed their firms, others, like Simon, sought to ratchet down the expectations of workers and their families and weaken their unions. Simon advocated making any federal aid to New York available only on terms "so punitive, the overall experience made so painful, that no city, no political subdivision would ever be tempted to go down the same road." Many members of Congress proved equally antagonistic, seeing New York as profligate, sinful, and irresponsible. A city made up mostly of blacks, Catholics, Jews, and Puerto Ricans found little empathy among many representatives of a country still dominated by white Protestants. President Gerald Ford, a conservative fearful of political challenges within his party from the right, aligned himself with Simon. Attacking New York's extensive public services and relatively generous compensation for its workers, he rejected a federal bailout in a speech summarized in a *Daily News* headline as "FORD TO CITY: DROP DEAD."

Ultimately, MAC found another source of capital, the large municipal employee pension funds, jointly controlled by the city and the public worker unions. Union leaders, fearing the adverse effect of a city bankruptcy on their members, agreed to purchase $2.5 billion dollars in MAC bonds with pension fund money. With that in hand, city and state leaders returned to Washington seeking seasonal loan guarantees to allow the city to manage fluctuations in its cash flow. The Ford administration, sobered by the realization that a New York City bankruptcy might have a disastrous impact on the national municipal bond market and even international finance, reversed course and agreed to the guarantees—but only after the state legislature raised taxes in the city and shifted some pension costs to employees.

During the next few years the city faced other moments when insolvency seemed imminent, but with the federal guarantees in place it had put its worst fiscal moments in the past. But at a price. The cutbacks in city services and large-scale layoffs of city workers, coming at the depth of the worst recession since the 1930s, made life in New York grim. Streets grew filthy, roads literally crumbled, crime shot up, subways broke down frequently, and libraries opened only a few days a week. In the public schools, teacher layoffs meant overcrowded classes, while guidance counselors, sports programs, art and music instruction, bilingual education, and summer school were severely curtailed.

With resources and population diminishing, one prominent city official advocated "planned shrinkage," cutting off municipal services to selected sections of the city. Never adopted as an official policy, New York instead experienced unplanned shrinkage, as neighborhoods like the South Bronx and East New York suffered massive waves of housing abandonment, arson, and population loss. Pictures taken in October 1977 of President Jimmy Carter standing on a rubble-strewn South Bronx block surrounded by gutted buildings shocked people across the country and abroad. The South Bronx became the national symbol of urban collapse, reinforced when a television broadcast of the World Series at Yankee Stadium featured aerial shots of buildings in the neighborhood ablaze.

Yet even as the economy and social fabric of New York became deeply strained, the creativity of the city flourished. The relatively low living expenses during the 1970s and the abandonment of many commercial buildings, by-products of depopulation and recession, allowed young artists to find spaces in which to live and work. A new generation of painters, punk rockers, jazz musicians, experimental theater groups, and dancers kept the city bubbling with artistic endeavors that often began on the margins but soon were taken up by mainstream cultural institutions. Many of the most impressive works to come out of New York during the period, such as Martin Scorsese's 1976 film *Taxi Driver*, had a decidedly dystopian air.

One of the most influential New York contributions to twentieth-century global culture, hip-hop, grew directly out of the hardship that hit poor and working-class communities during the 1970s. Break-dancing, graffiti art, and rap music sprung up in spite of, and in response to, the deterioration of living standards during the fiscal crisis years. When young spray-painters covered filthy subway cars and stations with ever-more elaborate and colorful graffiti, they engaged in a form of social criticism as well as the defacement of public property. Rap music, which exploded forth at block parties in the Bronx in the mid-1970s, mixed critiques of the hardship of daily life with boasting and boisterous celebration. Hip-hop brought a New York sensibility that emerged from African-American and Puerto Rican communities to national, and then international prominence, as the look, feel, and sound of New York in the 1970s was disseminated across the world.

In the late 1970s, New York began an economic recovery that lasted through most of the next decade. The growth of globally oriented finance companies and providers of business services powered the revival, complemented by an influx of immigrants who provided a low-wage work force that staffed restaurants and nursing homes, demolished buildings, drove taxis, took care of children, and labored in the diminishing but still substantial manufacturing sector. With more jobs available, the population again began to grow and the city government began restoring many of the jobs and services it had eliminated.

The fiscal crisis left behind changed attitudes and structures. The conservative politicians in Washington and financiers in New York who wanted to dismember New York's version of social democracy had only partial success: Rent control remained in place, municipal unions remained powerful if chastened, and the city continued to provide a range of social and cultural services well beyond the national norm. But the public sector did suffer grievous blows, as city colleges, schools, and health facilities could not maintain their standing as first-rate institutions serving a broad cross-section of the public. Starved for funds, public institutions came to be seen as second-rate alternatives to private providers. The fiscal crisis furthered the belief that the private sector could do things better and cheaper than the public sector, and that government served more as an obstacle to public good than as a means to obtain it. When Edward I. Koch, a liberal turned economic conservative, was elected mayor in 1977, he pursued fiscal prudence, a pro-business atmosphere, and a continuing effort to diminish the power of public sector unions, obviating the need for MAC, the EFCB, and other unelected oversight bodies to continue their heavy-handed role in setting public policy.

Conservatives across the country and in Europe saw in New York proof that even the most liberal policies could be moved toward a diminishment of state benefits through bold action. A city known through much of its history for its progressive and sometimes radical politics helped pave the way for the neo-liberalism that became increasingly influential throughout the world in the late twentieth century.

(LEFT) **PRO–VIETNAM WAR DEMONSTRATION, NEW YORK, 1970:** Although the Vietnam War inflamed passions on both sides, it was the war's opponents who generally commanded the scene and the press if not the corridors of power. On April 4, 1970, some 50,000 people marched up Pennsylvania Avenue to a rally at the Washington Monument to advocate victory in Vietnam. On May 8, kindred spirits also rallied around the flag in New York's financial district. PHOTOGRAPH © BENEDICT J. FERNANDEZ. GIFT OF THE PHOTOGRAPHER.

JOSHUA B. FREEMAN IS PROFESSOR OF HISTORY AT QUEENS COLLEGE AND THE GRADUATE CENTER, CITY UNIVERSITY OF NEW YORK. HIS BOOKS INCLUDE *WORKING-CLASS NEW YORK: LIFE AND LABOR SINCE WORLD WAR II* AND *IN TRANSIT: THE TRANSPORT WORKERS UNION IN NEW YORK CITY, 1933-1966*. HE IS CURRENTLY WRITING A HISTORY OF THE UNITED STATES SINCE WORLD WAR II.

NO SMOKING

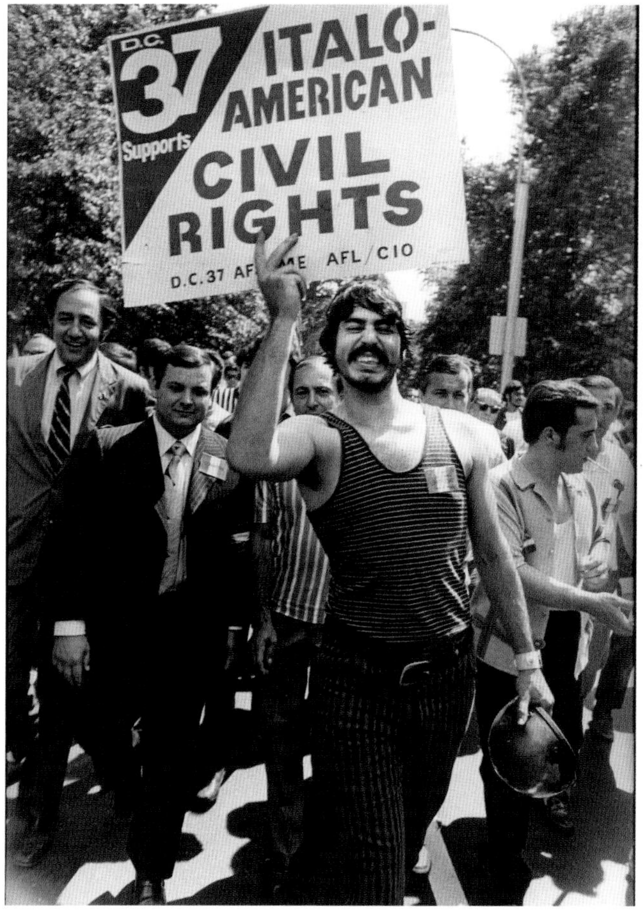

[BELLA ABZUG CAMPAIGNING], 1974: Bella Abzug (1920–98) was active in the civil rights and feminist movements. As a young attorney, she felt unnoticed in large gatherings with male counterparts and adopted the practice of wearing a hat to help her to stand out from her colleagues. These hats, along with her outspoken voice, became her signature style. Abzug served in Congress for three terms (1971–77) and despite losses in subsequent electoral efforts, she remained a political force until her death. PHOTOGRAPHER UNKNOWN. GIFT OF LIZ AND EVE ABZUG. 02.1.1.73.

(LEFT) **STATEN ISLAND FERRY, 1977:** It is a brisk and breezy ride across the bay from Manhattan's Whitehall to Staten Island's St. George, enough to force one's concentration or test one's resolve. Of the current fleet of ten ferries, one is named for a photographer—Staten Island's Alice Austen. PHOTOGRAPH BY DEBORAH FREEMAN. GIFT OF MRS. ZINA FREEMAN. 82.14.2.

ITALIAN-AMERICAN DEMONSTRATION, CENTRAL PARK, 1972: The Black Pride movement of the late 1960s led to resurgent factional identification by other hyphenated groups, from Native Americans and Hispanic Americans to second- and third-generation Irish Americans and Italian Americans. The Italian-American campaign of 1972 to combat stereotyping was stimulated in some measure by the success of the film *The Godfather*, released in that year. Note that the sign was issued by District Council 37, the largest municipal workers union in the city, testimony that ethnic identification cross-cut with all kinds of other social institutions in this period, including organized labor. PHOTOGRAPH BY CATHERINE URSILLO. 03.104.2.

THEATER TICKET SALES, TIMES SQUARE, 1979: Created in 1968 to help strengthen Broadway and Off Broadway, in particular productions of serious dramatic plays, the Theater Development Fund has developed a wide-ranging variety of programs to serve audiences and theaters. Perhaps none has been as successful for as long a period as TKTS, a booth selling same-day tickets to live theatrical performances discounted by as much as half of listed price. While today there are locations in Brooklyn and at the South Street Seaport, bargain-hunting theater lovers have for decades flocked to this bold signage at Father Duffy Square on Broadway and 47th Street. PHOTOGRAPH © ANDREAS FEININGER. GIFT OF THE PHOTOGRAPHER. 90.40.27.

PREPARATIONS FOR MACY'S THANKSGIVING DAY PARADE, 1972: The highlight of each Thanksgiving Day in New York since 1924 has been the Macy's Parade. At the end of that first parade, as has been the case with every parade since, Santa Claus was ushered into Herald Square to symbolize the start of the winter holidays and, perhaps more significantly, the shopping season. Felix the Cat, the first large-scale balloon float, was introduced in 1927; Mickey Mouse followed seven years later. PHOTOGRAPH BY PAULA WRIGHT. GIFT OF THE PHOTOGRAPHER. 98.121.3.

KITCHEN OF SILVER PALACE RESTAURANT, 52 BOWERY, 1977: This 900-seat dim sum parlor and banquet hall at 52 Bowery, also known as Dong Khanh, was famed for its fine fare. However, enduring renown may be accorded it for a twenty-year-long labor dispute over anti-union hiring practices and tip-skimming. In 2003 a federal judge awarded $2.3 million to seventeen aggrieved waiters and busboys, but by then the restaurant had filed for bankruptcy. PHOTOGRAPH BY CARIN DRECHSLER-MARX. MUSEUM PURCHASE. 82.143.78.

NINTH AVENUE AT 40TH STREET, CA. 1976: Escaping from the heat at their windows or on the fire escape, these denizens of Hell's Kitchen stare out at the southwest end of the massive Port Authority Bus Terminal. PHOTOGRAPH BY JAN LUKAS. GIFT OF THE PHOTOGRAPHER. 93.92.8.

PARK

(LEFT) **WEST HOUSTON AND WEST BROADWAY, LOOKING SOUTH, 1978:** This was the time of a booming arts scene in SoHo (echoing the name of the London district, but really named for its being the area *So*uth of *Ho*uston Street). Galleries and boutiques lined West Broadway and the cross streets (Prince, Spring, Broome, et al.). The old industrial lofts and walkups fit the make-it-new spirit of those moving to the city's hottest neighborhood, in the shadow of the World Trade Center to the south. Victor Laredo (1910–2003) took this image one year after his retirement from teaching at a photographic school he had organized in East Harlem. GIFT OF THE PHOTOGRAPHER. 82.74.8.

DESTRUCTION OF THE WEST SIDE HIGHWAY [II], CA. 1977: On December 16, 1973, a cement truck going to make a repair on another stretch of the highway triggered a collapse of a sixty-foot section of the northbound roadway at Gansevoort Street. While engineers figured out what it would cost to make the needed repairs, the highway was closed from the Battery to 57th Street. When the price tag came in at $88 million, the decision was made not to reopen the highway and to begin dismantling it. A replacement plan labeled Westway was bruited about for years until 1990, when it was killed despite its powerful backers. PHOTOGRAPH BY ROBERT BIANCHI. GIFT OF THE PHOTOGRAPHER. 83.106.1.

(LEFT) **SOUTH BRONX, 1978:** The South Bronx—a region famous as the home of Yankee Stadium and the cradle of hip hop—consisted originally of only Mott Haven and Melrose, then came to encompass Hunts Point, Morrisania, and Highbridge as well. Historically a place for working-class families, in 1930 it was 49 per cent Jewish. But beginning in the late 1940s suburbanization accelerated and the South Bronx went from being two-thirds white in 1950 to being two-thirds black and Puerto Rican only ten years later. By 1978, the year depicted in this image, the South Bronx was infamous nationwide. Widespread arson of troubled buildings, preceded by looting of its wiring, plumbing, and anything else of value gave the impression that the whole Bronx was burning. PHOTOGRAPH BY SUSAN KATZ. GIFT OF THE PHOTOGRAPHER. 84.203.86.

BAR INTERIOR, CA. 1974: The opportunity of being alone together, at a bar stool or a ballgame, on the subway or Fifth Avenue, is one of New York's amenities. The city is famous for its ancient and intimate taprooms, from McSorley's to P. J. Clarke's to Pete's Tavern and too many more to mention. These form the ordinary man or woman's answer to the Union Club. PHOTOGRAPH BY DONALD GREENHAUS. GIFT OF THE PHOTOGRAPHER. 80.65.55.

CHAPTER XV | 1980–1989

GOODBYE TO ALL THAT

JED PERL

I DOUBT THERE IS ANYBODY WHO FEELS MUCH NOSTALGIA FOR THE NEW YORK ART WORLD OF THE 1980S. NOSTALGIA IS A PRIVATE FEELING, AND BACK THEN ART WAS BECOMING AN INCREASINGLY PUBLIC AFFAIR. WHEN I REMEMBER THOSE TIMES I SEE WEST BROADWAY BETWEEN PRINCE AND SPRING STREETS, A STRETCH OF REAL ESTATE THAT WAS HOME TO THE MOST TALKED-ABOUT CONTEMPORARY GALLERIES: CASTELLI, SONNABEND, AND BOONE. I CANNOT SAY I LIKED VERY MUCH OF WHAT I SAW THERE. I HAVE A MEMORY OF COMING OUT OF ONE OF DAVID SALLE'S EARLY SHOWS AT MARY BOONE, SO PISSED OFF AT HIS TRUMPED-UP PROFUNDITY THAT AS I WALKED DOWN WEST BROADWAY WITH A FRIEND, I STARTED TEARING UP THE ANNOUNCEMENT FOR THE SHOW TO LITTLE PIECES, WHICH I TRIUMPHANTLY DEPOSITED IN A TRASH CAN. SOMETHING ABOUT WEST BROADWAY—THE STREET TOO WIDE FOR CHARM AND TOO NARROW FOR GRANDEUR, THE GRACELESS BUILDING FAÇADES, THE LIGHT THAT WAS FLAT AND HARSH NO MATTER THE SEASON—CRYSTALLIZED THE UNEASY ATMOSPHERE OF THE 1980S. ANY DECADE IS A MIXED BAG, AND THOSE YEARS WERE ALMOST IMPOSSIBLY MIXED, TOO ABRASIVE, TOO AGGRESSIVE, TOO CRISSCROSSED BY CONTROVERSY TO EVER PRESENT, EVEN TO THE RETROSPECTIVE GAZE, ANYTHING LIKE A COHERENT PICTURE. AN EDITOR AT *ARTFORUM*, WRITING IN 2003, GOT IT RIGHT WHEN HE SAID "THE '80S REMAIN SOMETHING OF AN OPEN WOUND."

THERE WAS CERTAINLY A LOT TO SEE. NEW YORK WAS HONEYCOMBED WITH SO MANY GALLERIES THAT EVEN IN A COUPLE OF DAYS IT WAS IMPOSSIBLE TO COME CLOSE to visiting them all. There were the traditional locales, on 57th Street and along Madison Avenue. In the early 1980s, the East Village developed its own gallery scene, which didn't last. My feeling was that the paying customers never really took to the neighborhood, and in any event, as the galleries began to prosper they wanted bigger spaces, which were easier to find in SoHo. Many galleries still had an appealing mom-and-pop quality. The buying and selling of art was to some degree seen as a local matter, a New York phenomenon with a New York accent. SoHo kept the memories of the old industrial city alive, with its rattletrap elevators and endless, often fairly decrepit flights of wooden stairs. Then there was Dean and Deluca, where gourmet food was presented in a freshly conceived, casually hi-tech setting; and Jaap Rietman's bookstore, with its beautiful volumes laid out on wide tables and filling endless shelves. Many who lived in SoHo felt both triumphant and bemused—triumphant at being ensconced in terrific spaces that they had bought for a song or lived in with some form of rent control, bemused that the neighborhood, week by week, was becoming unrecognizable.

Looking back, I am reminded of the last line of an essay that Edwin Denby wrote in the 1950s about the New York art world of the 1930s: "Private life goes on regardless," he observed, thinking of the differences between one decade and another. And so it does. The thing about public life in the 1980s, though, was that it gave so little sustenance to private life. It was public in the most extreme way. One of the controversies that dragged on through the decade centered around Richard Serra's *Tilted Arc*, the huge Cor-Ten steel sculpture installed in Federal Plaza in Lower Manhattan in 1981, which proved wildly unpopular among the office workers in the neighborhood, who said it was ugly, intimidating, and interfered with their movement around the plaza. By the time it was finally removed in 1989, *Tilted Arc* had become the flash point for arguments about populism and elitism and an embarrassment to New York's reputation for live-and-let-live liberalism. My feeling was that the artist and his public were both at least partly to blame. Although a quarter of a century later Serra has turned out to be a crowd pleaser, he was one of SoHo's original irascibles. One evening long before the neighborhood had begun its rise, he was seen standing on the corner of West Broadway and Spring, snarling, "Some day all this will be fucking *boutiques*!" Bohemianism was not necessarily dead. Even as the years passed, it was still possible, if you walked up those creaky wooden SoHo staircases, to feel some old sense of the art world as a band of outsiders. The act of creation, however, was increasingly prey to the forces of Warholism and Reaganomics, which sometimes looked like the same thing: a Gilded Age that wanted nothing so much as one of Julian Schnabel's smashed plate paintings to hang on the wall.

And the best memories? The decade began with one of the greatest of all museum shows, the Museum of Modern Art's 1980 Picasso retrospective, an extravaganza that filled the entire building on West 53rd Street and brought New York's long-running love affair with the Spaniard who had never visited Manhattan to a fever pitch not seen before or since. The Courbet retrospective at the Brooklyn Museum in 1988 was another notable event among museum shows. It was there that Courbet's *The Origin of the World*, that close-up view between a woman's legs, was exhibited for the first time in public. It confounded all the art world's arguments about sexual politics, which were by then fueled not so much by heartfelt anger as by a taste for ideas that were elegantly abstruse. In the contemporary galleries, I watched as artists who had come of age in the mid-century years, among them Leland Bell and Louisa Matthiasdottir, reached the climaxes of their careers, and younger painters and sculptors—Joan Snyder, Bill Jensen, Barbara Goodstein—gave the decade's restless, relentless spirit some persuasive formal logic. If I were to generalize about the artists who mattered most in the 1980s, whether historical or contemporary, I would say each of them had a certain boldness of attack; it was a time when a contemplative or classicizing spirit was difficult to believe in, much less sustain. Once upon a time, New York's artists and writers had found in the lyric mode a way of drawing together public fact and personal fantasy. This passionately dreamy feeling for the hurly burly of the city had perhaps last been expressed in some of Frank O'Hara's poems or in the paintings of the city's streets that Fairfield Porter was working on in the early 1970s. One can argue that lyric New York was dying a natural death in the 1980s, although I'm inclined to believe it was mugged, with Warholism and Reaganomics doing the dirty work.

The business of art, which in the mid-twentieth century had still been as much a European as an American affair, was increasingly concentrated on this side of the Atlantic, and so Manhattan became the place where artists from many different countries hoped to see their work warmly received. New York now had all the characteristics of Paris a hundred years earlier; it was a vast marketplace for the visual arts, with a bewildering concentration of dealers and promoters, auctions and exhibitions, amid which the real work of art went on. Many of the finest artists living in New York in 1985 were as little known to the broad public as Cézanne was in Paris in 1885. Many wanted to believe that art was first and foremost a spectacle, and although artists were producing many remarkable works, there was nothing that could really satisfy this desire for a wide-angle, all-embracing vision, which had more to do with the movies than with modern art. What was mostly discussed were the trends—the art stars; the rise and fall of the East Village; postmodernism in all its varieties; Neo-Expressionism; political correctness—and in such an overheated environment the victory involved in painting a good painting could be dismissed as a minor accomplishment. The art world was bigger than ever before, more divided within itself—and against itself. The writing was on the wall. By the end of the 1980s the New York that was the center of the art world had lost touch with the inner lives of the artists. They still lived there and showed there. But it was no longer their city.

(RIGHT) GALLERY IN SOHO, 1983: The viewer is challenged: which silhouettes are live and which art? PHOTOGRAPH © ANDREAS FEININGER. GIFT OF THE PHOTOGRAPHER. 90.40.99.

JED PERL IS THE ART CRITIC FOR *THE NEW REPUBLIC*. IN 2005 HE PUBLISHED A PANORAMIC STUDY OF ART AND CULTURE IN TWENTIETH-CENTURY NEW YORK, *NEW ART CITY: MANHATTAN AT MID-CENTURY*. AMONG HIS OTHER BOOKS ARE *PARIS WITHOUT END*, *EYEWITNESS*, AND *ANTOINE'S ALPHABET*. MR. PERL HAS WRITTEN FOR *HARPER'S*, *THE ATLANTIC*, *THE NEW YORK TIMES BOOK REVIEW*, *THE YALE REVIEW*, *SALMAGUNDI*, AND WAS THE ART CRITIC FOR *VOGUE* DURING THE 1980S. HE IS A VISITING PROFESSOR OF LIBERAL STUDIES AT THE NEW SCHOOL IN NEW YORK.

Graffiti is a art
And if art
is a crime,
Let GOD
Forgive all

(LEFT) ***HOWARD THE DUCK*, 1989:** Graffiti started to appear on subway walls, cars, underpasses, and other public spaces in the 1970s. Despite infuriating the establishment, a few of the "aerosol artists" came to prominence in the gallery scene of the 1980s. The artist who tagged himself LEE commenced his graffiti career with *Doomsday* (1976), a piece that covered two subway cars parked at the Lexington Avenue yards. *Howard the Duck* (1978) was actually a commissioned piece, painted at the behest of the school principal on the handball-court wall of Corlears Junior High School 56 on Henry Street. More than a decade later, the artist replicated his work in acrylic on canvas. PAINTING BY LEE (LEE GEORGE QUIÑONES). GIFT OF MARTIN WONG, 58 x 88. 94.114.1.

BROADWAY AND 14TH STREET, 1982: This had once been the northern border of residential New York. Subsequently it became the shopping district, the hotbed of labor and political activism, and the home to theaters and restaurants and bargain meccas such as, respectively, the Academy of Music, Lüchow's, and S. Klein. By the time this urban landscape was taken, they were gone or gasping. PHOTOGRAPH BY ROBERT SHERWIN. GIFT OF THE PHOTOGRAPHER. 85.74.

(LEFT) YUGOSLAVIAN MEN PLAYING LOPTA, ASTORIA PARK, 1982: "Lopta" means *ball* in the Croatian or Stovakian languages, and is to be distinguished from "lapta," a Russian name for a game of bat and ball. PHOTOGRAPH © AGNES ZELLIN. GIFT OF THE PHOTOGRAPHER. 85.8.12.

TIMES SQUARE, 1980: Beneath the bronze statue of entertainer and songwriter George M. Cohan, erected in 1959 at the southern point of the triangle known as Duffy Square, a group of tourists awaits instructions from its leader. The late lamented Howard Johnson's became a famous family spot for its twenty-eight flavors of ice cream. By 1980, its neighbors reflected different tastes. PHOTOGRAPH © ANDREAS FEININGER. GIFT OF THE PHOTOGRAPHER. 90.40.23.

[TIMES SQUARE], 1983: The traditional honky-tonk aspects of Broadway were still strong in the 1980s, and the frisson of touring Sin City was not without appeal, to out-of-towners and natives alike. The young woman in the foreground wears a button that proclaims, "I ♥ Irv," but her button is an extension (unlicensed, surely) from a spectacularly long-lived publicity campaign. Although the logo for "I ♥ New York" was designed by Milton Glaser and the jingle was written by Steve Karmen as part of a New York State publicity effort in 1977, both quickly became identified with the city. T-shirts and buttons with the logo still abound citywide. PHOTOGRAPH © ANDREAS FEININGER. GIFT OF THE PHOTOGRAPHER. 90.40.4.

FOLLOW THE LEADER, 1981: "We beg delinquents for our life./ Behind each bush, perhaps a knife;/ each landscaped crag, each flowering shrub,/ hides a policeman with a club." So wrote poet Robert Lowell in "Central Park" in 1965, when the crime problems of the city and the park seemed intractable. From purse snatching to vandalism to violent assaults, the Park became viewed not as a respite from the city but a den of all its ills. By the time of this image of unconcerned youth busily at play, the city had begun to tighten its policy on petty crime in the park and by decade's end, despite the occasional outrage, safety improved. PHOTOGRAPH BY BROR KARLSSON. GIFT OF THE PHOTOGRAPHER. 89.94.10.

(RIGHT) **GAME OF SKELLIE, EAST HARLEM, 1987:** This street game, a New York favorite for generations, is variantly spelled as skully, skelly, and skelsy; it is also called caps because bottle caps or checker-like objects are generally employed to execute the moves of this asphalt board game. (It is said that the game has existed as long as the crown-rimmed bottle cap.) The number of boxes and playing rules will vary according to neighborhood, custom, and availability of space, so it will be enough here to note that a skellie board and a pool table have much in common—in pool, the balls are numbered; in skellie, the boxes. Both balls and caps hit each other, and the various angles and speeds at which the objects move determine success or failure. PHOTOGRAPH BY JOSEPH RODRIGUEZ. GIFT OF THE PHOTOGRAPHER. 2007.8.1.

GIRL, CONEY ISLAND, 1989: Some things about New York don't change, and they continue to shape the life of the city. PHOTOGRAPH BY MATT BIALER. GIFT OF THE PHOTOGRAPHER. 01.14.2.

CENTRAL PARK, SHEEP MEADOW, LOOKING TOWARD CENTRAL PARK SOUTH BUILDINGS, 1980: On an early spring day, the Sheep Meadow offers recreation to the young and contemplation to those no longer so. To deter physical activity and promote green thoughts, Frederick Law Olmsted and Calvert Vaux actually introduced a flock of sheep to the meadow in 1864. Not until seventy years later did Robert Moses exile the woolly ones to Brooklyn, at which point the sheepfold was taken down to permit construction of the Tavern on the Green restaurant. PHOTOGRAPH BY VICTOR LAREDO. GIFT OF THE PHOTOGRAPHER. 82.74.2.

WATER TOWERS, 1984: Water towers provided water above the sixth floor, at which point the gravity drop from the reservoirs no longer works. The wooden water towers may contain 5,000–10,000 gallons of water, only the topmost fraction of which is used on a daily basis, with the rest held in reserve in the event of fire. These largely unutilized examples of the cooperage trade of the nineteenth century provide a pleasing vista, historically and aesthetically.
PHOTOGRAPH © ANDREAS FEININGER. GIFT OF THE PHOTOGRAPHER. 90.40.69.

REFLECTIONS, 1981: Photographer Andreas Feininger had executed a dazzling series of morning-sun reflections in the windows of the United Nations Building for *Life* in June 1951. Here the depicted building may be different, and the date is thirty years distant, but the play of reflected light clearly continued to fascinate. PHOTOGRAPH © ANDREAS FEININGER. GIFT OF THE PHOTOGRAPHER. 90.40.41.

MIDTOWN MANHATTAN, 1981: The vision is upward, beyond the steel and glass towers into the clouds. But the tableau is anchored by the roofline of the Racquet and Tennis Club, a members-only enclave on Park Avenue between 52nd and 53rd Streets. Designed in the Italian Renaissance style by McKim, Mead, and White and completed in 1918, the building is a neighborhood anomaly for not extending into the stratosphere. PHOTOGRAPH © ANDREAS FEININGER. GIFT OF THE PHOTOGRAPHER. 90.40.52.

[CHILDREN LOOKING THROUGH SUBWAY WINDOW AT WONDER WHEEL], 1980: A wonderful day at Coney Island ends with a subway ride home at dusk. The graffiti is invisible. Bruce Davidson, a Magnum photographer since 1958, received the first photography grant from the National Endowment for the Arts. After a two-year project of documenting a single block in East Harlem, *East 100th Street*, Davidson followed with *Subway* (1980), in which this image was included. PHOTOGRAPH BY BRUCE DAVIDSON, MAGNUM PHOTOS. GIFT OF JEANNE & RICHARD S. PRESS. 2006.25.22.

FRANKFURTERS-HAMBURGERS (FROM THE COTTINGHAM SUITE), 1980: The pop-art movement of the 1960s turned heads away from abstract expressionism and minimalism to superrealism (also known as hyperrealism or photorealism). Imitations of photography or CMYK printing were among the approaches of artists like Chuck Close, Richard Estes, and Malcolm Morley; or Robert Cottingham, whose graphics-dominated lithograph is depicted here. Like Andy Warhol, Cottingham came to fine art through New York's advertising-agency world. LITHOGRAPH BY ROBERT COTTINGHAM. MUSEUM PURCHASE. 84.82.

[WOMAN SEATED BELOW GRAFFITI], 1980: In this image from Davidson's *Subway* series, there is no escaping the scrawls of the vandals, who at this tipping point in New York's history seemed to be sacking the city. PHOTOGRAPH BY BRUCE DAVIDSON, MAGNUM PHOTOS. GIFT OF HALUK & ELISA SOYKAN. 2006.26.8.

CHAPTER XVI | 1990–2009

IMMIGRANTS RESHAPE THE CITY

DAVID DYSSEGAARD KALLICK

THROUGHOUT ITS HISTORY, NEW YORK'S DYNAMIC ECONOMY HAS BEEN RECHARGED BY PERIODIC INFUSIONS OF THE ENERGY AND CULTURES BROUGHT BY IMMIGRANTS. IN THE FIRST DECADE OF THE TWENTY-FIRST CENTURY, IMMIGRANTS ARE AGAIN CHANGING NEW YORK, BRINGING TO THE CITY VIBRANT SOUNDS, FRESH TASTES, AND NEW IDEAS. TODAY, 37 PERCENT OF PEOPLE LIVING IN NEW YORK CITY WERE BORN IN ANOTHER COUNTRY, AND MORE THAN HALF OF NEW YORK CHILDREN ARE GROWING UP IN FAMILIES WITH AT LEAST ONE IMMIGRANT ADULT. MORE IMMIGRANTS ARE COMING TO THE UNITED STATES TODAY THAN IN THE HEYDAY OF ELLIS ISLAND, AND IMMIGRANTS TODAY MAKE UP ALMOST AS GREAT A SHARE OF THE OVERALL POPULATION OF THE COUNTRY AS THEY DID A HUNDRED YEARS AGO. NOWHERE IS THE CHURNING OF IMMIGRATION MORE VISIBLE THAN IN AMERICA'S LARGEST CITY.

IN ITS ORIGINS FOUR CENTURIES AGO AS AN OUTPOST OF THE DUTCH WEST INDIA COMPANY, NEW YORK WAS ALREADY A LOCUS OF CULTURAL BLENDING. MUCH LIKE AMSTERDAM IN THE SEVENTEENTH CENTURY, NEW AMSTERDAM QUICKLY CAME TO BE KNOWN AS A CENTER FOR GLOBAL CONNECTEDNESS AND A GREATER DEGREE OF DIVERSITY THAN ITS NEIGHBORS.

IN THE NINETEENTH CENTURY, NEW YORK WAS THE MAIN PORT OF ENTRY FOR IMMIGRANTS COMING TO THE UNITED STATES. THE CITY WAS RESHAPED AS IT BECAME HOME TO SUBSTANTIAL NUMBERS OF CATHOLICS FROM IRELAND AND GERMANY AND LATER FROM ITALY AND TO JEWS AND OTHERS FROM EASTERN EUROPE; THEY TENDED THE PUSHCARTS, BUILT THE SUBWAYS, staffed the police force, dug water tunnels, and worked in the garment factories of the Lower East Side.

The Depression and World War II, as well as restrictive immigration laws passed in the 1920s, dramatically narrowed the door for immigrants for much of the middle of the twentieth century. But that didn't mean New York stopped drawing newcomers, as Puerto Ricans and African Americans from the South moved in.

But something changed profoundly in the years that followed. Indeed, the *absence* of immigration is an important part of the 1970s story of suburbanization, white flight, and fiscal crisis—though it is rarely seen in this light. A quick look at what has happened in the years since the city's most famous tabloid headline ("Ford to City: Drop Dead") shows a strong resurgence fueled largely by immigrants. Population in the city had reached a historic low by the end of the 1970s, weakening the tax base, leaving neighborhoods full of abandoned buildings, and hurting the economy.

Since the era when the Bronx was burning, New York has regained its patina as a vibrant, global city. Real estate problems now revolve around high rents, not abandoned buildings.

Surprisingly, however, throughout the two and a half decades since the '70s ended, the U.S.-born part of the population has remained essentially flat—in fact, it's declined a little. What has changed is the immigrant portion. The city population grew by 1.2 million between 1980 and 2005; the number of immigrants in the city grew by 1.3 million. Clearly, immigrants have played an enormous role in helping New York get its groove back. A lively music scene, restaurants with food from around the world, inexpensive laundry service, the sense of being in a global city, and delivery of just about anything at 2:00 am—all fueled by immigration—are all very appealing to bright college graduates, ambitious entrepreneurs, and global business leaders.[1]

Today's immigrants are perhaps the most ethnically, racially, and culturally diverse ever. Immigrants come to New York from around the world—no single region of the world dominates. Today the country of origin for the largest share of immigrants is the Dominican Republic, followed in rapid succession by China, Jamaica, Mexico, Guyana, Haiti, India, Trinidad and Tobago, Colombia, Ukraine, and the list goes on and on. Immigrants to New York City are a little less than a quarter white, a quarter black and a quarter Asian, while not quite a third are Hispanic.

The portrait of immigrants in New York today is exciting and colorful, but it is not always a pretty picture. In this city of great extremes, immigrants are subject to the same economic and social trends as the rest of the population. At the very lowest end of today's immigrant economy, people are working in appalling conditions. Sweatshops, not far removed from those of the Lower East Side before the 1911 Triangle Shirtwaist fire that killed 146 young immigrant women workers, are out of the sight of pedestrians but not hard to find in Manhattan's Chinatown and along Seventh Avenue, or in Sunset Park in Brooklyn or Long Island City in Queens. Rows of workers—nearly always women—sit behind sewing machines straining their eyes and fingers. They are frequently paid below the minimum wage, and sometimes not paid at all when factory owners suddenly close up shop, only to reopen under new premises across the street. If workers are in a union, their wages are still not great, but a very substantial advantage is that they are then likely to have the availability of health insurance for their families. The number of jobs in apparel manufacturing has decreased drastically in New York City, but there are still 26,000 sewing-machine operators here, and another 9,000 tailors, dressmakers, and sewers—very nearly all of whom are immigrants.

Studies show that, in an astonishing number of New York industries, violations of workers' rights are common and sometimes even the norm. Immigrant workers don't create low standards—employers do, particularly when government regulators fail to do their job. But immigrants and U.S.-born workers are equally affected by unregulated labor markets in such sectors as retail, restaurants, low-wage construction, domestic-work, taxi driving, personal services, and laundry and dry cleaning, to name but a few.

Estimates of undocumented immigrants are inherently imprecise, but there is little doubt that unauthorized immigrants are among the lowest-paid workers in the city, sometimes working under dangerous conditions. About half of dishwashers in the city are estimated to be undocumented, as are about a third of sewing-machine operators, painters, cooks, construction laborers, and food preparation workers.[2] There are plenty of immigrants in "regular" low-end jobs as well—jobs not marked by widespread violations of labor laws, but where wages are low, benefits rare, and working conditions substandard.

What is surprising, perhaps, is the extent to which immigrants are helping bolster the city's middle class. New York is often described as having an "hourglass economy," with a bulge at the top and bottom, and few in the middle. Immigrant families—that is to say, families in which at least one adult is born in another country—are clustered in the *middle* of the income distribution. More than half (55 percent) of people in immigrant families have an annual family income between $20,000 and $80,000. By comparison, just 44 percent of people living in families where all adults were born in the United States are in this income bracket. People in U.S.-born families are more likely to be at the two extremes of the hourglass, while people in immigrant families are making the hourglass a little broader in the middle.

Although immigrants generally earn wages that are somewhat lower than their U.S.-born counterparts at the same educational levels, lower wages don't necessarily mean lower family income. This is due in part to the fact that, compared to U.S.-born New Yorkers, immigrants are more likely to be in the workforce, typically work slightly longer hours, and live in families with more working adults.

At the same time, immigrants work in a wide range of midlevel jobs. As of 2005, immigrants account for one out of every three elementary school teachers living in New York City, for example, and one out of three secretaries and administrative assistants. Half of all accountants and auditors are foreign-born, as are a third of all designers.

In addition, immigrants are well represented among the professional classes. Half of all doctors living in New

York are foreign-born, as are nearly four out of ten architects and professors. Immigrants make up four in ten financial managers, property managers, and software engineers. Discussions about the H1B visa, for foreign nationals who have a job offer in a field requiring specialized knowledge, has traditionally been driven in the U.S. by Silicon Valley. But, as the Partnership for New York points out, a larger number of H1B visas are for jobs in the New York tri-state area than for all of California.[3]

New York's immigrants are also playing a big role at every economic level as entrepreneurs. The vast majority of street vendors in New York are immigrants, working hard just to make ends meet—adding to the character, street life, and level of service in the city. Other immigrants have opened stores, started restaurants, or set up businesses manufacturing products, providing services, or importing goods. A study by the Center for an Urban Future, in fact, found that immigrants are much more likely to be entrepreneurs than U.S.-born Americans. Between 1994 and 2004, the number of businesses in New York City as a whole increased by just under 10 percent, while in heavily immigrant neighborhoods it increased several times faster—in Flushing by 55 percent, in Sunset Park by 47 percent, and in Sheepshead Bay-Brighton Beach by 34 percent. In some cases this may be simply providing for the needs of a growing population. In others, the same mixture of ambition and risk-taking that brings immigrants here may also drive them to start their own ventures. Some immigrant groups also come with an added boost, drawing on rotating credit associations or other traditions brought with them from abroad.[4]

For immigrants who don't own their own business, joining labor unions can be an important step toward social integration, promoting better conditions for all workers and expanding the middle class. In New York City, immigrants are represented by unions at nearly the same rate as U.S.-born workers. Unions such as those representing hospital workers, transportation workers, or building service workers are among the many very visible unions with large immigrant memberships. Unions are helping immigrants adjust to American culture, and by the same token, immigrants are helping shape the culture of New York unions. In all, 44 percent of union members in the city are immigrants.

What about commuters? Nearly a third of the people who travel from other areas to work in New York City are immigrants. Foreign-born commuters tend to be in the professions or management, business, and finance in about the same proportion as the U.S.-born workers sharing the highway or train ride with them in the morning.

Even in the highest reaches of the economy, immigrants are playing an important role. Taking a quick tour of the top echelons of New York business in 2008: Alain Belda, born in Brazil, is chair of Alcoa; Shoba Purushothaman, born in Malaysia, is CEO of the Newsmarket; Mort Zuckerman, born in Canada, is publisher of the *Daily News* and CEO of Boston Properties; Charles Wang, born in China, is co-founder of Computer Associates International and owner of the New York Islanders hockey team; and George Soros, born in Hungary, is chair of Soros Fund Management as well as of the philanthropic Open Society Institute. In all, a quarter of all CEOs living in New York City are foreign-born. New York draws on a global pool of talent; immigrants help connect New York business to global markets; and New York provides the environment in which many immigrants thrive.

New York's political leaders generally appreciate the importance of immigrants to the economy, culture, and society of the city. As mayor, Michael R. Bloomberg has spoken out strongly about the importance of immigrants, even undocumented immigrants, to the New York economy. "Although they broke the law by illegally crossing the borders or overstaying their visas, our economy would be a shell of itself had they not," Bloomberg wrote in a 2006 article for the *Wall Street Journal*.

Certainly the city could do more to boost the contribution of immigrants to the economy. It's hard to understand why the city isn't overflowing with opportunities to learn English at every school, library, and community center. Still, at least the government doesn't err in the other direction, trying to micromanage immigrants' lives. A midlevel official summed up New York's approach recently, responding to European visitors who asked how the city government helps immigrants.

"Mostly," he said, "we just try to stay out of their way."

DAVID DYSSEGAARD KALLICK IS SENIOR FELLOW OF THE FISCAL POLICY INSTITUTE AND PRINCIPAL AUTHOR OF *WORKING FOR A BETTER LIFE: A PROFILE OF IMMIGRANTS IN THE NEW YORK STATE ECONOMY*. KALLICK WAS PREVIOUSLY EDITOR OF *SOCIAL POLICY* MAGAZINE, AND HE HAS WRITTEN EXTENSIVELY ON GLOBALIZATION, CIVIC PARTICIPATION, ELECTORAL REFORM, URBAN PLANNING IN NEW YORK AFTER SEPTEMBER 11, AND A RANGE OF SOCIAL AND ECONOMIC ISSUES.

(LEFT) **COMMUNICANT, GRAND STREET, BROOKLYN, 1996:** Photographer Régina Monfort writes, "The teens I photograph in South Williamsburg are second- or third-generation immigrants. They identify themselves as Puerto Ricans, as Dominicans, as Americans, but they are from Brooklyn. . . . From Grand Street to Lindsay Park, my lens found hope and frustration. I am often asked 'Why are you here? Why are you interested in our lives? What is there to see here? Nothing is beautiful here!' These photographs are my answer." PHOTOGRAPH BY RÉGINA MONFORT. GIFT OF THE PHOTOGRAPHER. 01.20.1.

CIGARS (QUISQUEYANA), 2000: Dominican hand-rolled cigars became the symbol of masculinity in the boom years on Wall Street, especially before the city banned smoking in public and commercial spaces. *Quisqueya* is a name for the island of Hispaniola in the Taíno language meaning "mother of the earth," but also is used to refer to the Dominican Republic. PHOTOGRAPH BY EDWIN MARTIN. GIFT OF THE PHOTOGRAPHER. 01.63.11.

STILL OPEN, 1994: The city that never sleeps actually does, of course, in its neighborhoods if not its vast public spaces. But even the sleepiest of the city's streets possesses a nightlife unknown in the suburbs or exurbs. The painter's bird's-eye vantage—from his apartment window—and glowing foreground bring intimacy to this large-scale view of the Greenpoint neighborhood of Brooklyn. EGG TEMPERA ON PANEL BY DOUGLAS SAFRANEK, 4¾ x 4. MUSEUM PURCHASE, NEW YORK. 95.6.

[FROM THE SERIES *BAR PICTURES*, GREENPOINT, BROOKLYN], 1998: "Still Life with Beer," one might term this, with the invisible television set commanding its communicants. PHOTOGRAPH BY DARIN MICKEY. GIFT OF THE PHOTOGRAPHER. 04.32.1.

[FROM THE SERIES *THE VIADUCT PAINTERS*], 1995: Sophie Rivera recalls her subject: "The viaduct subway station at 125th Street is seventy-five feet off the ground. One morning a group of bridgework painters came with their tarpaulins and paint equipment. They hoisted the tarpaulins seventy-five feet and tied them to the station. For a month I followed them as they painted a primer coat and a finishing coat. I used my Nikon camera lenses 24mm, 50mm, and 90mm to photograph them. . . . They coated their faces with Vaseline and wore several layers of clothing in the hot sun and worked hour after hour bantering among themselves, climbing up and down the structure as though they were at home on it. There seemed to be a camaraderie and a trust among them that was a great inspiration."

PHOTOGRAPH BY SOPHIE RIVERA. GIFT OF THE PHOTOGRAPHER. 00.77.2.

SANTA AT ROLL CALL, 6TH PRECINCT, 1996: New York's finest, and the North Pole's. The undercover Santa will be expected to know who's been naughty and who's been nice. PHOTOGRAPH BY STEFFEN A. KAPLAN. GIFT OF THE PHOTOGRAPHER. 01.3.2.

POLICE OFFICER AND CROWD AT 11:59PM, NEW YEAR'S EVE, 1997: Times Square is a happy place for revelers and their monitors too, as amiability reigns and crime is minimal despite the size and density of the crowd. PHOTOGRAPH BY STEFFEN A. KAPLAN. GIFT OF THE PHOTOGRAPHER. 01.3.5.

EASTER PARADE, 1998: "In your Easter bonnet with all the frills upon it,/ You'll be the grandest lady in the Easter Parade." This may not be precisely what Irving Berlin had in mind, but parades celebrating gay pride have been staged in New York since 1970, commemorating the previous year's "Stonewall Riots"—protests that followed upon a police raid on the Stonewall Inn in Greenwich Village on June 28, 1969. Ever since, gay-pride rallies have been held worldwide in June, but in several cities the Easter Parade has become a notable gay event, too. PHOTOGRAPH BY EDWIN MARTIN. ANONYMOUS GIFT. 99.17.2.

JUMP ON SOUTH 1ST STREET, WILLIAMSBURG, BROOKLYN, CA. 1995: Vincent Cianni documented in photographs and video how in-line skating—blading—became the rallying force for Hispanic teens growing up in a challenging part of the city. The photo exhibition, documentary film, and book bore the title *We Skate Hardcore*. "Think 'West Side Story' with skates," offered the *Boston Sunday Globe* in its review. PHOTOGRAPH BY VINCENT CIANNI.

[NEWSSTAND], 1993: *Sidewalk* was the name of the book that collected Jeff Mermelstein's unusual street pictures, and it presented the city's denizens as driven and more than a little eccentric. In this image, the news hound does not chase the story, he is the story. PHOTOGRAPH BY JEFF MERMELSTEIN.

[SUBWAY ENTRANCE], CA. 1995: For more than twenty years Jeff Mermelstein has prowled the streets capturing the off-kilter moments that are distinctive to New York City. With a wry sense of humor he takes a magnifying lens to the city's eccentricities. PHOTOGRAPH BY JEFF MERMELSTEIN.

(RIGHT) **THE REBBE, 1992:** Rabbi Schneerson addresses his followers at the Eastern Parkway, Brooklyn headquarters of the Lubavitch movement. This image first appeared as part of Michael Specter's "The Oracle of Crown Heights," in the *New York Times Sunday Magazine*. "In my fifteen years working as a photojournalist," photographer Marc Asnin wrote, "no project has had a more profound impact on my life. . . . From the moment of my initial contact with this group I was utterly swept away—both emotionally and visually—by their passionate approach to their belief in and worship of Judaism." PHOTOGRAPH BY MARC ASNIN. GIFT OF THE PHOTOGRAPHER. 01.71.1.

path
ONE WAY
7
NY
YORK

(LEFT) **FULTON AND CHURCH STREETS, SEPTEMBER 11, 2001:** The faces tell the story of the terror that gripped the city that day. Russian-born Gulnara Samoilova writes, "I was supposed to be in Russia on September 11 to photograph a family I was chronicling as part of a personal, ongoing project. Instead, I was nearly buried alive in the ash and debris from the World Trade Center as I documented the events of the day." PHOTOGRAPH BY GULNARA SAMOILOVA. GIFT OF THE PHOTOGRAPHER. 02.29.2.

TWIN TOWERS OF THE WORLD TRADE CENTER, SEPTEMBER 11, 2001: On this terrible day in the city's history, terrorists crashed two airliners into the World Trade Center; the savage blows brought the towers down. PHOTOGRAPH BY GULNARA SAMOILOVA. GIFT OF THE PHOTOGRAPHER. 02.29.1.

FIREMEN AT THE PILE LOOKING WEST, OCTOBER 24, 2001: Photographer Joel Meyerowitz came to Ground Zero with his view camera on September 23, 2001 and documented the cleanup effort daily for the next nine months. "It was important for me to try to do something that was helpful. After the event of September 11, I felt I had to contribute in some way. Of course it was impossible to really do anything a few days afterwards. The place was gated off. There were no volunteers that weren't necessary volunteers. When I heard that there was no photography allowed in there, I got the call in some way to make an archive. I understood that this was something that was being overlooked by the administration, and I thought, this is what I can give, I know how to make an archive. I called the Museum of the City of New York. I worked out an arrangement with them where I had a letter—it didn't do much good—but I had this letter to flag to the police and the state troopers who were down there." IMAGE COURTESY EDWYNN HOUK GALLERY.

(RIGHT) **TRIBUTE IN LIGHT MEMORIAL #5, 2002:** The Tribute in Light was an art installation of eighty-eight searchlights placed next to the site of the World Trade Center from March 11 to April 14, 2002 as a memorial of the September 11, 2001 attacks. Originally intended as a temporary commemoration, it was repeated in subsequent years. PHOTOGRAPH BY DANIEL HUANG. MUSEUM PURCHASE. 04.14.5.

[TIMES SQUARE], 1996: Street photographer Alex Webb writes, "I only know how to approach a place by walking. For what does a street photographer do but walk and watch and wait and talk, and then watch and wait some more, trying to remain confident that the unexpected, the unknown, or the secret heart of the known awaits just around the corner." At the secret heart of the Stardust Dine-O-Mat is a hazy recollection of the past ("Remember when?" asks the sign above the automat-like doors). The past is filtered, refracted, repackaged and rouged-up for the present. "Times Square is full of color," he says, "but it is really full of color to sell things." PHOTOGRAPH BY ALEX WEBB, MAGNUM PHOTOS.

IRON FRAMEWORK OF THE NEW CORTLANDT STREET STATION, LOOKING NORTH, 2002: This is from the photographer's forty-five image series "Rebuilding the 1 & 9," about the reconstruction of the Cortlandt Street subway station, which was destroyed in the September 11 attacks. Only a few months earlier, the entire area was still covered with smoking debris. The horizontal tracks in the foreground are part of the original track bed. In record time, workers rebuilt the 1 & 9 subway line that ran underneath the World Trade Center, reconnecting Lower Manhattan into the larger city subway network. The Cortlandt Street station reopened on September 15, 2002. PHOTOGRAPH BY SAM HOLLENSHEAD. MUSEUM PURCHASE. 2006.1.41.

PROCESSION OF PATRON SAINT FILIPPO OF LIMINA, SICILY, ST. LUCY'S CHURCH, BRONX, 1996: San Filippo d'Agira is the patron saint of Limina in Sicily, a small town of rapidly shrinking population from which many of the original parishioners of St. Lucy's emigrated. PHOTOGRAPH BY LIANA MIUCCIO. GIFT OF THE PHOTOGRAPHER. 02.114.1.

WEDDING KISS, 1997: As the photographer describes the image, "Photographed on Nostrand Avenue in the heart of Bed-Stuy [the Bedford-Stuyvesant neighborhood of Brooklyn]. A wedding party passing through while continuing to share their celebration with the community at large." PHOTOGRAPH BY RON CAMPBELL. GIFT OF THE PHOTOGRAPHER. 97.162.3.

CROSS BRONX EXPRESSWAY (NIGHT), 2006: Few highways have been so roundly criticized as this one, Robert Moses's prescription for traffic congestion. "The path of the great road lay across 113 streets, avenues, and boulevards," wrote Robert Caro in *The Power Broker*, "sewer and water and utility mains numbering in the hundreds; one subway and three railroads, five elevated rapid transit lines, and seven other expressways or parkways, some of which were being built by Moses simultaneously." Construction, which began in 1948, was completed in 1963. Middle-class residents were displaced from the South Bronx and slums came in their wake; blame was placed on the lowered property values caused by the Expressway. As anyone who drives it knows, traffic congestion on the Cross Bronx is dreadful—except late at night, after rush hour, when it can seem almost pretty. PHOTOGRAPH BY ANDREW MOORE. 2007.10.4.

WEST INDIAN KIDDIE CARNIVAL, CA. 2001: Brooklyn's annual West Indian American Day Parade & Carnival, first staged more than forty years ago, is the city's largest. As it evolved in recent years, Jamaican and Haitian entertainment increasingly competed with and then complemented the traditional Trinidadian program. Kiddie Carnival, an event modeled on the vast children's carnival of Trinidad, was born in New York in 1988 and has remained a Brooklyn favorite. PHOTOGRAPH BY MARTHA COOPER.

ENDNOTES

CHAPTER 1

This article first appeared in Dutch in *Biografie Bulletin* (*Dutch Journal of Biography*), Volume 18, Issue 2 (Summer 2008), pages 30–36, under the title "Het ongrijpbare stuifzand," and is reproduced here with permission.

CHAPTER 2

[1] James Alexander to Cadwallader Colden, February 10, 1744–45, New-York Historical Society, *Collections*, 52 (1919): 107–109.

[2] Guerbois's advertisement: *New-York Weekly Post-Boy*, October 30, 1752.

[3] Duyckinck's advertisement: *New-York Weekly Journal*, October 16, 1749; Hardenbrook's: *New-York Mercury*, September 25, 1758.

[4] Dr. Stork's advertisement: *New-York Mercury*, December 6, 1762.

[5] Radish-hand story: *New-York Gazette*, May 15, 1732.

[6] Johnson, William. *A Course of Experiments, In that Curious and Entertaining Branch of Natural Philosophy, call'd Electricity*. New-York: Hugh Gaine, 1765.

[7] "treated with kindness" and "monstrous ingratitude": Daniel Horsmanden, *Journal of the Proceedings in the Detection of the Conspiracy . . .*, ed. Thomas J. Davis (1744, reprint: Boston: Beacon Press, 1971), 105–106, 109–110.

SUGGESTED READING:

Lepore, Jill. *New York Burning: Liberty, Slavery, and Conspiracy in Eighteenth-Century Manhattan*. New York: Alfred A. Knopf, 2005.

Zabin, Serena. *Dangerous Economies: Status and Commerce in Imperial New York*. Philadelphia: University of Pennsylvania Press, 2009.

Stidstone Gronim, Sara. *Everyday Nature: Knowledge of the Natural World in Colonial New York*. New Brunswick, NJ: Rutgers University Press, 2007.

CHAPTER 4

[1] Isenberg, Nancy. *Fallen Founder: The Life of Aaron Burr*. New York: Viking, 2007: 347–48; and Andrew Burstein, *The Original Knickerbocker: The Life of Washington Irving*. New York: Basic Books, 2007: 33.

[2] See Washington Irving to James Kirk Paulding, June 22, 1807, in Pierre M. Irving, ed., *The Life and Letters of Washington Irving*. New York, 1862, I: 194–95; and Isenberg, *Fallen Founder*, 347–48.

[3] Isenberg, *Fallen Founder*, 88, 91–92, 193–195, 329, 237–243, 385–386.

[4] Isenberg, *Fallen Founder*, 266–68; and Agnes Addison Gilchrist, "John McComb, Sr. and Jr., in New York, 1784–1799," *The Journal of the Society of Architectural Historians*, 31, no. 1 (March, 1972), 14.

[5] Sandoval-Strausz, A. K. "A Public House for a New Republic: The Architecture of Accommodation and the American State, 1789–1809," *Perspectives in Vernacular Architecture*, Vol. 9, Constructing Image, Identity, and Place (2003): 57–58; Gilchrist, "John McComb," 16; and for the importance of coffee houses in the merchant culture of the early republic, see Jane Kamensky, *The Exchange Artist: A Tale of High-Flying Speculation and America's First Bank Collapse*. New York: Viking Press, 2008: 86–87, 188–190.

[6] Gilchrist, "John McComb," 18; *Commercial Advertiser*, January 31, 1798; and Edward Burrows and Mike Wallace, *Gotham: A History of New York City to 1898*. New York: Oxford, 1999: 375.

[7] Gilchrist, "John McComb," 14–15; Burrows and Wallace, *Gotham*, 301; Kenneth R. Bowling, "New York City, Capital of the United States, 1785–1790," in Stephen L. Schechter and Wendell Tripp, eds., *World of the Founders: New York Communities in the Federal Period*. Albany, NY, 1990: 13–17; Catherine Allgor, *Parlor Politics: In Which the Ladies of Washington Help Build a City and a Government*. Charlottesville, Va., 2000: 18–20; and Rufus Griswold, *The Republican Court, or American Society in the Days of Washington*. New York, 1855, 215.

[8] Wagner, John. "New York City Concert Life, 1801–1805," *American Music*, 2, no. 2 (Summer 1984): 55–57, 60, 65; Burrows and Wallace, *Gotham*, 300, 372–74; and John Lambert, *Travels Through Canada and the United States of North America in the Years 1806, 1807, 1808*. London, 1816, II: 55.

[9] Burstein, *The Original Knickerbocker*, 21, 47–49.

[10] "Letter of Jonathan Oldstyle, Gent.," Letter I, *Morning Chronicle*, November 15, 1802, in *Washington Irving: Letters of Jonathan Oldstyle, Gent.: Salamagundi; or The Whim-whams and Opinions of Launcelot Langstaff, Esq. & Others*, eds. Bruce I. Granger and Martha Hartzog. Boston: Twayne, 1977: 3–4.

[11] "Letter of Jonathan Oldstyle, Gent.," Letter IX, *Morning Chronicle*, April 23, 1803, in Granger and Hartzog, eds., *Washington Irving*, 32–35.

[12] See "Character of a Beau," *The Weekly Visitor, or Ladies' Miscellany* (New York), June 23, 1804; and "Character of a Beau," *The Lady's Weekly Miscellany* (New York), December 6, 1806.

[13] See Philip Carter, "Men about Town: Representations of Foppery and Masculinity in early Eighteen-Century Urban Society," in Hannah Barker and Elaine Chalus, eds., *Gender in Eighteenth-Century England: Roles, Representations and Responsibilities*. London: Longman, 1997: 31–57; Susan C. Shapiro, "'Yon Plumbed Danderbrat': Male Effeminacy in English Satire and Criticism," *Reviews of English Studies*, 39 (1988): 400–412.

[14] See Timothy Gilfoyle, *City of Eros: New York City, Prostitution, and the Commercialization of Sex, 1790–1920*. New York, 1992: 24–26; Kenneth Roberts and Anna M. Roberts, eds. *Moreau de St. Méry's American Journal, 1793–1798*. Garden City, NY, 1947: 156, 176–78.

[15] Gilfoyle, *City of Eros*, 43–44; Cogan, Jacob Katz. "The Reynolds Affair and the Politics of Character," *Journal of the Early Republic*, 16 (Fall 1996): 389–90, 396, 402–403; and Aaron Burr to Theodosia Burr Alston, July 10, 1804, in Matthew L. Davis, ed., *Memoirs of Aaron Burr*, 2 vols. New York, 1836: II: 322–23.

[16] For a description of the estate, see Isaac Newton Phelps Stokes, *Iconography of Manhattan Island*, 6 vols. New York, 1926: V: 1440; and for furnishings, Deed to Sir John Temple, June 17, 1797, Burr Papers, microfilm, reel 4.

[17] Isenberg, *Fallen Founder*, 158–59.

[18] Ibid., 159.

[19] Lambert, *Travels*, II: 91.

[20] See "Biography of a Modern Beau," *The Polyanthos* (Boston), March 1806; and "He Cuts a Figure," *The Weekly Visitor, or Ladies' Miscellany* (New York), June 9, 1803; and see Kamensky, *The Exchange Artist*, 45–46.

[21] See "Portrait of Burr," *Port Folio*, May 16, 1807, 314–15.

[22] See Isenberg, "The 'Little Emperor': Aaron Burr, Dandyism, and the Sexual Politics of Treason," in *Beyond the Founders: New Approaches to the Political History of the Early Republic*, eds. Jeffery L. Pasley, Andrew W. Robertson, and David Waldstreicher. Chapel Hill: University of North Carolina Press, 2004: 142–44; and *Fallen Founder*, 348.

CHAPTER 7

[1] There are conflicting estimates of the number of deaths attributable to the riots. Some scholars have suggested that the toll may have reached a thousand, while estimates of under a hundred have also

been offered. The truth undoubtedly lies somewhere in between, but probably closer to the lower estimate.

SUGGESTED READING:

Gutfreund, Owen. *The New York City Draft Riots of 1863*. Bedford/St.Martins Press, 2009.

Bernstein, Iver. *The New York Draft Riots: Their Significance for American Society and Politics in the Age of the Civil War*. Oxford University Press, 1990.

Schecter, Barnet. *The Devils Own Work: The Civil War Draft Riots and the Fight to Reconstruct America*. Walker & Co, 2005.

Burrows, Edwin and Mike Wallace. *Gotham: A History of New York City to 1898*. New York: Oxford University Press, 1999.

CHAPTER 8

[1] Parkhurst, Rev. Charles H. *Our Fight with Tammany*. New York, 1895: 10, 14.

None of the newspaper accounts printed the full text of the sermon, and there were considerable differences among them. I have relied upon this published version for direct quotes; but it no doubt included some changes from the sermon Reverend Parkhurst preached in church.

[2] New York State Senate. *Report and Proceedings of the Senate Committee Appointed to Investigate the Police Department of the City of New York*. Albany, 1895, 5 vols. Hereafter cited as LC (Lexow Committee).

[3] M. R. Werner to Mark Hanna, December 10, 1955, in M. R. Werner Papers, Box 2, Rare Books and Manuscript Collection, New York Public Library. The *New Yorker* series was eventually published in book form as "Dr. Parkhurst's Crusade," in Werner's *It Happened in New York*, 1957: 36–116. Werner's *Tammany Hall* (1928) remains one of the most frequently cited sources for the history of Tammany.

[4] Asbury, Herbert. *The Gangs of NewYork: An Informal History of the Underworld*. New York, 1928; Sante, Luc. *Low Life: Lures and Snares of Old New York*. New York, 1991; Martin Scorsese, director, *Gangs of New York* (2004). For a critical review of Scorsese's film and its debt to this tradition, see Daniel Czitrom, *"Gangs of New York," Labor History* 44 (August 2003): 301–04.

[5] Parkhurst quoted in Introduction to *Report of the Society for the Prevention of Crime* (1896): 6.

[6] Godkin, E. L. "Criminal Politics," *North American Review* 150 (June 1890): 713, 714, 708.

[7] For Martin's testimony, see LC I: 418–475.

[8] Argersinger, Peter. "New Perspectives on Election Fraud in the Gilded Age," *Political Science Quarterly* 100 (Winter 1985–6): 687. See also Howard W. Allen and Kay Warren Allen, "Vote Fraud and Data Validity," in *Analyzing Electoral History*, Jerome M. Clubb, et.al., eds. Beverly Hills, 1981: 153–93, and Gary W. Cox, Jr. and J. Morgan Kousser, "Turnout and Rural Corruption: New York as a Test Case," *American Journal of Political Science* 25 (November 1981): 646–63.

[9] The Federal Elections Commission and John I. Davenport's career are badly neglected topics. The best available overview remains Albie Burke, "Federal Regulation of Congressional Elections in Northern Cities, 1874–1894," PhD. diss, University of Chicago, 1968. For the broader Reconstruction context of the Federal Elections Law, see Everette Swinney, "Enforcing the Fifteenth Amendment, 1870–1877," *Journal of Southern History* 28 (May 1962): 202–218. See also Jerome Mushkat, *The Reconstruction of the New York Democracy, 1861–1874*. East Brunswick, 1981: 161–208, and John I. Davenport, *The Election and Naturalization Frauds in New York City, 1860–1870*. New York, 1894, 2nd. ed. On the strategic importance of New York state in this era, see Mark Wahlgren Summers, *Party Games: Getting, Keeping, and Using Power in Gilded Age Politics*. Chapel Hill, 2004; and George Harmon Knoles, *The Presidential Campaign and Election of 1892*. Palo Alto, 1942.

[10] "Politics of the Police," *New York World*, April 6, 1892: 8.

[11] "Harry Hill Gets Even," *New York World*, June 21, 1894: 1–2; for Hill's testimony, see LC II, pp.1926–1950. For George Appo's testimony, see LC II: 1621–1664. Timothy Gilfoyle's insightful and deeply researched biography of Appo, *A Pickpocket's Tale: The Underworld of Nineteenth Century New York* (2006), is also the best social history of the urban underworld.

[12] Costello, Augustin. *Our Police Protectors: History of the New York Police From the Earliest Period to the Present Time*. New York, 1885; Byrnes, Thomas F. Byrnes. *Professional Criminals of America*, New York, 1886; reprint edition, 1969.

CHAPTER 10

SUGGESTED READING:

Crouse, Joan M. *The Homeless Transient in the Great Depression: New York State*. Albany: State University of New York Press, 1986.

Depastino, Todd. *Citizen Hobo: How a Century of Homelessness Shaped America*. Chicago: University of Chicago Press, 2003.

Greenberg, Cheryl. *"Or Does it Explode?" Black Harlem in the Great Depression*. New York: Oxford University Press, 1997.

Kusmer, Kenneth L. *Down and Out, On the Road: The Homeless in American History*. New York: Oxford University Press, 2002.

Wenger, Beth S. *New York Jews and the Great Depression: Uncertain Promise*. Syracuse: Syracuse University Press, 1999.

CHAPTER 12

This essay is modified from one published in 2001 in a catalog accompanying the exhibit *John Koch: Painting a New York Life, at the New-York Historical Society*.

CHAPTER 16

[1] All statistics in this report, unless otherwise noted, are drawn from *Working for a Better Life: A Profile of Immigra--nts in the New York State Economy*, published by the Fiscal Policy Institute in 2007.

[2] The array of jobs subject to rampant workers rights violations is well documented in *Unregulated Work in the Global City*, by Annette Bernhardt, Siobhán McGrath, and James DeFilippis, New York: Brennan Center for Justice at New York University School of Law, 2007.

[3] *Winning the Global Race for Talent: How U.S. Visa & Immigration Policies Threaten the New York Economy & Cost American Jobs—And How We Can Fix It*. Partnership for New York City, March 2008.

[4] *A World of Opportunity*. New York: Center for an Urban Future, 2007.

ADDITIONAL PHOTO CREDITS

Page 287: Image Courtesy Rea Irvin/The New Yorker, © Conde Naste Publications.

Page 329: © Estate of Reginald Marsh/Art Students League, NY/Artist Rights Society, NY.

Pages 332, 344: Images used with permission of the Van Vechten Estate.

Pg 369: © the Lisette Model Foundation, Inc., 1983. Image used with permission of the Foundation.

Pages 395, 396: Dan Weiner: © Sandra Weiner.

Page 395: © Ruth Orkin, 1952. Image courtesy of the Ruth Orkin Photo Archive.

Pages 405, 407: Images used with permission of David M. Bernstein, Aesthetic Realism Photographer.

Page 427: © 2009 Estate of Donald Greenhaus/Artists Rights Society, NY.

Page 433: © 2009 Artist Rights Society, New York, VI$COPY, Australia.

Page 445: © 2009 Robert Cottingham, courtesy of Forum Gallery, New York, NY.

Page 452: Image used with permission of ACA Gallery.

Page 455 (right): Image courtesy of Vincent Cianni.

Page 456: Both images courtesy of Jeff Mermelstein.

Page 460: Image courtesy of Edwynn Houck Gallery.

AFTERWORD

It has been a special pleasure—indeed a duty—for the Museum of the City of New York to consider 400 years of New York's history through the lens of new scholarship and images from our vast holdings. The Museum's mission is to connect the past, present, and future of this great city, and to explore its heritage of diversity, opportunity, and perpetual transformation. All of these qualities are vividly manifest in the pages of *New York 400*. The astonishing changes that have taken place over the course of four centuries in the city's built environment, its population, and its culture are presented in these pages, as are both the beauty and the grimness of the New York experience. We hope that you have enjoyed this journey through the high and the low, the sublime and the surreal, the everyday and the extraordinary—all of the contrasts that define the New York *gestalt*. The book drew on the interpretive talents of some of today's best scholars and observers of New York and on the visual riches of the Museum of the City of New York's own treasures. The Museum's extensive iconographic collections—photographs, prints, paintings, drawings, and maps that portray the city—constitute an extraordinary record of the development of New York and the history of its people. Among the jewels of the more than half a million images of the city in the collection are photographs by Berenice Abbott, Jessie Tarbox Beals, Samuel H. Gottscho, Victor Prevost, Jacob Riis, and the Wurts Brothers; paintings by Asher B. Durand, William Earl, and Childe Hassam, and prints by James Bennett, Currier & Ives, and William Guy Wall. But equally compelling are the hundreds of thousands of images by unidentified photographers and artists documenting streets corners, buildings, public events, and the life of New Yorkers over the centuries. These collections were assembled by some remarkably forward-looking people, starting with Henry Collins Brown, who in 1923 spearheaded the creation of the Museum and became its first director, and the early curators, especially Grace M. Mayer, whose tenure as curator of prints from 1932 to 1959 saw the creation of one of the first major collections of photographs in the country as well as a major collection of etchings, lithographs, maps, and other works on paper. She and her colleagues benefited from the generosity of the individuals who generously donated major collections to the Museum, notably J. Clarence Davies, whose gift of some 15,000 items in 1929 formed the foundation of the prints, paintings, and photography collections; as well as Percy C. Byron, who gave thousands of photographs by the Byron firm, and Harry T. Peters, who gave the Museum the nation's largest collection of prints by Currier & Ives. Work to preserve and make the Museum's collections accessible on the web is now ongoing, with the generous support of the Institute for Museum and Library Services, the National Endowment for the Humanities, the Upper Manhattan Empowerment Zone Corporation, and we are especially grateful to Daryl Brown Uber of the William E. Weiss Foundation for helping to initiate and support these many projects.

The present book is a tremendous achievement and the product of enormously hard work. Thanks go first to John Thorn, the book's editor, who conceived of the project, championed it, and did an astonishing job of marshalling the resources to capture the complex stories of New York in word and image, including researching and writing the extensive captions. Sarah Henry, the Museum's Deputy Director and Chief Curator, comes next in our list of thanks for overseeing the project and providing crucial support and resources. As the Museum's Manager of Collections Access, Melanie Bower served as the book's picture editor and heroically combed through literally tens of thousands of prints and photographs to choose the highlights from among the vast collection. Senior Curatorial Associate Autumn Nyiri provided key assistance. Museum colleagues Kathleen Benson, Sean Corcoran, Andrea Henderson Fahnestock, and Thomas Mellins all helped shape the selection.

We are also grateful for the expertise of Mike Wallace, co-author of *Gotham* and founder of the Gotham Center for New York City History, for his counsel and guidance in shaping this project, as in so many others that we undertake at the Museum. And most of all, I am grateful to the historians and journalists of New York who contributed essays to the volume and to the countless photographers, printmakers, painters, mapmakers, and other artists who have labored over the centuries to ensure that we have a visual record of our vibrant city and its evolution.

The Museum of the City of New York is committed to being a place where the past informs the future. We hope that this volume, *New York 400*, provides an enjoyable and informative journey through the city's past for all of us who will help shape its tomorrows.

SUSAN HENSHAW JONES

RONAY MENSCHEL DIRECTOR OF THE MUSEUM OF THE CITY OF NEW YORK

ABOUT THE MUSEUM OF THE CITY OF NEW YORK

THE MUSEUM OF THE CITY OF NEW YORK CELEBRATES AND INTERPRETS THE CITY, EDUCATING THE PUBLIC ABOUT ITS DISTINCTIVE CHARACTER, ESPECIALLY ITS HERITAGE OF DIVERSITY, OPPORTUNITY, AND PERPETUAL TRANSFORMATION. FOUNDED IN 1923 AS A PRIVATE, NONPROFIT CORPORATION, THE MUSEUM CONNECTS THE PAST, PRESENT, AND FUTURE OF NEW YORK CITY. IT SERVES THE PEOPLE OF NEW YORK AND VISITORS FROM AROUND THE WORLD THROUGH EXHIBITIONS, SCHOOL AND PUBLIC PROGRAMS, PUBLICATIONS, AND COLLECTIONS.

SPECIAL THANKS

The Museum of the City of New York would like to thank the following for their contributions to the creation of *New York 400*:

Cindy De La Hoz, our editor at Running Press, who oversaw this complex project with unfailing skill and composure.

Joshua McDonnell, designer at Running Press, who created a handsome picture frame for all of our disparate images and text formats.

Publishers Jon Anderson and Craig Herman at Running Press, who showed faith in the book at all stages.

Mark Thorn, able research assistant.

Matt Flynn, C. Bay Milin, Chris Murtha and Matt Pinto, who aided in the task of digitizing the images in this book.

Steven H. Jaffe, whose knowledge of New York City history was invaluable.

ORDERING IMAGES FROM THIS PUBLICATION

If you found an image in this publication that you would like to hang in your home, the Museum's Department of Rights and Reproductions provides custom made, archive-quality prints for personal use. Reproductions from the Museum's collections of 1.5 million objects may also be ordered for scholarly or commercial use. For more information, please visit www.mcny.org or call 212.534.1672 x 3375.

INDEX

Note: Page references in italics indicate illustrations and captions.

H

I

N